Proceedings of the American

Intelligence and the Philosophy of Mind

Volume 80, 2006

Edited by:

Michael Baur
Fordham University

Papers for the regular sessions were selected by the program committee:

Michael Gorman
Douglas Rasmussen
James South

Issued by the National Office of the American Catholic Philosophical Association
Fordham University
Bronx, NY 10458

The *Proceedings of the American Catholic Philosophical Association* are published as an annual supplement to the *American Catholic Philosophical Quarterly* and distributed to members of the ACPA as a benefit of membership. The *Proceedings* are also available for purchase to libraries, departments, institutions, and individuals. For information regarding subscriptions and/or back issues, please contact:

Philosophy Documentation Center
P.O. Box 7147
Charlottesville, VA 22906-7147
Phone: 800-444-2419 (U.S. and Canada); 434-220-3300
Fax: 434-220-3301
E-mail: order@pdcnet.org
Web: www.pdcnet.org

The *Proceedings of the American Catholic Philosophical Association* are indexed in *Academic Search Premier, American Humanities Index, Catholic Periodical and Literature Index, Current Abstracts, Expanded Academic ASAP, Index Philosophicus, Index to Social Science & Humanities Proceedings, InfoTrac OneFile, International Bibliography of Periodical Literature* (*IBZ*), *International Philosophical Bibliography, ISI Alerting Services, Periodicals Index Online, Philosopher's Index, Reference and Research Book News*, and *Religious & Theological Abstracts.*
The *Proceedings of the American Catholic Philosophical Association* are also available in POIESIS: Philosophy Online Serials, and the full text of over thirty volumes is available online to libraries that subscribe both to the *Proceedings* and to POIESIS. For more information, contact the Philosophy Documentation Center at order@pdcnet.org.

ISSN 0065-7638
ISBN 978-1-889680-58-3

Published by the Philosophy Documentation Center, Charlottesville, Virginia.

Proceedings of the American Catholic Philosophical Association

Intelligence and the Philosophy of Mind

Volume 80, 2006

Table of Contents

A Look at Inner Sense in Aquinas: A Long-Neglected Faculty Psychology

Anthony J. Lisska

Abstract: This paper investigates Aquinas's thought on the *vis cogitativa*, in order to determine whether Aquinas's use of the inner sense of the *vis cogitative* is an embarrassment (as Dorothea Frede recently suggested), or whether it is rather an important element in Aquinas's philosophy of mind that calls for serious study (as John Haldane argued several years ago in an ACPA plenary address). An examination of Aquinas's theory of inner sense (as found in the *Commentary on Aristotle's De Anima*) reveals that, for Aquinas, the *vis cogitativa* has two cognitive functions: (1) to be aware of an individual as an individual, and (2) to recognize an individual as a member of a kind. If Aquinas' philosophy of mind did not include some account of the *vis cogitativa*, then it would not be able to accommodate what for Aquinas is a principal ontological category (namely, primary substance).

In her recent article, "Aquinas on *Phantasia*," Dorothea Frede remarked that Aquinas's use of the inner sense of the *vis cogitativa* is "an embarrassment" in his over all philosophy of mind: "This ability is something of an embarrassment for it seems to be an ability that is somehow *in between* sense-perception and thought."[1] Why, we might ask, is the *vis cogitativa* an embarrassment? In an ACPA plenary address several years ago on contemporary naturalist epistemology, John Haldane, to the contrary, argued that serious discussion was needed in this area of inner sense in Aquinas.

> What is now needed, however, is a fully perspicuous philosophical account . . . of the nature and operations of what in [Aquinas's philosophy of mind] are spoken of as the "cogitative powers" and the "active intellect." That might be one of our tasks for the next century.[2]

These are two contrasting positions, to be sure. One of the purposes of this presidential address is to sort out some of these differences and see if the *vis cogitativa* is "an embarrassment" like Frede purports, or following Haldane, an item for serious study in the history of philosophy that is "one of our tasks for the next century."

The late twentieth century witnessed a renewed interest in Aquinas's philosophy of mind within the context of analytic philosophy. Much of this was due, I suggest, to four philosophers from the United Kingdom: Peter Geach and Elizabeth Anscombe, and probably their most illustrious student, Anthony Kenny; and more recently John Haldane. Commenting on Aquinas's contribution to the philosophy of mind, Kenny once wrote:

> Aquinas's doctrine of the intentional existence of forms remains one the most interesting contributions ever made to the philosophical problem of the nature of thought.[3]

Kenny reiterates this point in his 2006 book, *What I Believe*.[4]

What is important in considering philosophy of mind issues in Aquinas is that this is, I submit, one arena in which Aquinas can be considered as a Philosopher. One need not take sides in that almost interminable set of issues on whether Aquinas was in fact primarily a theologian who just happened to be saying a few things of philosophical interest. This claim, of course, I need to spell out with this analysis. Furthermore, Aquinas is not only deeply indebted to Aristotle for his own take on the philosophy of mind, but in an important and significant sense, Aquinas moves beyond what are severe limits in Aristotle's own account, especially involving inner sense.

Recent Work on Aquinas and Inner Sense

Following on the coattails of recent work into Aristotle's philosophy of mind, substantial scholarship has developed on inner sense in Aquinas. This is a radical departure from much twentieth-century history of medieval philosophy, where Aquinas's general account of perception was for the most part relegated to the dustbins of forgotten theory. Dominik Perler's recently published *Ancient and Medieval Theories of Intentionality*,[5] for instance, contains four articles devoted almost exclusively to Aquinas's philosophy of mind, with the *vis cogitativa* occupying a central place in two of the essays: Frede's article noted above and Cyrille Michon's "Intentional Thoughts and Proto-thoughts." This is a far cry from the bemoaning title of an essay on inner sense in Aquinas that appeared some sixty plus years ago: "A Forgotten Sense: The Cogitative According to St. Thomas Aquinas."[6]

What do we know about Aquinas's work on inner sense? He treats these issues in the *Prima Pars* of the *Summa Theologiae*, the *Commentary on Aristotle's On the Soul*, and the *Summa Contra Gentiles*, among other places. R. -A. Gauthier notes that Aquinas wrote the passages in the *Summa Theologiae* on sensation and perception about the same time as he undertook his *Commentary on the Soul.* Gauthier suggests that Aquinas at least began if not completed this *Commentary* in late 1267, before leaving Rome in the autumn of 1268 for his second stint at the University of Paris. About this time, Aquinas undertook concurrently the composition of the *Prima Pars* of the *Summa Theologiae*, which contains his philosophy of mind discussions in Questions 78–79 and 84–89. Hence, Aquinas was figuring out his own take on issues in the philosophy of mind while wrestling with Aristotle's *De Anima*. Gauthier, along with Simon Tugwell, note that this was the first of Aquinas's Aristotelian commentaries.[7] The same method of proceeding holds for Aquinas's treatment of ethical naturalism in the *Prima Secundae* of the *Summa Theologiae* and the *Commentary on the Nicomachean Ethics*. Hence Aquinas developed several principal sections in the *Summa Theologiae* while constructing his fruitful commentaries on the works of Aristotle. Certainly this simultaneous writing of treatise and commentary contributed to the strong Aristotelian flavor found in much of Aquinas's work.

In this discussion, I am in general agreement with Alasdair MacIntyre, who, in his *Dependent Rational Animals*, wrote the following:

> I remain in general convinced by those commentators who have stressed the extent to which Aquinas in his philosophical enquiries was not just an Aristotelian, but often a keenly perceptive interpreter as well as an adapter of Aristotle.[8]

As this analysis unfolds, I intend to show how Aquinas is a "keenly perceptive interpreter as well as an adapter of Aristotle."

The analysis proposed in this address depends on the exposition of inner sense Aquinas puts forward in his extensive commentary on Aristotle's *De Anima*. Here, in my judgment, Aquinas offers his best explanatory account of perception theory, both for the external senses and for the inner senses. Writing on Aquinas's *Commentary*, Martha Nussbaum once wrote:

> Aquinas' commentary, . . . produced in the thirteenth century, is one of the very greatest commentaries on the work . . . , [and] Aquinas's commentary itself is very insightful; so too are the extensive remarks about Aristotelian soul-body issues contained in the *Summa Theologiae*.[9]

In my judgment, one needs to read carefully Aquinas's exposition and commentary on Aristotle's *De Anima* in order to witness Aquinas's wrestling at his best with issues in sensation, perception and concept formation. The account of Aquinas's philosophy of mind normally referred to in contemporary discussions is the short analysis in the *Prima Pars* of the *Summa Theologiae*,[10] plus occasional references to the somewhat whimsical discussions in the *Summa Contra Gentiles*. While the account of intellectual knowledge found in the *Prima Pars* of the *Summa Theologiae* is moderately developed, nonetheless Aquinas treats the important issues of sense knowledge in but two articles of Question Seventy-Eight: Article Three for the external senses and Article Four for the internal senses. Given the interest in philosophy of mind issues revolving around sensation and perception in both modern and contemporary philosophy, one needs to see where Aquinas considers these issues in more detail. It is to the *Sententia libri "De anima"* where one turns.[11] This Aristotelian *Sententia* account of a realist theory of sensation and perception is, in my judgment, more fully developed than in any other texts found in the Aquinian corpus.

Aquinas's Meta-Philosophy

In his philosophy of mind, Thomas adopts, to be sure, a different method and architectonic of proceeding from what one finds in most modern philosophy. Haldane, among others, notes this different meta-philosophical approach found in Aquinas:

> Our knowledge of the external world is the starting point for philosophical reflection, the task of which is not to *justify* this knowledge but to *explain* it; to give an account of the scope of cognition, its genesis and its operations.[12]

Scott MacDonald also brings to our attention this aspect of Aquinas's meta-philosophy:

> Aquinas does not build his philosophical system around a theory of knowledge. In fact the reverse is true: he builds his epistemology on the basis provided by other parts of his system, in particular, his metaphysics and psychology.[13]

Hence, Aquinas adopts the meta-philosophy of going from metaphysics to epistemology and philosophy of mind and not vice versa. Without being an epistemological foundationalist, Aquinas nonetheless maintains a strong sense of both ontological realism and epistemological realism.

Aquinas on *Phantasia*

In this essay, I intend to address Aquinas's account of sensation and perception. Hence, I am interested in concept-formation and the process of abstraction through the *intellectus agens* only in a periphery way. To be more specific, I shall focus our attention on Aquinas's fascinating and, I submit, long neglected account of inner sense, especially the wonderfully interesting cognitive faculty of the *vis cogitativa*.

There are two different interpretations of inner sense and *phantasia* in Aquinas. The text of the *Summa Theologiae* suggests one account of *phantasia*, while Aquinas's *Commentary on Aristotle's De Anima* offers a different account.

1. In the *Summa Theologiae*, the inner sense faculty of *phantasia* is identical with the imagination or *vis imaginativa*. Aquinas writes: "*Ad harum autem formarum retentionem aut conservationem ordinatur phantasia, sive imaginatio, quae idem sunt.*"[14]
2. In the *Commentary on the Soul*, *phantasia* is, I suggest, used as a generic concept or "place-holder" covering three distinct faculties of inner sense: the imagination, the *vis cogitativa* and the sense memory. Aquinas does, nonetheless, mention each of these faculties in his *Summa Theologiae* account.

Throughout these texts on inner sense, Aquinas links animal awareness with the rudimentary awarenesses of human beings. Aquinas, as we know, is neither a Cartesian nor dualist metaphysician. In *Dependent Rational Animals*, Alasdair MacIntyre writes about this set of issues, which he believes philosophers have too long neglected.

> But some commentators . . . have failed to ask the relevant questions about the relationship between our rationality and our animality. They have underestimated the importance of the fact that our bodies are animal bodies with the identity and continuities of animal bodies, and they have failed to recognize adequately that in this present life it is true of us that we do not merely have, but are our bodies.[15]

In reading these texts on inner sense, one notes immediately that Aquinas pays special attention to the knowing apparatus and the mental acts of non-human animals. This suggests strongly the anti-dualist characteristic of Thomas's meta-philosophy. Aquinas once wrote: "*Anima mea non est ego*."[16] In no sense of the term is Aquinas a Cartesian dualist in his metaphysics or his philosophy of mind. The analysis of inner sense enables us to tease out these important non-dualist properties.

Structure of the Objects of Sensation

In the *Commentary on the Soul* and in the *Summa Theologiae*, Aquinas, following Aristotle, provides a three-fold division of objects of sensation. Aquinas, as the passages below will clearly indicate, distinguished three generic kinds of objects of sense knowledge:

1. The proper or special sensibles.
2. The common sensibles.
3. The incidental objects of sense.

In his analysis of the objects of perception, therefore, Aquinas is more sophisticated, for instance, than the rather simplistic structure discussed by early twentieth-century proponents of the sense data theory or that articulated by the classical British Empiricists. The following passage from the *Summa Theologiae* spells out these three categories of sense objects:

> Sense powers know things by being impressed with their likeness (*similitudo*). However, this likeness can be understood in three different stages.
>
> 1. First, *immediately and directly*; this is when the likeness of color is in the faculty of sight. This is true of all the other *proper sensibles* in their appropriate sense faculties.
> 2. Secondly, *directly, but not immediately*, as when the likeness of shape or size is in the sight. This is true of all the other *common sensibles* shared through several different senses.
> 3. Thirdly, *neither immediately nor directly*, as when the likeness of man is in the faculty of sight. He is there—i.e., in the faculty of sight—not because he is a "man" but rather because he is a colored object. [This is the *incidental object of sense*.][17]

What is important for this discussion of the *vis cogitativa* is Aquinas's claim that the incidental object of sense *neither immediately nor directly* affects the external senses. This introduces the concept of an "*intentio non-sensata*," which is an important, albeit continuously overlooked, principle in Aquinas's philosophy of perception.

The *Vis Cogitativa*

The *vis cogitativa* contributes, I submit, an additional aspect to direct perception above and beyond that provided by the external senses alone; the object of the external senses is an awareness only of the proper and the common sensibles. An "*intentio non-sensata*" is important in providing an explanatory account of what I take to be Aquinas's unique contribution to the Aristotelian philosophy of perception: the incidental object of sense is known through the inner sense of the *vis cogitativa*. The following two passages from the *Commentary* texts explicate this act of awareness of the *vis cogitativa*.

> Aristotle next takes the third member of the division. We might, he says, call Darius or Socrates incidentally a sense object because each happens to be white: that is sensed *incidentally* which happens to belong to what is sensed *absolutely*. It is accidental to the white thing, which is sensed absolutely, that it should be Darius. Thus, Darius is a sense-object incidentally. *He does not, as such, act upon the sense at all.*[18]

Aquinas suggests that the act of awareness of the *vis cogitativa* is of "something incidental":

> Thus as soon as I see anyone talking or moving herself, my intellect tells me that she is alive and I can say that I see her alive. But if this apprehension is of something individual, *as when, seeing this particular coloured thing, I perceive this particular man or beast, then the cogitative faculty [in the case of human persons at least] is at work*, the power which is also called the "particular reason" because it correlates individualized notions, just as the "universal reason" correlates universal ideas.[19]

Aquinas writes that the *vis cogitativa* ". . . is aware of a human person as *this* human person, and of a tree as *this* tree."[20] The *vis cogitativa*, therefore, is aware of a human person as this particular human person and this tree as this particular tree.

> It remains to be seen how anything is a sense object "incidentally." Now for an object to be a sense object incidentally, it must first be connected accidentally with an *essential* sense object; as a human person, for instance, may happen to be white, or a white thing may happen to be sweet. Secondly, the one who is sensing must perceive it. If it were connected with the sense object without itself being perceived, it could not be said to be sensed incidentally. *But this implies that with respect to some cognitive*

> *faculty of the one sensing it, it is known, not incidentally, but absolutely. Now this latter faculty . . . [is] the vis cogitativa.*[21]
>
> But whatever makes no difference to the immediate modification of the faculty we call an incidental object of sense. Therefore, Aristotle says explicitly that *the senses are not affected at all by the incidental object of sense as such.*[22]

An awareness of "this particular, concrete thing" becomes important for Aquinas's theory of perception. The individual as an individual is more than a collection of sense qualities, a position articulated by both Berkeley and Hume and held subsequently by more than several twentieth century empiricists. In his discussion of the incidental object of sense, Aquinas advances the analysis from Aristotle's more limited treatment of the faculties of inner sense.

The Awareness of the Individual as of a Kind

For Aquinas, the *vis cogitativa* has two cognitive functions.

1. To be aware of an individual as an individual.
2. To recognize an individual as a member of a kind.

In his *Commentary on Aristotle's Metaphysics*, Aquinas also notes this cognitive role of the mental act of the *vis cogitativa*. Thus, it is not only in the *Prima Pars* of the *Summa Theologiae* and the *Commentary on the Soul* that Aquinas discussed the importance of this faculty of inner sense. In the *Commentary on the Soul*, Aquinas introduces this awareness of an individual of a natural kind. Moreover, he offers a distinction between instinct through the *vis aestimativa* and an awareness of an individual as a natural kind through the *vis cogitativa*. The *vis aestimativa* also uses an *intentio non-sensata*, which is Aquinas's explication for animal instinct.

> The *vis cogitativa* apprehends the individual thing as existing in a common nature, and this is because it is united to intellect in one and the same subject. . . . Instinct, on the other hand, is not aware of an individual thing as in a common nature.[23]

The important question concerns the significance of these texts in offering a consistent analysis of Aquinas's theory of sensation and perception. It appears that Aquinas provides a modified Kantian or Gestalt-like account for the perception of an individual. Since the *intentiones non sensatae* cannot be known through the external senses, it appears to follow that there must be some active contribution, what might be called a "conditioning" or "structuring" of the mental act, on the part of the *vis cogitativa*. This faculty enables one to perceive individuals as substantial wholes of a natural kind and not just as mere bundles of sensations. In this case, Aquinas's epistemological account is not a reception of a form immaterially in a simple-minded isomorphic way. There is, however, a kind of isomorphism, but it is with the individual primary substance, which is the principal ontological entity in Aquinas's metaphysics. This individual—a primary substance—is an individual of a natural kind. Without the awareness of the *vis cogitativa*, Aquinas's philosophy of mind would lack the ability to be aware of what is his principal ontological category; this inability in turn would entail a huge philosophical lacuna. Furthermore, the *vis cogitativa* enables Aquinas to distinguish between sensation and perception; he provides the philosophy of mind machinery for the very same distinction that Thomas Reid affirmed against Hume but justified only by calling it, as John Haldane once explained, "miraculous!"

The Importance of this Account

Without this structured awareness on the part of the *vis cogitativa*, a human knower would be, I submit, deficient in at least two ways. Aquinas, to be sure, was not one to permit philosophical deficiencies to appear in his ontological accounts.

1. A human knower would be unable to be aware directly of the fundamental ontological category in Aquinas's metaphysics, the category pertaining to individuals of natural kinds; these are, of course, primary substances.
2. A human knower would be less able to "abstract" the essence from the phantasms in the sense memory using the *intellectus agens*.

The *explicatio textus* suggested here is remarkably similar, it would seem, to the method articulated by James Gibson in discussing the evolutionary development of human sense organs. It is through this evolutionary development that a human knower can make one's way around the environment. While Gibson does not affirm an ontology of primary substances, nonetheless he does consider the role the environment plays in determining how sense organs and faculties have developed and function. The same is true, *mutatis mutandis*, for Aquinas.[24] Haldane is quite explicit about this epistemological naturalism in Aquinas, especially when he once suggested that Aquinas and Willard Quine share some important meta-philosophical themes, since in the philosophy of mind, "both are philosophical naturalists."[25]

According to the texts, it appears that for Aquinas, the *vis cogitativa* is the faculty of inner sense by which we are aware of an individual as a member of a particular kind. This mental act, it must be emphasized, is neither identical with nor co-extensive with the mental act of concept-formation, which, of course, is what Aquinas identifies with the role of abstraction through the *intellectus agens*. To know a concept is to have an awareness of the "nature" or "essence" of a thing, which is reducible to an understanding of the set of sortal properties. This nature is common to many; hence, the individual *concretum* as individual is precluded from being the intentional object of the *intellectus agens* (abstracting the essence) or the *intellectus possibilis* (knowing the essence). Aquinas articulates this position in the *Summa Theologiae* with the following proposition: "*Unde intellectus noster directe non est cognoscitivus nisi universalium*."[26] It is precisely at this point in the discussion that the *vis cogitativa* comes into play. It is this inner sense faculty that conditions the mental act to be aware of an individual as a member of a "kind." This does not mean that the *vis cogitativa* has an awareness of a "nature" or "essence." This is the role of first intentional awareness on the part of the *intellectus possibilis*. In other words, the *vis cogitativa* is not aware of "human nature as human nature," but rather as Megan the human person and Elin the human person. This awareness comes about through the working of the phantasms in the *vis cogitativa*. The phantasm peculiar to the *vis cogitativa* "conditions" or "colors" the mental awareness of the *vis cogitativa* so that it interprets the object—the primary substance—in the external world in a unique way. Parenthetically, in my judgment, there are at least three different conceptual uses of phantasm in the writings of Thomas, but that tedious *explicatio textus* is more than can be undertaken in this present discussion.

To be sure, this suggests an almost Kantian interpretation regarding a structured act of awareness. The structure of the act of awareness of the *vis cogitativa* is determined by the phantasms; the phantasms in turn come about only because of the range of the perceiver's experience. In other words, the *vis cogitativa* "interprets" an object as an individual of a kind and not merely as a unified concrete whole composed of a set of proper and common sensibles. This, in effect, distinguishes the *vis cogitativa* from the *sensus communis*. This is evidence for placing the *sensus communis* in the external sensorium and not in the *internal sensorium* even though Aquinas classifies it as an internal sense.[27]

Ontological Realism

I suggest that this interpretation of Aquinas on inner sense saves the metaphysical realism on which he builds his philosophical system. This is, it would appear, neither an arcane nor an idle philosophical question. Writing in *New Blackfriars*, Catherine Pickstock asked the following question, and I think not rhetorically:

> How should one respond to the death of realism, the death of the idea that thoughts in our minds can represent to us the way things actually are in the world? For such a death seems to be widely proclaimed by contemporary philosophers.[28]

To reiterate briefly, Aquinas, like Gibson, assumes that there is a world around us. He asks, like Gibson does, what must be necessary in order for us to know and understand this world of individuals. Gibson would appeal to evolutionary development in order to explain how our perceptual apparatus developed. Nonetheless, Gibson—and if Haldane is correct, Quine too—and Aquinas adopt, I submit, the same meta-philosophical approach—i.e., how do we explain our awareness of the world around us?[29] As Haldane once noted in his "metaphysics and cognitive psychology, . . . Aquinas advocates strong versions of both epistemological and ontological realism.[30]

This account renders more perspicuous the structural connections between the *vis cogitativa* and its phantasms, the sense memory and its phantasms, and the power of abstraction with the *intellectus agens*. I will discuss this set of connections near the end of this inquiry.

Substance and Classical British Empiricism

If this analysis is correct, it would appear that the paramount example of "inner sense" for Aquinas is the *vis cogitativa*. It is by means of this faculty that Aquinas is able to transcend the limits of most empiricist and certainly all phenomenalist accounts of sensation and perception.

An important corollary of this discussion is the role that primary substance plays in the functioning of the *vis cogitativa*. In his ontology, Aquinas, in the manner of Aristotelian realism, suggests that the basic and fundamental things in the external world are primary substances. We have seen that Aquinas, following Aristotle, adopts a three-fold division for the objects of sense knowledge: the proper sensibles, the common sensibles, and the incidental object of sense. There is no analogue in classical British empiricism for the incidental object of sense. Given the bundle view of perception espoused by Berkeley in *The Principles* and Hume in *The Inquiry*, among other places, theoretically there is no room left for the incidental object of sense. Berkeley and Hume analyze an individual in terms of a collection or "heap" of sensible properties. Berkeley wrote as follows in *The Principles*:

> Thus, for example, a certain color, taste, smell, figure and consistency, having been observed to go together, are accounted one distinct thing, signified by the name "apple." Other collections of ideas constitute a stone, a tree, a book, and like sensible things.[31]

In his *An Inquiry Concerning Human Understanding*, Hume used the same analysis, substituting a peach for an apple:

> As our idea of any body, a peach, for instance, is only that of a particular taste, color, figure, size, consistency, etc., so our idea of any mind is only that of particular perceptions without the notion of anything we call substance, either simple or compound.[32]

These texts from Berkeley and Hume indicate that the paradigm of perception accepted by these empiricists is what we might call "the bundle view." A physical object is nothing more than a collection—i.e., a set of sense qualities—that in British empiricism would be the set of primary and secondary qualities. On the other hand, Aquinas, in espousing a "thing consciousness" paradigm, goes beyond the limits of the bundle view paradigm. The *vis cogitativa* is what provides for this more sophisticated account.

In his *De Anima*, Aristotle spells out in some detail the structure and content of the proper and the common sensibles. But, as I suggested earlier in this discussion, when he comes to the incidental object of sense, Aristotle has precious little to say. Aquinas, in suggesting that it is by means of the *vis cogitativa* that we account for our perception of the incidental object of sense, goes beyond the limits found in Aristotle's account of sensation and perception. Moreover, and this is the important cash value claim of this analysis for work in the philosophy of mind, both Aristotle and Aquinas transcend the limits entailed by the bundle view paradigm adopted by the British empiricists. This is what, I submit, Aquinas would say to Thomas Reid in offering a more thorough analysis of the sensation/perception distinction than Reid was able to muster.

A primary substance, to reiterate briefly, is an individual thing of a certain natural kind. The "natural kind" refers to a species that is determined by the substantial form of the thing. The *vis cogitativa* appears to be the faculty by which the perceiver is aware of a primary substance as a thing and not merely as a bundle of sensations. This, again, requires an interpretive function on the part of the *vis cogitativa*. In effect, inner sense goes beyond the data of the external sensorium. This is accomplished through an *intentio non-sensata* and the structured mental act of the *vis cogitativa*.

Accordingly, Aquinas not only has primary substances in his ontology, but his philosophy of mind is structured so that the perceiver can be aware of these primary substances. Simply put, the *vis cogitativa* explains the possibility of the awareness of individual substances. The end result is that Aquinas asserts the two following propositions:

1. There are individual things (primary substances) in the external world.
2. We are aware of these individual things (primary substances) as individuals and not as mere collections of proper and common sensibles.

The possibility of our being aware of individual things is accounted for by means of the phantasm-structured *vis cogitativa*. The external sensorium is aware of unified wholes of proper and common sensibles. The *vis cogitativa*, however, is aware of the primary substance as a primary substance—an individual. The mental act of the *vis cogitativa* renders the awareness of "unified whole" into awareness of an individual of a natural kind. In effect, it is because of the *vis cogitativa* that Aquinas can distinguish between sensation and perception, and, *a fortiori*, transcend the limits of modern and contemporary British empiricism.

The importance of this inner sense faculty in Aquinas's philosophy of mind is obvious. An experienced datum of our perceptual lives, the pre-analytic datum, is that we, as perceivers, seem to be directed primarily towards things rather than just to collections of qualities. Accordingly, Megan—as a *perceiver*—is aware of Elin—as an *individual*—and not merely a collection of proper and common sensibles. Contemporary philosophers who claim that we ordinarily talk as if we perceive things and not sense data point out this same pre-analytic datum. John Wisdom, for example, once remarked that philosophers must consider the difference between what he called "sense statements" and "thing statements."[33] In addition, this distinction was reiterated often in the writings of Roderick Chisholm.[34] Of course, this analysis squares with the data used in Gestalt Psychology.

With his discussion of the *vis cogitativa* and its mental act, Aquinas accepts in principle Wisdom's distinction and is concerned about the same set of issues. Through his analysis of the *vis cogitativa*, Aquinas undercuts the sense data theories of early twentieth-century epistemology found in the writings of Russell, Moore,

Price and Ayer, and also the early modern empiricism of Locke, Berkeley and Hume. Aquinas accomplishes this by suggesting, in effect, that our experience is of things rather than of sense data. In addition, by using a meta-philosophical methodology entailing a cognitive faculty psychology, Aquinas provides the philosophy of mind cognitive machinery necessary to explain the possibility of an act of awareness of an object beyond the immediate data of the proper and the common sensibles. There is a similarity with Peter Strawson, who once claimed that "particulars" are the basic elements of a human perceiver's conceptual scheme. Accordingly, Aquinas, like Strawson, suggests that it is a mistake to claim that human perceivers are primarily and fundamentally aware of bundles of sense data. To the contrary, human perceivers have a direct "thing consciousness" or "individual consciousness." Furthermore, this "consciousness" and "intentional awareness" are rudimentary for human perceivers.

It is appropriate, I suggest, to compare the acts of awareness of the *vis cogitativa* with what is common sensibly referred to as "experience." Recall once again the "army in retreat" metaphor in the *Posterior Analytics*. The first time Megan sees Elin, she obviously does not recognize her as Elin. Nonetheless, the *vis cogitativa* is already geared—or structured—towards interpreting this object of awareness as an individual, and an individual of a natural kind. After Megan has begun to know Elin, then she immediately recognizes Elin "as Elin" as soon as Elin comes into view. It is important to realize that Aquinas does not claim that we remember this particular bundle of sensations—i.e., the concrete whole—as Elin. Rather, we *perceive* her immediately to be Elin. Yet "being Elin" is not some type of discrete, identifiable individuating property, which is directly perceivable in the external world. "Being Elin" is not a proper or a common sensible. Elin is, however, an incidental object of sense. This is an important part of Aquinas's theory of sense perception.

Accordingly, Aquinas claims that it is by means of the internal sense of the *vis cogitativa* that a human perceiver is able to "immediately perceive" an individual as an individual. In other words, when Megan is directly aware of Elin, she is not remembering what she saw earlier as this same bundle of sensations nor is Megan exercising any act of judgment. Quite the contrary, she is directly aware that this "concrete whole" is Elin—a particular individual of a natural kind. That such an individual property is imperceivable *per se* is, furthermore, consistent with Aquinas's position on individuation. The ontological problem of individuation is resolved in Aquinas's metaphysics by the assertion that "*materia prima*" is the principle of individuation. Accordingly, there is no postulation of an individualizing form similar to the *haeccaeitas* of Duns Scotus. It follows from what I take to be Aquinas's "axioms of intentionality" that only a form can be knowable directly. Since *materia signata quantitate*, which is the direct opposite of a form, is the individuator, there is nothing as such in the external world, which could be the object of the mental act of direct sensation regarding an individual as an individual. Therefore, Aquinas makes use of the *vis cogitativa* as the faculty of the internal sensorium, which accomplishes our awareness of individuals, and not just of "concrete wholes." Indeed Aquinas's analysis develops substantially Aristotle's limited account of both the cognitive faculties of inner sense and the incidental object of sense.

Michon on Proto-Thought and Proto-Judgment

In his "Intentional Thoughts and Proto-Thoughts," Cyrille Michon recently remarked, incorporating suggestions from Davidson, among others, that some sense of judgment is necessary for the workings of the *vis cogitativa*:

> The presentation of phantasms to the intellect, for abstraction or conversion, does not involve any kind of judgement. However, the cogitative power is needed for a direct and non-intellectual knowledge of the singular, which is a complex knowledge, a judgement.[35]

Michon is correct, I believe, in suggesting that there is a non-intellectual knowledge of the particular, which would be a primary substance.[36] However, the claim of this paper is that this awareness is neither a judgment nor a proposition but rather a Gestalt-like perception based on a structured mental act using the *vis cogitativa*. Aquinas does not refer to a "judgment" in these texts. Hence, the proposal here is that a "conditioning" or "structuring" of the mental act in a Gestalt manner provides for the awareness of an individual of a natural kind. In this way, Aquinas saves his epistemological realism and his ontological realism.

The Klubertanz/Kneale Analysis of the *Vis Cogitativa*

In his *The Discursive Power*, George Klubertanz argued that the function of the *vis cogitativa*, in a manner analogous to the *vis aestimativa*, is that which recognizes the good to be done here and now in a particular situation. William Kneale, in commenting on perception in Aquinas, offered the same suggestion regarding an elucidation of *intentiones non-sensatae* with the *vis cogitativa*. It is through these unsensed intentions, so Kneale argued, that a human perceiver discerns the useful or the good in particular situations. Kneale wrote as follows.

> Animals are said to have a faculty other than sense by which they perceive *intentiones* of usefulness and harmfulness. But the peculiar talk of perceiving *intentiones* into which St. Thomas falls here seems to have been suggested to him by the peculiarity of the mental occurrence we call seeing a thing as useful or harmful.[37]

The analysis suggested in this essay, however, is that the awareness of the individual as an individual is the first and primary purpose of the *vis cogitativa*. The apprehension of "the useful or the good" is a second order awareness following upon the primary awareness which is of a specific individual primary substance. This is how Aquinas accounts for the awareness of the principal ontological category in his metaphysics—the primary substance. In his classic account of sensation and perception in Albert, Aquinas and Siger, Edward Mahoney appears to agree with the Klubertanz and Kneale account of the intentional awareness of the *vis cogitativa*.[38]

Connection with the *Intellectus Agens*

Often in Book II of the *Summa Contra Gentiles*, Aquinas, in considering the relation between the *vis cogitativa* and the formation and exercise of concepts, writes statements like the following: "phantasms [are] prepared by the *vis cogitativa* in order that they may become actually intelligible and move the possible intellect."[39] In addition, Aquinas discusses the connection with the awareness of the *vis cogitativa* to the *intellectus agens* and the *intellectus possibilis*:

> The *vis cogitativa* is . . . directed to the possible intellect . . . only through its act by which the phantasms are prepared, so that by the *intellectus agens* they may be made actually intelligible; in this way, the possible intellect is perfected.[40]

In the following passage, Aquinas brings in all three inner sense faculties:

> It is through the *vis cogitativa*, together with the imagination and the memory, that the phantasms are prepared to receive the addition of the *intellectus agens*, whereby they are made actually intelligible.[41]

Aquinas adopts, I submit, a theory of intentionality espousing what might be called "structured mental acts." There are two important intentional structures in Aquinas's philosophy of mind:

1. The *intellectus agens*.
2. The *vis cogitativa*.

Both of these intentional structures are necessary conditions in order for Aquinas to provide an account of an awareness of essential properties. Both transcend direct data from the external senses. The *intellectus agens* is the power of abstraction. In discussing Gilson on Aquinas's philosophy of mind, John Peterson once wrote: "the senses carry a message which they cannot themselves interpret."[42] Peterson and Gilson refer only to the *intellectus agens*. The thrust of this essay suggests unequivocally that the *vis cogitativa* also must be included in this philosophy of mind characteristic or intentional structure proposed by Gilson. Hence, the working of the *vis cogitativa* enables the *intellectus agens* to engage in the process of abstraction. If the *vis cogitativa* were not aware of individuals of a natural kind, then it is unclear how the abstractive process would be anything but an empty process scattered among bunches of discrete and unconnected sensible qualities. The *vis cogitativa* prepares the way for abstraction. This important function of this faculty of inner sense is, then, hardly an embarrassment.

Concluding Propositions from this Analysis

In this discussion of Aquinas and the perception of individuals through the *vis cogitativa*, the following seven propositions offer a convenient summary analysis:

1. The *vis cogitativa* is the faculty of inner sense by means of which the human perceiver is aware of the individuals of the world. In Aquinas's ontology, these individuals are the primary substances, each of which is a *hoc aliquid* of a natural kind.
2. The perception is of an individual of a natural kind.
3. This awareness transcends the limits of the external senses. The external senses are limited, given the structure of Aquinas's philosophy of mind, only to an awareness of proper and common sensibles.
4. The awareness by the *vis cogitativa* is an "active contribution" to the perceiving process necessary to be aware of individuals as individuals and not bundles of sensations; this process justifies distinguishing sensation from perception.
5. It follows from 1 through 4 that Aquinas developed a philosophy of mind on the perceptual level necessary to provide for an awareness of individuals.
6. This account of the awareness of an individual through the structured mental act of the *vis cogitativa* is not reducible to the account of the reflexive awareness of the intellect so common in explications of Aquinas's philosophy of mind.[43] These two mental acts are categorically distinct.
7. It follows that Aquinas offers an account for the awareness of individuals as individual *hoc aliquids* on the level of sense perception.

The Inner Sense Theory and Contemporary Scientific Explanation

Before closing this journey into medieval cognitive theory, I suggest that we historians of philosophy might learn from a historian of psychology, Simon Kemp. Kemp offers several significant suggestions in his evaluation of the medieval theory of inner sense as elucidated in several Aristotelian commentators. First of all, inner sense is, Kemp suggests, an "information-processing model." Secondly, the theory is consistent with "discrete stage-processing models," which, Kemp notes, have been important in twentieth century cognitive psychology. These models argue that cognitive information is transformed in discrete stages. Thirdly, contemporary psychologists distinguish between "episodic memory" and "semantic memory."[44] For Aquinas, the former would be located in the inner sense faculties and the latter in the mind; this "semantic memory" would be, I submit, an example Peter Geach's account of the development of concepts in Aquinas's philosophy of mind as cognitive abilities.[45]

Kemp suggests, furthermore, that when considering the value of medieval theories of the inner sense faculties, one needs to approach this set of issues using the meta-scientific theory articulated by recent philosophers of science.[46] The necessary conditions for an adequate scientific theory include: (a) explanatory depth; (b) unifying power; (c) consistency and coherence; and (d) application. The theory of inner sense as developed in medieval cognitive theory, Kemp argues, did attempt to offer substantive explanations of perception theory. In addition, this sustained analysis of inner sense provided a unified position covering the developing stages of phantasm formation. Moreover the discussions of inner sense by many of the medieval Aristotelians appeared to be consistent internally. Lastly, Kemp writes that the theory generally assisted in offering an account for certain mental aberrations that interest psychologists so much—nightmares, delusions, *et al.* Such intentional events were explained through the malfunctioning of the *vis cogitativa* or the *phantasia*. This entire analysis of inner sense is in turn a naturalist account of a philosophy of mind resting on a theory of cognitive faculty psychology.

In closing, I recommend that we historians of medieval philosophy reflect on Kemp's rejoinder to historians of psychology—and also, I might add, contemporary philosophers of mind—who too readily dismiss medieval cognitive theories as trivial:

> However, we would claim that the theory of the inner senses was an elaborate and innovative exposition that, even in retrospect, can be regarded as a considerable scientific achievement.[47]

The texts from the *Summa Theologiae* and the *Commentary on the Soul*, I submit, justify this explanatory analysis put forward in this essay. The incidental object of sense is an *intentio non-sensata* known through the intentional activity of the *vis cogitativa*.[48] Given this analysis, I submit that the *vis cogitativa*, in an explanatory mode within the context of a naturalist philosophy of mind, is hardly an embarrassment to Aquinas. On the contrary, this faculty provides the possibility for the awareness of an individual of a natural kind on the level of perception. This, in turn, renders the entire abstraction process, which is part of the intellect, more coherent.[49] Given this analysis, Aquinas holds that the *vis cogitativa* is a necessary component between sense perception and thought through abstraction, which Frede calls an embarrassment. Without the *vis cogitativa*, indeed Aquinas's philosophy of mind would be an embarrassment.

This concludes my analysis—an *explicatio textus*—into the somewhat murky region of inner sense—*phantasia*—in Thomas Aquinas. This is a bit of philosophy of mind rooted in Aristotle's *De Anima*, but an account developed more intensely than the Aristotelian discussion. I trust this account is sufficiently perspicuous in order to help meet what John Haldane suggested as "one of the tasks for the next century."

Denison University

Note of Acknowledgement

The author first began worrying about Thomas Aquinas on sensation and perception more than several years ago. Aquinas's analysis of these issues did not seem to fit into the regular patterns or paradigms used by analytic philosophers undertaking work in medieval philosophy of mind. It was the late Professor Robert G. Turnbull who urged the author to venture into what in some sense was uncharted territory. This presidential address is part of a larger book length monograph on Aquinas's account of the intentionality of sensation and perception. The author is saddened that Professor Turnbull did not live long enough to see this long-term project that he supported with great enthusiasm brought to completion. In addition, the author has profited immensely from discussions on these issues with Alan Hausman, James South, Sir Anthony Kenny and John Haldane, among others. It is in the context of this sustained work that the theme for the 2006 ACPA meetings on "Intelligence and the Philosophy of Mind" took root. The author acknowledges a deep and abiding sense of gratitude to these philosophers who took time to assist the author as he worked through a set of somewhat messy issues in Aquinas's very important and substantial cognitive theory of inner sense.

Notes

1. Dorothea Frede, "Aquinas on *Phantasia*," in *Ancient and Medieval Theories of Intentionality*, ed. Dominik Perler (Leiden: Brill, 2001), 170.

2. John Haldane, "Insight, Inference and Intellection," in *Proceedings of the American Catholic Philosophical Association*, Vol. 75, 1999 (Bronx, NY: Fordham University, 2000), 43.

3. Anthony Kenny, *Aquinas* (Past Masters Series): (Oxford: Oxford University Press, 1980), 80.

4. Kenny, *What I Believe* (London: Continuum, 2006), 10.

5. Dominik Perler, Editor, *Ancient and Medieval Theories of Intentionality* (Leiden: Brill, 2001).

6. Julien Peghaire, *The Modern Schoolman*, 20 (1942–3), 123–140, 210–229.

7. The recently published English translation of Jean-Pierre Torrell's *St. Thomas Aquinas: The Person and His Work* (Washington, DC: The Catholic University of America Press, 1996), 172, contains a thoughtful discussion of Gauthier's research.

8. Alasdair MacIntyre, *Dependent Rational Animals* (Chicago: Open Court, 1999), xi.

9. Martha C. Nussbaum, "The Text of Aristotle's *De Anima*," in *Essays on Aristotle's De Anima*, ed. Martha C. Nussbaum and Amelie Oksenberg Rorty (Oxford: The Clarendon Press, 1992, 1995), 4.

10. Questions 78–79 and 84–89

11. This is the exposition and commentary from Chapter/*Lectio* Ten of Book Two forward and also major sections of Book Three. This corresponds to Book Two, Chapter Five and following in Aristotle.

12. Haldane, "Insight, Inference and Intellection," 38.

13. Scott MacDonald, "Theory of Knowledge," found in *The Cambridge Companion to Aquinas*, ed. Norman Kretzmann and Eleonore Stump (Cambridge: Cambridge University Press, 1993), 160.

14. *Summa Theologiae*, Ia, Q. 78, art. 4.

15. MacIntyre, *Dependent Rational Animals*, 6; Patrick Lee argues in a similar manner in his article, "Human Beings are Animals," in *Natural Law and Moral Inquiry*, ed. Robert P. George (Washington, DC: Georgetown University Press, 1998), 135–151.

16. *Commentary on St. Paul's First Letter to the Corinthians*, 15: 17–19, found in *Aquinas: Selected Philosophical Writings*, ed. Timothy McDermott (Oxford: Oxford University Press, 1993), 192–193.

17. *Summa Theologiae*, Ia, Q. 17, a. 2. (Italics not in the original.)

18. *Commentary on the Soul*, # 387. (Italics not in the original.)

19. Ibid., # 396.

20. Ibid., # 398

21. Ibid., # 395.

22. Ibid., #393 (Italics not in the original).

23. Ibid., # 398.

24. I wish to acknowledge the assistance my Denison colleague, Harry Heft, provided in this discussion of James Gibson's work.

25. Haldane, "Insight, Inference and Intellection," 39.

26. *Summa Theologiae*, Ia, Q. 86, a. 1.

27. One needs here to distinguish the external senses from the internal senses, and the external sensorium from the internal sensorium. The former pair is distinguished by the location of the sense faculties, while the latter pair is distinguished by the intentional act itself. The faculties of the internal sensorium—the imagination, the *vis cogitativa* and the sense memory—all require phantasms.

28. Catherine Pickstock, "Imitating God: The Truth of Things According to Thomas Aquinas," The 1999 Aquinas Lecture, *New Blackfriars*, July/August, 2000 (Vol. 81: Nos. 953/954), 308; this is the first chapter of Pickstock and John Milbank's *Truth in Aquinas* (London: Routledge, 2000).

29. While I have suggested a certain affinity with Kant on inner sense, this does not entail that my analysis of Aquinas on the *vis cogitativa* is either connected with or dependent upon what has been called "Transcendental Thomism."

30. Haldane, "Mind-World Identity Theory and the Anti-Realist Challenge," in *Reality, Representation and Projection*, ed. John Haldane and Crispin Wright (Oxford: Oxford University Press, 1993), 24.

31. George Berkeley, *A Treatise Concerning the Principles of Human Understanding*, # 1.

32. David Hume, *An Inquiry Concerning Human Understanding* (Hendel Edition), 194.

33. John Wisdom, "Philosophical Perplexity," found in Morris Weitz, *20th Century Philosophy: The Analytic Tradition* (New York: The Free Press, 1966), 292.

34. For example, Roderick M. Chisholm, "On the Observability of the Self," *Philosophy and Phenomenological Research*," 30 (1969), 7–21.

35. Cyrille Michon, "Intentional Thoughts and Proto-Thoughts," in Dominik Perler, editor, *Ancient and Medieval Theories of Intentionality* (Leiden: Brill, 2001), 339.

36. Michon attempts to incorporate recent work from Davidson and others on the matter of proto-thoughts. He suggests that the workings of the *vis cogitativa* would be an example of a proto-thought mechanism.

37. William Kneale, "Analysis of Perceiving," found in *Perception*, ed. F. N. Sibley (London: Methuen & Co Ltd, 1971), 68.

38. Edward Mahoney, "Sense, Intellect and Imagination in Albert, Thomas, and Siger," found in *The Cambridge History of Later Medieval Philosophy*, ed. Norman Kretzmann, Anthony Kenny and Jan Pinborg (Cambridge: Cambridge University Press, 1982; 1984), 602–622.

39. *Summa Contra Gentiles* Book II, chap. 76.

40. Ibid., Book II, chap. 73.

41. Ibid., Book II, chap. 60.

42. John Peterson, *Realism and Logical Atomism*: (University, AL: The University of Alabama Press, 1976), 7.

43. *Summa Theologiae*, Ia, Q. 86, a 1: "Whether the Intellect knows Particulars"—i.e., "*Utrum Cognoscat Singularia*."

44. Simon Kemp, "The Medieval Theory of the Inner Senses," with Garth Fletcher, in "History of Psychology" section, *American Journal of Psychology*, Vol. 106, No. 4 (Winter: 1993), 568–569. The author's good friend, Professor of Psychology Harry Heft, introduced the author to the important historical studies undertaken by Kemp.

45. Peter Geach, *Mental Acts* (London: Routledge & Kegan Paul, 1957; revised edition, 1971), 11–17; this important book has been reissued recently by St. Augustine Press.

46. Kemp here refers to the work of Larry Laudan; "The Medieval Theory of the Inner Senses," 572.

47. Ibid., 572–573.

48. Furthermore, in some texts of Aquinas, the particular reason is equated with the *vis cogitativa*. In none of these texts, however, is the *ratio particularis* identified with the *intellectus possibilis*. Hence, all of this is undertaken on the level of sense perception.

49. Historians of medieval philosophy need to mine deeper the substantial lode offered in Aquinas's *Commentary on the Soul*, where Aquinas treats sensation and perception issues in greater detail and depth than found in his other works.

Presentation of the Aquinas Medal

Alexander Eodice

It is my distinct pleasure to introduce Sir Anthony Kenny as the 2006 recipient of the Aquinas Medal, given each year by the American Catholic Philosophical Association to a philosopher of note. Anthony Kenny is a figure of great significance. We can hardly think of contemporary philosophical thought without thinking of some way in which he has shaped our common discourse about the central concepts of mind, will, action, emotion and belief; or the way he has reawakened the importance of philosophy's past by enlivening our sense of what is of enduring value in the work of the ancient, medieval and modern philosophers; or of the way in which he could, with uncanny clarity, lay bare the sense of an otherwise seemingly inscrutable passage from Wittgenstein.

I am further humbled to make this introduction by the fact that many of you here seem already to know Sir Anthony, while he and I have only just met this evening. Yet I feel as if I know him as well, at least as much as one can know a person through the words he writes. My undergraduate and graduate reading lists read, in part, like some subsection of the publications contained in his *curriculum vitae*. Professors would recommend reading Kenny on Descartes, Kenny on Aquinas's Five Ways, Kenny on Aristotle, Kenny on Wittgenstein; get Pitcher's volume of essays on Wittgenstein, one suggested, and read Kenny's "Cartesian Privacy"; I picked up Vesey's collection as well and read the first article—Kenny on "The Ghost of the *Tractatus*."

I was very pleased in 1977 to purchase a hardcover first edition of Sir Anthony's work, *Action, Emotion and Will*, published in 1963 round about the time my parents let me stay up late on a school night to watch some other fellows from Liverpool sing songs on the Ed Sullivan show. For me and many in my generation, the Beatles spurred a British invasion that framed our sensibilities about popular culture. Years later I was subject to another British invasion, one that would help frame my philosophical sensibilities, thanks to Anthony Kenny and his analytic compatriots. Even on this day, I marveled at his ability to quicken our sense of the meaning of words. This morning he lectured on the origin of the intellectual soul and started his talk by asking "when did I begin?" I was immediately tempted to respond "just now," until I realized how he meant the question.

My acquaintance was strengthened when I began to assign my own students readings from Anthony Kenny—read Kenny on Descartes, on Aquinas, on Aristotle, on Wittgenstein, I'd tell them. In 1999, while Director of Honors at Iona College, I was fortunate enough to mentor a student, a brilliant young woman, who won a Rhodes Scholarship, the first in Iona's history. I saw that Sir Anthony Kenny was then Warden of Rhodes House and I thought, in anticipation, I might finally get to meet him should I visit my student. When I visited her the following year at New College, Sir Anthony had left his position at Rhodes and was gone from Oxford. Elusive fellow, I thought, much like "the ghost of the *Tractatus*." I still had not met Anthony Kenny, at least not until now on my first trip to, of all places, Granville, Ohio. It is my pleasure to put flesh and blood to his name.

I recently read an account of Sir Anthony's visit to Prague not long ago. He was there, the account went, to give a lecture about European identity throughout the ages. This was not, however, his first visit to the city, for he and a number of other Oxford philosophers visited communist Czechoslovakia in the 1970s and 1980s to take part in the underground "living room seminars." On this recent trip he was asked by a reporter about his earlier visits and experiences. He and other members of the philosophy faculty in Oxford were invited to attend an informal philosophy group, he indicated and responded further that:

> So many people from Oxford came, and some from other universities. My own visit was in itself no way remarkable, except that it was one of two or three over a period of years, and was actually interrupted by the police, broken up and I was extradited from the country under an article forbidding hooliganism, which I had not realized included lecturing on Aristotle in private rooms.

I mention this story because we honor Sir Anthony not only for his prolific philosophical writings and his extraordinary contributions to education as Pro-Vice Chancellor of Oxford, Curator of the Bodleian Library, Warden of Rhodes House and Fellow of St. John's College (to name only a few), but also for the breadth of his experience and for the character and quality of his public intellectual life. In this, he is an exemplar for all of us.

I am honored to present this year's Aquinas Medal to Sir Anthony Kenny.

Aquinas Medalist's Address

Anthony Kenny

Abstract: The author begins by observing that he has often been described as an analytical Thomist. He proceeds to argue that—regardless of what school one belongs to—genuine philosophical engagement with Aquinas's texts means one should be both reverent and critical. If we are to consider the relevance of Aquinas's thought for contemporary philosophy, the author suggests, the best way for us to write about Aquinas is the way in which he wrote about Aristotle: stating his views as clearly and sympathetically as possible, showing their connection with current concerns, and contesting them politely but firmly if they appear to be erroneous.

The thought of St. Thomas Aquinas continues to exercise and fascinate the minds of many. After the Second Vatican Council Thomism lost the commanding position that it had for nearly a century occupied in the training of Catholic clergy; but in compensation many philosophers outside the Roman fold took up the serious study of the *Summa Theologiae* and the *Summa contra Gentiles*. The seminary manuals had, in any case, functioned at some distance from Thomas' actual writings, and the disrepute that has overtaken manual Thomism has in the long run served the Saint's reputation well.

In the English speaking world it is possible to distinguish four different schools among contemporary admirers of Aquinas.

First, there are the conservatives who continue to work in the neo-scholastic tradition of Gilson and Maritain, albeit in a chastened and less triumphalist form. A doughty exponent of this school of thought is Ralph McInerny, who has sought to make Thomism accessible in many works, and whose recent Gifford lectures presented a popular defence of traditional natural theology in its relation to theoretical and practical reasoning.

Second, there are the transcendental Thomists who combine close and sympathetic appreciation of the writings of St. Thomas with a respect for the importance of the critical insights of Immanuel Kant. Prominent leaders of this line of thought were the Jesuits Joseph Marechal and Peter Hoenen, and at the present time the school is represented above all by followers of the late Bernard Lonergan, S.J.

Third, there are those who follow an agenda drawn from post-modernism, among whom are the members of the theological movement that styles itself "Radical Orthodoxy." John Milbank and Catherine Pickstock are vociferous proponents of this tendency, which has gained influence in the Church of England.

Finally, there are several philosophers in the analytic tradition, who seek to interpret Aquinas in the light of recent currents of thought in philosophy of language and philosophy of mind. Many of these have been heavily influenced by Wittgenstein, who like Aquinas stands at the opposite pole of philosophy from the Cartesian tradition which sees epistemology as the basic philosophical discipline and private consciousness as the fundamental datum of epistemology. There is by now an impressive corpus of works of this so-called analytical Thomism. Some of the leading practitioners are Catholics, such as Peter Geach and John Finnis; some indeed, like the late Herbert McCabe, were members of St. Thomas's own Dominican Order. But there have been other influential writers of this school who—like Norman Kretzmann—have never been Catholics or—like Alasdair MacIntyre—have held varying religious allegiance.

I find that I am myself from time to time described as an analytical Thomist. I am happy to be called a Thomist if that means a person who admires and studies St. Thomas. But I have never been a Thomist if a Thomist is a paid-up member of a particular philosophical party. I first met Thomism in the scholastic manuals of the Gregorian university in Rome, and took an instant and lasting dislike to it. It was Bernard Lonergan, at the end of my Roman course, and Peter Geach and Herbert McCabe in Oxford, who taught me to distinguish between Thomas and Thomism.

There are some Thomists who so swear by the words of the Saint that they resent any criticism of him and will not accept any contradiction of him (unless it comes from a Pope, as when Pius IX defined the immaculate conception). Such an entrenched position is sometimes called "citadel Thomism." I believe that it represents a misunderstanding of the nature of philosophy. The student of philosophy is not called on to subscribe to one or other philosophical "ism", but rather, in the light of the varied teachings of the great philosophers of the past, to make up her own mind on each philosophical issue that presents itself. Philosophy is such a difficult subject that to achieve a consistent overall philosophical *Weltanschaung* has proved beyond the reach of even the greatest geniuses such as Plato, Aristotle, Descartes and Kant. A fortiori, we lesser mortals cannot help but be eclectic.

I regard Aquinas as ranking, as a philosopher, with the greatest geniuses of the discipline, but I think that our engagement with him, as with them, must be critical as well as reverent. In a number of books I have tried to present his thought in a manner that shows its relevance to the issues that occupy philosophers working in the contemporary analytic tradition. There are those who argue that the conceptual world of the thirteenth century was so different from that of the twentieth century that any attempt at such bridge-building is bound to fail. I disagree: I think that philosophy is perennial in the sense that many of the conceptual problems that we confront today are the very same problems as those that faced Plato and Aristotle.

Other issues are as it were the descendants of the ancient issues, and can best be understood by tracing their provenance. Aquinas's thought, I believe, is just as relevant to the twenty-first century as Aristotle's thought was to the thirteenth century. And the best way for us to write about Aquinas is the way in which he wrote about Aristotle: stating his views as clearly and sympathetically as possible, showing their connection with current concerns, and contesting them politely but firmly if they appear to be erroneous.

Of course much that was written by ancient and medieval philosophers has been superannuated by the progress of science, but there remains a substantial corpus that is as relevant today as ever. Those of us who call ourselves philosophers today can genuinely lay claim to be the heirs of Plato and Aristotle. But we are only a small subset of their heirs. What distinguishes us from the other heirs of the great Greeks, and what entitles us to inherit their name, is that unlike the physicists, the astronomers, the medics, the linguists, we philosophers pursue the goals of Plato and Aristotle only by the same methods as were already available to them.

Aquinas stands in a similar relation to today's philosophers. His philosophy of nature has been antiquated, in great part, by the swift progress of natural science since the Renaissance. His philosophy of logic and language has been enormously improved on by the work of logicians and mathematicians in recent centuries. But his writings on metaphysics, philosophical theology, philosophy of mind, and ethics are still as rewarding to read as anything written on those topics by philosophers between his age and ours.

Much writing on ethics in contemporary Anglophone philosophy draws its ultimate inspiration from Jeremy Bentham. On the one hand it is consequentialist: no form of action is absolutely ruled out as immoral, for a sufficiently imposing end may justify the most abhorrent of means. On the other hand it is sensationalist: the ultimate criteria of right and wrong are pain and pleasure, conceived as private experiences. It follows that animals belong to the same moral community as humans, because they like us can feel pain and pleasure. Fetuses, however, do not, since they are incapable of feeling either.

Aquinas's ethics stands in splendid contrast to this noxious utilitarianism. While the calculation of consequences has its place in his system, this is within a framework which rules out certain actions as absolutely forbidden. It is rationality, not sensation, that is the mark of human beings, so that animals form no part of our moral community. A creature's potentialities, no less than its experiences, are relevant to the evaluation of its moral worth, and they should be our guide in deciding how to treat a fetus.

Only Aquinas's fellow Christians can endorse the whole of Aquinas's ethical system, with its emphasis on theological as well as moral virtues. But his treatment of the moral virtues, and his analysis of human actions and intentions, commends itself to secular as well as to religious readers. This is unsurprising, since much of the ethical parts of the *Summa Theologiae* read like a commentary on the *Nicomachean Ethics* of the pagan Aristotle.

The first book that I wrote on Aquinas, *The Five Ways* (1969), was a discussion of the proofs of God's existence to be found at the beginning of the *Summa Theologiae*. I concluded that none of them achieved its object. I continue to believe this, but I now think that it might have been better to concentrate my attention on the *Summa contra Gentiles* as Norman Kretzmann later did in his magisterial *The Metaphysics of Theism*.

Later I was invited to write a brief introduction to Aquinas in the Oxford series *Past Masters* (1969). The book contained three chapters, the first a summary of the Saint's life and works, the second devoted to Being and the third to Mind. I argued that St. Thomas's philosophical psychology was equal to anything currently on the philosophical market, but I took a critical view of the real distinction between essence and existence and the thesis that God was self-subsistent being.

Later I expanded each of these judgements in full-length books. In *Aquinas on Mind* (1993), I spelt out that for Aquinas the intellect is the capacity for thought, for the particular kind of thought peculiar to language-users. The agent intellect, or concept-forming ability is species-specific in humans; the receptive intellect is the set of concepts and beliefs possessed by an individual. Aquinas's account places him between empiricists who regard ideas as arising simply from experience, and rationalists who postulate innate ideas. He also stands in the middle between realists and idealists. He agrees with the realists that the human mind is capable of genuine knowledge of an extra-mental world. But he agrees with the idealists that the universals that the mind uses to conceptualise experience have no existence, as universals, outside the mind. His map of the mind is a complicated one but it is superior to that offered by many another famous philosopher.

My attitude to Aquinas's metaphysics is an ambiguous one. There run through his works two grand Aristotelian principles. The first is that there is no actualisation without individuation; the second is that there is no individuation without actualisation. The first principle is anti-Platonic; the second, anachronistically, we can call anti-Leibnizian. These principles seem to me to be fundamental to any sound ontology, and they are key elements of Aquinas's philosophy of creation.

But if Aquinas is an Aristotelian on earth, he is a Platonist in heaven. I argued in *Aquinas on Being* (2002) that the idea of God as pure Being is vulnerable to all the arguments that can be brought against Plato's theory of Ideas, and that the distinction between essence and existence embodies a deep philosophical confusion between different senses of the verb "to be." That book, not unnaturally, attracted a hail of criticism from citadel Thomists.

It is, therefore, highly magnanimous of the American Catholic Philosophical Association to award me the Aquinas medal. I value it highly not only because my admiration of Aquinas's gigantic achievement far outweighs my criticism of aspects of his apparatus, but also because it is an honour to be enrolled in the same company as those distinguished scholars and philosophers who have won the medal in the past. I am most grateful to you all and offer you my warmest thanks.

I must end, however, on a note of caution. You will remember that shortly after his death a number of Aquinas's teachings incurred academic and ecclesiastical sanction. On March 7, 1277, they were condemned by Bishop Tempier in Paris and ten days later by a special congregation of the university of Oxford. The Oxford condemnation specified that those who taught the Thomist theses were to be allowed forty days to recant, and if they continued to uphold them they were to be deprived of their degrees.

The Paris condemnation was revoked two years after the Saint's canonization. The Oxford one, so far as I know, has never been withdrawn. So when I get back to Oxford I had better not boast of having received the Aquinas medal, for fear of losing my M.A.

University of Oxford

The Beginning of Individual Human Life

Anthony Kenny

Abstract: This paper explores the issue of when human life begins, giving special attention to the thought of St. Thomas Aquinas. Aquinas's position is contrasted with the position defended by many Catholics today. After considering the evidence and a variety of arguments, the paper suggests that the individuated human being begins to exist at roughly fourteen days after the moment of conception.

When did I begin? When does any individual human being begin? At what stage of its development does a human organism become entitled to the moral and legal protection which we give to the life of human adults? Is it at conception, or at birth, or somewhere between the two?

In this lecture I will discuss the question in general terms, but I will pay particular attention to Aquinas's account. I will contrast his position with the one currently adopted by most Catholics, and then I will present my own answer to the question, which is midway between the Catholic one and the Thomist one.

The three alternatives—at conception, at birth, or between—do not in fact exhaust the possibilities. Plato, and some Jewish and Christian admirers of Plato, thought that individual human persons existed as souls before the conception of the bodies they would eventually inhabit. This idea found expression in the Book of Wisdom, where Solomon says "I was a boy of happy disposition: I had received a good soul as my lot, or rather, being good, I had entered an undefiled body." Clement of Alexandria records an early Christian notion that the soul is introduced by an angel into a suitably purified womb.

Aquinas rejects this position in Ia 118, 3, where he discusses whether human souls were created at the beginning of the world. He argues against it in three stages. First, if a soul existed perfectly well before being embodied, then a human being would be only an *ens per accidens*. Second, if it is natural for a soul to be united to a body, God in creating a bodiless soul would be making something imperfect, just as if he were to make a human being without legs. But if someone says that it is not natural for a soul to be united to a body, then, third, there would be no good reason for it ever to be so united, whether voluntarily or involuntarily. Aquinas is surely right to reject these fantasies, and they have little relevance to any contemporary moral debate.

But in addition to those who thought that the individual soul existed before conception, there have been those who thought that the individual body existed before conception, in the shape of the father's semen. Onan, in Genesis, spilt his seed on the ground; in Jewish tradition this was seen not only as a form of sexual pollution but an offence against life. Aquinas, in the *Summa contra Gentiles*, in a chapter on "the disordered emission of semen" treats both masturbation and contraception as a crime against humanity, second only to homicide. Such a view is natural in the context of a biological belief that only the male gamete provides the active element in conception, so that the sperm is an early stage of the very same individual as eventually comes to birth. Masturbation is then the same kind of thing, on a minor scale, as the exposure of an infant. The high point of this line of thinking was the bull *Effraenatam* of Pope Sixtus V (1588) which imposed an excommunication, revocable only by the Pope himself, on all forms of contraception as well as on abortion. But the view that masturbation is a poor man's homicide cannot survive the knowledge that both male and female gametes contribute equally to the genetic constitution of the offspring. And, as we shall see, Aquinas himself seems to have had second thoughts.

At the other extreme are those who maintain that it is not until some time after birth that human rights arise. In pagan antiquity infanticide was very broadly accepted. No sharp line was drawn between infanticide and abortion, and as a method of population control abortion was sometimes regarded as inferior to infanticide, since it did not distinguish between healthy and unhealthy offspring.

In our own time a number of secular philosophers have been prepared to defend infanticide of severely deformed and disabled children. They have based their position on a theory of personality that goes back to John Locke. Only persons have rights, and not every human being is a person: only one who, as Locke puts it, "has reason and reflection, and considers itself as itself, the same thinking thing, in different times and different places." Very young infants clearly do not possess this degree of self-awareness, and hence, it is argued, they are not persons and do not have an inviolable right to life.

Defenders of infanticide are still, mercifully, very few in number. It is more common for moralists to take the rejection of infanticide as a starting point for the evaluation of other positions. Any argument that is used to justify abortion, or IVF, or stem-cell research must undergo the following test: would the same argument justify infanticide? If so, then it must be rejected.

The central issue, then, is to record, and decide between, the three alternatives from which we began: should we take individual human life as beginning at conception, at birth, or at some point in between? If the correct alternative is the third one, then we must ask further questions. What, in the course of pregnancy, is the crucial moment? Is it the point of formation (when the fetus has acquired distinct organs), or is it the point of quickening (when the movements of the fetus are perceptible to the mother)? Can we identify the moment by specifying a number of days from the beginning of pregnancy?

Some familiar texts from the Bible suggest that we should opt for conception as the beginning of the individual life of the person. "In sin did my mother conceive me" sang the Psalmist (51,5). Job cursed not only the day on which he was born but also "the night that said 'there is a man-child conceived'" (3,3). Since 1869 it has been the dominant position among Roman Catholics, but for most of the history of the Catholic Church it was a minority view.

It has been much less common to regard personality and human rights as beginning only at the moment of birth. But one important rabbinic text allows abortion up to, but not including, the time when a child's head has emerged from the womb. Some Stoics seem to have taught that the human soul was received when a baby drew its first breath, just as it departs when a man draws his last breath.

Through most of the history of Western Europe, however, the majority opinion has been that individual human life begins at some time after conception and before birth. In the terminology that for centuries seemed most natural, the "ensoulment" of the individual could be dated at a certain period after the intercourse that produced the offspring. Among Christian thinkers the general consensus was that the human soul was directly created by God and that it was infused into the embryo when the form of the body was completed which was generally held to occur around forty days after conception.

Thomas Aquinas held a particularly complicated version of this consensus position. He did not believe that individual human life began at conception; the developing human fetus, for him, does not count as a human being until it possessed a human soul, and that does not happen until some way into pregnancy. For him the first substance distinct from the mother is the embryo living a plant life with a vegetative soul. This vegetable substance disappears and is succeeded by a substance with an animal soul, capable of nutrition and sensation. Only at an advanced stage is the rational soul infused by God, turning this animal into a human being.

His fullest account is given in Ia 118, 1, when he is discussing the origin of the sensitive soul in individual human beings. This soul, he tells us, is neither directly created by God nor directly caused by a human father: it is the result of an active power inherent in the father's semen. This power, he says, is a motion of the father's soul, a motion whose vehicle is the white bubbly spirit contained in the semen. This spirit also contains heat deriving from the heavenly bodies, thus verifying the Aristotelian dictum "man and the sun begets man."

> In perfect animals that are generated by copulation, the active power is in the semen of the male, as Aristotle tells us. The matter of the fetus is what is given by the woman. In this matter there is, right from the outset, a vegetative soul, not in second act but in first act in the way that the sensitive soul is in people who are asleep. When it begins to draw nourishment, then it comes into an actual operation. By the power that is in the male semen this matter is transformed until it reaches the actuality of a sensitive soul. It is not that the actual power that was in the semen turns into a sensitive soul—that would make the begetter and the begotten one and the same. . . . But once a sensitive soul has been produced in the begotten in respect of its main parts, the soul of

> the offspring begins to operate to complete its own body by means of nutrition and growth.[1]

The whole process of development, according to Aquinas, is supervised by the father's semen, which he believed to remain present and active throughout the first forty days of pregnancy. For this biological narrative Aquinas claimed, on slender grounds, the authority of Aristotle. He added to Aristotle's account a crucial element: after the sensitive soul has brought the body to an appropriate stage of perfection, then an intellectual soul is infused directly by God. This soul is in no way caused by the father's semen.

On the topic of abortion, Aquinas has remarkably little to say directly, mentioning it at most thrice in the vast expanse of his corpus. His relevance to the contemporary debate centres on his teaching about the origin of human life. He is not an ally of those at the present time who claim that human life begins at conception. The developing human fetus does not count as a human being until it possesses a human soul, and this does not occur until pregnancy is considerably advanced. Aquinas clearly believed that late abortion (even if caused unintentionally) was homicide. A person who strikes a pregnant woman, he says, will not be excused from homicide. But at an earlier stage abortion, on his account, is wrong only for the same reason as masturbation and contraception: it is the destruction of an individual that is potentially a human being.

The theory of three successive entities at different stages of pregnancy, each with its own soul, does not seem entitled to any great respect. It is too closely linked to the idea that only the male is the active cause of the human generative process, and to the theory that the intellectual soul must be divinely infused because it is immaterial. The theory obscures the fact that there is an uninterrupted history of development linking conception with the eventual life of the adult.

In his book *Thomas Aquinas on Human Nature*,[2] Robert Pasnau emphasizes the discontinuity Aquinas sees in the development of the fetus. It is not a human being, he says, until it has developed its brain and sensory systems to the point where it can support the distinctive intellectual capacities of a human being. What quite does this mean? Surely a child can only exercise these capacities after learning language. Does this mean that infanticide, no less than first-trimester abortion, can be absolved from the charge of murder?

Aquinas can reject this, Pasnau believes, only on the basis of a controversial empirical claim, namely that at some point around mid-gestation a fetus begins to engage in conceptual cognitive activity. I am very doubtful whether Aquinas ever made such a claim; but Pasnau is surely right to believe that it is a very implausible one.

He offers Aquinas a fall-back position. Perhaps what Aquinas is doing is simply, out of a cautious respect for human life, to place its beginning at the point where the fetus conceivably has the potential for conceptualisation. "His policy is like that of a union that protects all of its members, apprentice and skilled craftsman alike." Our own respect for human life, Pasnau believes, should lead us to endorse something like Aquinas's account.

Few I think, whether pro-life or tolerant of abortion, will find Pasnau's account here convincing. It is surely the potential for, not the actuality of, intellectual activity that makes the late-term fetus and the newborn entitled to the respect due to human life. It is possible to accept this while agreeing with Aquinas that there is not an unbroken continuity of substantial identity between the moment of conception and the full development of the fetus.

If we turn from Aquinas to other Christian thinkers, a survey of the history of the topic makes it abundantly clear that there is no such thing as *the* Christian consensus on the timing of the origin of the human individual.[3] There was, indeed, a consensus among all denominations until well into the twentieth century that abortion was sinful, and that late abortion was homicide. There was no agreement whether early abortion was homicide. However those who denied that it was homicide still regarded it as wrong because it was the destruction of a potential, if not an actual, human individual. There was again no agreement whether the wrongfulness of early abortion carried over into the destruction of semen prior to any conception. Even within the Roman Catholic Church, different Popes can be cited in support of each option.

The question at issue is often posed in the confused form "When does life begin?" If this means "At what stage of the process between conception and birth are we dealing with living matter?" the answer is obvious: at every stage. At fertilization egg and sperm unite to form a single cell: that is a living cell just as the egg and sperm were themselves alive before their fusion. But this is clearly not the question which is relevant to the moral status of the embryo: worms and rosebuds are equally indubitably alive, but no one seeks to give their lives the protection of the law.

So perhaps we should reformulate the question: "When does human life begin?" Here too, the answer is obvious but inadequate: the newly formed conceptus is a *human* conceptus, not a canine or leonine one, so in that sense its life is a human life. But equally the sperm and the ovum from which the conceptus originated were human sperm and human ovum; but no one nowadays wishes to describe them as human beings or unborn children. If asked "When does life begin?" We must respond with another question "When does the life *of what* begin?"

Sometimes the question is formulated not in terms of life, but in terms of animation or personhood. Thus it is asked "When does the soul enter the body?" or "when does an embryo become a human person?" Modern discussions of the morality of abortion or of the status of the embryo often shy away from these questions, regarding them as matters of theology or metaphysics. Thus the Warnock Committee, whose report on human fertilization and embryology paved the way in England for the legalisation of experimentation on embryos, observed that some people thought that if it could be decided when an embryo became a person it would also be decided when it might, or might not, be permissible for scientific research to be undertaken upon embryos. The committee did not agree.

> Although the questions of when life or personhood begin appear to be questions of fact susceptible of straightforward answers, we hold that the

> answers to such questions in fact are complex amalgams of factual and moral judgements. Instead of trying to answer these questions directly we have therefore gone straight to the question of *how it is right to treat the human embryo*.

A philosopher writing on these matters cannot evade, as a politician or a committee may do, the question of personhood. It is indeed a metaphysical question when personhood begins: that does not mean that it is an unanswerable question, but that it is a question for the metaphysician to answer. To answer it we must deploy concepts that are fundamental to our thinking over a wide range of disciplines, such as those of actuality and potentiality, identity and individuation: and these are the subject matter of metaphysics.

The question about personhood is also the same as the question about life, rightly understood. For "when does life begin?" must mean "When does the life of the individual person begin?"

The question is a philosophical one, but in order to answer it one does not need to appeal to any elaborate philosophical system, or appeal to quasi-theological concepts such as the soul. As so often in philosophical perplexity what is needed is not recondite information, or elaborate technicalities, but reflection on truths which are obvious and for that reason easily overlooked.

If a mother looks at her daughter, six months off her twenty-first birthday, she can say with truth "If I had had an abortion twenty-one years ago today, I would have killed you." Each of us, looking back to the date of our birthday, can say with truth "If my mother had had an abortion six months before that date, I would have been killed." Truths of this kind are obvious, and can be formulated without any philosophical technicality, and involve no smuggled moral judgements.

Taking this as our starting point, however, it is easier to find our way through the moral maze. Let us consider first fetuses, and then embryos. Those who defend abortion on the grounds that fetuses are not human beings or human persons are arguing, in effect, that they are not members of the same moral community as ourselves But truths of the kind that we have just illustrated show that fetuses are identical with the adult humans that are the prime examples of members of the moral community.

It is true that a fetus cannot yet engage in moral thinking or the rational judgement of action that enables adults to interrelate morally with each other. But neither can a young child or baby, but this temporary inability does not give us the right to take the life of a child or a baby. It is the long-term capacity for rationality that makes us accord to the child the same moral protection as the adult, and which should make us accord the like respect to whatever has the same long-term capacity, even before birth.

To be sure, there can be goodness or badness in human actions with regard to beings that are not members of the human moral community. Those who believe in God do not think of him as on terms of moral equality with us, and yet regard humans as having a duty towards him of worship. Non-human animals are not part of our moral community, and yet it is wrong to be cruel to them. But the moral respect we accord to children, and, if I am right, should accord to fetuses, is something quite different to the circumspection proper in our relation with animals. For the individual that is now a fetus or a child will, if all goes well, take its place with us, as the animal never will, as an equal member of the moral community. As Kant might say, it will become a fellow-legislator in the kingdom of ends.

I have claimed it as an obvious truth that a fetus six months from term is the same individual as the human child and adult into which, in the natural course of events, it will grow after birth. This seems true in exactly the same sense as it is true that the child is the same individual as the adult into which it will grow, all being well, after adolescence. But if we trace the history of the individual from the fetus back towards conception, then matters cease to be similarly obvious.

Many people do not seem aware of the difficulty here. In 1985 in the UK the report of a committee chaired by Mary Warnock recommended the legalisation of experimentation on pre-implantation embryos; the committee's recommendation was put into effect by the Human Embryology and Fertilization Act of 1990. In a parliamentary debate triggered by the report of the Warnock Committee one Member of Parliament, Sir Gerald Vaughan, had this to say in opposition to experimentation on embryos.

> It is unarguable that at the point of fertilization something occurs which is not present in the sperm or the unfertilized ovum. What occurs is the potential for human life—not for life in general, but life for a specific person. That fertilized ovum carries the strucutue of a specific human being—the height, the colour, the colour of his or her eyes, and all the other details of a specific person. I do not think that there can be any argument against that. The fact that the embryo at that stage does not bear a human form seems to me to beg the issue and to be quite irrelevant. It carries the potential, and, just as the child is to the adult human, so the embryo must be to the child.

Sir Gerald concluded that human rights were applicable to an embryo from the first moment of conception.

It is undoubtedly true that in the conceptus there is the blueprint for "the structure of a specific human being." But to establish the conclusion that an embryo has full human rights, a different premise is needed, namely, that the conceptus contains the structure of an individual human being. A specific human being is not an individual human being. This is an instance of a very general point about the difference between specification and individuation. The general point is that nothing is ever individuated merely by a specification of its properties, however detailed or complete this may be—as it is in the case of the DNA of an embryo. It is always at least logically possible that there should be two or more individuals answering to the same specification; any blueprint may be used more than once. Two peas in a pod may be as alike as you please: what makes them two individuals rather than one is that they are two parcels of matter, not necessarily that they differ in description.

In the case of human beings the possibility of two individuals answering to the same specification is not just a logical possibility: it is a possibility that is realised in the case of identical twins. For this reason an embryo in the early days after fertilization cannot be regarded as an individual human being. The single cell after fusion is totipotential, in the sense that from it develop all the different tissues and organs of the human body, as well as the tissues that become the placenta. In its early days a single embryo may turn into something that is not a human being at all, or something that is one human being, or something that is two people or more.

It is important to be on guard here against an ambiguity in the word "identical": there is a difference between specific identity and individual identity. Two things may be identical in the sense that they answer to the same specification, and yet not be identical in the sense that they are two separate things, not a single thing. When we say that Peter and Paul are identical twins we mean that they are alike in every specific respect, not that they are a single individual.

Between an embryo and an adult there is not an interrupted history of a single individual life, as there is linking foetal life with the present life of an adult. There is indeed an uninterrupted history of development from conception to adult; but there is equally an uninterrupted history of development back from the adult to the origination of each of the gametes that fussed at conception. But this is not the uninterrupted history of an individual. For each of the gametes might, in different cicumstances, have fused to form a single conceptus, and the conceptus might, in different circumstances, have turned into more or less than the single individual that it did in fact turn into.

Of course, all development, if it is to proceed, depends on factors in the environment: an adult may die if diseased and a child may die if not nourished, just as an ovum will die if not fertilized and an embryo will die if not implanted. But though children and adults may die, they cannot become part of something else or turn into someone else. Fetus, child, and adult have a continuous *individual* development that gamete and embryo do not have.

The moral status of the embryo and the question whether its destruction is homicide was and is important, because if it is not, then the rights and interests of human beings may legitimately be allowed to override the protection that by common consent should in normal circumstances be extended to the early embryo. The preservation of the life of the mother, the fertilisation of otherwise barren couples, and the furthering of medical research may all, it may be argued, provide reasons to override the embryo's protected status.

The line of argument I have outlined was found convincing in the United Kingdom not only by the Warnock committee but also by the later Harries committee.[4] These committees made a significant contribution to the debate by offering a *terminus ante quem* for the origin of individual human life—one which was much earlier in pregnancy than the forty days set by the pre-reformation Christian consensus. Experimentation on embryos, they thought, should be impermissible after the fourteenth day. The Warnock committee's reasons were well summarized in the House of Commons by the then Secretary of State for Health, the Rt. Hon. Kenneth Clarke.

> A cell that will become a human being—an embryo or conceptus—will do so within fourteen days. If it is not implanted within fourteen days it will never have a birth. . . . The basis for the fourteen day limit was that it related to the stage of implantation which I have just described, and to the stage at which it is still uncertain whether an embryo will divide into one or more individuals, and thus up to the stage before true individual development has begun. Up to fourteen days that embryo could become one person, two people, or even more. (*Hansard*, vol 73, col. 686)

This ethical reasoning is rejected by those Catholics who insist that individual human life begins at conception. An embryo, from the first moment of its existence, has the potential to become a rational human being, and therefore should be allotted full human rights. To be sure, an embryo cannot think or reason or exhibit any of the other activities that define rationality: but neither can a new born baby. The protection that we afford to infants shows that we accept that it is potentiality, rather than actuality, that determines the conferment of human rights.

Undoubtedly, whatever Aquinas may have thought, there is an uninterrupted history of development linking conception with the eventual life of the adult. However, the line of development from conception to fetal life is not the uninterrupted history *of an individual*. In its early days, as Kenneth Clarke indicated, a single zygote may turn into something that is not a human being at all, or something that is one human being, or something that is two people or more. Fetus, child and adult have a continuous individual development which gamete and zygote do not have. To count embryos is not the same as to count human beings, and in the case of twinning there will be two different human individuals each of whom will be able to trace their life story back to the same embryo, but neither of whom will be the same individual as that embryo.

Those who argue for conception as the moment of origin stress that before fertilisation we have two entities (two different gametes) and after it we have a single one (one zygote). A moment at which one entity (a single embryo) splits into two entities (two identical twins) is surely equally entitled to be regarded as a defining moment. It is true that in the vast majority of cases twinning does not actuallly take place; but surely the strongest element in the Catholic position is the emphasis it places on the ethical importance of potentiality. It is the potentiality of twinning, not its actuality, that gives reason for doubting that an early embryo is an individual human being.

In my view, the balance of the arguments lead us to place the individuation of the human being somewhere around the fourteenth day of pregnancy. But there are two sides to the reasoning that leads to that conclusion. If the course of development of the embryo gives good reason to believe that before the fourteenth day it is not an individual human being, it gives equally good reason to believe that after that time it *is* an individual human being. If so, then late abortion is indeed homicide—and abortion becomes "late" at an earlier date than was ever dreamt of by Aquinas.

Since most abortion in practice takes place well after the stage at which the embryo has become an individual human being, it may seem that the philosophical and theological argument about the moment of ensoulment has little practical moral relevance. That is not so. If the life of an individual human being begins at conception, then all practices which involve the deliberate destruction of embryos, at whatever stage, deserve condemnation. That is why there has been official Catholic opposition to various forms of IVF and to scientific research involving stem cells. But if the embryo, in its earliest days, is not yet an individual human being, then it need not necessarily be immoral to sacrifice it to the greater good of actual human beings who wish to conceive a child or reap the benefits of medical research.

University of Oxford

Notes

1. In animalibus perfectis, quae generantur ex coitu, virtus activa est in semine maris, secundum Philosophum in libro de Generat. Animal; materia autem fetus est illud quod ministratur a femina. In qua quidem materia statim a principio est anima vegetabilis, non quidem secundum actum secundum, sed secundum actum primum, sicut anima sensitiva est in dormientibus. Cum autem incipit attrahere alimentum, tunc iam actu operatur. Huiusmodi igitur materia transmutatur a virtute quae est in semine maris, quousque perducatur in actum animae sensitivae; non quod ipsamet vis quae erat in semine, fiat anima sensitiva, quia sic idem esset generans et generatum. . . . Postquam autem per virtutem principii activi quod erat in semine, producta est anima sensitiva in generato quantum ad aliquam partem eius principalem, tunc iam illa anima sensitiva prolis incipit operari ad complementum proprii corporis, per modum nutritionis et augmenti. (Ia, 118, 1 and 4).

2. Cambridge University Press, 2002, 105–120.

3. Such a survey has been carried out with great care by David Albert Jones in his book, *The Soul of the Embryo* (London, Continuum 2004), to which I am greatly indebted for much historical information.

4. *Report of the Committee of Inquiry into Human Fertilization and Embryology* (chaired by M. Warnock), London, HMSO, 1984; *Report of the House of Lords Select Committee on Stem Cell Research* (chaired R. Harries), London, HMSO, 2002.

The Metaphysics of Intellect(ion)

John Haldane

Abstract: In the heyday of conceptual analysis philosophical psychology was practised without regard to the ontology of mind as that was associated with disputes between materialism and non-materialism. The rise of functionalism, however, led philosophical psychology in the direction of materialism, though with a residue deriving from phenomenal consciousness. This is now widely viewed as 'the hard problem' for physicalism and probably an insuperable one for it, raising the spectre of epiphenomenalism. I argue that in fact sensory consciousness is not the greatest challenge to materialism, for that lies with the conceptual intentionality of abstract thought. I make these points in connection with the views of Aquinas and consider two of his arguments (from *ST*, Ia, q. 75) for the immateriality of intellectual acts. While finding one inadequate for reasons internal to the Thomist account of cognition, I defend the second against recent critics.

Philosophical Psychology and Philosophy of Mind

On a broad interpretation, 'philosophy of mind' encompasses the philosophical study of the nature of mindedness, its powers and operations; and to that extent it includes epistemology, philosophy of language and action, and the study of psychological concepts such as consciousness, imagination, and memory, as well as the metaphysics of mind. In the course of the twentieth century, however, a division developed between *philosophical psychology*, understood as the analysis and assessment of psychological concepts and theories, and *philosophy of mind* as the study of ontological status of mental phenomena. To some extent this was a separation of convenience, a division of labour, but it also reflected some significant meta-philosophical assumptions.

One such was the idea that the proper role of philosophy is to clarify concepts, not to make existential claims. Thus, while a philosopher might determine that a given concept is relational, or substantival say, or identify an ambiguity between ideas of process and of product, it is not his or her business to assert whether such relations, substances, processes or products actually exist, or what their ontological nature might be. It is hard at this point, when philosophy is again commitedly metaphysical, to recover the mid-century Anglo-American sense of it as pure conceptual analysis; and even if one could enter into this way of thinking it is an understanding that deserves to be repudiated. For one thing it rested on an untenable version of the analytic/synthetic distinction, assuming that there is such a thing as pure meaning unsullied by extra-linguistic fact. For another, it tended to be both ahistorical in its understanding of concepts, supposing, for example that the idea of imagination, or of ideas themselves, say, are essentially the same as they occur in Plato, Aristotle, Plotinus, Augustine, Aquinas, Descartes, and Kant; while yet being rather parochial, blithely favouring current understandings without asking where they came from or what interests they might serve.

There was also a concern, however, that if philosophy were to try to say how things are in reality then it might be embarrassed by the counter-claims of empirical scientists whose very business is to investigate the nature of the world, and whose practice had carried them far beyond simple observation into complex causal theories of the contents and character of the universe. Furthermore there was the thought, somewhat more plausible I believe, that the character of various psychological concepts such as perception and imagination can be understood independently of considering whether the subjects to which they are applied, perceivers and imaginers, are or could be immaterial or material.

The Rise and Varieties of Functionalism

Something of this last consideration served as an inspiration for a philosophical theory of mind that bridged the gap between old-style conceptual analysis and the new style (of scientifically-inclined) philosophical psychology practiced today, viz. functionalism. Here, however, it is necessary to mark a distinction that is not always observed between two varieties of functionalist theory: *logical* and *causal*, associated in the first instance with Hilary Putnam and David Armstrong, respectively.[1] According to the former, such central cognitive concepts as thought and deliberation are to be understood computationally, that is, as defined over contents which they process in various logical ways. So, for example, the mental activity of mathematical calculation is a process defined over representations of numerical quantities such that given a certain input ('2,' say) and a certain function (e.g., squaring) a certain output ('4') is produced. Such a (partial) definition of 'calculating' is metaphysically neutral inasmuch as it abstracts from such questions as whether calculators are natural or artificial, material or immaterial. So far as this kind of functional analysis is concerned, a calculator might be a pocket instrument, a human brain, a Cartesian 'ego,' or an angelic intellect. Such ontological neutrality was thought to be an advantage, since to focus on the issue of whether mental states are material or not, simply fails to address the prior issue of what makes them mental.

The other kind of functionalism, causal functionalism, is superficially similar inasmuch as it begins with an analysis of psychological concepts, proposing, for example, that the concept of belief is that of a state of a psychological system that intervenes between certain inputs to it, paradigmatically, perceptions, and certain outputs of it, again typically actions (intentionally characterised behaviour), and which mediates between them. At first sight this appears to be equally ontologically neutral, identifying psychological states by their functional roles, not by their composition or by the medium in which they occur. Against that, however, the concepts of intervention and mediation are causal ones, and their analysis has generally been taken to imply that instances of them could only be realized physically. This conclusion can be arrived at in several ways. Causing is making to occur (in the case of an event or a process) or making to be such and such in some respect or another. But occurrences, and substantial and accidental changes involve times, locations, and transformations and these are inter-connected as part of the spatio-temporal field. Causality is thus implicitly defined as part of the material domain. Relatedly, the initiation, direction or cessation of a process involves the expenditure of energy (an 'impulsion'), but energy is a physical quantum, so causality is inseparable from, even if not perhaps identical with physicality.

So, by two steps: 1) causal functionalism; and 2) causal materialism, psychology is rendered materialist. Arguably these reasonings beg the question by defining causality in relation to the physical, but a defender of the position has a powerful reply. Whenever a causal process is identified, those wishing to understand or make use of it do so by looking for physical mechanisms. That tendency may be inductively based or it may have an a priori foundation, but in either event it is real and at the very least it establishes a burden of proof on those who wish to argue that causality need not be physical. And since it is agreed that psychological states exist within causal networks, so the case is made for 'minimal materialism.'

Minimal Materialism

I introduce this expression because nothing in the line of argument described so far accounts for the intrinsic nature of mental states in physicalist terms. Indeed, it may properly be thought of as only engaging with the psychological through its extrinsic character. Here one needs to distinguish between intrinsic/extrinsic and essential/accidental. It may be essential to a state or entity that it is capable of certain kinds of causal commerce, but it does not follow that this is part of its intrinsic, non-relational character (though the causal capacity will supervene, at least in part, on the intrinsic nature). So even if it can be argued that the active and passive powers of psychological states imply their physicality this, by itself, does not show either a) how being physical explains being psychological, or even b) that every attribute of a psychological state is a physical attribute. That is to say, causal functionalism, at least as expounded here, is (apparently) compatible with some of the intrinsic features of psychological states not being physical. (I say 'apparently' in anticipation of some worries about how material and immaterial properties might be conjoined which I shall mention later in connection with epiphenomenalism).

This is where analytical philosophy of mind had got to by the early 1980s, i.e., it had disavowed the willful innocence of pure conceptual analysis and begun to connect accounts of psychological phenomena with philosophical analyses of causality (thus reuniting philosophical psychology and philosophy of mind). An important influence during this period, though one independent of the development of functionalism, was Donald Davidson's argument that while psychology as a descriptive-interpretative-explanatory field is governed by rationalistic criteria rather than by causal laws, nonetheless reflection on psychological explanations (of perception, deliberation and action) shows them to be in part causal, and hence it again implies that the referents of such explanations fall under physical laws and thus are themselves physical.[2] The anomality of the mental, as Davidson identified it, relates to psychological discourse, but the events that are described and interpreted in that scheme are not anomalous per se, and indeed are actually physicalistically explicable—though not in a manner useful for (or even intelligible to) the purposes of psychology.

Davidson's version of minimal materialism was sometimes construed as a case of property dualism according to which physical events also have non-physical, mental attributes; but that was not at all his own position, as he later made clear:

> I agree that it is because [basic psychological] concepts operate in a conceptual domain that psychology is different [from the hard sciences] but I see this difference as due to our special interest in interpreting human agents as rational agents rather than to special powers of those agents.[3]

In other words, not only are the events rationalistically accounted for by actually physical events, but rationality is a characteristic of the descriptive scheme and not of what it describes. So, far from being any kind of ontological dualism, Davidson's position was one of strict materialist monism rendered humanistic by the idea that our ways of describing and interpreting human behaviour are not reducible by analysis, or by inter-theoretic reduction, to physical explanation. The sense of a relaxed reconciliation of the psychological with the physical is captured in the following representative statement of non-reductionist orthodoxy.

> [1] There are minds; [2] there is matter; [3] mind and matter are fundamentally distinct kinds of things. The three combined underpin classical dualism. . . . [however] one can simply assert the negation of the unwelcome [3], and hang on to [1] and [2]. We may as well call this bland position a version of materialism, and I am sure that we should all be materialists in this bland sense. . . . Basically it's just the claim: No Spooks! . . . Davidson and Sartre, in their no doubt different ways, combine bland materialism with the thought that there is knowledge to be had of minds that is not available to the physical scientist. . . . [this] dualism is not (perniciously) ontological, but rather (benignly) epistemological.[4]

A further pressure in the direction of ontological materialism came from the investigation of perception. In the earlier part of the twentieth century philosophical understandings of the idea of perceiving were heavily influenced by phenomenalism, so it was assumed that the question of perceptual content was quite separate from considerations about how the physical world might actually be external to the perceiver. After all, so far as phenomenalism was concerned, there might not even be a material world. But this approach was challenged by the claim that in order for perception to be veridical it had better be the case that how things are with the perceiver corresponds to how things are in his or her environment, such that the former is dependent upon the latter (in a manner that would license the counterfactual that if things were otherwise objectively, so would they be different subjectively). This seemed intrinsic to the idea of the veridical, but it also suggested that a condition on a state being perceptual, as contrasted with its being imaginative, is that its object be present and that it be a cause (in a non-deviant manner) of the experiential state. And once again the idea of a causal connection was naturalized, making it the case that perception was only a possibility where physical causality was in play. And what has a physical source has a physical terminus, or else we face the interactionist problem pressed upon Descartes by the Princess Elizabeth of Bohemia:

> For it seems every determination of movement happens from the impulsion of a thing moved, according to the manner in which it is pushed by that which moves it, or else, depends on the qualification and figures of the superficies of the latter. Contact is required for the first two conditions, extension is required for the third. You entirely exclude extension from your notion of the soul, and contact seems to me incompatible with an immaterial thing.[5]

Materialism and the Problem of Consciousness

So, having begun with a division between philosophy of psychology and philosophy of mind, the two were reunited via the place of causality in the analysis of mental phenomena, and that reunification led in the direction of materialism, though not to the extent of explaining the psychological in physicalist terms. For Davidson, what is non-reducible is the practice of intentional ascription and interpretation; for others, however, there is something in the very nature of the objective reality that psychology describes which resists physicalism, namely phenomenal consciousness. Let beliefs and desires be functionalistically analysed not just to the extent of being shown to have causal roles, but even to the point of being identified exhaustively with types of physical realisers of those roles; still there remain qualia, the felt qualitative aspects of conscious states. This, it is widely said, is the stumbling block to materialism.

> It is consciousness, and in particular phenomenal consciousness, that makes the mind-body relation so deeply perplexing . . . it is consciousness that gives rise to the explanatory gap. . . . We all have a grasp of the subjective or phenomenal character of such states as the visual experience of orange, the feeling of anger, the sensation of being about to sneeze. Our grasp of what it is like to undergo these and other experiential states is

> supplied to us by introspection. We also have a grasp, albeit an incomplete one, of what goes on objectively in the brain and the body. But there is, it seems, a vast chasm between the two.[6]

This puts the point in terms of an explanatory gap between brain science and phenomenal awareness, and recalling Davidson's position one might wonder why a conceptual or epistemological deficiency should be thought to threaten ontological materialism. The answer lies with the claim that we have introspective access to a domain of phenomenal reality: we know that qualia exist and that they are irreducibly 'subjective' or 'apparitional,' whereas we also know that material realities are objective, their intrinsic natures being constituted independently of how or whether they are experienced. Put in Cartesian style, the argument is that while qualia are essentially subjective and necessarily experienced, material states or objects are neither and hence qualia are not material.

Interestingly, Davidson does not discuss phenomenal consciousness, and his own argument against reductionism is confined to intentional, that is to say, conceptually-informed states. He writes: "We may call those verbs mental that express propositional attitudes like believing, intending, desiring, hoping, knowing, perceiving, noticing, remembering, and so on."[7] Yet for the currently fashionable forms of anti-materialism, or non-reductionism, the intentional per se seems to present no problem. Galen Strawson represents a widespread orthodoxy when he writes:

> The existence of experience is the *only* hard part of the mind-body problem for materialists. . . . The things we think of as higher intellectual achievements are just not a philosophical problem, except in so far as they involve a capacity for experience. (my emphasis)[8]

This last is to be understood as saying that dispositional and occurrent intentional states such as believing and thinking can be adequately accounted for in causal functionalist terms, and hence materialistically; but that experiential states such as pure phenomenal consciousness, or intentional states that have an inextricable phenomenal aspect are materialistically inexplicable. In the face of this prospect there are two broad responses: 1) give up materialism as a fully comprehensive account of the mental; or 2) give up the idea that we can determine the intrinsic nature of the mental and its realization in the physical in a manner that satisfies materialist explanatory ambitions. So far as the first of these is concerned, and allowing the link between the causal and the material, this amounts to the idea that if qualia are real then they are non-physical and causally inert. In short they are epiphenomenal.[9] The second skeptical response meanwhile has earned the title 'mysterianism' and been generally viewed as defeatist.[10] Some 'all but' materialists regard the epiphenomenalist implication of the first position with a weary shrug of resignation as if to suggest that while regrettable it is a tolerable inconvenience. That, however, is disingenuous for three reasons.

First, like pregnancy, materialism is an all or nothing state of affairs. If any part of reality resists materialist accommodation then materialism is false, and that being established with regard to qualia, one might wonder whether it fails elsewhere also. Second, if there are non-material aspects of reality the issue arises of their relation to physical parts and processes. If qualia are particulars then there is the question of how they are affected by material objects, events and operations. Saying they are epiphenomeanal only disconnects them from one half of the causing/being caused pairing. So the interactionist problem reappears. If qualia are properties of material particulars (physical events, say) then in addition to the foregoing there is the issue of inherence: just how do immaterial attributes attach to material subjects? These difficulties feed a further mystery: where do qualia come from? If they have not always existed then either they were superadded to the material world or they came into existence from within it it. If superaddition, then from whence and by what power? If emergence, then how? For that would involve material causes having immaterial effects. If interactionism is a problem for Descartes, it is no less a problem for the 'all but' materialist.

The third problem is that epiphenomenalism with regard to qualitative consciousness runs contrary to common sense and informed philosophical reflection. If a rapidly combustible substance is ignited close to my face I hear the ignition, see the material burst into flames, smell the vapour, feel the surge of heat and pull back sharply. How so? Well, sensing the ignition, the flames, the vapour and the heat I react, drawing away from what I recognize to be a danger. This explanation mixes qualia, judgements, causes and effects in a naturally intelligible manner. But if epiphenomenalism were true then my drawing back would not be explained by my felt experience since that can have no effects. Instead some other causal story would have to be told in which my conscious experience is at most an effect and never a cause. It is not just that any such story will be hard to construct, it is rather that however well it may be done it will remain less plausible than the simple story according to which I drew back because of what I felt. This is how things seem, and arguably it is such primitive sense-response reactions that are the foundations of the human concept of causality. Take those away and it is hard to see how the concept might ever have arisen.

Consciousness not the Hardest Problem

Having said all of this this, however, I also want to suggest that sensory consciousness is the easier part of mindedness to account for materialistically. In proposing this I should add that I am agnostic on the question of whether consciousness is indeed physicalistically explicable but I see reason to think that it might be, while at the same time, and in opposition to the prevailing orthodoxy (though in keeping with what I suspect was Davidson's inclination), I think that the part of human psychology that is least amenable to physicalist analysis is that to which belong what Galen Strawson termed "higher intellectual achievements," and in particular intellection.

In this I am following, or at least siding with the ancients and medievals for whom mind properly concerned abstract general judgement rather than embedded, particular sensory activity which was deemed to be exercised through the body. In his essay 'Why Isn't the Mind-Body Problem Ancient,' Wallace Matson writes:

> [I]n the whole classical corpus there exists no denial of the view that sensing is a bodily process throughout. . . . The Greeks did not lack a concept of mind, even of a mind separable from the body. But from Homer to Aristotle the line between mind and body, when drawn at all, was drawn so as to put the processes of sense-perception on the side of the body.[11]

And Anthony Kenny carries the point forward to cover the period prior to Descartes:

> The old, or Aristotelian, kingdom of the mind had rather narrower boundaries than the new or Cartesian kingdom. . . . Intellectual activity was in a particular sense immaterial, whereas sense-perception was impossible without a material body. For Descartes, and for many others after him, the boundary between mind and matter was set elsewhere. . . . For every form of human sensation, according to Descartes, included an element that was spiritual rather than material, a phenomenal component which was no more than contingently connected with bodily causes, expressions and mechanisms.[12]

Of course, between Aristotle and Descartes came the neo-Platonists and it is arguable that for Plotinus consciousness is non-material. He offers two considerations concerning it which he seems to think tell against its being a material process and which merit some examination. The first is that consciousness is not distributed in parts but is unified across sense modalities: 'perception demands a common gathering place.' Considering the example discussed above, it is in and through one and the same act of perceptual consciousness that I see, hear, and smell the burning substance. But if the senses were material they would be spatially distributed and form at best an aggregate and not an intrinsic and indivisible unity. Second and related is the consideration that consciousness involves reflexive self-awareness which again would be impossible if it were a material process, for the most that could then occur is that a second-level activity operated upon a first-level one and that would only provide higher-order consciousness rather than self-consciousness *per se* (see *Enneads* IV.3.3).

This style of reasoning, involving reflection on the knowing subject, warrants the claim that Plotinus anticipates the turn in philosophy to subjective consciousness represented by Descartes. Mine is not a new observation. Writing almost a century ago, G. S. Brett remarked that, 'In Plotinus, for the first time in its history, psychology becomes the science of the phenomena of consciousness, conceived as self-consciousness'.[13] Certainly, although he knew and used extensively works of Aristotle and of Aristotelian commentators, Plotinus departed significantly from them and he is a notable exception to the rule that for ancient and medieval authors sense-perception belonged unambiguously on the bodily side of things.

Still the general point holds good and it is a useful reminder that the present-day orthodoxy according to which consciousness is the hard problem for materialism stands in marked contrast to major pre-modern traditions. More than siding with the scholastic Aristotelians, however, I wish to consider arguments associated with them, more precisely with Aquinas. But before that I should indicate, if only briefly, why I believe the matter of phenomenal consciousness may lend itself to materialist explanation.

Following a widely-favoured terminology let me distinguish objective facts from subjective ones and, correspondingly, objective from subjective 'spaces.' The distinction is best drawn by use of example. Consider then the situation in which you are seated on a winter evening by an open fire, with music playing through a sound system, and dimmer-controlled artificial lighting illuminating the room. That describes the objective situation but it has a counterpart in a description of a corresponding phenomenal array. You are aware of variation in felt warmth, of a sequence of heard melodies and rhythms, and of levels of visible illumination. Such is the character of your subjective, phenomenal 'space.' The question for the materialist is how these are related, or rather since he is supposing that experiences and their contents are themselves physical it is that of showing how the subjective is (part of) the objective. I am not concerned to try to carry through that project but I do wish to suggest why, quite apart from any prejudice towards materialism, it seems a possible one.

Put most briefly, the hope lies in the fact that the structure and contents of the two 'spaces' look to be isomorphic. The sources of heat, sound and light are physically located and the directions of phenomenal receptivity are analogously oriented. If you want to feel the heat more intensely then you should move towards the fire or pile on more logs. If you want to hear the music more clearly then you should incline towards the speakers or turn up the volume. If you want to see more clearly then you should move into the light or raise the level of it. In other words, the way to change one's experience is by adjusting one's location in physical space or by intensifying or diminishing the physical sources of felt experience. 'Stoke up the fire, I'm cold,' 'turn up the music, I can't hear it,' 'increase the light, I can't see'—all of these presume a correspondence between actions taken in the objective domain and effects registered in the subjective one. Arguably they do more, since it is no mere conjunction that the two spaces and the events within them are structurally related. It is not just an accident (even a regular one) that if I incline my head towards the speaker the heard sound intensifies. Rather, the two are related in a manner that is intrinsically intelligible. Subjective experience represents itself to itself as openness to objective space. More radically, subjective space is objective space *as experienced*. The correspondences of location and intensity point towards identities. If there is a residue it may be looked for not in a dualism of spaces but in one of perspectives or modes of origination and reception. Rather, as in scholastic cognitive psychology, it was customary to distinguish between subjective and objective being, saying, as Descartes does in his reply to Caterus, that '[T]he idea of the sun will be the sun itself existing in the understanding, not indeed formally, as it exists in the sky, but objectively in the way in which objects normally exist in the mind.'[14] It may be countered that this is a dualism all the same. Perhaps it is, but if so it is a formal rather than a material one. This incidentally is one way of interpreting what Aquinas says in the following passage:

> For even in sensible things it is to be observed that the form is otherwise in one sensible than in another: for instance, whiteness may be of great intensity in one, and of a less intensity in another: in one we find whiteness with sweetness, in another without sweetness. In the same way the sensible form is conditioned differently in the thing which is external to the soul, and in the senses which receive the forms of sensible things without receiving matter, such as the color of gold without receiving gold. [15]

Being 'conditioned differently' (*alio modo est in re et in sensu*) is compatible with being material in both instances, and for Aquinas the reception of a sensible form in the sense faculty was a material process, be it that the particular matter in which the form was received into the sense was not that of the subject in which it originated. With this encouragement offered to the project of materializing consciousness, let me now turn to the matter of intellection concerning which I think (again with Aquinas) that there is no prospect of materialist analysis or explanation (by which I mean neither an epistemological nor an ontological accommodation).

The Immateriality of the Intellect Proposed and Challenged

Consider then two arguments for the immateriality of intellectual operations that recur within Aquinas's writings. In each case I present a passage from the *Summa Theologiae* Prima Pars, question 75 (articles 2 and 5 respectively), and then a gloss or formulation of what I take to be the skeletal structure of the argument.

First, then, the argument from *conceptual omniscience*:

> It must necessarily be allowed that the principle of intellectual operation which we call the soul, is a principle both incorporeal and subsistent. For it is clear that by means of the intellect man can have knowledge of all corporeal things. Now whatever knows certain things cannot have any of them in its own nature; because that which is in it naturally would impede the knowledge of anything else. Thus we observe that a sick man's tongue being vitiated by a feverish and bitter humor, is insensible to anything sweet, and everything seems bitter to it. Therefore, if the intellectual principle contained the nature of a body it would be unable to know all bodies. Now every body has its own determinate nature. Therefore it is impossible for the intellectual principle to be a body.[16]

Gloss:

1. The intellect is able to acquire concepts corresponding to the nature of any material entity or property, and in that respect is potentially conceptually omniscient.

2. In order for the intellect to acquire a concept corresponding to a nature it cannot already have that nature itself.
3. Therefore, the intellect cannot have any material nature itself.

Second, the argument from concepts as universals:

> Whatever is received into something is received according to the condition of the recipient. Now a thing is known in so far as its form is in the knower. But the intellect knows a thing in its nature absolutely: . . . Therefore the intellectual soul itself is an absolute form, and not something composed of matter and form. For if the intellectual soul were composed of matter and form, the forms of things would be received into it as individuals, and so it would only know the individual: just as it happens with the sensitive powers which receive forms in a corporeal organ; since matter is the principle by which forms are individualized. It follows, therefore, that the intellectual soul, and every intellectual substance which has knowledge of forms absolutely, is exempt from composition of matter and form.[17]
>
> Gloss:
>
> 1. Intellectual acts are essentially constituted by conceptualized universal natures.
> 2. No materially instantiated property is universal.
> 3. Therefore, conceptualized universal natures are not materially instantiated.
> 4. What is essentially constituted by non-materials is itself non-material.

Much could be said by way of exposition and criticism of these arguments, and there is already a small but useful literature of that sort.[18] Here, however, I shall be brief, not discussing fine details of interpretation but dealing with the arguments directly: in the case of the first rejecting it for reasons internal to Aquinas's own account of intentionality; and in the case of the second defending it against two recent critics.

The argument from conceptual omniscience depends on the Thomistic thesis that cognition involves a reception of the form of the thing known into the intellect where it is deployed as a concept informing an intellectual act.[19] That is a development of an analogous claim made by Aristotle and adopted by Aquinas that in the case of sense-cognition the sensible form of the object is received into the sense. As noted, however, in the case of the latter St. Thomas holds that the process of reception and the realization of the form in the sense (which come to the same thing) are material processes. So the hand that was cold, in grasping the warm cup receives heat into the organ (the skin) and in that way itself takes on the sensible form, i.e. it becomes warm. This process of change exemplifies the general Thomistic formula according to which that which is potentially f becomes actually f through that which is already in act with respect to f. Accordingly, one cannot become what one already is actually, but only what one is potentially. Of course, intensification with respect to a form already possessed is possible but this might be accounted for either by saying that previously the form was only received partially, or by saying that one form is replaced by another from along the same sensible range. These possibilities would correspond to the difference between greater saturation of a given hue, and replacement of one shade by a darker one of the same colour. In any event it is clear why one cannot become that which one already is, or equivalently take on within a given location a form already residing there.

As Aquinas presents the argument, it is as if the form already present in the sense excludes the possibility of receiving other forms by obstructing them through some natural opposition, as in the example the bitterness already in the tongue blocks the reception of sweetness. While that may be true, it is also and more pertinently the case that existing bitterness precludes the reception of further bitterness also, though as I noted it might allow intensification (or diminution of it). The antecedently bitter tongue is unable to taste something else bitter, or something else sweet: if bitterness already, then, for so long as it remains, (that) bitterness only. This implies restriction with regard to the senses as their existing conditions limit what can be sensed. But since, let us suppose, the intellect can think of any material nature, which is to say be informed by any and every intelligible form of a material body (carbon, gold, marble, flesh, etc.), therefore it cannot have any material nature.

Leaving aside the adequacy of the account of sensation and material change more generally, the problem with this argument is that it overlooks a distinction essential for the application of the theory of form reception to the case of conceptual intentionality. As a human being I have the form humanity. If I think about the nature of dogs I am informed by caninicity, the form of dogness. But in this event my humanity is not displaced by caninncity. I do not become a dog in the respect in which I am already a man. So in addition to the idea of form inherence and reception, Aquinas needs a distinction between two ways in which a form can feature in or characterise a substance, an accident, or an act; and he has such: the distinction between possession *in esse naturale* and *in esse intentionale* (with natural and with intentional being respectively). I am naturally informed by humanity in being a man and intentionally informed by caninicity in thinking of a dog. But that necessary distinction having been drawn it is no longer possible to say, without qualification, that if you are already f you cannot become f, or that being f prohibits becoming g. Since a man may think of a dog while naturally remaining a man, why may not the intellect receive the form of a dog while naturally being made of, or being exhaustively realized by movements of flesh and blood? If there is a reason why that cannot be so, it is not demonstrated by the first proof of intellectual immateriality.[20]

How then stands the second argument? Aquinas holds a mediate position between *universalia in rebus* and nominalistic conceptualism. For him natures are as such neither one nor many, but many in things and one in the mind (*De ente et essentia*, and *Commentary on the Metaphysics*, V, 1). To each member of a natural kind K belongs an individualized nature: the kness-of-a, the kness-of-b, and so on. These natures are numerically distinct, being individuated by the matter they inform; but they are formally or specifically alike, and this formal identity provides the basis for a general nature produced by the mind in abstraction from particulars. In sense cognition individualised forms corresponding to those in the objects of sense are formed under the material conditions appropriate to the particular sense organ. In intellectual cognition, by contrast, the principle of cognition is not an individualized form but the universal. When I look at Molly the cat, both Molly and my eyes feature individualsed sensible forms of the colours of her fur. When I think that cats are animals, by contrast, the content of my mental act is not a particular cat, or the members of the set of existing cats; rather it is catness, *per se*. Catness, *per se*, however, is an abstract entity, an immaterial universal. So if intellection involves a cognitive faculty receiving forms in this way, then that faculty and its acts are themselves immaterial. Put another way, if purely conceptual thought involves universals and is thereby immaterial, then since acting follows upon being (*agere sequitur esse*) the faculty or power is itself immaterial.

Unlike the previous argument, this one does not depend upon an analysis of change, or an analogy with the causality of sensation. It rests instead on the pure metaphysics of form and nature. Yet it has recently been criticised for committing a fallacy of equivocation reminiscent of that with which I charged the first proof—in brief, the accusation is that it confuses two senses of receiving a form, in this case a universal formed by abstraction. Though taken up by Robert Pasnau in an article and in his book on *Summa Theologiae* Ia 75–89,[21] the originator of this criticism (so far as I am aware) is Joseph Novak who writes:

> The difficulty in Aquinas's argument does not lie [in the claim that] spiritual accidents must have spiritual substances in which they inhere . . . one can readily grant [this]. Rather the problem lies in attributing the property of being immaterial [intentionally] and immaterial [ontologically] in the same sense. A representation seems to possess the property of being immaterial [intentionally] while the intellect itself seems to possess the property of being immaterial [ontologically]. Moreover, one cannot argue from the immaterial quality of the form as representation to its immaterial quality as inhering accident, since the former possesses only intentional, while the latter possesses ontological, immateriality.[22]

Pasnau formulates the same point as follows:

> It seems to me that Aquinas has fallen victim to what I call the content fallacy: the fallacy of conflating facts about the content of our thoughts with facts about what shape or form those thoughts take in our mind. When Aquinas characterizes the soul as having one power through which it makes things actually immaterial by abstracting from the conditions of individual matter, a power which is called the agent intellect (79.4 ad 4), it seems to me that he has fallen victim to an ambiguity in the phrase "abstracting from the conditions of individual matter." That phrase might mean that the agent intellect produces an entity that is immaterial rather than material . . . or that the agent intellect changes the representational

> content . . . making it so that the newly formed intelligible species no longer represents "the conditions of individual matter."[23]

The general suggestion, then, is that there is a distinction between epistemological or representational abstraction on the one hand, as when one moves from an idea or representation of Molly to a concept or representation of catness, and metaphysical or ontological abstraction on the other, whereby a material particular yields an abstract universal. In the case of the latter there is an existential difference between a material and an immaterial entity, while in the case of the former the difference is in intentional content. And granting that the process of intellectual abstraction may effect the latter, producing universal ideas (concepts) from particular representations (percepts), it does not follow that in crossing this intentional divide one has also crossed the ontological one between the material and the immaterial.

Conclusion

What is to be made of this? Here I must leave aside exegetical questions as requiring too lengthy a treatment and deal only with the philosophical possibilities. So far as the former are concerned the fact is that St. Thomas says many things in different places suggesting different interpretations and it may well be that he never fully reconciled these. It would be highly worthwhile and very useful if someone were to take up the work of cataloguing, analyzing, evaluating and integrating Aquinas's stated positions on these issues, but that is not something I can even begin here. Instead I wish to suggest a response to the fallacy objection that does credit to the originality of Aquinas's metaphysics of cognition and leaves the original argument standing.

Distinguish then between thoughts as mental acts and thoughts as intentional contents. If at exactly the same time during a particular day in AD 50, Peter and Paul both thought that Andrew had progressed from being a catcher of fish to being a fisher of men, then we can say that they had the same thought (content) while yet having different thoughts (episodes). Different criteria of identity and individuation apply to acts and to contents, though they may be mixed as when we say that A thought of B while walking home at midnight. For the strict materialist, whatever thoughts (as mental acts or states) are about, angels, say, they themselves are certainly material entities; whereas for an absolute idealist whatever thoughts may be about, rocks, for example, in themselves they are immaterial. For Aquinas, as we have seen, sensory acts have particular sensibles as their objects and are themselves sensible particulars. Both sensings and what they represent exist under material conditions, individuated by the quantities of stuff that they characterise. Through a process of intellectual abstraction, however, particulars (states of the sense-faculties) having particular contents (being of this or that individualsied sensible form) are used to form general conceptions. There is no disagreement about this. The challenge of the critics is that Aquinas fallaciously moves from content de-particularisation to ontological dematerialisation, whereas there is nothing in the former that requires or supports the latter, and so far as abstractness of content is concerned that is compatible with it being carried by a material representation. Just as for Berkeley thoughts of rocks were made of mind, so for the materialist Aquinas's thoughts of angels may be made of brain.

One might respond with three points. First, whereas in the case of sensory consciousness I argued that the phenomenal content presents itself as openness to a material world, in the case of conceptual thought there is no corresponding environment shaped phenomenology. Acts of intellectual judgement may be accompanied by all sorts of conscious imagery or by none, but their intrinsic content is abstract. Relatedly, while the conceptual contents of such acts may have actual or possible empirical extensions (as in the judgement that cats are animals), equally they may be such as could not possibly have anything like empirical realization conditions since they concern *abstracta* or *entia immaterialia*: as in a universally quantified mathematical formula, or in the judgement that every angel is a species unto itself. A reply to these first two points might be to reassert the distinction between thoughts as acts and as contents and to insist that the non-intimation of the materiality of an act by its content, and even the apparent opposition to materiality by a content, are compatible with the act itself being material.

These issues deserve further consideration but I omit that now since my third point undercuts the distinction deployed in the charge of equivocation against Aquinas and in the anticipated responses to the previous rejoinders. In the case of sensory-cognition Aquinas's account of this involves material causation and therefore encourages the thought that presentational content *per se* is compatible with materiality. A generalisation from that might take the form of distinguishing act and content and deploying this in the ways considered above. But there is another possibility compatible with the materiality of sensory cognition but which blocks the act/content distinction as formulated and thereby denies the critic's use of it against Aquinas. Suppose that instead of distinguishing representations as vehicles of content from representational content as such, one identifies sensory acts with their sensuous contents, and intellectual acts with their conceptual contents, treating both as pure *Vorstellungen* or cognitive presentations. On that account the presentation of a material particular as content is identical with the occurrence of a material particular, a state of the sensory system of the subject. Similarly, the presentation of an abstract universal, being immaterial in content is thereby immaterial in substance.

This possibility has several features to commend it. First, it explains the asymmetry in phenomenology between sensory and intellectual cognition: in the former one is aware of a synthesis of received material form and sentient corporeality; in the latter there is nothing sensible of which to be aware. Second, it is also conducive to intentional realism, not requiring cognitive states to be internal to the subject but allowing them to be actualizations of a potentiality to receive external forms, the very reception of which may constitute direct knowledge of reality. Third, it provides an interpretation of Aquinas's second argument in which it does it not rest on a fallacy, a suggestion that, as Pasnau remarks of his own analysis, involves a 'not very charitable explanation'[24] of Aquinas's linking of intentional and ontological abstraction. Finally, it provides the basis for a re-examination of an argument that deserves close attention not only as key to an important theme in Aquinas's work but as a route into the issue of materialism and immaterialism: one that reunites philosophical psychology and philosophy of mind, but which also bypasses something of the blockage arising from the neo-Cartesian obsession with phenomenal consciousness.[25]

St. Andrews University

Notes

1. See Hilary Putnam, "Psychological Predicates" in *Art, Mind and Religion*, ed. W. H. Capitan and D. D. Merrill (Pittsburgh: University of Pittsburgh Press, 1967); and David Armstrong, "The Causal Theory of Mind" in Armstrong, *The Nature of Mind and Other Essays* (Ithaca: Cornell University Press, 1981).

2. The locus classicus for the presentation of this argument is Donald Davidson, "Mental Events" in *Experience and Theory*, ed. L. Foster and J. W. Swanson (Amherst: University of Massachusetts Press, 1970).

3. Donald Davidson, "Reply to Peter Lanz" in *Reflecting Davidson*, ed. Ralph Stoeker (Berlin: de Gruyter, 1993) 303.

4. Gregory McCullough, *Philosophical Books*, vol. 42, no. 4, 2001, 264 and 267.

5. John J. Blom, *Descartes, his Moral Philosophy and Psychology* (New York: New York University Press, 1978), 106.

6. Michael Tye, "Absent Qualia and the Mind-Body Problem," *Philosophical Review*, vol. 115, no. 2, 2006, 139 and 163.

7. Donald Davidson, "Mental Events," 83.

8. Galen Strawson. *Mental Reality* (Cambridge, Mass.: MIT Press.1994).

9. In this connection see Jaegwon Kim, *Physicalism or Something Near Enough* (Princeton, N.J.: Princeton University Press, 2005).

10. See Colin McGinn, *The Mysterious Flame* (New York: Basic Books, 1999).

11. Wallace Matson, "Why Isn't the Mind-Body Problem Ancient?" in *Mind, Matter and Method*, ed. P. Feyerabend and G. Maxwell (Minneapolis, Minn: University of Minnesota Press, 1996), 93 and 96.

12. Anthony Kenny, *Aquinas on Mind* (London: Routledge, 1993).

13. G. S. Brett, *A History of Psychology* (London: Allen and Unwin, 1912) vol. 1, 302. For an interesting discussion of consciousness in Plotinus see Richard E. Aquila, "On Plotinus and the 'Togetherness' of Consciousness" *Journal of the History of Philosophy*, vol. 30, 1992, to which I owe the reference to Brett's work.

14. See Descartes, *Philosophical Works*, trans. E. Haldane and G. R. T. Ross (London: Cambridge University Press, 1967) vol. II., 10

15. Aquinas, *Summa Theologiae*, literally translated by Fathers of the English Dominican Province (London: R & T. Washbourne, Ltd. 1912) Ia, q.84, a 1.

16. *Summa Theologiae*, Ia, q.75, a 2.

17. Ibid.

18. See J. Deely, "The Immateriality of the Intentional as Such," *New Scholasticism*, vol. 42, 1968; David Ruel Foster, "Aquinas on the Immateriality of the Intellect," *The Thomist*, Vol. 55, 1991, and "Aquinas's Arguments for Spirit," in *Religions and the Virtue of Religion*, ACPA Proceedings vol. 65, 1991; Matthew Kelly, "Aquinas and the Subsistence of the Soul: Notes on a Difficulty," *Franciscan Studies*, vol. 27, 1967; Anthony Kenny, *Aquinas on Mind*, op. cit. chap. 11 "The Nature of the Soul"; Herbert McCabe, "The Immortality of the Soul" in *Aquinas: A Collection of Critical Essays*, ed. Anthony Kenny (Garden City, N.Y.: Doubleday, 1969); Joseph Novak, "Aquinas and the Incorruptibility of the Soul," *History of Philosophy Quarterly*, vol. 4, 1987; and Robert Pasnau, "Aquinas and the Content Fallacy," *Modern Schoolman*, vol. 75, 1998, and *Thomas Aquinas on Human Nature* (Cambridge: Cambridge University Press, 2002) chap. 10.3 "Abstraction."

19. The analysis of cognition in terms of the reception and exercise of species becomes particularly intricate in the writings of later Thomists, often involving additions to and changes of terminology. The best account of the subject as it is treated by St. Thomas himself is Bernard Lonergan, *Verbum: Word and Idea in Aquinas*, ed. David Burrell (London: Darton, Longman and Todd, 1968), and for Aquinas and later Thomism more generally see John Peifer, *The Concept in Thomism* (New York, N.Y.: Record Press, 1952) reprinted as Volume 3 of *Modern Writings on Thomism*, selected and introduced by John Haldane (London: Thoemmes Continuum, 2004). Piefer's book is unduly neglected and rewards study.

20. For further criticisms of this first argument see David Ruel Foster, "Aquinas on the Immateriality of the Intellect," op. cit. Foster also believes that it requires supplementation by the second argument which he expounds but does not critically assess, but of which he writes, "I believe that this is the most fundamental argument for the immateriality of the intellect and is the one that promises to be most useful in the present day" (418).

21. Robert Pasnau, "Aquinas and the Content Fallacy," op. cit., and *Thomas Aquinas on Human Nature*, op. cit.

22. Joseph Novak, "Aquinas and the Incorruptibility of the Soul," 413.

23. Robert Pasnau, *Thomas Aquinas on Human Nature*, 315–316.

24. Ibid., 351.

25. I am grateful to Tony Lisska for the invitation to deliver the lecture to the 2006 meeting of the ACPA in Granville, Ohio, upon which this text is based. His friendly hospitality and intellectual encouragement were much appreciated. The writing of this essay was made possible by research support from the Institute for the Psychological Sciences. I am grateful to Dr. Gladys Sweeney, Dean of the Institute, for facilitating this support.

The Place of Intellect in Aristotle

Kurt Pritzl

Abstract: This paper explores Aristotle's account of the human intellect, with special emphasis on how this account relates to Aristotle's treatment of nature. In his complex account of the intellect, Aristotle distinguishes very broadly between two types of intellection. One type (*nous*) involves the reception of what things are and is non-discursive in character, while the other type (*dianoia*) is the result of intellectual activity and is discursive in character. While Aristotle affirms that both types of thinking are distinctive and essential functions of the intellect, it is also clear that *dianoia* presupposes *nous*, insofar as *dianoia* assumes as given what *nous* has received. This paper also investigates Aristotle's account of truth, arguing that the very principles of the intellect's functioning are naturally given to the intellect. Given Aristotle's account of the intellect as well as his account of truth and the principle of non-contradiction, one can see that, for Aristotle, nature has a primacy relative to the intellect.

> From these facts one might think that the only cause is the so-called material cause; but as men thus advanced, the very facts (*auto to pragma*) showed them the way and joined in forcing them to investigate the subject (*sunênangkase zêtein*).
>
> —*Metaphysics 1.3.984a18–19*

> The first of those who studied philosophy were misled in their search for truth and the nature of things by their inexperience (*hupo apeirias*), which as it were thrust them into another path.
>
> —*Physics 1.8.191a24–27*

> It is evident, then, even from what we have said before, that all men seem to seek the causes named in the *Physics*, and that we cannot name (*eipein*) any beyond these; but they seek these vaguely; and though in a sense they have all been described (*eirêntai*) before, in a sense they have not been described at all.
>
> —*Metaphysics 1.10.993a11–15*

1

I am honored by the invitation to give this paper about Aristotle's account of the human intellect. I want to get underway by outlining contrasts between Aristotle and Nietzsche developed by Thomas Prufer, my late colleague at Catholic University, whose brilliant, carefully crafted pieces of philosophical writing defy paraphrase and deserve to be long studied for what Hans-Georg Gadamer called their "unique vision."[1]

Prufer observes that in Aristotle nature has primacy and that un-naturalness is included within and subordinate to nature. By contrast, Nietzsche gives creativity primacy rather than nature and "reduces nature to the unarticulated and the indeterminate" (*to aoriston*, 1007b27–29; *a-horos*) so that creativity will face minimal resistance in its workings.[2]

Prufer develops these contrasts by reference to Aristotle's treatment of the principle of non-contradiction in *Metaphysics* 4. He notes with Aristotle that everyone, including the philosopher, accepts or takes as granted a *doxa* (4.3.1005b33) which is first (*archê*, 1005b33; indeed first by nature [*phusei . . . archê*]), last (*eschatên*, 1005b33), presuppositionless (*anupotheton*, 1005b14), and unsubordinated (*ouch hupothesis*, 1005b16), namely, the principle of non-contradiction. The philosopher is different from other people, however, for always seeking to provide an account or *logos*, even of a *doxa* that is first, last, presuppositionless and unsubordinated. To do so in such a special case, Aristotle requires according to Prufer "the un-naturalness of a freak or monster, the opponent who opposes in speech the differences . . . without which there is no *logos*."[3] The differences necessary for *logos* are (a) the differences among kinds (*sêmainein ti*, 4.4.1006a21) and (b) the difference between truth and falsity (4.5.1009a9). The un-naturalness of the opponent of the principle of non-contradiction entails denying these two differences. The first difference, the differences among kinds, in Aristotle's philosophy depends upon the forms of natural things.[4] The second difference, the difference between truth and falsity, depends upon the cognition of the differences among kinds. Prufer fills out the meaning of nature, with respect to which the opponent of the principle of non-contradiction is un-natural, in a way that bridges natural things and their cognition as natural. He writes that nature is "being as *eidos*, *horos* (boundary, term, demarcation, definition), *logos*, and *nous*-ing the first and last *doxa*."[5] Prufer then discusses how the opponent's un-naturalness—denying nature in speech—is actually subordinate to nature.[6] The subordination of the un-naturalness of the opponent to nature is clear in the way in which the philosopher achieves the justification or *logos* of the *nous*-ed first, last, presuppositionless, and unsubordinated *doxa*. It is achieved not by arguing on the basis of some other *doxa*, but "only by displaying in speech the self-refutation in speech of such an opponent."[7]

In a footnote to this description of the special non-demonstrative justification or *logos* of the *nous*-ed *doxa* Prufer raises a question about the nature of the *nous* or intellection through which humans are granted a first, last, presuppositionless, and unsubordinated *doxa*. He writes: "Does rest (*nous*, *intellectus*, *intuitus*) include a potentiality for being complemented by motion (*logos, ratio, discursus*)?"[8] The *nous*-ed *doxa* is a matter of rest, not motion. Motion and activity of the intellect from other beliefs, presuppositions, principles, or hypotheses does not account for *nous* in this case. Nevertheless, even the rest that is the *nous*-ed *doxa* finds a justification, a peculiar one, by the peculiar motion of "using the freakish and monstrous un-naturalness of the opponent" to display how voicing a denial of nature refutes itself.[9]

Thus the primacy of nature recognized by Aristotle includes the natural acceptance by the human intellect of a first, last, presuppositionless, and unsubordinated *doxa*. This natural acceptance is a form of rest rather than intellectual motion or creativity. Prufer does not question that such *nous* is rest but asks rather whether this rest includes *within itself* the potential to be complemented by the motion that is *logos, ratio, discursus*. This question is one focus of my paper. Prufer's observation that even the un-naturalness of the opponent of the principle of non-contradiction is subordinate to nature draws attention as a special case to the larger issue of this paper, namely, the extent to which all intellectual motion and creativity is subordinate to nature in its primacy, a primacy entailing the differences of kinds and the difference between truth and falsity.

With the primacy of nature as framework and context I want to consider Aristotle's account of the human intellect with respect to rest, on the one hand, and motion, activity, or creativity, on the other. Within his complex analysis of the intellect Aristotle distinguishes very broadly between two types of intellection—one type, *nous*, that is a reception and is non-discursive in character and another type, *dianoia*, that is the result of intellectual activity and is discursive in character. The former is rest with the potentiality within it, indeed the impetus, to be complemented by motion. The latter is motion—indeed, the results of this latter intellection are "made" by the intellect, as *De Anima* 3.6.430b5–6 puts it—but this motion is subordinate to intellection as rest in identifiable ways.[10] My paper is an attempt to explain these claims, which are controversial as an interpretation of Aristotle, and thereby to display some of the strength of Aristotle's position over the alternatives. The starkest foil to this picture of Aristotle, as Prufer realizes, is Nietzsche, precisely because he so decidedly gives primacy to creativity in the human person—to doing and making—and denies nature its sharp edges and its power to shape and form.[11] From the beginning of modernity to this day there are other foils (for example, Descartes, Kant, cognitive science).[12] Aristotle's position is an important one to stake out. The principal texts for my discussion are Aristotle's account of the intellect in *De Anima* 3.4–8 and Aristotle's treatment of truth in *Metaphysics* 6.4 and 9.10.

2

Aristotle's account of the intellect and thinking in *De Anima* 3.4–8 concentrates in a thoroughgoing, almost extreme way, on thinking as passive reception of form (*De Anima* 3.4.429a13–18) and on the intellect as the power or faculty capable of receiving form. The intellect is the "place of forms" according to *De Anima* 3.4.429a27–29.[13] The first positive move in the *De Anima* 3.4–8 account is to compare thinking to sensing as a manner of being affected by its object (3.4.429a13–14). Aristotle first discusses cognitive passivity in the discussion of sensation in *De Anima* 2.5, where after some initial considerations he makes what he calls a beginning: "To begin with let us speak as if there were no difference between being moved or affected, and being active" (*proton men oun hôs tou autou ontos tou paschein kai tou kinesthai kai tou energein legômen*, 417a14–16). One of the things I take this beginning statement to mean and that is borne out later is that the being moved or affected, that is, the receiving, *is* the cognizing (what is received both in sensation and intellection is form, the form of the known thing: 2.12.424a18; 3.4.429a15–16; 4.8.431b26–432a3). Neither the sense faculty nor the intellect as a cognizing faculty looks at or grasps the received form as its cognitive object (for the intellect what Michael Wedin calls the "searchlight model"[14]); the receiving *is* the cognizing of the object in the world.

Some interpreters of Aristotle's account of the intellect diminish the importance of the opening comparison between sensing and thinking and argue that Aristotle labors to backpedal from it. They seem motivated principally by worries that accepting the comparison at face value saddles Aristotle with an unacceptably occult ontology of the intellect, the specter of an immaterial entity rather than a material organ receiving forms. Whatever the solution to the anxiety, the fundamental point of the comparison, the first thing he chooses to say about the intellect, is that reception of form *is* thinking most fundamentally and foundationally.[15] The intellect does not do anything except receive, in order to be alive with awareness.

This crucial first point perfectly suits Aristotle's remarkable emphasis on the passive dimensions of intellection. This passive account supports Aristotle's direct realism,[16] since it supports an account of the identity of knower and known in actual knowledge. The forms of the things in the world, the principles that make those things to be what they are, are received by the intellect and the having of them in the intellect is the primary intellectual cognition of the thing.

This crucial first point is also immediately amplified by Aristotle in two key ways as he proceeds in *De Anima* 3.4. (1) He argues that the intellect "can have no nature (*physin mêdemian*) of its own, other than that of having a certain capacity (*dunatos*)" and that "before it thinks" it is "not actually any real thing" (429a21–22, 24). (2) He concludes that the intellect, now understood as potential to forms, is well-named as the "place of forms" (*topon eidôn*, 429a27–29).[17] There is remarkably little commentary on this key phrase.[18] In the *Physics* Aristotle describes place as neither form nor matter, but rather as a surrounding vessel or container (*Ph.* 4.1.209a19–22; 4.2.209b21–32; 4.3.210b27–31; 4.4.212a1–2, a14–16). A place neither adds to nor takes away from what it holds. In the intellect as a place forms can exercise their specific actuality (a) without material generation or alteration occurring, (b) without the intellect actively doing anything to or with the form received, and (c) without distortion or interference.

The intellect as a place, that is, what receives forms without acting on them, is consequently a place of rest. Aristotle explicitly states at a point in the *De Anima* 1 arguments against a moved or self-moved soul that the process of thinking is serial rather than continuous. Thinking is thinking one thing at a time, one thing after another, and in each instance thinking resembles "a sort of rest or coming to a halt, and not motion" (*De An.* 1.3.407a32–33).[19] More than any other case of thinking, thinking as pure reception of form is rest. Yves Simon ends his account of Aristotle's position that sensation is not motion, that is, that it is an immanent rather than a transitive action, in a memorable and far-seeing way: "Unlike movement, sensation is an activity by way of rest. It is the first image of heaven."[20] Intellection as reception of form in the place that is the intellect is an activity by way of rest. It is, also, a closer image of heaven than sensation. Aristotelian heaven is populated with separate substance as pure actuality without matter, which is the ultimate instance of life as "the actuality of thought" (*hê gar nou energeia zôê, Metaph.* 12.7.1072b26–27) and thought thinking itself (*hauton ara voei . . . kai estin hê noêsis noêseôs noêsis,* 12.9.1074b33–35). This ultimate instance of cognition is absolutely free of motion and is not wearisome (12.9.1074b25–27, 29). It is the prime instance and analogue for all acts of cognition, sensible or intellectual.

Indeed, the initial fundamental account in *De Anima* 3.4 of human thinking as reception of form and thus a type of rest in the place that is intellect should be directly read off of this prime and ultimate instance of cognition—pure actuality without motion which is actual living thinking without distinction of subject and object, knower and known.[21] *De Anima* 2.4.415a29–b2 explains that any natural being as natural does whatever it does so that "as far as its nature allows, it may partake in the eternal and divine." Human thinking as reception of form in the place that is the intellect is arguably the closest and most direct instance of eternal and divine actuality in the realm of nature.[22] The human intellect must be self-effacing, having no nature of its own except to be potential and existing as a place of forms, for this to be the case.

It is worth emphasizing how unusual a notion of thinking this is and consequently how unusual a notion of intellect. Thinking is usually conceived as something done by an intellect, not by a thing.[23]

3

The other half of noting Aristotle's emphasis on thinking as a passive reception of form in his account of intellect in *De Anima* 3.4–8 is pointing out that Aristotle also concerns himself with the ways in which we normally and naturally understand the intellect to be active. These normal modes of discursive intellectual activity include judgment or proposition formation, reasoning and inferring, shifts in attention and the direction of the flow of thought, and so on.

The texts of the *De Anima* amply acknowledge that the human intellect is active in such ways. It mentions being able to think at will (*De Anima* 3.4.429b7) and makes much of the stages of actualization of the intellect upon thinking and learning (e.g., *De Anima* 2.5.417a21–b2). The verb *dianoeisthai,* which denotes discursive thinking in contradistinction to *noein,* is explicitly attributed to the intellect (*De Anima* 3.4.429a23; see also 1.4.408b3, b9, b14, b25 and 3.3.427b13) and used frequently.[24]

Aristotle discusses a variety of intellectual objects and the discursive intellectual activity appropriate to them in *De Anima* 3.6. As a first instance he considers judgments or propositions. The obvious discursive activity of judgment or proposition formation, which opens up the logical space for falsity, is the result of combining and separating by the intellect. Aristotle wants to treat both of these as different expressions of the same operation ("It is possible also to call all these cases [of combination or union] division" [430b3–4].) and the operation that he has in mind is making or forming a unity. In his most explicit statement in the *De Anima* of how the intellect does something, he writes with respect to propositions: "In each and every case that which unifies [*to de hen poioun*] is thought [*ho nous*]" (430b5–6). A literal rendering says that the intellect *makes* one. In fact, the unitary or the indivisible is the rubric according to which Aristotle carries on the entire discussion of discursive thought in *De Anima* 3.6.

Aristotle amplifies what he means by this operation of the intellect in *Metaphysics* 6.4 where he makes the following point about the intellect's activity of combining and dividing: "it is another question, how it happens that we think things together or apart; by 'together' and 'apart' I mean thinking them so that there is no succession in the thoughts but they become a unity" (1027b23–25). The actual discursive thinking of a combination or a division is the thinking of a unity or oneness (*hen ti*, 6.4.1027b25). As a psychological achievement it is an actual unity; there is no passage from concept to concept; a proposition is thought as a whole. The linear linguistic expression of the logical structure of subject, predicate, copula, temporal aspect, and so on, is not the psychological character of the proposition as it is entertained in *dianoia*. This is why the *De Anima* 3.6 discussion of discursive objects of thought considers them as indivisibles or unitaries[25] and says in its most explicit statement of how the intellect works that in each case the intellect makes one. But in what sense does the intellect *make* this unity in thought? How does combining and separating *effect* such a unity in thought?

While it is possible that Aristotle is positing a genuine creative power of the human intellect to fuse or bind the parts of propositions into the psychological unity achieved in propositional thinking, rather like the Love of Empedocles mentioned in the *De Anima* 3.6 passage that can put anything together with anything else (430a28–31), it is more likely, I think, that discursive thinking is thinking of things themselves, in their complexity, which are actual unities in some form or other. The axiom of Aristotle's account of cognition is the identity of soul with its object, not mere representation, which is effected primarily in thinking as reception of form. Somehow the basis for the "products" of discursive thought, which are unitary, are the actual unitary things in the world in their complexity.[26] Aristotle's treatment of intelligible objects keeps its center of gravity on things, and not on propositions or beliefs about things, which are themselves treated rather as things considered in the complexities of their being. Actual states of affairs, for Aristotle, are things insofar as they are complex or composite.[27] The discursive unity achieved by the intellect in proposition formation, say, is a unity derivative from the unity of things themselves in their natures and in their complex relationships with other things.

Aristotle goes on in *De Anima* 3.6 to consider a number of other intellectual performances besides judgment, all of which require discursive activity by the intellect, namely, the cognition of mathematical points, of privations, and of generic universals.[28] This last type—the cognition of generic universals such as animal—is particularly noteworthy. Aristotle treats even it as a discursive achievement of the intellect. He does not think that there is a form in the strict sense of a physical or metaphysical principle for every common name. There is in this strict sense no form "animal" and therefore the thinking of "animal" and the intellectual awareness of animals as animals cannot be the result simply of the intellect's receiving the form "animal." It must be the result of discursive activity based upon the reception of the forms of specific animals.[29] Thus discursive activity by the intellect is much more pervasive in Aristotle's account of intellectual cognition than most recognize, though it is not thoroughly pervasive. The cut occurs between the intellection that is reception of form in the place that is the intellect and the intellection achieved by the intellect that makes one (the cognition of generic universals, mathematical points, privations, and so on, as well as propositions).

Aristotle's recognition of higher-order discursive activity by the intellect in company with sheer reception of form is importantly linked to Aristotle's position that thinking is a form of life. Aristotle considers life to be an equivocal *pros hen* or by reference (*De An.* 2.2.413a22–25). As noted above, the primary instance of life to which the other instances of life refer, including the life of the human intellect, is that of divine separate substance ("And life also belongs to God; for the actuality of thought [the *energeia* of *nous*] is life," *Metaph.* 12.7.1072b27).[30] To see human thinking as a form of life is to attribute to it a teleologically driven momentum toward full truth. Aristotle says explicitly that the intellect is "a special faculty dealing with truth" (*tôi nôi hôs dunamei tini peri tên alêtheian, De An.* 1.4.404a30–31) and that truth is the *telos* of all theoretical inquiry.[31] The theoretical life of the intellect includes the discursive activities necessary to recognize facts, achieve inductions, make inferences, discover causes, and in general develop bodies of knowledge and so possess greater and more articulate truth.[32] Thinking as a form of life means that it is striving for a fulfillment in truth.[33] Thus Aristotle's writings present a complex account of partial and full truth, vague and clear truth, and truth in degrees, which is adequate to the teleologically driven life of the intellect and far from the modern non-teleological correspondence theory of truth, for which Aristotle's account of truth is often held to be the precursor or pioneer.[34] Alasdair MacIntyre, for one, nicely distinguishes the modern "epistemological enterprise" which is first-person and non-teleological from the "Aristotelian or Thomistic enterprise" which is third-person and teleological. He notes that "as a given soul moves successfully towards its successive intellectual goals in a teleologically ordered way" it increasingly achieves as one intellect among many cognition that is "adequate" to "the objects of its knowledge."[35] Both the third-person and the teleological characteristics of intellection in the Aristotelian account ultimately derive from intellection as reception of form in the place of the intellect. Things through their forms provide intellectual life, including the drive to further articulation and comprehension achieved by the intellect itself through its discursive activities. These discursive activities are within and subordinate to the life provided by the reception of the forms of things in the place of the intellect. Because things have primacy in this way and because thinking does not begin immediately in the doings or makings of the individual intellect the public and teleological character of the "Aristotelian enterprise" is possible. The teleological cognitional life afforded human persons together by their intellects is lived out and advanced over time by a wide range of discursive activities whose *telos* is fuller and eventually full truth. Aristotle's account of truth sheds light on this process and on the interrelationship of the two types of intellection, *nous* and *dianoia*, which together constitute intellectual life according to Aristotle. To this we now turn.

4

Let me make two preliminary points about Aristotle's account of truth.

[1] Aristotle considers truth a type of being, along with three other types of being (the categories; actuality and potentiality; and accidental being).[36] This conforms to Greek linguistic usage where the *alêtheia* words can mean reality and the real, and where the veridical sense of *esti* ("is" as "is true") is arguably the most ancient sense of the verb.[37] It also perfectly fits Aristotle's claims [1] that thinking is reception of form, since form is the principle that makes a thing what it is, and [2] that in cognition "the soul is in a way all things" (*De An*. 3.8.431b21).

[2] Aristotle's writings contain what I call both an explicit and an implicit account of truth. The explicit account of truth consists chiefly of two cross-referenced discussions in *Metaphysics* 6.4 and *Metaphysics* 9.10, which present two types of truth answering to two types of thing. The implicit account of truth consists of references to and remarks about partial and full truth, vague and clear truth, and truth in degrees scattered throughout his writings. These references and remarks can usefully be considered in relation to what Aristotle says about dialectic and to his dialectical practice, whose concerns include displaying and exploiting the partial, vague, and degree of truth present in beliefs people hold. Study of Aristotle's dialectical practice, in particular, reveals how difficult it is to find completely false propositions. Truth exists in abundance in Aristotle's view. It is a door hard not to hit (*Metaph*. 2. 1.993b5). As he puts it when discussing the partial and limited views of his predecessors, the facts (*auto to pragma*) lead the way as humans form judgments, make inferences, and characterize matters under consideration (*Metaph*. 1.3.984a18–19).

In Aristotle's explicit account of truth one type of truth, the familiar type, is often called propositional or logical truth. Its opposite is falsity and it is ordered to composite things. It is founded in the discursive combining and dividing activity of thought, which Aristotle calls *dianoia*, done in relation to the combinations and divisions existing in things ("A is b" is true when A is b, and so on). In my view, this type of truth is more accurately called dianoetic truth, since, as I have pointed out above, Aristotle does not limit discursive thinking to thinking propositions.

The other type of truth is sometimes called metaphysical truth. I prefer to call it noetic truth, because Aristotle uses *nous* and *noein* rather than *dianoia* and *dianoeisthai* with respect to it, and I do not find it any more or less metaphysical than dianoetic truth. It is an ordinary part of thinking. Noetic truth relates to incomposite things. Its opposite is not falsity but ignorance. It takes the form of "contact and saying" (*thigein kai phanai*, *Metaph.* 9.10.1051b24; the Oxford translation has "assertion," which does not capture Aristotle's intended meaning of the utterance of a single word, as the later contrast with *kataphasis* or "affirmation" at 1051b24–25 shows), in contradistinction to dianoetic combination or division as affirmation or denial. A *phasis* or "saying" is the smallest significant unit of speech contained in a statement. Aristotle at one place gives the example of "man" (*Int.* 4.16b27; cf. 5.17a17; 1.16a10–12, 16a30). To have truth with respect to incomposite or simple things is to be in contact with them. To lack this truth is to be ignorant of them, not to be in error. This contact is like saying or speaking the most elemental units of significance among things. It is also like sensing, for Aristotle says at *De Anima* 3.7.431a8 that "sensing (*to aisthanesthai*) . . . is like bare asserting or thinking (*phanai monon kai noein*)." This contact is not to be construed as the intellect making contact or getting itself into contact with the incomposite thing, but rather as there being contact between thing or intellect, or better, like sensation, as the incomposite thing making contact with the intellect (this reading is supported by considerations in *Metaphysics* 12.7.1072b15–22[38]). All this connects with the first thing Aristotle says about *noein* in *De Anima* 3.4 when he compares it to sensing and describes it as reception of form.[39] It also connects to the active intellect as light: with an intellect ready to go and awake, thinking as contact begins just as when we open our eyes where there is light and immediately see colored things.

There is dispute about what Aristotle means by incomposite things. He refers to "simple things and essences" (*ta hapla kai ti estin*, 6.4.1027b27–28), "incomposites' (*ta asuntheta*, 9.10.1051b17), "what a thing is" (*to ti estin*, 9.10.1051b26, b32), and "non-composite substances" (*tas mê sunthetas ousias*, 9.10.1051b27).[40] Some have argued that incomposite things here refer solely to separate substances, with Werner Jaeger saying that noetic truth for Aristotle constitutes a special metaphysical intuition of "a being that is not an object of experience"[41] as a vestige of Platonism. I see no reason for restriction to separate substance. Sensible physical substances as composites of form and matter do not qualify, but the forms of physical substances, considered in themselves, meet the qualifications for incomposites specified by Aristotle.[42] They are *ousiai* or substances in a non-composite sense (*De Anima* 2.1.412a6–8); they are actualities (*De Anima* 2.1.412a10; *Metaph.* 10.8.1050b2–3); and they are neither generated nor corrupted (*Metaph.* 7.8.1033b8; 7.10.1035a25–31; 7.15.1039b20–27; 8.1.1041a23; 8.3.1043b15).[43] These are the forms that are received by the intellect when it thinks in the sense of thinking as *noein*. *De Anima* 3.6, whose subject is discursive thought and dianoetic truth, closes with a reminder that there is also non-discursive thought. It states that in addition to assertion and denial, which is either true or false, there is thought akin to mere saying, which is infallible like the perception of a special object of sense in contradistinction to an incidental object of sense. Aristotle identifies this thought as the thinking (*nous*) of the essence (*ti esti*) in the sense of the form (*to ti ên einai*).[44] This matches perfectly with the account of noetic thought given in *Metaphysics* 9.10 and there is no hint in the passage of esoteric intelligible objects like separate substances.[45]

There is also considerable dispute about whether noetic thinking is non-discursive or not. Non-discursive thought or intuition is anathema to many contemporary philosophers, who cannot allow a good philosopher like Aristotle to endorse it.[46] To claim that there can be thinking something (to think *x*) that is not thinking something about that something (to think that *x* is *y*) is considered philosophically incoherent. One argument for this view is that every request for information about what one thinks when one says "I think *x*" is answered in the form "I think that *x* is *y*." Consequently intuition is denied to *noein* in *Metaphysics* 9.10 or at the end of *De Anima* 3.6[47] despite Aristotle's distinctions in those texts [1] between saying versus affirming or denying and [2] between contact versus combining or dividing, and also despite [3] the claim of infallibility for *noein* whose opposite is ignorance rather than falsity and [4] the many texts where Aristotle literally talks about knowing things rather than propositions (*De Anima* 3.8.431b25–432a1 is an instructive instance: knowledge and sensation correspond to things—*ta pragmata*—and the "thing" offered as an example is a stone; the issue is whether in intellectual knowledge the stone or the form of the stone is in the soul; there are no propositions in sight). In place of an intuitive or non-discursive grasp of incomposite things Aristotle is said to be denoting the thinking of definitions. Definitions, as identity statements rather than predications, are not propositions in the requisite sense for dianoetic truth and falsity (it is argued) but they are discursively grasped. If intuition is ruled out, and with it, Aristotle's apparent strong determination to center cognition, including intellectual cognition, on things acting on the intellect rather than propositions, then this is a sensible answer to what is going on with noetic thought. For it is a good question what is the content of a simple apprehension of an incomposite thing—an essence, a form, an *ousia*. To articulate and communicate the content of noetic contact would require discursive intellectual performances, of which the definition holds pride of place, since it expresses precisely and fully *what* the thing is. This fact does not seem to me to carry the argument for the anti-intuitionists, however, since it either begs the question (there just is no such thing as intuition) or presumes (falsely, I think) that whatever content noetic contact conveys should be fully expressible without remainder by articulations of its meaning, just because we cannot articulate its meaning without discursion and propositions.[48] The anti-intuitionist interpretation of Aristotle on noetic truth, in any case, commits him to the views that humans never conceive of false definitions or of partially true ones and that the thinking of a proposition that defines an essence either hits the mark fully or fails completely.

What is noetic contact like and what is its content? What is its relation to dianoetic truth and falsity? Aristotle presents this extra-predicative and non-propositional intellectual apprehension or intuition in *Metaphysics* 9.10 and attributes truth to it. Textual evidence identifies it with the passive immaterial reception of form by the intellect described in *De Anima* 3.4 as the foundational and fundamental account of all thinking.

Form, as the principle of intelligibility in an existing thing, is directly connected to form's oneness. Aristotle at *Metaphysics* 5.17.1022a8–10 (cf. *Physics* 4.4.211b13) says that *ousia* (substance) in the sense of *to ti ên einai* (form) is a limit (*peras*) as the limit of knowledge. It is a limit of knowledge because it is the limit of the thing itself (*pragmatos*). At *Metaphysics* 5.6.1016b17–24 Aristotle says that for every class of object there is a specific measure from which knowledge of that class takes its start. This measure is a one, and the one is always indivisible or unitary either in quantity or in *eidos*. He further states at *Metaphysics* 10.1.1052b19–20 that with respect to intellectual knowledge, the notion of a measure, which originates in the category of quantity with respect to the unit, is extended to the other categories. Aristotle speaks of measure to reverse Protagoras, who claimed that man is the measure of all things (*Metaphysics* 10.1.1053a35–b32). Human knowledge and perception do not measure things but are measured by them (*Metaphysics* 10.1.1053a31–36; 11.6.1062b12–14, b19, 1063a4). The world measures the intellect and not the other way around. This is not merely a rhetorical move, however, since Aristotle considers the form in its oneness received by the intellect to be the measure or determinant of discursive thinking and any subsequent learning.

Aristotle uses the notion of the one or the simple unit with respect to form as the principle of knowledge analogously. It is not a blank counter like a quantitative unit, but simple or one as a specific content (*Metaphyics* 12.7.1072a30–34; *Metaphysics* 8.3.1043b32–34 with 1044a2–9; *Metaphysics* 8.6.1045a36–b7[49]).[50] Form is a unity as an actuality and a definite nature. Thus it is the cause of the unity of the thing and of the unity of the definition and is not reducible to their parts (*Metaphysics* 8.6.1045a36–b7[51]). The definite and specific unity that is each definite thing, whose cause is the form, is not reducible to the components or elements united to constitute that thing. The unity of the definition that expresses the nature of a thing, a unity which is propositional in character and whose parts are related as actuality and potentiality,[52] is derived from the unity of the form which is its cause and is not identical to it. Form as an ultimately indivisible actuality and nature is the cause of this unity in things and in the definition of things. The forms of things ultimately account for how reality is divided up into identifiable definite things and how we take reality as divided up into those specific things.

This gets us to what noetic contact with incomposite things as non-discursive awareness is like. The reception of form in the intellect as the foundational act of thinking is contact with these things in their irreducible uniqueness and unity as definite natures and not collections of attributes spelled out in propositions. It constitutes their registration with the intellect, a registration that is not a blank unit the same for all things. If this registration did not occur, the business of articulating meaning, forming propositions, and other discursive activity would never get off the ground. When it occurs, when we are no longer in ignorance about this or that cut of reality, the intellect possesses an endowment that leads to, indeed forces, discursive articulation of all kinds. In *Metaphysics* 9.10, after Aristotle repeats that it is not possible to be in error about "the things . . . which are essences and exist in actuality . . . only to think them or not to think them," he goes on to talk in an adversative clause about an inquiry regarding them: "but inquiry about their 'what' takes the form of asking whether they are of such and such a nature or not" (*Metaphysics* 9.10.1051b30–33; translation emended to express the adversative *alla* at 1051b32). This inquiry into the nature of simple things ultimately seeks their definitions and is distinct from noetic contact itself (as the anti-intuitionists see, even definitions are propositional in character[53]). Due to the registration achieved by noetic contact with the irreducible and definite unities of meaning and truth that are the things of the world, as this text says, inquiry follows towards the definitions of things in themselves.[54] But reception of form accounts not only for moves towards definitions, but for all manner of dianoetic discursive recognition and articulation of things, insofar as they are composite entities with relations to other things.

This cannot be a case, however, of *nous* simply providing and turning over content to *dianoia*, which then performs operations of combining and dividing with respect to it.

For one thing, the noetic contact that is reception of form perdures through all exercises of intellectual life, because it is the foundational registration for any intellectual rather than strictly perceptual seeing of the world. This infallible, extra-predicative awareness, as it perdures, is that to which the intellect also has recourse as it carries on its dianoetic life. This infallible noetic awareness must be the evidence for the truth of propositional first principles, once they are explicitly articulated, since they are known in themselves only through *nous*, and the means with sense perception for the verification or falsification of other discursive products, such as propositions expressing contingent states of affairs.

More importantly, indeed crucially, noetic contact as reception of form is the driving force for further intellectual activity. Form is actuality and energy. This specific content that is the endowment of each form, given completely as a whole in the infallible contact of extra-predicative awareness, evokes its own articulation in definition, as Aristotle points out at *Metaphysics* 9.10.1051b30–33 quoted above. This is the finest work of *dianoia*, since then sciences can be established and the *telos* of the intellect in truth can be reached. It also evokes other articulations as well because of the complex being it causes in composite substance of which it is the form and the relations and interactions the composite substance has with other things. Form present in the intellect, that place of forms, causing the type of being that is truth, that is, as the cause of noetic contact, accounts for the teleological character of truth in Aristotle, since it explains the impetus and drive towards articulation, where the intellect makes new unities through the unities given by received forms in the ongoing life of experience. Aristotle says that things themselves force us along in rational inquiry; they do so through their forms received by the intellect.

5

This discussion of the place of the intellect in Aristotle can conclude with some remarks about the primacy of nature and the subordinate character of making and doing with respect to nature. Aristotle holds, unlike rival accounts, that in actual thinking much more is done by the natural things known than by the knower. This is the primacy of nature through *eidos* received in the place of intellect. Things themselves due to their forms provide content, push and direction to the life of the mind, to which the intellect responds. One consequence of this view, which Aristotle frequently exploits in his philosophical writings, is that our thinking can be better, that is more truthful, than our linguistic reports of our thinking may seem to indicate. There is a distinction between our thinking, which, actual thought by actual thought, is always unitary,[55] and our speech, which must express our dianoetic thoughts (for example, propositions) in linear fashion extended over time.[56] Thus Aristotle develops dialectic and finds much (surprising much) truth in what others say, both all people and the wise, although it is partial truth and it may lisp. One of the rival accounts that Aristotle is rejecting is that of Plato, who says that thinking is a dialogue that the soul has with itself (*Theaetetus* 189d6–7; *Sophist* 263e3–5; cf. *Posterior Analytics* 1.10.76b24–27) and who sees the Good, the cause of all intelligibility and necessity to being, providing truth like a light extrinsically yoking knower and known, rather than a type of being where knower and known are one intrinsically (*Republic* 6.508a–d, 509b). Aristotle does not speak in these ways. He considers thinking resting with an object (see, e.g., *De Anima* 1.3.407a6–9, a20–34) and truth a mode of being, being the thing known and being the thing known in a living, teleological manner. Another rival account that Aristotle's position opposes more radically is that of Nietzsche. The active doings and makings of the intellect are subordinate to the cognitive deposit of the specific natures of things given through reception of form. The results or products of all intellectual activity, when they are successful, that is, truthful, are versions of oneness and resting derivative from the more primary instances, in pure reception of form and ultimately in the cognition that is separate substance as thought thinking itself. Things themselves, with which the intellect is directly engaged, propel the intellect to the articulations that complete and fulfill the teleological drive to fuller truth given in the forms of nature themselves.

Aristotle's account of the intellect described here as the power both of *nous* and *dianoia* cedes much to *dianoia*, much more than is commonly recognized by interpreters of Aristotle. The discursive activity of the intellect extends to the recognition of generic universals, privations, and so on. The threshold for discursion, as opposed to what is given non-discursively to the intellect, is not proposition formation. There is much taking-as in Aristotle's account, even at what is commonly taken to be the conceptual and non-propositional level. Yet interpreters often are also loath to find non-discursive thought in Aristotle's account. I have argued that *nous* as non-discursive intellection consisting of the reception of the actual forms of nature in the place of the intellect is the basis for all thinking according to Aristotle and the engine for the articulations, makings, and advances that constitute the life of the human intellect whose *telos* is truth, especially the truth of science. This is primacy of nature with creativity subordinate to it.[57]

The Catholic University of America

Notes

1. The following two paragraphs are drawn from "Scholium I (Chapter 11): Two Doxologies: Argument and Praise," 103–104, in Thomas Prufer, *Recapitulations: Essays in Philosophy* (Washington, D. C.: The Catholic University of America Press, 1993).

2. Prufer, 103.

3. Ibid.

4. See, e.g., *De An.* 2.1.412a8–9; *Ph.* 2.1.193b6–12. This is the sophisticated version of what was recognized by predecessors about the soul, as *De An.* 1.2.404b8–10 notes: "All, on the other hand, who looked to the fact that what has soul in it knows or perceives what is, identify soul with the principle or principles of Nature, according as they admit several such principles or only one."

5. Prufer, 103.

6. Ibid.

7. Ibid.

8. Ibid, 103, n1.

9. Ibid, 103.

10. This motion will be a form of rest, in a derivative sense, as discussed on pages 60–61 below.

11. Robert Sokolowski has pointed out to me that Nietzsche may be the starkest foil for Aristotle by completely removing rest from the intellect, but that Machiavelli is first, citing the work of Francis Slade: "Machiavelli, of course, had been here before Hobbes and before everyone else. Machiavelli's *verità effetuale* is that there is no 'best form of rule,' a form of rule that of itself reason would have to approve as superior to any other form. Any instance of rule exercised according to its intrinsic necessities is *the product of reason*. There is no 'best.' Nothing measures rule except rule itself" (emphasis added). See Francis Slade, "Rule as Sovereignity: The Universal and Homogeneous State," 165 in *The Truthful and the Good: Essays in Honor of Robert Sokolowski*, ed. John J. Drummond and James G. Hart (Dordrecht: Kluwer Academic Publishers, 1996), 159–180.

12. Cf. Hilary Putnam's defense of Aristotle as a direct realist in "Aristotle's Mind and the Contemporary Mind," 7–28, in Demetra Sfendoni-Mentzou, ed., *Aristotle and Contemporary Science*, vol. 1 (New York: Peter Lang, 2000). Recognition of Aristotle's direct realism is connected to the points made in this paper, despite possible differences about the nature of Aristotle's essentialism. As I attempt to do in a different way, Putnam is presenting aspects of the "'Aristotelian' alternative" in philosophy of mind, for which there is "a systematic neglect" from Descartes "to the present day" (Putnam, 8).

13. All translations of Aristotle's works are from *The Complete Works of Aristotle: The Revised Oxford Translation*, ed. Jonathan Barnes, 2 volumes (Princeton, N. J.: Princeton University Press, 1984), unless otherwise noted.

14. Michael Wedin, *Mind and Imagination in Aristotle* (New Haven and London: Yale University Press, 1988), 168.

15. Cf. Wedin, *Mind and Imagination*, 163.

16. See, e.g., Vasilis Politis, "Aristotle's Account of the Intellect as Pure Capacity," *Ancient Philosophy* 21 (2001): 401, who usefully quotes Terence Irwin's strong statement of Aristotle's

realism in *Aristotle's First Principles* (Oxford: Clarendon Press, 1988), §2. Politis distinguishes pure passivity or receptivity (my concern) from pure capacity (his interest) and recognizes that claims of strong realism for Aristotle depend on the former. See also, Putnam, 7–8.

17. The full text of *De An.* 3.4.429a27–29 reads: "It was a good idea to call the soul 'the place of forms', though this description holds only for the thinking soul, and even this is the forms only potentially,not actually" (*kai eu dê hoi legontes tên psuchên einai topon eidôn, plên hoti oute hole all' hê noêtikê, oute entelecheia, alla dunamei ta eidê*).

18. For example, Hicks, 482–483, in Aristotle, *De Anima*, with trans., intro., and notes by R. D. Hicks (Cambridge: Cambridge University Press, 1907), debates a Platonic provenance and adds a few details but does not discuss the meaning, while Ross, 292, in Aristotle, *De Anima*, ed., with intro. and comm. David Ross (Oxford: Clarendon Press, 1961), limits himself to supposed Platonic provenance; Alan Code and Julius Moravcsik, "Explaining Various Forms of Living," 138, in the invaluable *Essays on Aristotle's* De Anima, ed. Martha C. Nussbaum and Amélie Oksenberg Rorty (Oxford: Clarendon Press, 1992), mention the "many difficulties of interpretation" but merely note that "the whole tenor of this remark resists both functionalist and materialist readings;" the phrase is nowhere else discussed in the volume; I have found no explicit discussion of it in Michael V. Wedin, *Mind and Imagination*; Politis, 394, contains the only reference in Politis's otherwise detailed study.

19. Translation from Hicks. In the *De An.* 1.3 polemic against Plato's account of soul as self-moved magnitude, Aristotle argues that the process of thinking consists of thinking one thing at a time (407a6–10) in linear fashion, where each thought entertained, each conclusion reached, each definition conceived, is a form of rest and halting with the object, rather than motion (407a23–31). He notes that "all theoretical processes come to a close in the same way as accounts do" (407a24–25).

20. Y. R. Simon, "An Essay on Sensation," 61–64, in *Philosophy of Knowledge: Selected Readings*, ed. Roland Houde and Joseph Mullally (Chicago, Philadelphia, and New York: J. B. Lippencott Company, 1960).

21. The *De Anima* account of soul is often read in a bottom-up manner with inanimate physical change as the baseline. These considerations show that top-down analysis is equally necessary.

22. *De An.* 1.4.408b24–29 says thinking as *noein* is divine in contradistinction to thinking as *dianoeisthai*.

23. It is also worth noting that Aristotle holds that this foundational purely receptive activity of the intellect, like the perception of particular sensible objects, is infallibly true. It is only when the intellect does something, is active in a further and more obvious way, as when it combines or separates to form a judgment, that falsity is possible as well as truth. See *De An.* 3.6.430a26–28, 430b26–30; cf. 2.6.418a12; 3.3.427b11–14.

24. For *dianoeisthai* as discursive thinking, consider *De An.* 3.3.427b13 with *De An.* 3.6.430a27–b3, *Metaph.* 4.7.1012a2–3, 5.7.1017a31–35, 6.4.1027b18–23, 9.10.1051b1–17, 11.8.1065a21–23 and the distinction between *noein* and *dianoeisthai* developed in *De An.* 1.4.408b3–27.

25. The recommended translation of David Ross in his edition and commentary, *De Anima* (Oxford: Clarendon Press, 1961), 300.

26. These remarks are sufficient so far as they go but not adequate for understanding Aristotle's account with respect to cases of falsity, negative states of affairs, and so on.

27. Paolo Crivelli, *Aristotle on Truth* (Cambridge: Cambridge University Press), 3–5. Irwin, *Aristotle's First Principles*, 2, makes this point about knowing things ("non-linguistic, non-psychological, non-propositional entities") as well as beliefs and propositions as first principles, with beliefs and propositions describing things.

28. I have argued that *De Anima* 3.6 extends the discussion of intelligible objects begun in *De Anima* 3.4 to handle all these cases of discursive thinking in "The Cognition of Indivisibles and the Argument of *De Anima* 3.4–8," *Practical Reason: Proceedings of the American Catholic Philosophical Association* 58 (1984): 140–150.

29. Pritzl, "Cognition of Indivisibles," 146–147.

30. Other instances are the life of celestial bodies, the life of sensation, the life of nutrition and reproduction, and even by extension the "kind of life" (*hoion zôê tis*) that inanimate bodies have inasmuch as they are in motion. See *De Anima* 2.4.415a23–26; *GA* 5.1.788b31–32; 1.23.731b2–4; *EE* 2.1.1219a23–25; 7.12.1244b23–25; *EN* 9.9.1170a18–19; *Cael.* 2.12.292a18–21; *Ph.* 8.1.250b11–15, 259b25–26. For a discussion of univocals and equivocals in Aristotle, see J. Owens, *The Doctrine of Being in the Aristotelian 'Metaphysics'*, 3rd ed., rev. (Toronto: Pontifical Institute of Mediaeval Studies, 1978), 107–128. An important text for the reference of all soul activity to divine separate substance is *De Anima* 2.4.415a25–b7: "The acts in which it manifests itself are reproduction and the use of food, because for any living thing that has reached its normal development and which is unmutilated, and whose mode of generation is not spontaneous, the most natural act is the production of another like itself, an animal producing an animal, a plant a plant, in order that, as far as nature allows, it may partake in the eternal and divine. That is the goal towards which all things strive, that for the sake of which they do whatsoever their nature renders possible. The phrase 'for the sake of which' is ambiguous; it may mean either the end to achieve which, or the being in whose interest, the act is done. Since then no living thing is able to partake in what is eternal and divine by uninterrupted continuance (for nothing perishable can for ever remain one and the same), it tries to achieve that end in the only way possible to it, and success is possible in varying degrees; so it remains not indeed as the self-same individual but continues its existence in something like itself—not numerically but specifically one."

31. *Metaph.* 2.1.993b20–21.

32. *Metaph.* 2.1.993b23–31; for the analogue in practical thinking, see *EN* 6.2.1139a21–31.

33. Aristotle criticizes Democritus at *De An.* 1.2.404a30–31 for considering soul and intellect (*nous*) to be the same by saying that Democritus "does not employ mind (*nous*) as a special faculty dealing with truth."

34. See, e.g., Richard Kirkham, *Theories of Truth: A Critical Introduction* (Cambridge, Mass.: M.I.T. Press, 1992), 119–120; Frederick F. Schmitt, *Truth: A Primer* (Boulder, San Francisco, and Oxford: Westview Press, 1995), 145. For a detailed assessment, see Crivelli, *Aristotle on Truth*, 129–138.

35. Alasdair MacIntyre, *First Principles, Final Ends and Contemporary Philosophical Issues* (Milwaukee: Marquette University Press, 1990), 12.

36. *Metaph.* 5.7.1017a31–35; 6.2.1026a33–35; 6.4.1027b18; 9.10.1051a34–b2.

37. Charles Kahn, "The Greek Verb 'To Be' and the Concept of Being, *Foundations of Language* 2 (1966): 250–254.

38. *Thigganein* is a synonym for *haptesthai*, to touch. There are instances where Aristotle uses the word not merely to express physical contact but action and passion in touching, one thing pressing itself on another, including a passage where Aristotle talks of nature touching like a modeler of clay with her own hands rather than like a carpenter who uses tools (*GA* 2.4.740b22; 1.22.730b30; *HA* 6.14.568b7; 4.7.532a13; *De Insomn.* 2.459a30). Contact can imply the action of one thing touching another.

39. For the infallibility of the sense perception of proper sensible objects, which parallels that ascribed to noetic contact with simple things, see *De Anima* 2.6.418a16 and cf. 3.6.430b29–30.

40. It is worth adding that when Aristotle says that they are not composite (*ou gar estin suntheton*, 9.10.1051b19), the meaning seems to be a thing in its individual being ("as truth is not the same in these cases, so also being is not the same," 9.10.1051b22–23) considered apart from positive (combinations) or negative (separations) states of affairs (9.10.1051b19–20). They exist actually, not potentially, and neither come to be nor cease to be (9.10.1051b28); as such, they are "being itself" (*to on auto*, 9.10.1051b29), a phrase W. D. Ross, *Aristotle's Metaphysics*, 2 volumes (Oxford: Clarendon Press, 1924): 2, 278, points out designates "the pure form." They are things that *nous* is in contact with (*thigein*, *thigganein*, 9.10.1051b24, 25), in the sense that they are simply thought or not thought ("but only to think them or not to think them" [*ê noein ê mê*], 9.10.1051b31–32).

41. Werner Jaeger, *Aristotle: Fundamentals of the History of His Development*, trans. Richard Robinson, 2nd edition (Oxford: Clarendon Press, 1948), 204–205; cf. Owens, *Doctrine of Being*, 413.

42. As stated in a previous note, Ross, *Aristotle's Metaphysics* 2:278 says, the phrase "being itself" (*to on auto*, 9.10.1051b29) applied to incomposite things designates "the pure form."

43. For a fuller argument of this claim, see Kurt Pritzl, "Being True in Aristotle's Thinking," *Proceedings of the Boston Area Colloquium for Ancient Philosophy* 14 (1998): 188–190.

44. That *to ti ên einai* always means "form" in Aristotle, see Owens, *Doctrine of Being*, 181–188.

45. I also think that the discussion of the *nous* of primitive universals in *Posterior Analytics* 2.19 also matches up with the *Metaphysics* 9.10 account of noetic truth, though there is no space to present the argument here.

46. See, e.g., A. C. Lloyd, "Non-Discursive Thought—An Enigma of Greek Philosophy," *Proceedings of the Aristotelian Society* N.S. 70 (1969/70): 261–276; Richard Sorabji, "Myths about Non-Propositional Thought," chapter 10 in *Time, Creation, and the Continuum: Theories in Antiquity and the Early Middle Ages* (Ithaca, N.Y.: Cornell University Press, 1983), 138–156.

47. This holds also for the end of the *Posterior Analytics*.

48. Aristotle, *Metaphysics* 9.10.1051b30–33, distinguishes the apprehension of a form from the articulation of the definition of that form: "About the things, then, which are essences and exist in actuality, it is not possible to be in error, but only to think them or not to think them. Inquiry about their 'what' takes the form of asking whether they are of such and such a nature or not."

49. *Metaphysics* 12.7.1072a30–34: "And thought (*nous*) is moved by the object of thought (*noêtou*); and in this, substance (*ousia*) is first, and in substance, that which is simple and exists actually. (The one and the simple [*to hen and to haploun*] are not the same; for 'one' means measure, but 'simple' means that the thing itself has a certain nature.)."

Metaphysics 8.3.1043b32–34 with 1044a2–9, which reads: "And the number must have something in virtue of which it is one thing, while our opponents cannot say if it is one (for either it is not one but a sort of heap, or if it is, we ought to say what it is that makes one out of the many); and the definition is one, but similarly they cannot say what makes *it* one. And this is natural; for the same reason is applicable, and substance is one in the sense which we have explained, and not, as some say, by being a sort of unit or point; each is a complete reality and a definite nature (*all' entelecheia kai phusis tis hekastê*, 1044a9).

Metaphysics 8.6.1045a36–b7: "But of the things which have no matter, either for reason or for sense, each is by its nature essentially a kind of unity, as it is essentially a kind of being—a 'this,' a quality, or a quantity. And neither 'existent' or 'one' is present in definitions, and an essence (*to ti ên einai*) is by its very nature a kind of unity as it is a kind of being. This is why none of these has any reason outside itself for being one, or for being a kind of being; for each is by its nature a kind of being and a kind of unity, not as being in the genus 'being' or 'one' nor in the sense that being and unity can exist apart from particulars."

50. On the tendency to see form as a blank see Owens, *Doctrine of Being*, 458n23: "Modern thought is strongly inclined to equate 'content' with matter. Form as such is considered 'empty.' The Aristotelian conception is directly the opposite. Matter as such has no intelligible content whatsoever. The whole 'content' is the form."

51. *Metaphysics* 8.6.1045a36–b7.

52. A definition is divisible in itself (*Metaph.* 5.6.1016a35), since it is composed of parts in terms of genus and difference. Its parts are the parts of the form (*Metaph.* 7.10.1035b31–1036a1; 5.25.1023b22–25; 5.14.1023b2), which has parts in the sense that its being can be spelled out dianoetically by appropriate common characteristics. These parts are related to each other as form and matter (*Metaph.* 8.6.1045a33–35).

53. Sorabji, "Myths about Non-Propositional Thought," 141.

54. It is important to note that thinking definitions and recognizing propositional first principles are cases needing special consideration. With the ambiguity between first principles as things or propositions acknowledged, it may still be the case that Aristotle holds that intellectual cognition even of propositional first principles is a matter of *nous* rather than *dianoia*. For example, in *Topics* 1.2.101a37–b4 Aristotle says that dialectic, which is dianoetic thinking, provides "a process of criticism wherein lies the path to the principles of all inquiries." Dialectic cannot establish or prove first principles, but just lead to them. Precisely as first principles they are known in themselves by *nous*, whatever discursive dialectical work occasions this noetic recognition. There has to be a special proprietary relationship between the *nous* as noetic contact of a first principle as a thing and the unique type of articulation that is the proposition expressing the being of the first principle. I do not think this is an insurmountable task, in light of the texts cited above about forms (which are not propositions) as the units and measures from which knowledge with respect to the respective classes of things begins. It must be the case, for instance, that the noetic grasp of a form, which is never left behind, is the confirmatory awareness for the correct articulation of that essence. This would not be the case with other propositions, whether propositions derived within a science from first principles, where the character of the deduction is crucial, or propositions expressing factual states of affairs, where empirical observation is crucial.

55. Aristotle says explicitly that we can only think one thing at a time (*De An.* 1.3.407a6–10; *Metaph.* 4.4.1006b10; also consider that the meaning of *phanai* is applied to *noein* at *De An.* 3.7.431a8 in relation to *Metaph.* 9.10.1051b24, *Int.* 5.17a17, and 4.16b27).

56. Aristotle says at *SE* 7.169a38–40: "an inquiry with someone else is carried on by means of words, whereas in our own minds it is carried on quite as much by means of the thing itself" (*di' autou tou pragmatos*; Loeb trans.).

57. I am grateful to Jean De Groot and Robert Sokolowski for comments on drafts of this paper. The essay is much better thanks to them; its deficiencies are entirely due to me.

Aristotle's Divided Mind: Some Thoughts on Intellectual Virtue and Aristotle's Occasional Dualism

Jonathan J. Sanford

Abstract: In this paper I focus on a few of the passages in the *Nicomachean Ethics* that challenge the standard hylomorphic interpretation of Aristotle's anthropology. I proceed by reflecting on the manner in which Aristotle's two ways of characterizing the human person follow from his accounts of the two most important intellectual virtues, *phronesis* and *sophia*. I attempt to argue for the following three points: first, that Aristotle's presentation of a divided mind is the result of his consistency rather than inconsistency; second, that there is not a clear way found in his *Nicomachean Ethics* to overcome this dual anthropology without doing violence to his account of intellectual virtue; and third, that there are several reasons why this dual anthropology should not be regarded as an aporetic failure.

We have grown accustomed to thinking of Aristotle as an incorrigible anthropological hylomorphist. The standard procedure in the classroom, for instance, is to pit this hylomorphism against Platonic or Cartesian dualism, and for good reason. But it has not always been customary to regard Aristotle as so stridently opposed to Platonic anthropology, as Lloyd Gerson has so ably demonstrated in his recent effort, *Aristotle and Other Platonists.*[1] Of course, how one defines Platonism is a matter of some contention and pertinent to any judgment we should make on the extent of Aristotle's Platonism. But, this important issue of defining Platonism, and Aristotle's many criticisms of Platonic doctrines notwithstanding, there is plenty of evidence in the texts of Aristotle we possess to give some credence to the Neoplatonic judgment that Aristotle was one of their own. Jaeger's claims that such evidence can be explained away as the avowals of a young Aristotle, still under the sway of his master, which found their way into his mature writings through editorial oversight have come under tremendous critical scrutiny in recent years.[2] As well they should, since those points where professions of dualism emerge alongside Aristotle's hylomorphism are no mere sidelines. We find them at the summit of Aristotle's investigations into how we know (*DA* III.5), what or who ultimately we ought to know (*Meta.* XII.6–9), and why we ought to strive to know (*EN* X.7–8; *EE* VII, 15).

In this paper I focus on a few of the passages in the *Nicomachean Ethics* that challenge the standard hylomorphic interpretation of Aristotle's anthropology. I proceed by reflecting on the way in which Aristotle's two ways of characterizing the human person follow from his accounts of the two most important intellectual virtues, φρόνησις and σοφία. I attempt to argue for the following three points: first, that Aristotle's presentation of a divided mind is the result of his consistency rather than inconsistency; second, that there is not a clear way found in his *Nicomachean Ethics* to overcome this dual anthropology without doing violence to his account of intellectual virtue; and third, that there are several good reasons not to regard this dual anthropology as an aporetic failure.

Prudence as Supreme Virtue for the Hylomorphic Political Animal

Aristotle explores two classes of virtues, moral and intellectual. Moral virtues are the proper attunements of our psychosomatic complex: they are what make us well disposed so that we might perform morally virtuous actions. Intellectual virtues, on the other hand, are not so easily classified. One of them, practical wisdom or prudence (φρόνησις), works hand in hand with the moral virtues: by means of it we assess when morally virtuous actions are required and how they are to be carried through. But other intellectual virtues, such as craft knowledge (τέχνη), have little to do with moral virtues *per se*, even if, for instance, only a fairly temperate man makes for a dependable carpenter. Both prudence and craft knowledge are knowledge directed at things that are brought into being by human activity, and are thereby very different from those sorts of intellectual virtues which are directed at objects ontologically distinct from human intervention. Those other intellectual virtues are concerned with such stable entities as the definitions of various living things or an eternal and unchanging God. The greatest of these sorts of intellectual virtues is philosophical wisdom (σοφία). There are good reasons for thinking prudence to hold pride of place over philosophical wisdom, and in this section some of these are considered.

The study of ethics is, for Aristotle, a subset of the study of politics. This is why Aristotle in *NE* I.2, 1094a27 claims that inquiry into the greatest good falls within the most authoritative architectonic or master-art, politics; and why he ends the *Nicomachean Ethics* with a prelude to the *Politics*, telling us that we must turn to the *Politics* "so that we can, insofar as we are able, complete the philosophy of human things" (*NE* X.9, 1181b15–16).[3] Happiness, the ultimate good, falls within politics because it is within the *polis* that human beings work out their quest for the good life, a quest that is directed by legislation about "what we are to do and what we are to abstain from" and so the end of politics "must include the end of the other [sciences], so that this end must be the good for man" (*NE* I.2, 1094b5–7).[4] Politics, it would seem, is the guarantor of happiness. It is for this reason that the student of politics studies human virtue above all else, since virtue leads us to and is constitutive of happiness (*NE* I.13, 1102a6-10, 14–17).

Characterizing ethics as a subset of politics and making politics the guarantor of happiness does not imply that happiness is only achieved through social actions within a *polis*: It could be the case, for instance, that politics is responsible for legislating for the possibility of the best sort of life, even if such a life is not properly speaking a political life. Nevertheless, Aristotle does seem to suggest in several places that perhaps the best sort of life, that is a life that achieves our highest good, is in fact a political life, that is, a life of social actions within a *polis*.[5] Such, for instance, seems to be the implication of Aristotle's discussion of the μεγαλόψυχος—the person of pride, or the great-souled individual—who is "good in the highest degree," and has "greatness in every excellence" (*NE* IV.3, 1123b29–30). Such too seems to be the conclusion of Aristotle's discussion of prudence.

In a sense, prudence is the greatest intellectual virtue. It is concerned with things human, that is, with things which are up to human beings to bring about or not to bring about, and it is the chief virtue of "the person who is without qualification good at deliberating," for such is the individual "who is capable of aiming in accordance with calculation at the best for a human being of things attainable by action" (*NE* VI.7, 1141b12–14). It is by the intellectual virtue of prudence, then, that a person exercises the moral virtues. So tight does Aristotle consider the relationship between prudence and the moral virtues that he claims that "it is not possible to be good in the strict sense without prudence, nor prudent without moral virtue" (*NE* VI.13, 1144b30–32). Insofar as the development of a strong moral character is the aim of ethics, as Aristotle understands it, prudence is not only foremost in the attainment of that end, but is in large measure constitutive of it.

It appears that prudence is chiefly responsible for attaining happiness, rather than philosophical wisdom, for "wisdom [σοφία] will contemplate none of the things that will make a man happy (for it is not concerned with any coming into being), . . . though prudence [φρόνησις] has this merit" (*NE* VI. 12, 1143b19-20). Only prudence, and not wisdom, can make us happy, because it is prudence that deliberates about how to achieve our end and our end is something we hope to bring into being. Our end seems to be that of flourishing within the *polis* since, "political wisdom and prudence are the same state of mind" (*NE* VI.8, 1141b23), and the performance of virtuous actions, especially the greatest moral virtue, justice, requires a *polis*. It would seem, then, that the political life would be the best sort of life, for it is only through such a life that happiness can be attained for we deliberative and hylomorphic political animals.

Philosophical Wisdom as the Supreme Virtue for the Non-hylomorphic Self

The question of which intellectual virtue is superior, φρόνησις or σοφία, prudence or wisdom, turns in part on what is entailed by 'superior.' A superior virtue would be one that has more to do with our attainment of the ultimate end of happiness than an inferior virtue. A superior virtue would also be one which Aristotle ranks higher within the functional scheme of the human person, where differences in rank are made on the principle that some virtues require higher order functioning than others. Wisdom, it becomes clear especially in the last book of the *Nicomachean Ethics*, is superior to prudence for both these reasons. Finally, wisdom is superior because of the superior content of the intellectual activity itself: the 'what' of which one is thinking.[6] These last two sorts of superiority presage Husserl's noesis/noema distinction, the roots of which are found in Aristotle's *De Anima*.[7] The case for the superiority of wisdom has, then, three stages: Wisdom is tied more intimately than anything else to our happiness, it is the noetically superior activity, and it has the noematically superior content. All three of these stages in Aristotle's case for the superiority of wisdom take their orientation from his characterization of human function.

Though much rehearsed in Aristotelian scholarship of the last forty years it is worthwhile to look briefly at Aristotle's function argument, both as a reminder and to clarify how I am reading it.[8] Acquiring our chief good, happiness, is a matter of attaining our end (τέλος), and doing this is a matter of performing our function (ἔργον) well (*NE* I.7, 1097b22-7). By function, Aristotle does not mean performing well in some aspect or other of our person, it is not the actualization of just one of our talents, but rather it is a matter of doing well *qua* human being. This doing well *qua* human being must have something to do with the rational principle of soul—as opposed to the nutritive or perceptive principles, which are lower parts of the human soul[9]—since the rational principle of soul is the better part of us:

> Now if the function of a human being is an activity of soul in accordance with, or not without, rational principle, and if we say a so-and-so and a good so-and-so have a function which is the same in kind, . . . human good turns out to be activity of soul in conformity with excellence, and if there are more than one excellence, in conformity with the best and most complete. (*NE* I 7, 1098a7-17)

Whatever our rational principle of soul has made us fit to do, if we are doing it well or excellently, then we are being happy. But Aristotle leaves open here the possibility that there may be more than one excellence, and that our highest human good consists in an activity that is "in conformity with the best (ἀρίστην) and most complete (τελειοτάτην)."

Happiness has then much, or perhaps even everything, to do with this most complete activity. The most complete activity is, at least on one way of stressing key passages in Aristotle's text, the activity of contemplative wisdom. One of the ways this activity is distinguished from the activity of prudence is that it is the activity of a different part of the soul, since, "prudence and wisdom are . . . each the excellence of a different part of the soul [ὅτι ἄλλου τῆς ψυχῆς μορίου ἀρετὴ ἑκατέρα]" (*NE* VI.11, 1143b15-17). What are these parts of the soul?

Aristotle's investigations in *De Anima*, whether or not this work was composed before *NE*, elucidates principles foundational to his treatment of human excellence in the *Nicomachean Ethics*; as he himself suggests when admonishing students of politics to "study the soul" (*NE* I.13, 1102a22). In Book I, chapter 13 of the *NE*, Aristotle distinguishes between the irrational (ἄλογον) and rational (λόγον) parts of the soul. The irrational part includes both the nutritive and the perceptive or appetitive.[10] It is indeed a good thing to have the nutritive part of the soul function well, for its well-functioning is largely responsible for our physical health. Nevertheless, the excellence of the nutritive part is common to all plants and animals, and so not indicative of our function *qua* human being. The appetitive part of the human soul, however, shares in a rational principle insofar as it can be controlled. It is the rational part of the soul which can control the appetites. All of the moral virtues are states concerned with choice in which the rational part of the soul controls the appetites in accordance with the mean relative to us as determined by right reason.[11] Just as the irrational part of the soul admits of divisions, so too does the rational part. The most basic difference in types of virtue correspond to these divisions within both rational and irrational parts of the soul, "for we say that some virtues are intellectual and others moral, philosophic wisdom and understanding [σύνεσιν] and prudence being intellectual, liberality and temperance moral" (*NE* I.13, 1103a4-7). It is the intellectual virtue of prudence that governs moral virtues,[12] and it is this which is the rational principle of the soul governing the irrational. So it is prudence that, with the aid of good moral training,[13] establishes and maintains moral character. Wisdom, on the other hand, has nothing to do with our character, for, "in speaking about a man's character we do not say that he is wise or has understanding" (*NE* I.13, 1103a8). Wisdom has nothing to do with character because it is neither a habit nor a governor of habits. Wisdom, it turns out, has very little if anything to do with a human being considered as a social animal.[14]

How could this be? If a human being is a social animal, this is because it is a logical animal, which is to say that it is an animal which speaks and so can bind itself to others in pursuit of some common good. If it is the case that wisdom has nothing to do with our social and moral life, then it would have to be the activity of some part of our rational nature that has nothing to do with the social and moral life. It would have to be the activity of that part of our rational nature that rises to contemplation of the divine substance in *Metaphysics* XII.7 and 9, which is *the* goal of human life that Aristotle presents to us to in the *Nicomachean Ethics* X. 7–8. Achieving this goal is a matter of achieving wisdom. The activity of wisdom would seem to be the actualization, the full functioning, of that separable part of soul discussed in several passages in *DA*.

In *De Anima* II.1 Aristotle tells us that there are two senses of our having a soul as an actualizing force. On the one hand the soul actualizes, gives life to, the body: "Hence the soul must be a substance in the sense of the form of a natural body having life potentially within it. But substance is actuality, and thus soul is the actuality of a body as above characterized" (*DA* 412a20-22). We are most familiar with this understanding of the soul, for it plays the critical role in Aristotle's hylomorphism. The soul gives life to the potential body.

Yet there is, Aristotle argues, an additional part of the soul that plays no part in actualizing the body:

> From this it is clear that the soul is inseparable from its body, or at any rate that certain parts of it are (if it has parts)--for the actuality of some of them is the actuality of the parts themselves. *Yet some may be separable, because they are not the actualities of any body at all* [διὰ τὸ μηθενὸς εἶναι σώματος ἐντελεχείας]. (*DA* II.1, 413a4-7, my emphasis)

This part of the soul is separable from the body insofar as it plays no role in the function of actualizing it. This idea of a separable part of the soul is made even more explicit in the following:

> We have no evidence as yet about thought [τοῦ νοῦ] or the power of reflection [τῆς θεωρητικῆς δυνάμεως]; *it seems to be a different kind of soul* [ἀλλ' ἔοικε ψυχῆς γένος ἕτερον εἶναι], it alone is capable of being separated, differing as what is eternal from what is perishable. All the other parts of soul, it is evident from what we have said, are, in spite of certain statements to the contrary, incapable of separate existence though, of course, distinguishable by definition. (*DA* II.2, 413b25–29, my emphasis)

That part of the soul that seems almost as though it is an entirely different soul is that part which engages in thought or reflection. Again, it is primarily separable in the sense of not taking part in the process of actualizing the body, though it may be separable in other ways as well.

It is our separable rational principle of soul that enables us to pursue science, for doing so requires a faculty that is capable of bearing a certain likeness or kinship with the objects of science, which are the way they are by necessity.[15] When we speak of knowledge, we are also speaking of that part of the soul that makes us capable of achieving knowledge since the expression, "that whereby we know" has two meanings, "[it] may mean either knowledge or the soul, for we can speak of knowing by either" (*DA* II.2, 414a 4-6). We know insofar as we have knowledge. But we have knowledge insofar as we have a rational soul capable of achieving it. Aristotle explains this further: "And in fact the intellect [νοῦς], as we have described it, is what it is *by virtue of becoming all things* [πάντα γίνεσθαι]. . . . Actual knowledge is identical with its object" (*DA* III.5, 430a14, 20, my emphasis).

The separable principle of soul is what makes actual knowledge possible. When this knowledge is achieved, there is a relationship of identity between this part of our soul and the object of knowledge. This relationship of identity holds even in the case of our knowledge of God. It is this relationship that prompts Aristotle to claim that we can engage in God's activity because "something divine is present in" us (*NE* X.7, 1177b28). We must have some measure of the divine in us if we are able to know God himself through sharing in his own activity of contemplation. The goal for our lives, then, becomes one of seeking to become more like God (*NE* X.7, 1177b29–1178a8). Wisdom, it turns out, is superior to prudence in the way in which God is superior to a human person, and the philosophical life is divine in comparison with the political.

The Mind Divided

The dialectic between prudence and wisdom has now brought us to a point at which Aristotle's competing descriptions of our nature can come into clearer focus. We know that a human being is what it is because it has a rational soul. But there are two main parts of the rational soul. The first is that part which is capable of governing the appetites and can thereby facilitate the acquisition of moral virtue. When functioning well, this part of the rational soul is prudence. Prudence is incapable of pursuing science, but it is the intellectual virtue without which we could not function excellently as political animals. Prudence, then corresponds to our composite nature, to ourselves considered as social and rational animals:

> Prudence, too, is linked to virtue of character, and this to prudence, since the principles of prudence are in accordance with the moral virtues and rightness in the moral virtues is in accordance with prudence. Being connected with the passions also, the moral virtues must belong to our composite nature [περὶ τὸ σύνθετον]; and *the virtues of our composite nature are human; so therefore, are the life and the happiness which correspond to these*. (*NE* X.8, 1178a15–21, my emphasis)

Notice that Aristotle claims not only that prudence is our greatest intellectual virtue insofar as we are considered as composite animals, but that there is a happiness that corresponds to the life of prudence, which is necessarily the life of the moral virtues as well since prudence and the moral virtues always go hand in hand. Prudence and the moral virtues are the exclusively human virtues, for neither animals—since they lack reason, nor God—because he lacks a body, share in them.

The second part of the rational soul is separable or separate from the lower parts of our nature, as well as from the part of the soul of which prudence is the activity. It alone is capable of pursuing knowledge in the strict sense. This part of the soul is the intellect *simpliciter*, νοῦς considered in and of itself, and it achieves its greatest completion in wisdom. Aristotle stresses, in the sentence just after where the last quotation ends, that "the virtue of the intellect [τοῦ νοῦ] is a thing separated [κεχωρισμένη]" (*NE* X. 8, 1178a22). That is, it is separated from the virtues which are the proper functions of a human animal considered as a composite being. It is separated because the intellect, when considered in its purest condition, is differentiated from the rest of the composite nature, as Aristotle puts it when he says that, "for a human being, therefore, the life according to intellect [κατὰ τὸν νοῦν] is best and pleasantest, since *this* most of all *is anthropos* [εἴπερ τοῦτο μάλιστα ἄνθρωπος] (*NE* X.7, 1178a6–7). The intellect, more than anything else, is *anthropos*, is a human being, and its proper functioning is the best of all possible activities. But such a human being is no animal, and its best work is not exclusively human insofar as it most perfectly belongs to God.

The two ways in which Aristotle describes the human being, as composite and social on the one hand, and as an intellect on the other, leads him to claim that there are two, and not just one ultimate goals. On the one hand, there is the ultimate end of happiness which corresponds to our composite nature. Aristotle calls this a secondary sort of happiness, for "in a secondary degree the life in accordance with the other kind of virtue [i.e., prudence] is happy; for the activities in accordance with this befit our human estate" (*NE* X.8, 1178a9–10). This merely human happiness is secondary in comparison with the primary and divine happiness, which is the activity of wisdom itself: "For this activity is the best since not only is intellect the best thing in us, but the objects of intellect are the best of knowable objects" (*NE* X.7, 1177a19–21). Aristotle admonishes us to ignore those advocates of the political life who advise us only to concern ourselves with human things, but instead we ought to "strain every nerve to live in accordance with the best thing in us; for even if it be small in bulk, much more does it in power and worth surpass everything. This would seem, too, to be each anthropos himself. . . . It would be strange, then, if he were to choose not the life of himself but that of something else" (*NE* X.7, 1178a2–5). The life of the intellect is the best and therefore the happiest life. This is the philosophical life, the life of wisdom, and the happiness of this life is of a dominant, intellectualist sort. Aristotle tells us that it would be strange not to choose this life, but to choose instead the life of political activity.

The life of political activity, a life in which we exercise the moral virtues and are guided throughout by prudence, is still a happy life, but only in a secondary and merely human way. The happiness of this human life is inclusivist, that is, it incorporates all the human goods as ingredients. Aristotle is arguing, then, that insofar as the secondary inclusivist sort of happiness—a life in which we perfect ourselves as hylomorphic political animals—is our ultimate goal, we are not yet seeking our ultimate goal. This ultimate goal is that of the happiness proper to a perfected intellect, but such a life is more divine than human.

What to Make of This

These issues have long been matters of great interpretative difficulty for Aristotle's commentators, and likely always will be. Aristotle brings us to a conclusion in the *Nicomachean Ethics* which is simultaneously exhilarating, at least for many, and deeply troubling. It is exhilarating because it presents us with an invitation to live the life of God, but it is troubling because he suggests that in living this life we must somehow abandon our composite selves. Troubling too, at least for those like myself who are critical of anthropological dualism, are the suggestions that in some significant ways we are not rational animals after all, but really just intellects. But it is important to remember that in stressing the ways in which prudence and wisdom are disconnected we have neglected some of the important ways in which they are interwoven. Aristotle's analysis of friendship presents one particularly rich field to harvest for the synthesizing of these two intellectual virtues. This is so since in a true friendship prudence and wisdom are both exercised insofar as morally good friends contemplate each other, as well other objects, in common.[16]

Another such point of intersection, and more pertinent to our present discussion, is wisdom's necessary dependence on prudence, insofar as one cannot have wisdom without first having prudence; and, I would add, this is not just so for the first acquisition of wisdom, but the successive or continued exercising of wisdom remains dependent on prudence. We need prudence to move towards our end, since prudence includes the whole of deliberating well, and deliberating is always concerned with means to an end. Our ultimate end, happiness, simply is the activity of wisdom, but we need prudence to establish the conditions whereby we might first exercise wisdom, and we need to continue to be prudent (and so too morally virtuous) if we are to continue to be wise.[17] It is for these reasons, amongst others, that Aristotle would count Gauguin—the artist who abandoned his family and other obligations to dedicate himself exclusively to art, not only morally vicious but also not truly wise, Bernard Williams's protestations to the contrary notwithstanding.[18] The collaboration of both prudence and wisdom in promoting the best of lives points to at least one way to combine Aristotle's hylomorphism with his dualism: achieving our highest end is the actualization of both our composite and our exclusively rational natures so that we might be happy both as hylomorphic animals and as intellects, simultaneously.

Yet this *rapprochement* between prudence and wisdom fails to mollify sufficiently that which is most destructive to a unified theory of the human being. After all, in saying that we can be happy simultaneously as rational animals and as intellects is still to say that we are rational animals on the one hand, and intellects on the other. Assuming that Aristotle has as a goal a unified theory of the human being, how are we to interpret those passages in which Aristotle suggests that we are our intellects?[19] I suggest there to be three general types of ways, each of which permits of much variation, in which we can attempt to approach these passages: We can regard them as (1) perhaps unintentionally inconsistent but nevertheless metaphorically exhortative, as (2) signposts to Aristotle's esoteric teachings, or as (3) deliberately inconclusive.

A metaphorical, yet exhortative, interpretation suggests that we ought not to take Aristotle literally when he says things like "man is his intellect."[20] He is just speaking metaphorically here. And, perhaps, this way of speaking amounts to philosophical slips-of-the-tongue caused by his Platonic heritage, as indeed Jaeger most formidably argued.[21] But the reason that he would speak thus is to encourage us, to give us a goal to work towards: Try to be like gods, and, well, maybe you'll get farther than you would otherwise.[22] Seen in this light, the metaphorical spin is the best face we can put on Aristotle's, or his editors', purported inconsistencies.

One problem with this line is that there is nothing in the texts themselves to suggest that Aristotle is being merely metaphorical. Moreover, Aristotle's remarks about the human person and the activity of contemplation in the *Nicomachean Ethics* are connected in important ways with his theory of God in *Metaphysics* XII. 7 and 9, as well as with remarks he makes regarding final causality in the *Physics* and some of his biological works. In other words, the case can and should be made that Aristotle's remarks in *Nicomachean Ethics* X are not atypical, but instead coalesce with other central claims. This being said, there is nonetheless no reason why Aristotle could not be sincere in his views regarding the identification of the human person with his or her intellect and at the same time exhorting us to be all we can be—even if that includes being somehow more than a man.

An esoteric variety of interpretation might run something like the following.[23] Aristotle has to be cautious. He emphatically believes the philosophical life to be the best, but is careful not to appear too emphatic when justifying this claim. This is because his audience is composed of two types of students, those already convinced and dedicated to the philosophical life, and a much larger group comprising the future politicians.[24] There could be economic reasons why Aristotle would want to appeal to the future politicians: there are more of them and they will almost to a man be rich. Self-preservation could also be a motivating factor here: Aristotle is not only a foreigner in Athens, but a Macedonian, and in Athens at a time when many Athenians are troubled by the military successes of Alexander.

Even if these ulterior pressures did affect Aristotle's philosophical writing, such an esoteric interpretation's exegetical usefulness seems quite limited. It suggests to us that Aristotle is intentionally opaque at times, but it does not give us a divining rod for finding those undercurrents that carry the true springs of his thought. How exactly are we to disentangle what Aristotle's true but hidden views are? With this type of interpretation we are encouraged to consider factors other than just the text before us, and that is not a bad thing to do. But this interpretative mode does little to help us adjudicate between Aristotle's hylomorphism and dualism. The suspicions it casts on Aristotle's fidelity to hylomorphism hardly seem to need be taken seriously when one considers that hylomorphism pervades most of Aristotle's works. It strains the imagination to think thousands of pages were written to throw the authorities off the scent, and it would make of Aristotle a paranoid cryptic rather than a focused researcher. And finally, if Aristotle really meant to hide his occasional dualism as well as his judgment that the philosophical life is superior to the political, he did a very poor job of it.

There is third the possibility of deliberate inconclusiveness. Perhaps Aristotle simply had not at the time of writing the *Nicomachean Ethics*, or thereafter as far as I can tell,[25] found a way adequately to integrate his observations concerning the activity of thinking—an activity truly peculiar in comparison to every other observed natural phenomenon—with his hylomorphic view of the human person. And so he let matters fall where they would.

Someone might object that Aristotle is too great a thinker to leave undecided so important a problem. This objection sticks only if one insisted that Aristotle is a great philosopher *and* that the determining mark of a great philosopher is the consummation of a complete system. There is much to be said for not sacrificing one's observations to a theory. We call the virtue enabling such an action intellectual honesty, and, in spite of certain examples to the contrary, Aristotle tends to exercise this virtue consistently in his works. In fact, Aristotle acknowledges the importance of this virtue not long past those passages we focused on in Book X.7–8 of the *Nicomachean Ethics*. He writes, reminiscent in many ways of Plato's own admissions of incertitude regarding his conclusions,[26] the following:

> The truth in practical matters is discerned from the facts of life; for these are the decisive factor. We must therefore survey what we have already said, bringing it to the test of the facts of life, and if it harmonizes with the facts we must accept it, but if it clashes with them we must suppose it to be mere theory. (*NE* X.9, 1179a19–23)

Admitting in the very last chapter that his claims in the *Nicomachean Ethics* could be nothing but mere theory is the sign of a philosopher well acquainted with the limits of human knowledge. Aristotle here acknowledges that there is a standard prior to the particular theories of any particular philosophers, and he submits himself to that standard.

The dialectic that Aristole pursues between prudence and wisdom does indeed lead to the troubling conclusion of divided ways of characterizing *anthropos* and its best sort of life. But avoiding this conclusion does violence to Aristotle's insights regarding intellectual virtue: Advocate a thoroughgoing hylomorphism and one cannot make sense of philosophical wisdom; abandon hylomorphism for the sake of a consistent dualism and one loses sight of the centrality of prudence and its role in promoting a genuinely happy political life. Perhaps Aristotle would have preferred not to have left us with this problem, but there it is nonetheless. Yet this aporia is not merely the result of Aristotle's intellectual honesty, for it throws before us the very practical problem of negotiating between the active and contemplative lives. And, by painting in contrasting colors the pictures of the two best sorts of life, this impasse serves as Aristotle's invitation to his readers to find their own solution to the problem of how best to live one's life.

The third interpretative template, the inconclusive one, has three advantages. First, with it one is not in any way compelled to think that Aristotle means to abandon anthropological hylomorphism, which is good because nowhere does he ever say that one ought to. Second, it does justice to the frankness of Aristotle's wonder at the activity of thinking in general, and of human thinking in particular. And third, it leaves some work for the rest of us.[27]

Franciscan University of Steubenville

Notes

1. Lloyd Gerson, *Aristotle and Other Platonists* (Ithaca, NY: Cornell University Press, 2005).

2. For examples see G. E. L. Owen's "The Platonism of Aristotle," *Proceedings of the British Academy*, Vol. 51 (London: Oxford University Press, 1965): 125–150; Giovanni Reale's *Il concetto di filosofia prima e l'unita della metafisica di Aristotele*, 4th Edition (Milano: Vita e pensiero, 1984), *The Concept of First Philosophy and the Unity of the* Metaphysics *of Aristotle*, English translation of the 3rd Edition by John R. Catan (Albany, NY: State University of New York Press, 1980); and Gerson's *Aristotle and Other Platonists*.

3. "ὅπως εἰς δύναμιν ἡ περὶ τὰ ἀνθρώινα φιλοσοφία τελειωθῇ." Ross renders this, "in order to complete to the best of our ability the philosophy of human nature" in *The Complete Works of Aristotle's Ethics*, two volumes, ed. Jonathan Barnes. (Princeton: Princeton University Press, 1984). Apostle has, "so that we may complete as best as we can the philosophy concerning human affairs" in *Aristotle's* Nicomachean Ethics. Translated with Commentaries and Glossary by Hippocrates G. Apostle. (Grinnell, Iowa: The Peripatetic Press, 1984).

4. This and the following translations follow, with modifications, the *The Complete Works of Aristotle's Ethics*, two volumes, ed. Jonathan Barnes. (Princeton: Princeton University Press, 1984). The Greek text I used for the *NE* is Bywater's (ed.), (Oxford: Clarendon Press, 1954 [1894]); for the *DA*, *The Loeb Classical Library*, 288 (Cambridge, MA: Harvard University Press, 1957).

5. We can see this also in the *Politics* VII.2, 1324a6–8; 3, 1325b30–32; and 15, 1334a11–15, where, as in the *Nicomachean Ethics* I.3, 1094b10–11, Aristotle suggests a convergence between the happiness of the individual citizen and the *polis*. But we also find in the *Politics* a distinction between the good citizen and the good human person, at III.4, 1276b31–1277a4, that bears on the distinction between the two accounts of a human being pursued in this essay.

6. *NE* VI.1, 1139a10

7. *DA* I. 3, 407a7

8. The interpretation of several key passages in *NE* I.7 is at the center of the debate about whether Aristotle's notion of happiness is intellectualist/dominant (being found in one best sort of activity) or inclusivist (comprising all virtuous activities). An incomplete list of some of the principal players in this debate includes the following: W. F. R. Hardie, "The Final Good in Aristotle's Ethics," *Philosophy* 40 (1965); John Ackrill, "Aristotle on *Eudaimonia*," *Proceedings of the British Academy* 60 (1974); John Cooper, *Reason and Human Good in Aristotle* (Cambridge, MA: Harvard University Press, 1975); Anthony Kenny, *The Aristotelian Ethics* (Oxford: Clarendon Press, 1978); John Cooper, "Contemplation and Happiness: A Reconsideration," *Synthese* 72 (1987): 187–216; Richard Kraut, *Aristotle on the Human Good* (Princeton: Princeton University Press, 1989); Anthony Kenny, *Aristotle on the Perfect Life* (Oxford: Clarendon Press, 1992); and Jeffrey S. Purinton, "Aristotle's Definition of Happiness (*NE* I, 7, 1098a16–18)," *Oxford Studies in Ancient Philosophy* 16 (1998).

9. *NE* I.7, 1098a1-3; 13, 1102a26-1102b28; *DA* II.1 and 3

10. However, it does not contain the whole of the appetitive part of the soul, since wish (βούλησις) is a rational appetite. See *NE* III.4, 1113a15, 25–33; and *DA* III.10, 433a23–24: "thought is never found producing movement without appetite, for wish is a form of appetite; and when movement is produced according to calculation it is also according to wish."

11. *NE* II.6, 1106b35–1107a1

12. *NE* VI.5, 1140a 30-b7; VI.7, 1141b8–23; VI.9, 1142b20–35; VI.12: "Practical wisdom is the quality of mind concerned with things just and noble and good for man, but these are the things which it is the mark of a *good* man to do" (1143b21–24); VI.13: "It is clear, then, from what has been said, that it is not possible to be good in the strict sense without practical wisdom, nor practically wise without moral excellence" (1144b30–32).

13. "It makes no small difference, then, whether we form habits of one kind or of another from our very youth; it makes a very great difference, or rather all the difference" (*NE* II.1, 1103b24-5).

14. Aristotle explicitly calls a human being the social animal at *NE* I.7, 1097b11, and *Politics* I.2, 1253a3.

15. *DA* III.7, 431a1, 431b16–17; *NE* VI.3, 1139b20–25; *DA* III.9, 432b27–28

16. See *NE* IX.9, 1169b 29–1170a4

17. I don't think *NE* VI.13, 1145b4–8, where Aristotle describes Thales and "others like him" as wise but imprudent, counts against my claim since in this passage Aristotle is referring to what other people say of Thales and others, rather than giving his own view on the matter.

18. Williams argues that Gauguin is following Aristotle's own prescriptions in *Moral Luck* (Cambridge: Cambridge University Press, 1981), 23.

19. One of the best treatment of ways to approach this question is found in the chap. 3, "Intellectualism in the *Nicomachean Ethics*," of John Cooper's *Reason and Human Good in Aristotle* (Indianapolis, IN: Hackett Publishing Company, 1986 [1975]), especially 157–160.

20. See for instance Julia Annas's impressive *The Morality of Happiness* (New York, NY: Oxford University Press, 1993). In this work Annas offhandedly dismisses any real problem of dualism in Aristotle, "In the ethical works he [Aristotle] sometimes tends to treat the agent as being the soul. This does not import dualism, or indeed any metaphysical view of the soul. . . ." (364).

21. Werner Jaeger, *Aristoteles: Grundlegung einer Geschichte seiner Entwicklung* (Berlin, 1923); *Aristotle: Fundamentals of the History of his Development*, English trans. R. Robinson (Oxford: Clarendon Press, 1934). Similarities to Plato's theories in Aristotle's later works, like the *NE*, are merely "old notes [which] sound again" (243, English version), of Aristotle's earlier Platonic allegiances occasionally being echoed in his mature period.

22. There are several precedents for such exhortative statements in Aristotle, such as in *Parts of Animals*, where he encourages his biologists-in-training not to shrink from studying the humblest of animals because "every realm of nature is marvellous," and that there is something divine in everything living thing so that "we should venture on the study of every kind of animal without distaste; for each and all will reveal to us something natural and something beautiful" (*Parts of Animals* I.5, 645b17, 22–23).

23. Strauss brings this interpretative template to light in *Persecution and the Art of Writing* (Chicago, IL: The University of Chicago Press, 1952). Strauss's aim is much broader than an approach to interpreting Aristotle, but Aristotle is explicitly brought under the ambit of this approach on 28 and 33.

24. See Aristide Tessitore's *Reading Aristotle's Ethics: Virtue, Rhetoric, and Political Philosophy* (Albany: State University of New York Press, 1996). See especially chaps. 1 and 5, "The Audience of the *Ethics*, Book I" and "Making the City Safe for Philosophy, Book X."

25. Whether or not Anthony Kenny is right in dating the *Eudemian Ethics* after the *Nicomachean Ethics*, I do not agree that the *EE* is as thoroughgoingly inclusivist in its account of happiness as he contends. See his *The Aristotelian Ethics* (Oxford: Clarendon Press, 1978). For his argument that the *EE* does, contra Jaeger's claim to the contrary, include Aristotle's distinction between prudence and wisdom see especially chap. 7, "Wisdom in *Aristotelian Ethics*." For his argument that the *EE* avoids the *NE*'s problem of competing accounts of happiness, see chap. 8, "Happiness in the *Aristotelian Ethics*," especially 213–214. His contentions are repeated and amplified in especially chap. 7, "The Contemplation and Service of God," in *Aristotle on the Perfect Life* (Oxford, Clarendon Press, 1992).

26. For instance, at *Meno* 86 b–c; and *Phaedo* 85 c–d, 107 a–b.

27. With special thanks to James Delaney and Jiyuan Yu for comments on an earlier version of this paper. With thanks also to participants of the 2006 SAGP conference, and to Fr. Daniel Gallagher, Andrew T. Seeley, and other participants of the 2006 ACPA conference, for comments on the last few revisions of this paper.

A Husserlian Perspective on Empirical Mathematics in Aristotle

Jean De Groot

Abstract: Examples are presented of Aristotle's use of non-idealized mathematics. Distinctions Husserl makes in *Crisis* help to delineate the features of this empirical mathematics, which include the non-persistence of mathematical aspects of things and the selective application of mathematical traits and proper accidents. In antiquity, non-abstracted mathematics was involved with practical sciences that treat motion. The suggestion is made that these sciences were incorporated by Aristotle into natural philosophy without first being abstracted as pure mathematics—a state of affairs not envisioned by Husserl, for whom science recast natural ontology by means of the idealization of pure mathematics. The relation of empirical mathematics to life-world ontology is considered.

A distinguishing characteristic of Husserl's life-world (*Lebenswelt*) is that all its activities take place with a pragmatic motivation.[1] The mathematization of nature in natural science is, in contrast, an advanced stage of *theoria*, the drive to understand things as they are for and in themselves. In what Husserl calls Galilean physics, an inherited tradition of developed geometry, a type of *theoria*, is taken to be the hidden structure of the natural world. The life-world remains the anchor of perceptual and mathematicized nature, however. Without it, there is nothing to explain. But to explain the life-world, in Husserl's view, means recasting it in new ontological terms, because the life-world is forgotten or obscured in the idealization that accompanies science.

Husserl was not an historian of science, and it is important for understanding his point of view that Galilean physics is a *type* for the modern physical sciences. He is describing what it means to take nature as a genuine mathematical manifold, intelligible in the terms of quantity, shape, and exactness. Nevertheless, it is worth pointing out that Galileo himself probably does not conform to the type of Galilean science, in which pure geometry is the model for physics.[2] In fact, it was often the ancient tradition of mechanics on which Galileo drew for his mathematical tools. Mechanics is a practical discipline, and the mechanical tradition on which Galileo drew was, from a modern standpoint, incomplete. There was not a systematic mathematical manifold to replace the life-world.[3]

An important difference between geometry and mechanics is that mechanics includes motion as part of its account. Plato, in *Republic* VII (527d–531d), testifies to the difficulty of fully mathematicizing such a science. Speaking of astronomy, he says there must be a geometry of solid figures, stereometry, something not yet developed, and then these bodies must be set in motion. In the order of the sciences, then, astronomy comes after this pure mathematics of solids in motion (528b–e).[4] The order of the mathematical sciences had not attained much more completeness than Plato describes by the time of Galileo. Another important difference between geometry and mechanics is that mechanics involves weight as a feature of explanation, and this introduces another dimension for measurement and abstraction beyond the metric of space and time. Weight is not so easily mapped onto the intuitively grasped dimensions of space that are the natural home for Euclidean geometry.[5]

The point of these remarks is not to contend that Husserl's account is simplistic and flawed, but rather to draw attention to the fact that there is a type of mathematical account that is *part of the life-world*. Mechanics, as the mathematics of simple machines, is end-oriented and pragmatic. Its mathematical aspect has as its import a clearly defined effect depending on motion, namely a body covering a distance. Because of these features, mechanics is not fully abstracted from experience. Husserl said that geometry arose from the art of measuring, specifically surveying, a practical activity. So he recognized the pragmatic nature of some mathematical projects. Husserl does not take into account, however, that a non-abstracted practical science might be appropriated into *theoria* without its first being idealized as pure mathematics.[6] Such an appropriation did take place in ancient thought by means of the sciences of astronomy and mechanics, and it is particularly prominent in the philosophy of Aristotle. In what follows, I will sketch, with the help of Husserlian notions, some of the features marking or setting apart this appropriation of a non-abstracted mathematical science into a philosophical treatment of the world. I will discuss Aristotle's treatment of the movement of limbs in *MA* 1, his remarks about measurement, astronomy, and geometry in *Metaphysics* B.2, and his composition of the continuum in *Physics* V.3.

Mixing Movement with Idealized Points and Lines

An extended example of Aristotle's recourse to mechanical notions is his treatment of animal motion. In *Movement of Animals* 1–7, Aristotle presents an analysis of animal movement based on two principles. One is that points on a moving radius cover different distances in the same time. This is illustrated in the radial movement of a limb (698a21–24), like the flexing of the forearm at the elbow joint, but it is also the principle behind levers of different descriptions, e.g., the rudder (701b26–27). The second principle at work in *MA* is that all movement requires something relatively unmoved against which a moved thing fixes or steadies itself in order to move (700a9–10). The unmoved component may be an outside object, as in the case of a man propelling a boat by pushing his staff on the shore (699a9–10); or it may be an unmoved part within an animal, like the joint (698b1–7). Although these two principles complement one another, they cannot form a single mathematical account. The center of a circle, or the limit of a line cannot be described as unmoved, since points, lacking magnitude, cannot change place. They can be neither at rest nor in motion. Secondly, that against which something to be moved braces itself must have magnitude and exert force, if it is to support a moving thing (699a32–99b1). As Aristotle says himself, nothing mathematical moves (698a26), nor can points and extremities have power (699a20). Accordingly, Aristotle describes the immobile origin of motion as relative (ἡ ἀρχὴ ἡ πρὸς ὅ ἡ ἀρχή)[7] and says that it changes in relation to the moving part (698b1–6).

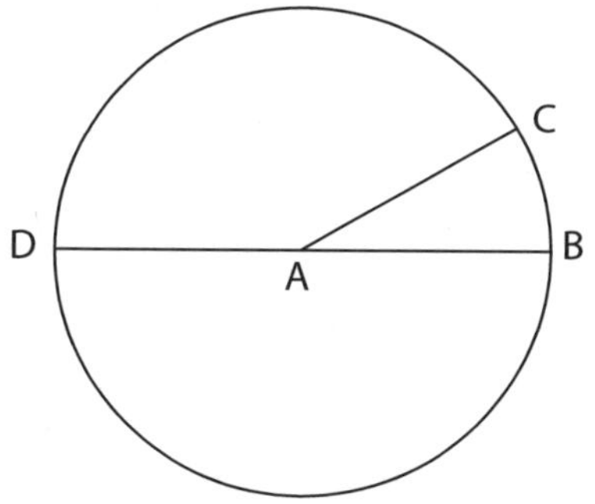

In his picture of radial motion in *MA* 1, a radius of a circle is made two from being one, by one point (σημεῖον) in the joint moving while another remains at rest. The joint is like a center (κέντρον) and the part containing the joint is what becomes "both one and two, both straight and bent, changing potentially and actually by reason of the joint" (698a18–20). This part, then, is represented by a line, as Aristotle makes explicit speaking of *AD* that remains and *B* that moves and generates *AC*. (See accompanying figure.) He qualifies his statement about points moving and resting, by citing anonymous authority or accepted practice: "For as they say, they apply a fictional motion to them (καὶ γὰρ τὸ κινεῖσθαι, ὥς φασί, πλάττουσιν ἐπ' αὐτῶν), for nothing mathematical moves" (698a25–26).[8] Given that the moving radius principle that figures so prominently in *MA* 1 and 7 is the explanatory principle of the lever, this remark by Aristotle may be drawing upon a received view of mathematical practice in mechanics. In any case, he here separates his own empirical geometry at work in understanding the movement of the lever from mathematics taken as a separated subject matter. One involves motion; the other, by the very nature of its entities, does not.

What is the meaning, then, of Aristotle's recourse to mathematical entities in this context of motion? It is not that, in mechanics, mathematical points *do* move but that points *do not persist* as elements of a situation of movement. The elbow is the stationary 'center' when the forearm moves, but the shoulder is, when the entire arm moves (698b1–3). So, what is an origin point of motion in one case becomes submerged in the continuous magnitude of the body part, when that part moves. This is because the end of a radius 'moves' but only to generate a second line (698a23). The linear magnitude represents the extended limb, and the end of the radius defines its displacement.

Empirical Shapes and Figures Versus Ideal Figures

Some of the things Husserl says, in tracing the origin of geometry to surveying and measurement, are helpful in understanding Aristotle's practice of empirical geometry here. Husserl says that there are shapes (*Gestalten*) of the surrounding world conceived as sensibly intuitable and there are types conceived at any level of generality (*die in jeder Allgemeinheitsstufe erdenklichen Typen*).[9] He makes two points. Shapes are not conceptualized apart from their sensible features. But also, shape defined generally, e.g.,'curved,' is as much a specific and clearly perceptible empirical shape as the more exact 'circular.' Practically speaking, he says, there can be a simple perfection (*ein Volkommenes schlechthin*) apart from idealization that is adequate to special practical interest.[10] Interestingly, he says that sensible shapes and the types in the world "fade into each another as a continuum (*gehen kontinuierlich ineinander über*)."[11] In this continuity, they fill out space-time (*Raumzeitlichkeit*) as their form. This means that, in our awareness, recognized shapes make up space, but loosely. Sensible shapes fade without continuous perceptual attention and overlap as we move from one place to another. Only as measured does a shape emerge with a form that can be similar to some other.[12] Husserl's description of empirical shapes recalls Aristotle's lines and points that figure in the account of animal motion but recede back into the corporeal when some other part moves. Husserl is describing perceptual and intellectual awareness of empirical shapes. Aristotle, on the other hand, is giving explanatory accounts that incorporate this kind of empirical awareness of mathematical objects. In these accounts, it would be correct to say that Aristotle does not objectify mathematical aspects of the motion of limbs, because he does not make them part of a mathematical subject matter. He also himself describes the status of these empirical shapes as not objectified, insofar as he says that the stationary point is an origin only in relation to another part, when that part moves.

Kjosavik presents a view of empirical lines and circles as "prototypes of perceptual organization." These schematic constructs are actually intuited lines and circles and "not merely degenerate derivatives of such shapes." Thus, a particular shape could be general, e.g., 'round,' without being unclear or imprecise.[13] Round is not just imperfectly a circle, according to the definition of circle. This is especially clear in Aristotle's application of the principle of the lever to the movement of joints. The radial motion of the limb is not poorly realized as radial motion or hard to perceive as such because it is not abstracted with the full complement of geometrical traits of the circle. The radial motion manifests with sufficient exactness whatever import is to be drawn from the features of the sensible shape.

Aristotle makes distinctions concerning mathematical objects that parallel the difference between ideal figures, in a Husserlian sense, and empirical shapes and figures. In *Metaphysics* B.2, he is puzzled about the status of astronomy and surveying (γεωδαισία) in relation to geometry. He says it cannot be the case that the only difference between geometry and surveying is that the latter deals with mathematical objects that are perceptible (997b27). For then there would be an intermediate type of being between the immovable imperceptible subject matter of mathematics and ordinary perceptible things. If these intermediate mathematical objects were *in* sensible things, then there would be immovables in what moves, an impossible suggestion for more than one reason. But Aristotle also rejects their existing separately. Yet, surveying—or measurement—is not measurement of perceptible and perishable magnitudes, he says; otherwise, the measure would perish along with those perceptibles (b33). By this, Aristotle must mean that the unit cannot be simply a perceptible thing belonging among the other perceptibles it measures. The unit is not something perceptible. Neither is astronomy concerned with perceptible magnitudes, he says. In this, both measurement and astronomy are like geometry, he says (997b32–98a6). He goes further and says that the accounts given by astronomy are not accounts of the very movements that the perceptible heavens in fact display. Indeed, perceptible magnitudes are subject to just the sort of limitations cited by Protagoras, that no sensible circle (κύκλος) touchs a straight edge (κανών) at a single point (998a7–11). Finally, it seems, it is the rules and definitions governing true mathematical objects that will apply to accounts in astronomy and surveying—just not all of those rules and not all the time. Aristotle does not speak of abstraction, ἀφαίρεσις, in this passage, nor does he use his elusive but ever reliable ᾗ, *qua*. Nevertheless, the generalizing regard without abstraction that he describes for these sciences is not an isolated case. It is illustrated in practice in Aristotle's treatment of the motion of limbs that we already examined.

The type of analysis Aristotle follows in these passages bears comparison to what Drummond calls generalizing abstraction.[14] In generalizing abstraction, we identify shapes predicatively but do not have a theoretical concern with them as exactly defined. Indeed, according to Drummond, we are not yet even engaged in measurement, though consistent with predicative interest, we make claims of similarity or dissimilarity between different instances. As Drummond delineates empirical abstraction, however, empirical shapes are not precise and do not support judgements about what is *necessarily* the same in similar cases (788). He seems to have in mind, for mathematical features, what Sokolowski calls 'associative judgment' in the case of ordinary concepts.[15] But the figures of Aristotle's mechanics and astronomy do implicate salient proper accidents and relational features of the circle and its parts, characteristics we recognize as geometrical. They are not inexact in the features they present. Nevertheless, the non-persistence of these features as part of a physical analysis indicates that, though they are conceptual, i.e. universalized, they are not conceptualized in a way that 'starts' idealization. This is perhaps consistent with Drummond's contention that empirical generalization is not the ground for idealization, which must originate in a return to the perceptible objects themselves.[16] Aristotle's use of mathematical entities and their features shows in practice the possibility of a non-idealized mathematics.

Selective Application of Mathematical Traits in Non-idealized Mathematics

Also revealing for Aristotle's non-idealized mathematical entities is another feature of Husserlian generalization, namely that there is an acceptable insouciance or inconsistency with respect to the way of defining shapes. In an early essay, Husserl treats the division of solids in physical space.[17] He says that, in the natural attitude, we make no distinction for division of bodies in physical space between dividing solids by surfaces that are lines or surfaces that are thin physical bodies.[18] It would seem to be a feature of non-idealizing mathematical treatments that there is no reason to consider these two ways of imagining the division of a body as different. Let us consider a case where Aristotle does what Husserl here describes, but in relation to composition not division.

In treating what we take to be the composition of the continuum in *Physics* V.3, Aristotle shifts between a mathematical and a physical characterization of the unity of endpoints of continuous segments of magnitude. In explicating the meaning of successive, contiguous, and continuous in terms of together and apart, touching, and between, he first treats parts of a continuum in mathematical terms. 'Together' (ἅμα) is to be in the same primary place (ἐν ἑνὶ τόπῳ πρώτῳ); parts touch when their extremities (τὰ ἄκρα) are together. The account is notoriously plagued by foundational difficulties.[19] Extremeties, being without magnitude, cannot touch, since things touch part to part not whole to whole, nor can two things occupy the same primary place without being the same thing. As he says elsewhere, one's primary place is the place that contains only you (*Physics* IV.2, 209b1). This inconsistency seems not to concern Aristotle in *Physics* V.3, however. He continues in mathematical style, defining 'contiguous' (τὸ ἐχόμενον) in terms of 'touching' (τὸ ἅπτεσθαι)and 'successive' (τὸ ἐφεξῆς).[20] But to illustrate, Aristotle uses examples that run the gamut from mathematics to craft: lines, something mathematical; units (μονάδες), a type for measurement; and houses. To define the continuous, Aristotle steps out of mathematical language almost entirely. The continuous has limits (τὸ πέρας), not extremities, that become one and the same. Πέρας is a term used in the *Physics* for the limit of a natural thing or the ending of a movement. Natural things, being finite, inevitably have endings in this sense. The term here refers to the natural boundaries of distinguishable parts making up a continuous thing. Shifting back into more rigorous terms, he lays down a requirement of continuity: "it is not possible that the touching extremes (τοῖν ἐσχάτοιν) are two." Having gotten this far, however, the priority of the natural in the account becomes apparent. Aristotle says, that once these things are defined, it becomes clear that the continuous is composed from things that can become a natural unity by contact (ἐξ ὧν ἕν τι πέφυκε γίγνεσθαι κατὰ τὴν σύναψιν). Here, Aristotle uses the language of the customary by nature, generation, and synthesis consequent upon contact.[21] He goes on, saying that continuous things are in essence what shall be one as a whole. His examples are wholes established by rivets, glue, contact (ἁφῇ), or growth (προσφύσει). As Aristotle says, natural union (σύμφυσις) is last in generation. For there to be natural union, extremities must meld, coalesce or grow together naturally (συμφύσεται), but not all things in contact form this sort of unity. Aristotle understands that continuity in magnitude for sensible and movable things just is not brought into effect by means of a mathematical conception. Aristotle's way of defining continuity illustrates in the the case of composition of bodies Husserl's point about an empirical conception of division of body. It does not matter whether we think of extremeties as points, limits with magnitude, or ends that can be glued or riveted. The relevance of the mathematical is guided by the real possibilities for natural things. The treatment of continuity in *Physics* V.3 is consequent upon an empirical abstraction of magnitude and its extremeties.

The points I have been making support two general conclusions. The first is that, even though Aristotle's application of mathematical notions to animal motion is practical and incompletely systematized, the conception of mathematical entities and their properties that is involved is not vague, in a pejorative sense, or imprecise. The non-abstracted character of mechanics does not consist in a confused notion of mathematics. Secondly, Aristotle consistently and consciously separates empirical geometry from abstracted mathematics. He does this, not because of the roughness and imprecision of empirical geometry but because of how the geometrical analysis must be conducted at all. So, 'mathematics in motion' will take some aspects of mathematical objects but not other as active and salient to its account. Finally, Aristotle is sufficiently in control of the differences in types of mathematical accounts to apply without comment the principle of the non-persistence of mathematicals. In accordance with the nature of empirical generalization, he disregards differences between the mathematical and the physical that need not affect the physical composition of the continuum.

To take seriously the possibility of a consistent generalizing regard without abstraction in Aristotle's approach to mathematical accounts in nature would enrich interpretation of a number of issues—e.g., his puzzling ascription of διότι status to mathematical explanations in physical science (*Po An* I.13) and his claim of a different standard of precision for a science of the ethical and social (*NE* I.3). There is another reason to consider the possibility of non-idealized mathematics. I would contend that the ancient μαθήματα, especially mechanics, provided for Aristotle conceptual resources for what Husserl would call a life-world ontology. To understand different types of mathematical accounts allows us to see that life-world ontology can be conceptually rich, and even mathematical, without what Husserl calls idealization. To the extent that we still lack a modern life-world ontology, Aristotle's sophistication about different types of explanation and his own natural philosophy provide an example of what life-world ontology is and how it is attained. I have also suggested, however, that one type of mathematical enterprise is not included in Husserl's own analysis. This is the incorporation of a non-idealized mathematical science into natural philosophy.

The Catholic University of America

Notes

1. Aron Gurwitsch, *Phenomenology and the Theory of Science*, ed. Lester Embree (Evanston: Northwestern University Press, 1974), 50. See also Robert Sokolowski, "Exact Science and the World in Which We Live," *Pictures, Quotations, and Distinctions* (Notre Dame: Notre Dame University Press, 1992), 155–172. For Husserl's presentation of the life-world, see his *Crisis of European Sciences and Transcendental Phenomenology*, trans. David Carr (Evanston: Northwestern University Press, 1970), 48–49; § 9h, and 34. German texts cited herein are from *Die Krisis der europäischen Wissenschaften und die transzendentale Phänomenologie*, herausgegeben von Elisabeth Ströker (Hamburg: Verlag, 1969).

2. As Patrick Heelan says, Husserl's Galilean science is "fundamentally a critique of the Cartesian spirit." See "Husserl's Later Philosophy of Natural Science," *Philosophy of Science* 54, no. 3 (Sept. 1987), 369. Gary Gutting criticizes Husserl's view of natural science as excessively idealized, not taking account of the scientist's aim to understand empirical realities. See Gutting's "Husserl and Scientific Realism," *Philosophy and Phenomenological Research* 39, no. 1 (Sept. 1978), 44.

3. It would be possible to overemphasize Galileo's dependence on the mechanical tradition. There is, of course, both modern novelty and idealization in Galileo's way of thinking. Galileo's debt to mechanics, in particular the theory of the balance that founds ancient mechanics, is especially prominent in *De Motu*, chap. 6, his *Mechanics*, and the inclined plane theorems of the Third Day of *Two New Sciences.* See the author's "Aspects of Aristotelian Statics in Galileo's Dynamics," *Studies in History and Philosophy of Science* 31, no. 4 (2000), 645–664.

4. On this topic, see Alexander Mourelatos, "Astronomy and Kinematics in Plato's Project of Rationalist Explanation," *Studies in History and Philosophy of Science* 12, no. 1 (March, 1981), 1–32, and "Plato's Real Astronomy: *Republic* 527d–531d," in John P. Anton, *Science and the Sciences in Plato* (New York: Eidos, 1980), 33–73.

5. Husserl comments on the mathematization of plena characteristics in *Crisis*, Part II, § 9c.

6. Aristotle does not have a notion of idealization in relation to the subject matter of mathematics. He speaks of abstraction (ἀφαίρεσις) instead. There is, nevertheless, a close parallel between idealization and abstraction in defining the subject matter of mathematics. For the purposes of this paper, I will sometimes speak of mathematics as idealized or non-idealized for Aristotle.

7. For alternate readings of this text, see Martha Nussbaum, *Aristotle's* De Motu Animalium, (Princeton: Princeton University Press, 1978), 284–285.

8. Reading κινεῖται with Nussbaum at a26 but understanding ὥς φασί as referring to those who practice or accept mechanical argumentation in the solution of mathematical or physical problems. Nussbaum takes the statement about mathematical entities to be a criticism by Aristotle of Plato's ideal astronomy (*Aristotle's* De Motu, 282–283).

9. *Krisis*, 26–27 (Carr, 27).

10. *Krisis*, 24 (Carr, 25). I do not follow Kjosavik's view that Husserl thought that "sensible shapes are inexact or vague, whereas geometrical shapes are exact or sharp." (See "Husserl's View of the Life-World and the World of Science," *Revue Internationale de Philosophie* 2/2003, no. 224, 195.) Kjosavik's notion of schematic construction of figures in a

kind of empirical geometry is, however, helpful in understanding Aristotle's use of mechanics and astronomy.

11. *Krisis*, 27 (Carr, 27).

12. *Krisis*, 27–28 (Carr, 27).

13. Kjosavik, 196–197.

14. John J. Drummond, "The Perceptual Roots of Geometric Idealizations," *Review of Metaphysics* 37, no. 4 (June 1984), 786–787.

15 Robert Sokolowski, *Husserlian Meditations* (Evanston: Northwestern University Press, 1974), chap. 3, § 19.

16. Drummond, "Idealizations" [see note 14], 801. An interesting issue is that the lines and circles describing movement of the limbs in *MA* 1 are not simply limits of bodies. Husserl treats empirical shapes and then idealization in terms of objects and their boundaries. But Aristotle is delineating mathematical elements descriptive of *movement* and, hence, the lines are like internal structures of bodies, not limits, and what is relevant to conceptualization is the path the line describes.

17. "Der anschauliche Raum," *Studien zur Arithmetik und Geometrie*, herausgegeben von Ingeborg Strohmeyer (*Husserliana* XXI) (The Hague: Martinus Nijhoff, 1983), 275–284.

18. "Raum," 279. Drummond discusses this passage in "Idealizations," 791.

19. For a brief survey of the problem and solutions, see Michael J. White, *The Continuous and the Discrete* (Oxford: Clarendon Press, 1992), 23–31.

20. One thing is 'in succession' to another when it is of the same sort as and comes after another, and there is nothing of the same sort between them. The contiguous is what, being in succession, is also touching.

21. The term σύναψις is used in the Aristotelian *Mechanics* for the common point where sides of a parallelogram meet (854b39). This is clearly a mathematical usage of the term, though even in this case, the context is motion. Here in *Physics* V, Aristotle uses the term for the coalescence of the limits of sensible things that can be a unity or form a whole by growth.

Thomas Aquinas on Truths about Nonbeings

Gloria Wasserman

Abstract: In *De veritate* I.2, Thomas Aquinas claims that "to every true act of understanding there must correspond some being and likewise to every being there corresponds a true act of understanding." For Aquinas, the *ratio* of truth consists in a conformity between intellect and being. This account of truth, however, does not appear to allow for a certain class of truths, namely those that are about nonbeings. Many think that it is true that 'no chimeras exist,' that 'blindness can be caused by exposure to bright lights,' and that 'evil should be avoided.' Yet, in each of these cases of truth, there does not appear to be a being to which the intellect conforms. In this paper, I will explore the ways in which Aquinas's notion of truth as "conformity to being" is able to accommodate truths about nonbeings.

Thomas Aquinas maintains that truth is found both in the intellect and in things: primarily in the human intellect in so far as it conforms to things and secondarily, in things in so far as they are apt to produce a true apprehension of themselves in the human intellect.[1] In the *De veritate,* for instance, Aquinas writes: "to every true act of understanding there must correspond some being and likewise to every being there corresponds a true act of understanding."[2] Throughout his works, he claims that the essence of truth of the human intellect consists in an adequation (or commensuration) of intellect and thing.[3] In the *Commentary on the Sentences*, Aquinas explains that, more precisely, it is the existence (*esse*) of a thing that enters into the relation of adequation and accordingly, causes truth to reside in the human intellect. He writes:

> But since in a thing there is its quiddity and its existence, truth is based more on the existence of a thing than on its quiddity, just as the name 'being' (*entis*) is derived from 'existence' (*esse*); and the relation of adequation in which the nature of truth consists is completed in the operation of the intellect which grasps the existence (*esse*) of a thing as it is by a certain assimilation to it. Accordingly, I say that the existence itself of a thing is the cause of truth insofar as it is in the cognition of the intellect.[4]

For Aquinas the truth of the human intellect is inextricably linked with existence.[5] This appears to present a problem, though, for a certain class of truths, namely, those that are about nonbeings. Most would not deny that 'blindness can result from getting certain chemicals in one's eyes,' that 'it is evil to torture innocent people' and that 'no unicorns exist.' It is difficult to see, however, how Aquinas's analysis can account for these truths since in these cases there is no being independent of the soul to which the intellect can conform. Moreover, there does not seem to be a fitting cause of truth in the intellect given that Aquinas claims that existence itself is the cause of truth. Yet, when Aquinas discusses the definition of truth, he never indicates that the nature of truth differs in the case of truths about nonbeings. In this paper, I will explore the ways in which Aquinas thought that his notion of truth could be preserved even in these cases.

In the first section, I will explore the possibility of asserting the existence of propositions about nonbeings. I will then address the question of how Aquinas thought that propositions about nonbeings could stand in the relation of conformity by analyzing his treatment of a widely discussed medieval paradox concerning the non-existence of truth. Next, I will address the question of what Aquinas took to be the cause of truths about nonbeings given that they cannot be caused by the existence of the subject of the proposition. In the final section, I will conclude that although truths about nonbeings are not instances of an intellect's conformity with a thing, they are not counter-examples to two fundamental tenets of Aquinas's theory of truth, namely that existence is the ultimate foundation of truth and that the nature of truth consists in adequation or conformity.

I. Propositions about Nonbeings

The first issue to consider is whether the assertion of the existence of propositions about nonbeings is even a coherent notion. If the idea of a proposition about a nonbeing is inherently self-contradictory, further questions about the truth of propositions about nonbeings do not arise since there will be no propositions of this sort. Some philosophers may be inclined to think that there are no propositions about nonbeings because if something does not *really* exist, there is no subject of which anything can be predicated or denied. On this view, even the claim that 'blindness is no real being' presupposes that there is some being called 'blindness' of which the predicate 'is a real being' can be denied. Aquinas, however, does not follow this line of reasoning when approaching the topic of our thought and speech about what is not. He begins with the assumption that we can talk about what is not. Beginning from that starting point, he tries to account for how our forming a proposition about something does not entail that it really exists. Aquinas blocks this inference by distinguishing two senses of 'being.'[6] In *De ente et essentia*, Aquinas writes:

> It should be known that, as the philosopher says in *Metaphysics* V, 'being *per se*' is said in two ways: one way as it is divided by the ten categories and in another way, as it signifies the truth of propositions. There is a difference between these because in the second way, 'being' can be said of

> everything that an affirmative proposition can be formed about, even if it posits nothing positive *in re*. It is in this way that privations and negations are said to be beings. For we say that affirmation is opposed to negation and that blindness is in the eye. But according to the first way, 'being' cannot be said except of that which posits something *in re*. Accordingly, in the first way, blindness and things of its kind are not beings.[7]

Aquinas is claiming that when we use 'being' in a proposition as, for example, when we say that 'blindness is in the eye,' we cannot infer the conclusion that blindness has real being *extra animam* because the 'is' of predication differs in sense from the 'is' of real being. He says that those who failed to recognize this distinction thought that in virtue of how we speak about evil, it must be a positive reality.[8]

Aquinas recognizes that the class of subjects that we can speak about has a wider extension than the class of real beings because the mind is able to treat as a being that which is *per se* a nonbeing.[9] For this reason, he thinks that subjects of predications, regardless of whether they exist *extra animam*, can be called 'beings,' albeit not in the same way that real beings are called 'beings.'[10] Accordingly, there is a trivial sense in which every proposition has a being as its subject. Yet, when 'being' is understood to mean 'real being' Aquinas does not hesitate in assuming that there are propositions that do not have beings as subjects. He does not see any contradiction in predicating or denying an attribute of a non existent subject.

There is a further difficulty that must be considered concerning propositions about nonbeings. The intellect can only assert and deny something of a subject it first apprehends. Yet, Aquinas holds that human cognition, like truth, depends on a being outside of the soul. Cognition takes place by means of an intelligible species that is abstracted from the form of a being existing independently of the soul.[11] The problem arises then of how nonbeings, which lack form, can be apprehended by the human intellect. If nonbeings cannot be apprehended by the human intellect, then they cannot be the subjects of propositions. Again, it appears that the problem of explaining the truth of propositions about nonbeings cannot even be generated since it seems that there cannot be any propositions of this sort.

Aquinas did not overlook the difficulty that his analysis of cognition appeared to present for explaining our thinking about what is not. As is well known, he held that privations are understood through the forms of their opposites since knowing some positive reality implies knowledge of what it would be for it to be absent.[12] Privations just are absences of forms in subjects that should possess them. It is in virtue of one's knowledge of sight that one understands what it would be for sight to be negated in an agent who should be able to see. Aquinas explains that privations are not known through their contraries as a conclusion is known through its premises, but rather as a thing is known through its definition.[13] Unlike a deductive inference, knowledge of a privation is a basic grasp of a complex concept that includes the concepts of a positive species and negation. For Aquinas, negation is one of the first concepts of the human intellect. In so far as we understand that something is a being, we understand that it is different from every other being. This transcendental notion of distinctness or *aliud* includes within itself the notion of negation. One being is distinct from another because it is *not* the other.[14] Accordingly, our notion of negation follows from our knowledge of being.

While Aquinas thinks that we can come to know that blindness is a lack of sight in a certain subject and that evil is a lack of good that should be present, he does not think that we can conceive of the form of blindness or evil in itself. This is because the very notion of privation is the non-existence of a form. The way in which we are able to think of privations and negations differs from the way in which we are able to conceive other nonbeings. In the *De veritate*, Aquinas writes:

> Something is said to be a nonbeing in two ways. In the first way, because nonbeing (*non esse*) is included in its definition, just as blindness is said to be a nonbeing. And a form of such nonbeing cannot be conceived neither in the imagination nor in the intellect, and evil is a nonbeing of this kind. In the other way, [something is called a nonbeing] because it is not found in the nature of things, although the very privation of entity is not included in its definition, and so, nothing prevents one from imagining such nonbeings and from conceiving of their forms.[15]

A fictional entity, such as a golden mountain, would be an example of the second type of nonbeing that Aquinas mentions. We create the form of a golden mountain by combining the forms of "gold" and "mountain." Non-existence is not included in the notion of a golden mountain. Accordingly, we can conceive of the form of a golden mountain. Despite the fact that we can imagine the forms of fictional nonbeings, our negative concepts of privative nonbeings have more of a foothold in reality. The union of our concepts of negation and sight has its foundation in real human persons who lack sight, whereas the unity of "gold" and "mountain" has its basis in the imagination alone. There will be more to say about this point later.

Since it has been shown that Aquinas thinks that nonbeings can be apprehended and that there can be propositions about nonbeings when this claim is understood to mean propositions whose subjects posit nothing positive *extra animam*, the question can now be raised of how these propositions about nonbeings can stand in the relation of conformity.

II. The Conformity of Propositions about Nonbeings

As mentioned in the introduction, Aquinas claims that the nature of truth consists in an adequation of intellect and thing. Moreover, in the *De veritate*, he claims that "to every true act of understanding there must correspond some being."[16] There is an approach that might be taken in order to avoid admitting that truths about nonbeings pose a clear exception to these claims. Recall that Aquinas holds that every subject of a proposition can be called a 'being' in a certain sense. It could be argued that truths about nonbeings *do* involve an adequation with a thing and *do* correspond to a being, namely a propositional being. I think, however, that Aquinas would reject this approach. The objects of thought and speech are called beings regardless of whether they also exist *extra animam*. If a subject of thought or speech does not posit anything *in re*, the only real being it has is the being in the intellect of the proposition of which it is the subject. Accordingly, to claim that the intellect corresponds to a propositional being in knowing a truth about a nonbeing is to claim that the intellect's predication conforms to the being of one of its own acts of predication. Aquinas would reject this suggestion since he holds that things must be sufficiently distinct in order to stand in the relation of conformity. It is for this reason that Aquinas claims that truth is found primarily in the second act of the intellect. In its second act, the intellect predicates or denies something of a subject that is simply apprehended. Accordingly, the intellect takes on a propositional structure that is proper to itself. Because of this difference, it is able to conform.[17] In the case of two propositions that both either affirm or deny the same predicate of the same subject, the necessary difference in one is not present in virtue of which it can be said to conform to the other.

Although he never says so when he is defining the nature of truth, Aquinas himself was content to deny that truths about nonbeings involve a conformity with a *being* or an adequation with a *thing*. This is seen in *De veritate* where Aquinas entertains a paradox concerning truth that many other medieval authors also addressed. The paradox is this: If there were no truth, then the statement that 'there is no truth' would be true.[18] This paradox is thought to show that truth must be eternal since it seems that there must be truth even when we posit that truth does not exist, but it is problematic for truth to be eternal because then God, the first truth, would not be the only eternal truth.

To solve the difficulty that the paradox raises, Aquinas notes that a distinction must be made between the way in which negations and privations and the way in which things that have real existence independent of the soul relate to the intellect. As we saw earlier, Aquinas thought that the existence of real beings causes truth in the intellect.[19] According to their definition, truths about nonbeings cannot similarly be caused by existence. We cannot claim that a real unicorn existing outside of the soul causes the truth of the proposition 'No unicorns exist' since if there were a real unicorn outside of the soul, the statement would no longer be true. In this reply, Aquinas writes: "Accordingly, if nonbeing is adequated to any intellect, it is not on account of the nonbeing itself, but rather on account of the intellect itself that grasps the intelligible character (*ratio*) of nonbeing in itself."[20] It is important to note that Aquinas does not deny here that there is an adequation when the intellect knows a truth about a nonbeing. In this passage, he assumes that it is possible for a nonbeing to be adequated to an intellect. Aquinas's point is that the intellect is ultimately responsible for its ability to be in the relationship of conformity that consists in a truth about a nonbeing.

Since the intellect itself, rather than a real being outside of the soul, is the cause of its truth about a nonbeing, Aquinas is able to claim that truth with respect to nonbeings resides only in the intellect. Recall that Aquinas holds that things only have truth in so far as they cause truth in the intellect. Nonbeings do not cause the intellect's truth, so they do not have truth of themselves. Accordingly, Aquinas solves the objection at hand by claiming that the statement that 'There is no truth' only posits truth in an eternal intellect, which for Aquinas is the first truth, God.[21] There is no really existing object outside of God that causes it to be true that 'there is no truth.' Furthermore, if there were no eternally existing intellect that could conceive of truth while it did not exist, it would not even be true that 'there is no truth.' For Aquinas, there can be no truth apart from an intellect.[22]

From Aquinas's treatment of the paradox about the non-existence of truth, some points can be drawn that are applicable to truths about nonbeings in general. The most important of these is that Aquinas thought that there could be a relationship of conformity and adequation even in the absence of a thing or being to which the intellect conforms. Aquinas's notion of "conformity" does not entail that conformity is a relation that requires two *relata*, each of which are real beings. Another key point to be taken from Aquinas's discussion of the paradox is that an intellect only has the possibility of conforming with the absence of a being or a lacking in a being, because of its own ability to form intelligible notions of what does not exist. Without this ability, the intellect would not be able to truly affirm or deny any lacking of real being because it would have no cognitive awareness of it. For this reason, Aquinas says that the intellect, rather than the existence of a thing, is the cause of truths about nonbeings. Yet, it will be shown that the intellect is not in every respect the cause of truths about nonbeings.

III. The Cause of Truths about Nonbeing

When Aquinas says that the existence of a thing is the cause of truth and that in the case of truths about nonbeings, the intellect itself is the cause of truth, he is talking more specifically about the *efficient* cause of truth.[23] An efficient cause is the primary source of motion or change in another. In the case of truths about beings, the existence of a being reduces the intellect from potency to an act of true judgment, while in the case of truths about nonbeings the intellect itself is the agent that causes truth to reside in itself by forming the intelligible notions of nonbeings. Aquinas does not think, however, that the intellect is in every respect the cause of truths about nonbeings. Although he does not offer much explanation, in the *De veritate* he indicates a certain respect in which a class of nonbeings can be considered causes of truth.

In reply to the question of whether every other truth is from the first truth, Aquinas brings up the issue of the truth of nonbeings.[24] Again, he claims that the conformity of the intellect to a nonbeing is due to the intellect that apprehends the intelligible character of it.[25] In one of the objections within this question, it is claimed that non-existence is the cause of the truth of negative propositions, just as existence is the cause of the truth of affirmative propositions.[26] In reply to this objection, Aquinas notes that a distinction must be made between the senses in which non-existence and existence are causes of truth. He denies that nonbeing efficiently causes truth to be in the intellect. The intellect does this itself by forming the intelligible notion of the nonbeing to which it conforms. He grants, however that "nonbeing existing outside of the soul" (*extra animam*) is the exemplar cause of truths in the intellect.[27] An exemplar is a principle for making something. It guides the efficient cause in its exercise of causality by functioning like an example or pattern. So Aquinas is claiming here that nonbeing existing outside of the soul provides a model for the intellect that acts as the efficient cause of truth.

Before it can be asked how nonbeing existing outside of the soul can be an exemplar cause of truth, we must ask what Aquinas means by "nonbeing existing *extra animam*." In the body of the reply to this question, Aquinas refers to negations and privations as existing independent of the soul (*existentes extra animam*).[28] Interestingly, Aquinas does not use this phrase "existing independent of the soul" to describe negations and privations in any other place in his corpus. Unfortunately, here Aquinas does not offer any explanation of what he means by this description. It is far from likely that he meant that some types of nonbeing have real being independent of the soul because this, of course, is certainly a contradiction. Moreover, it goes against what Aquinas clearly expresses elsewhere. In commenting on book IV of Aristotle's *Metaphysics*, Aquinas explains that the term being is used in many ways all with reference to one first being, namely substance, which has being through itself. He goes on to say that corruptions of substances can be called beings, as well as the privations in which these processes of corruption terminate. He also says that certain negations can be called beings because of their relationship to substances.[29] Yet, after categorizing the ways in which being can be said, he makes the point that the modes of being which he has enumerated can be reduced since the weakest (*debilissimum*) beings that he identified, namely negations and privations, only have being in reason.[30] Given the contrast Aquinas makes in this passage between negations and privations and the other modes of being, it seems unlikely that he meant to attribute real being to privations and certain negations by his usage of the phrase "nonbeing existing independent of the soul" in the *De veritate*.

Perhaps what Aquinas meant in saying that certain negations and privations exist *extra animam* is that they are nonbeings to which there corresponds a *fundamentum in re* for the concept that the intellect has in thinking them. Privations and qualified negations do not have being apart from an intellect, yet the intellect is not responsible for the unity of the intelligible character that privations have. The *fundamentum in re* for the concept of certain privations and negations is the real existence of subjects that lack certain forms that should be present in them. The real being that falls short of what it should be acts as the exemplar for the intellect's combining in one concept negation together with a species. In contrast, beings that are only dreamt of or imagined, such as a unicorn or a golden mountain, are also composed of notions that come from real being. Yet, the unity that is given these notions to form a single notion comes from the mind alone. There is no *fundamentum in re* for the unity of the notions of fictional beings. I suspect that is on account of the *fundamentum in re* that the unified concepts of privations and qualified negations have that Aquinas refers to nonbeings of this sort as "existing independent of the soul."

Now that we have a sense of what Aquinas means by nonbeing existing independent of the soul, we can ask how this nonbeing outside of the soul can be an exemplar cause of truths about nonbeings. I have claimed that nonbeings outside of the soul are those that have a foundation in real being, that is, they are negations or absences in real things. It is precisely on account of this nonbeing's foundation in real being that it is able to be an exemplar cause of truth. The *ratio* of blindness includes within itself the notion of being an absence *in* a subject, particularly one in the genus of animal to which sight is naturally present. The real unity between negation and a certain subject in the *ratio* of privation is the exemplar for the intellect's combining, for example, the notion of the negation of sight with the subject of Socrates.

Aquinas does not say whether nonbeing that is not "existing *extra animam*" similarly acts as exemplar cause of truth. I think, however, that he should deny that it does. The intelligible character of a nonbeing that lacks foundation in reality for its unity does not include within it any connection to something other than itself. Accordingly, there is no pattern in it that guides the intellect's joining or dividing it with other subjects and predicates. There is no sense in which an absolute nonbeing, like a fictional entity, can be said to cause a true predication in the human intellect.[31] The intelligible characters of fictional entities do not include within them the notion of nonbeing so by thinking the form of a unicorn, for example, the intellect is not even led to affirm the truth that "No unicorns exist."

We have seen that for Aquinas, while the intellect plays an integral role in causing truths about nonbeings, it is not the sole cause of these truths in every case. Because the essence of truth about nonbeings also consists in conformity to the way the world is independent of the intellect, the presence of a truth in the intellect about a nonbeing must in some respect be caused by that which does not depend on the intellect. Since that to which the intellect conforms in the case of a truth about a nonbeing does not have being, it cannot act as an efficient cause. In virtue of the real being of the subjects in which they are present, privations and negations, however, are able to act as exemplar causes for the intellect's own activity of rendering them intelligible and predicating them of a subject.

IV. Conclusion

At first sight it appears that Aquinas's analysis of truth cannot account for the case of truths about nonbeings given the close link that Aquinas posits between truth and existence. He claims that existence is the cause of truth and that the nature of truth consists in a conformity between intellect and a being. We have seen, however, that Aquinas can account for how the intellect can come to be adequated with reality even in situations where there is no real being outside of the soul to cause this adequation. Through its own activity, the intellect renders nonbeings intelligible by combining and negating the forms of real beings so that they can be predicated or denied in acts of judgment. Considering Aquinas's treatment of truths about nonbeings reveals something telling of his conception of intellect: The intellect is not merely a passive recipient of the structures that exist in the world. Its own activity is a necessary condition of its coming to be fully adequated with that which does not depend on itself. Without the intellect's activity of forming conceptions of that which does not exist in reality, there can be no adequation with and consequently, no true propositions about what is not.

While Aquinas can maintain that the intellect is adequated to reality when it knows a truth about a nonbeing, truths about nonbeings seem to be an exception to Aquinas's claim in the *De Veritate* that "every true act of understanding corresponds to a being."[32] In having a truth about a nonbeing, the intellect conforms to reality that does not depend on itself, yet what it is conforming to is not some real being, but rather a lacking in real being in the case of a privation or an absence of a real being in the case of affirming a truth that consists in the denial of a certain being's existence. In the *Sentences*, Aquinas claims that "The relation of adequation in which the nature of truth consists is completed in the operation of the intellect which grasps the existence (*esse*) of a thing as it is by a certain assimilation to it."[33] Truths about nonbeings cannot involve assimilation to or direct conformity with the real existence of the subject of the proposition since by definition the subject lacks real existence. Nevertheless, propositions about nonbeings do not contradict the claim that every truth has its foundation in actual existence.

In the context of discussing the convertibility of truth and being, Aquinas argues that truth does not in fact have a wider extension than being since in apprehending nonbeing, the intellect gives nonbeing a certain logical being.[34] What Aquinas is claiming here is that every true assertion has a being as its subject in so far as the intellect must treat a nonbeing as a being in order to affirm or deny anything of it. Aquinas's answer is not fully satisfying since it is the relation of truth to *real being* that is of interest when it is asked if every truth has a foundation in being. Yet, when the relationship of logical being to real being is considered, a further, more informative sense is revealed in which even truths about nonbeing have a basis in *real* being. Nonbeings can only be treated by the intellect as beings, and consequently, can only be the subjects of assertions and denials, on account of some real being. Concepts of privations are parasitic on the concepts of the real essence that is negated. The assertion that 'Socrates is blind' presupposes acquaintance with the real essence of sight. Even our concept of negation comes from our knowledge of being. Moreover, real essences are the sources of each element of our concepts of fictional entities.[35] Without real horses and horns, there can be no truths about unicorns. It is in this respect, that there can be no truth in the human intellect that does not depend on actual existence. It is also in this regard that every true act of understanding can be said to correspond to a being, or perhaps several beings.

While Aquinas's claim that the nature of truth consists in the intellect's conformity with a thing must be rejected for the slightly more modest claim that truth consists in the intellect's conformity with *the extra-mental world*, in order to allow for truths about nonbeings, it seems that the basic framework of his analysis of truth can remain in tact. It should also be noted that Aquinas has a very economical approach to explaining truths about nonbeings. Rather than positing additional entities, Aquinas reduces our concepts of nonbeings to the essences of real things. Given the building blocks of real essences, the intellect is able to form notions of privations, negations, and fictional beings of which predications and denials can then be made. These assertions and denials, like all other propositions, are then said to be true when they conform to a state of affairs *extra animam*, regardless of whether that state of affairs is a real being or the absence of one.[36]

University of Notre Dame

Notes

Through out this paper, I cite from following editions of Aquinas's texts: *Scriptum super Sententis* (*Sent.*), Mandonnett-Moos, Paris: 1929; *Summa contra Gentiles* (*ScG*), Taurin: 1961; *Summa Theologiae* (*ST*), Rome: 1888; *Quaestiones disputatae de veritate* (*De ver.*), Rome: 1970; *De Ente et Essentia* (*De ente*), Rome: 1976; *Sententia libri Metaphysicae* (*Meta.*), Taurin: 1950. Translations are my own.

1. See I *Sent.* 19.5.1, *De ver.* 1.2, *ST* Ia.16.2.

Many commentators have referred to these two notions of truth as "logical truth" and "ontological truth" respectively, although Thomas himself does not use these terms. See, for example, R. J. McCall, "St. Thomas on Ontological Truth," *The New Scholasticism* 12 (1938): 9–29. In order to have "ontological truth," things do not necessarily have to conform to a human intellect. Aquinas thought that relation to the Divine Intellect was a sufficient condition for a thing's truth. See for example *De ver.* 1.2.

2. *De ver*, 1.2 ad.1: "eo quod cuilibet intellectui vero oportet quod respondeat aliquod ens, et e converso."

3. See, for example, I *Sent.* 19.5.2, ad 2.; *De ver* 1.1, reply;

Thomas attributes this definition of truth to Isaac Israeli, but scholars have not been able to locate this definition in Isaac. See S. Rábade Romeo, *Verdad, conocimiento, y ser*, (Gredos: Madrid, 1965), 38 and J. T. Muckle, "Isaac Israeli's Definition of Truth," *Archives d'Histoire doctrinale et littéraire du Moyen Age* 8 (1933): 5–8.

4. I *Sent.* 19.5.1, reply: "Cum autem in re sit quidditas ejus et suum esse, veritas fundatur in esse rei magis quam in quidditate, sicut et nomen entis ab esse imponitur; et in ipsa operatione intellectus accipientis esse rei sicut est per quamdam similationem ad ipsum, completur relatio adaequationis, in qua consistit ratio veritatis. Unde dico, quod ipsum esse rei est causa veritatis, secundum quod est in cognitione intellectus."

John F. Wippel has pointed out that Thomas's use of the term *esse* in this passage is ambiguous. It could refer to the *actus essendi* unique to Thomas's metaphysics or rather "the fact that something exists." See "Truth in Thomas Aquinas," *Review of Metaphysics*, 43 (1990): 543–567, 550–555. Either understanding of the term *esse* will be compatible with the purposes of this paper since non-beings neither have an *actus essendi*, nor factual existence.

5. Armand Maurer has noted that in connecting truth with existence, Aquinas deviated from the tradition of Augustine and Bonaventure that viewed truth as an essence or a property of essences. After Aquinas, Suarez and Descartes also defended an essentialist view

of truth. See "St. Thomas and Eternal Truths," in *Being and Knowing: Studies in Thomas Aquinas and Later Medieval Philosophy*, (Toronto: 1990), 43–58, 46.

6. Here I am following Giorgio Pini's reading of this passage, which he suggested in his comments on this paper at the 2006 meeting of the American Catholic Philosophical Association.

7. *De ente*, c.1: "Sciendum est igitur quod sicut in V *methaphisice* Philosophus dicit, ens per se dupliciter dicitur: uno modo quod diuiditur per decem genera, alio modo quod significat propositionum ueritatem. Horum autem differentia est quia secundo modo potest dici ens omne illud de quo affirmatiua propositio formari potest, etiam si illud in re nichil ponat; per quem modum priuationes et negationes entia dicuntur: dicimus enim quod affirmatio est opposita negationi, et quod cecitas est in oculo. Sed primo modo non potest dici ens nisi quod aliquid in re ponit; unde primo modo cecitas et huiusmodi non sunt entia."

See also *In V Met.* n. 896.

8. *ST* Ia.48.2 ad 2: "Propter huius autem distinctionis ignorantiam, aliqui, considerantes quod aliquae res dicuntur malae, vel quod malum dicitur esse in rebus, crediderunt quod malum esset res quaedam."

9. *In V Met.* n. 896: "Sed, quia aliquid, quod est in se non ens, intellectus considerat ut quoddam ens, sicut negationem et huiusmodi, ideo quandoque dicitur esse de aliquo hoc secundo modo, et non primo."

10. *ST* Ia.48.2 ad 2: "Et sic caecitatem dicimus esse in oculo, vel quamcumque aliam privationem. Et hoc modo etiam malum dicitur ens."

11. See, for example, *ST* Ia.84.6 and 7.

12. *De ver* 2.15, reply: "Prima autem ratio distinctionis est in affirmatione et negatione: et ideo oportet quod quicumque scit affirmationem, cognoscat negationem; et quia privatio nihil aliud est quam negatio subiectum habens, ut dicitur in IV Metaphysicor., et alterum contrariorum semper est privatio, ut dicitur in eodem, et in I Physic., inde est quod ex hoc ipso quod cognoscitur aliquid, cognoscitur eius privatio et eius contrarium."

See also *ST* Ia.14.10 ad 4 and *ST* Ia.48.1 reply where Aquinas claims that God can know evil through the good.

13. *ScG* I, 71: "Nam bonum est quasi ratio cognitionis mali. Unde cognoscuntur mala per bona sicut res per suas definitiones: non sicut conclusiones per principia."

14. Ibid.: "Sed in ratione distinctionis est negatio: distincta enim sunt quorum unum non est aliud."

See also *In IV Met.* n. 566. On the derivation of the transcendentals, see *De ver* 1.1.

15. *De ver* 3.4 ad 6: "Ad sextum dicendum, quod aliquid dicitur non ens dupliciter. Uno modo, quia non esse cadit in definitione eius, sicut caecitas dicitur non ens; et talis non entis non potest concipi aliqua forma neque in intellectu neque in imaginatione; et huiusmodi non ens est malum. Alio modo, quia non invenitur in rerum natura, quamvis ipsa privatio entitatis non claudatur in eius definitione; et sic nihil prohibet imaginari non entia, et eorum formas concipere."

16. See footnote 2.

17. *De ver* 1.3, reply: "Veri enim ratio consistit in adaequatione rei et intellectus; idem autem non adaequatur sibi ipsi, sed aequalitas diversorum est; unde ibi primo invenitur ratio veritatis in intellectu ubi primo intellectus incipit aliquid proprium habere quod res

extra animam non habet, sed aliquid ei correspondens, inter quae adaequatio attendi potest. Intellectus autem formans quidditatem rerum, non habet nisi similitudinem rei existentis extra animam, sicut et sensus in quantum accipit speciem sensibilis;"

18. *De ver* 1.5 ob.2. See also I *Sent.* 19.5.3 ob. 3. For a study on medieval responses to this paradox see William Charron and John Doyle, "On the Self-Refuting Statement 'There is no Truth': A Medieval Treatment," in *Vivarium* 31:2 (1993): 241–266.

19. I *Sent.* 19.5.1, reply and *ST* Ia.16.1 ad 3.

20. *De ver* 1.5 ad 2: "Unde quod intellectui cuicumque aequetur, non est ex ipso non ente, sed ex ipso intellectu, qui rationem non entis accipit in seipso."

21. Ibid.

22. *De ver.* 1.2, reply, "Sed si uterque intellectus, rebus remanentibus per impossibile, intelligeretur auferri, nullo modo ratio veritatis remaneret."

In this passage, Aquinas is talking about "ontological truth," but clearly "logical truth" could not be apart from any intellects since it only resides in an intellect.

23. Aquinas is particularly clear in asserting that existence causes truth in *ST* Ia.16.1 ad 3: "Ad tertium dicendum quod, licet veritas intellectus nostri a re causetur, non tamen oportet quod in re per prius inveniatur ratio veritatis, sicut neque in medicina per prius invenitur ratio sanitatis quam in animali; virtus enim medicinae, non sanitas eius, causat sanitatem, cum non sit agens univocum. Et similiter esse rei, non veritas eius, causat veritatem intellectus. Unde philosophus dicit quod opinio et oratio vera est *ex eo quod res est, non ex eo quod res vera est.*"

24. *De ver* 1.8

25. Ibid.

26. *De ver* 1.8 ob.7

27. *De ver* 1.8 ad 7: "Ad sextum dicendum, quod non esse non est causa veritatis propositionum negativarum quasi faciens eas in intellectu; sed ipsa anima hoc facit conformans se non enti, quod est extra animam; unde non esse extra animam existens, non est causa efficiens veritatis in anima, sed quasi exemplaris. Obiectio autem procedebat de causa efficiente."

28. *De ver* 1.8, co.: "Sed negationes vel privationes existentes extra animam non habent aliquam formam, per quam vel imitentur exemplar artis divinae, vel ingerant sui notitiam in intellectu humano; sed quod adaequantur intellectui, est ex parte intellectus, qui earum rationes apprehendit."

29. *Meta.*, 4.1, n. 11.

30. *Meta.*, 4.1, n. 12: "Sciendum tamen quod praedicti modi essendi ad quatuor possunt reduci. Nam unum eorum quod est debilissimum, est tantum in ratione, scilicet negatio et privatio, quam dicimus in ratione esse, quia ratio de eis negociatur quasi de quibusdam entibus, dum de eis affirmat vel negat aliquid."

31. This is not to deny that, of course, our concepts of fictional entities have a basis in reality in so far as each element of them is taken from a real essence. My point is that the concept of the fictional entity as a whole does not contain a conceptual connection to a real being in the same way that the concept of blindness is linked to a real subject in the genus of animal. It is in virtue of the conceptual connection between blindness and an animal subject that I am claiming that blindness can be an exemplar cause of truth.

32. *De ver.* 1.2 ad 1: "eo quod cuilibet intellectui vero oportet quod respondeat aliquod ens, et e converso."

33. I *Sent.* 19.5.1, reply: "et in ipsa operatione intellectus accipientis esse rei sicut est per quamdam similationem ad ipsum, completur relatio adaequationis, in qua consistit ratio veritatis."

34. *ST* Ia.16.3 ad 2: Ad secundum dicendum quod non ens non habet in se unde cognoscatur, sed cognoscitur inquantum intellectus facit illud cognoscibile. Unde verum fundatur in ente, inquantum non ens est quoddam ens rationis, apprehensum scilicet a ratione. See also *De ver.* 1.1 ad 7.

35. See, for example, *De Ver*, 19.1, reply: "Unde nec etiam imaginatio aut intellectus aliquam formam de novo componit nisi ex aliquibus praeexistentibus; sicut componit formam montis aurei ex praeexistentibus similitudinibus auri et montis."

36. I am grateful to Stephen Dumont and Msgr. John Wippel for helpful comments on earlier drafts of this paper, as well as to Giorgio Pini who commented on it at the 2006 meeting of the A.C.P.A. I am especially thankful to John O'Callaghan for insightful comments and discussion in his graduate seminar on the *De veritate* in the spring of 2006 for which this paper was originally written.

Formal Identity as Isomorphism in Thomistic Philosophy of Mind

Stephen Pimentel

Abstract: A central problem within an influential strand of recent philosophy of mind has been to explain the "conformity of mind to thing" that characterizes knowledge. John Haldane has argued that this problem can be best addressed by a development of Thomas Aquinas's account of the "formal identity" of the knowing subject with the object known. However, such a development is difficult to present in a manner perspicuous to a contemporary audience. This paper seeks to present a persuasive account of formal identity, taking sensory cognition of the individual object as the primary case for examination. Formal identity is initially explored using the notion of encoding, or the systematic transfer of information reflecting efficient and formal causal processes. The mathematical notion of "isomorphism" is then employed to describe precisely the features of encoding needed for formal identity. Forms are defined as formally identical if and only if they are isomorphic.

1. Introduction

A central problem within an influential strand of recent philosophy of mind has been to characterize the "conformity of mind to thing" that takes place in the act of knowledge.[1] John Haldane has argued that this problem can be best addressed by a development of Thomas Aquinas's account of the "formal identity" of the knowing subject with the object known.[2] However, such a development poses significant challenges. Thomas's account of formal identity in the act of knowledge is dependent upon the conceptual framework of his natural philosophy, derived chiefly from Aristotle, and employs that framework in an analogical manner that is further intertwined with his metaphysics. These dependencies make it difficult to present an account of formal identity that is perspicuous to a contemporary audience.

A brief overview of the leading themes of Thomas's account of knowledge will highlight the difficulties. Thomas emphasizes that a certain immateriality or "freedom from matter" on the part of the knower is foundational for knowledge.

The knower must not be so immersed in matter as to be limited to a single form. Rather, "the nature of cognitive things has a greater amplitude and extension" that allows them to take on the forms of the things known.[3] Of course, the forms of the things known cannot simply be received materially in a manner that would involve substantial change. Rather, the knower is said to take on the form of the known "intentionally." Thus, Thomas posits two distinct modes of existence, the intentional and the real, and the form of the object exists within the knower with the intentional rather than real mode.

On the Thomistic account, this intentional existence of a object's form within a subject is a necessary condition for knowledge in creatures.[4] A knower must have the necessary "amplitude and extension" to support within itself the intentional existence of other forms. The form existing intentionally in the knower is "formally identical" to the form existing really in the object, though the two remain numerically distinct. In this way, the knower is intentionally united to the known. Yet, due to the freedom from matter that characterizes the act of knowledge, the knower and known remain substantially unchanged. Thomas applies this account of knowledge, in analogical ways, to both sensory and intellectual knowledge.

A major challenge posed by such an account centers on the notions of intentional existence and formal identity. Peter King has asserted that Thomas never really explains what it means for a form to be present only intentionally and that this failure renders the Thomistic account of cognition fundamentally obscure and mysterious.[5] Whether or not one concurs with King's negative evaluation, one can certainly agree that the persuasiveness of the Thomistic account depends on its ability to answer two closely correlated questions. First, how can the essence of an individual object have a different mode of existence in the knowing subject? Second, how can forms with numerically distinct acts of existence nevertheless be formally identical?

These two questions interact in ways that complicate each other. For example, does a form existing intentionally in a knower also have some distinct real existence in that knower? In particular, when Thomas speaks of a sensible object as causing an "animate immutation" in a sense organ so as to impress its species in that organ,[6] does this impression involve the real acquisition of an accidental form by the organ? If so, then the form existing intentionally in the knower, when considered in terms of its *real* existence in the knower, would seem obviously to *differ* from the form of the object. This discrepancy is just what is meant by the qualification that the knower becomes the known not in real existence but only in intentional existence. Thus, an account along these lines must explain how a really differing form in the knower can nevertheless be formally identical to the form of the object known.

There has been a natural tendency in philosophy of mind to focus attention on intellectual cognition. Nevertheless, from the Aristotelian perspective adopted by Thomas, intellectual cognition is a special case of the broader phenomenon of cognition. Human cognitive powers span both the intellectual powers unique to humans and the sensory powers possessed in common with other animals. Moreover, the central issues of intentional existence and formal identity arise already in the case of sensory cognition. If an adequate treatment of these issues cannot be found for the more primitive case of sensory cognition, it is unlikely that one will be forthcoming for the higher-level case of intellectual cognition. Therefore, the most promising approach will be to take sensory cognition of the individual object as the paradigmatic case to be explained.[7] After an adequate account of intentional existence and formal identity has been offered for sensory cognition, it should be possible to extend the account to intellectual cognition.[8]

The remainder of the paper will be organized as follows. Section 2 describes Thomas's account of the "intention" of the individual object, as it is received within the interior senses by the estimative or cogitative power. Section 3 examines the notion of "representation" by which the individual intention relates to its object. Representation can be defined in terms of the intentional existence of the object's form within the subject. The paper advances the claim that intentional existence supervenes on real existence. According to this view, an intentionally existing form is a really existing form that is formally identical to the object. However, such a claim requires further explanation of formal identity, which is pursued in section 4 through the notion of encoding. Sensory cognition relies on a causal process of encoding that transfers information from object to subject. Encoding rests on both efficient and, crucially, formal causality. Formal identity is initially described in terms of the sameness of information with respect to the relevant encoding. Section 4 employs the notion of an isomorphism, drawn from category theory, to give a more precise definition of formal identity. The final section situates cognition in the context of the act-potency hierarchy and summarizes the paper's conclusions.

2. Sensory Cognition

Thomas distinguishes among the various exterior[9] and interior[10] senses. Among the interior senses, he calls the highest sense the cogitative power in man and the estimative power in other animals. In both man and other animals, this power has the core function of receiving the "intention" of an individual object. The estimative power in animals will be examined first, as its essential features also apply to the case of man.

The notion of the estimative power entered Latin scholasticism from Avicenna's commentary on the *De Anima*. Avicenna infers the necessity of an estimative power to receive intentions from Aristotle's discussion of the "incidental" objects of sense in *De Anima* 418a20–25.[11] Thomas largely concurs with Avicenna's analysis. In his own commentary on the *De Anima*,[12] he interprets Aristotle's text as requiring "a faculty which apprehends natures, not as universals, but as present in singulars."[13] The estimative power is such a faculty.

According to Thomas, the incidental objects of sense are those objects that are "perceived by the one sensing" and yet are only "connected accidentally with an essential sense-object; as a man, for instance, may happen to be white."[14] One properly sees only a pattern of color (a proper sensible) arranged in a particular shape (a common sensible),[15] and yet one quickly perceives an individual man, say "this man Socrates." The individual, considered as such, is the incidental object of sense.

These objects, as incidental, are perceived via "intentions which are not received through the senses" directly; rather, the need to perceive such objects, "which the exterior sense does not perceive," is supplied by the estimative power.[16] Thus, the incidental object of sense is the direct object of awareness of the estimative power. It is also the highest of the three classes of sensibles, above the proper sensibles, such as color, and the common sensibles, such as shape.[17]

The incidental object of sense is perceived by means of an "intention." Avicenna distinguishes between the forms of proper and common sensibles and the intention of the individual object itself. While the lower sense powers receive the forms of proper and common sensibles, the estimative power receives the intentions.[18] Averroes, in turn, specifies that the type of intention in question is "that which conveys awareness of an individual *as* an individual."[19] Thomas integrates these aspects of Avicenna's and Averroes's accounts into his own. The intention, then, corresponds to the individual essence of its object.[20]

In reference to man, Thomas speaks of the cogitative rather than estimative power. Indeed, the cogitative power "becomes in many respects the focal point for Aquinas's interest in the internal senses in the explanation of human cognition."[21] However, considered strictly as a sense power, the cogitative power is identical to the estimative power in other animals. Thomas holds that "regarding sensible forms, there is no difference between man and other animals."[22] Gilson glosses this point as follows: "The sensitive powers of the soul are of exactly the same nature in animals and in men, if only what is properly sensitive in them is considered. Their higher efficacy in man comes from the intellect with which they are in contact."[23] In particular, the cogitative power "apprehends the individual thing as existing in a common nature, and this is because it is united to intellect in one and the same subject," whereas the estimative power "is not aware of an individual thing as in a common nature."[24]

The cogitative power, then, "belongs to sensitivity," although it is "sensitivity at its highest."[25] By this power, man perceives "something individual, as when, seeing this particular colored thing, I perceive this particular man or beast."[26] The cogitative power allows one "to distinguish individual intentions and to compare them with one another."[27] Yet, "since the cogitative power is operationally limited to particular things, makes its judgments on the basis of particular intentions, and acts by means of a bodily organ, it is not above the generic level of the sensitive soul."[28]

3. Representation

This account of sensory cognition raises the problem of the relation between the intention received by the estimative or cognitive power and the object. While Thomas does not give a detailed explanation of this relation, he does provide clarification by ruling out certain possibilities. First, he rules out the notion that there is a numerical identity between the form in the knower and the form of the known. "The conformity of the knower to the known, which produces knowledge, is not to be understood in terms of identity, but in terms of representation."[29] What then is "representation"? Again, no detailed explanation is forthcoming, but Thomas does insist on a crucial distinction: while commonly called a "likeness" by scholastics, representation differs from the ordinary sense of "likeness" as a shared feature or nature. "The likeness holding between two things can be understood in two ways. In one way, as an agreement in nature; . . . In another way, as representation; and this is the likeness required of the knower to the known."[30]

Thomas provides little more in terms of a positive description of representation. Can a coherent and persuasive description be given that fleshes out Thomas's account, or, as King suggests, is the Thomistic approach hopelessly obscure? Such a positive description of representation can indeed be provided, but, in order to do so, the issues of intentional existence and formal identity have to be squarely faced. At the most basic level, a representation is the form of an object existing in another thing, the subject, with the crucial qualification that the form exists really in the object but intentionally in the subject.[31] What does it mean for a form to exist intentionally? How can the form of a material object exist in a manner that does not structure matter in the ordinary way?

The key insight is that the form existing intentionally in the subject is nothing but a form also existing *really* within the subject that bears an appropriate relation to the form of the object.[32] The "appropriate relation" to the object will be considered in the next section, but first the dual nature of the form as intentional and real within the subject should be examined. The position here proposed can be summarized with the slogan that "the intentional supervenes on the real."[33] In other words, intentional existence, while a distinct mode of existence, nevertheless supervenes on real existence, so that no form can come to exist intentionally within a subject without some real change being effected in that subject. The real change will be the acquisition of some accidental form that serves as the intention by which the object is known. In the case of the individual intention received by the estimative or cogitative power, the accidental form "intends" or represents the individual essence of the object.[34]

However, this position raises another problem. The individual intention, considered as a really existing form, obviously differs from the individual essence of the object. When a dog sees a cat across the yard, its estimative power receives the intention of 'that cat across the yard.' The intention, considered as a form really existing in the dog's interior sense, presumably corresponds to some pattern of neural activation, which pattern is obviously not a cat, nor even superficially resembles a cat. Yet, the intention is supposed to be somehow "formally identical" to its object. In order to satisfy these conditions, formal identity must be a relation that can coincide with difference at the level of real existence.

In his brief treatment of representation, Thomas has already hinted that exactly such is the case. A representation, Thomas holds, is not a "likeness" of the object in the usual sense of possessing shared ostensible features, but in some other sense. By supplying an account of representation that both secures formal identity with the object and allows for real difference from the object, the air of mystery surrounding this "other sense" of likeness can be dispelled.

4. Formal Identity

A representation was described above as an accidental form that exists intentionally, but also really, within a subject and that bears an "appropriate relation" to the form of the object. The appropriate relation can be described as follows: a representation must be the result of a causal process that transfers information about the object to the subject.[35] This causal process integrally depends on the capacity of the subject to record faithfully the information received, although the manner in which the information is recorded will typically occlude the ostensible features of the object. The occlusion of ostensible features, which is characteristic of representation, is possible because a form can be received in many kinds of matter without detriment to the form itself. Information can be recorded without loss in different media and in different ways.

The causal process by which information is faithfully transferred from object to subject, while possibly altering its ostensible features, is called "impression"[36] or "animate immutation"[37] by Thomas. Gyula Klima has felicitously described such a process as *encoding*.[38] Neurobiologists speak of "the transformation of physical signals (such as light and sound) into a pattern of neural impulses," such that there is a systematic "relationship (the 'neural code') between these neural responses and the sensory signals they represent."[39] On this perspective, the knower *encodes* the form of the known. The remaining task is to explain how the causal process that transfers information can ground a persuasive account of formal identity and, thus, intentional existence.

Formal causality plays a crucial role in this account. The causal processes in question are themselves subject to formality. An intention is not merely the product of efficient causality but also of formal causality. Through formal causality, encoding establishes a relation that is not merely extrinsic. "Efficient causality is the vehicle for the communication of form; form is what structures the object, the thought, and the movement between them."[40] The causal process, with its formal as well as efficient aspects, couples the singular object with the intention as its representation. The transfer of information through a causal process subject to formality differentiates this account of knowledge from a "representationalism" of a post-Cartesian sort.

The formal identity of intention and object is defined, not by the sameness of their ostensible features, but by "the sameness of information" conveyed by the causal process acting upon and within the senses.[41] In other words, the causal process faithfully transfers information from the object via an encoding proper to the subject and so produces the intention. This faithful transfer of information results in the "sameness" that constitutes formal identity.

This description of formal identity acknowledges that the ostensible features of two things can differ greatly, so much so that there is no evident similarity between them, while nevertheless retaining (in different ways) the same form. James Ross observes that "a form, say a song, structure, or a shape, can typically be received in many kinds of matter." As a result, "forms can be transmitted and stored physically without exercising their definitive causal powers (e.g., mailed recording of a song), and sometimes without informing the medium at all (as when color is naturally transmitted through the atmosphere, or software through the internet.)"[42]

Formal identity, so understood, clarifies the description of representation given above. A representation, as a form existing in the subject, is formally identical to its object. The formal identity of the representation and its object grounds the veridical character of knowledge.[43] Most importantly, formal identity makes possible the formulation of a definition of intentional existence: the form of an object exists *intentionally* in a subject if and only if there *really* exists a representation in the subject that is formally identical to the object.

The interpretation of formal identity as resting on the sameness of information (apart from any shared ostensible features of the material bodies in question) accords with the Thomistic understanding of forms as real principles of things rather than things themselves. A form, considered absolutely, has no existence; it acquires existence only in union with a distinct material principle. Therefore, where there is formal identity, numerical difference can arise only as a result of differences in matter.[44]

5. Isomorphism

The definition of formal identity in terms of the sameness of information can be made more precise by describing the *maps* established by the relevant causal processes. Here the term "map" is being used in the mathematical sense of a systematic correspondence of one class of entities with another. Klima describes the causal processes as establishing "a system of encoding" that maps objects to the intentions that represent them.[45] However, the maps in question are not arbitrary; a particular sort of map is needed to establish a formal identity between the object and intention, namely, an *isomorphism*.[46]

Isomorphisms, along with other kinds of maps, are defined and studied within the branch of mathematics known as *category theory*.[47] Roughly speaking, an isomorphism is a map for which there exists an inverse map, which produces an identity when the two are composed.[48] For a map to possess an inverse, it must faithfully convey all information from the original object; only then will the inverse be able fully to recover that information. For example, if an visual image can be fully regenerated by "decoding" a representation, then the "encoding" must have preserved all the essential information in producing the representation. If there exists an isomorphism between two entities, then those entities are said to be isomorphic to each other.

In the case of sensory knowledge, the fundamental map is that of *impressing*, by which the form of an object is encoded to produce an intention. To establish formal identity, impressing must possess an inverse, *intending*, that maps the intention back to the object. When such an inverse exists, the map of impressing is an isomorphism, and the intention is formally identical to its object. It is just the capacity to form this inverse map of intending that distinguishes the cogitative power from a mere medium of species. While a medium may receive an impressed species that is formally identical to its object,[49] the medium has no capacity to determine the inverse map so as to intend the object.

Isomorphisms precisely identify the intrinsic content (or "information") of forms. Formal difference can arise only due to the intrinsic content of the form, as opposed to numerical difference, which can arise due to differences of matter extrinsic to the form. Thus, isomorphism, as defined in category theory in terms of a map with an identity-preserving inverse, can be used to give an exact characterization of the Thomistic notion of formal identity: two forms that exist separately in matter are formally identical if and only if there is an isomorphism between them.[50]

6. Conclusion

As noted above, Thomas describes the "nature of cognitive things" as possessing a greater "amplitude" than other natures. According to the proposed account of knowledge, this "amplitude" consists in the capacity of a subject's essence to acquire accidental forms that are isomorphic to other material objects. The essence of a knower possesses a structure that is sufficiently complex to encode within itself other forms. Using a technological metaphor, one can picture encoding as taking place in layers, analogous to the "stack" of communication protocols used in computer networks.

However, the deepest understanding of knowledge comes from situating it within the *act-potency hierarchy* that Thomas holds to constitute the metaphysical structure of finite beings.[51] W. Norris Clarke describes this hierarchy as an "interlocking system of metaphysical compositions on different levels within a single real being," with the composition of substantial form and prime matter at the lowest level and the composition of accidental form and substance at a higher level.[52] In representation, the form of an object is elevated by encoding to a higher level in the act-potency hierarchy. When a man sees a dog, the form that is substantial in the dog becomes accidental in the man. Nevertheless, the forms are isomorphic and so formally identical.

This paper has sought to present a persuasive account of formal identity and intentional existence within the context of Thomistic philosophy of mind. Sensory cognition of the individual object was taken as the paradigmatic case for examining the fundamental characteristics of formal identity and intentional existence. The paper reviewed Thomas's account of the estimative power in animals and the cogitative power in man, both of which receive the intention of the individual object. Thomas describes the individual intention as a representation, which is a likeness of the object, not in the usual sense of a shared quality or nature, but in some other sense. A representation can be further described as the form of the object existing intentionally in the subject.

An intentionally existing form was then analyzed as a really existing form that encodes the form of the object, although it differs in itself from the latter. Encoding was described as a transfer of information from object to subject through a causal process with both efficient and, crucially, formal aspects. Formal identity was initially described as sameness of information with respect to the relevant encoding. Given the notion of formal identity, an intentionally existing form was defined as a really existing form that is formally identical to its object. The paper then introduced the notion of an isomorphism, or map that possesses an identity-preserving inverse, with the relevant maps in the case of sensory cognition being those of impressing and intending. Finally, two forms were defined as formally identical if and only if they are isomorphic under those maps.

Notes

1. Hilary Putnam, *The Threefold Cord: Mind, Body, and World*, The John Dewey Essays in Philosophy, vol. 5 (New York: Columbia University Press, 1999); John McDowell, *Mind and World* (Cambridge, MA: Harvard University Press, 1994).

2. John Haldane, "The Philosophies of Mind and Nature," in *Recovering Nature: Essays in Natural Philosophy, Ethics, and Metaphysics in Honor of Ralph Mcinerny*, ed. Thomas Hibbs and John O'Callaghan (Notre Dame: University of Notre Dame Press, 1999), 37–51 at 43.

3. "Nautura autem rerum cognoscentium habet maiorem amplitudinem et extensionem." Thomas Aquinas, *Summa Theologiae* I, 14, 1.

4. However, Thomas denies that the intentional reception of form is a *sufficient* condition for cognition. In discussing air as a medium by which forms are communicated to sense organs, he states that the air does not sense "since it has no sensitive potency," indicating that cognition in creatures also requires some power beyond mere receptivity to intentional form. Thomas Aquinas, *Commentary on Aristotle's* De Anima, trans. Kenelm Foster and Silvester Humphries, Aristotelian Commentary Series (Notre Dame, IN: Dumb Ox Books, 1994), paragraph 563.

5. Peter King, "Rethinking Representation in the Middle Ages," in *Representation and Objects of Thought in Medieval Philosophy*, ed. Henrik Lagerlund (Ashgate Press, 2005), 5. Page references are to the on-line version at <http://individual.utoronto.ca/pking/articles/Rethinking_Representation.pdf>.

6. Thomas Aquinas, *ST* I, 78, 3.

7. James Ross has advocated just such an approach. See James Ross, "The Fate of the Analysts: Aristotle's Revenge," *Proceedings of the American Catholic Philosophical Association: Ways to World Meaning* 64 (1990), 9. Page references are to the on-line version at <http://www.sas.upenn.edu/~jross/aristotlesrevenge.htm>.

8. Ibid., 11. However, the treatment of intellectual cognition is beyond the scope of the present paper.

9. Thomas Aquinas, *ST* I, 78, 3.

10. Ibid., *ST* I, 78, 4.

11. Deborah L. Black, "Imagination and Estimation: Arabic Paradigms and Western Transformation," *Topoi* 19, no. 1 (2000), 1, 3. Page references are to the on-line version at <http://philosophy.utoronto.ca/documents/cvs/works/1130950711.pdf>.

12. Thomas Aquinas, *De Anima*, 395–398.

13. Black, 14.

14. Thomas Aquinas, *De Anima*, 395.

15. On the common sensibles, such as shape, see ibid., 575–578.

16. Thomas Aquinas, *ST* I, 78, 4.

17. Ibid., *ST* I, 17, 2.

18. Black, 2.

19. Ibid., 6.

20. The "individual essence" refers here to the whole essence of the individual, including designated matter as well as form, as opposed to the specific essence, which includes only undesignated matter and form. Thomas notes that "designated matter would be included in the definition of Socrates, if Socrates had a definition," and so "the essence of man and the essence of Socrates do not differ, except as the designated differs from the undesignated." Thomas Aquinas, *De Ente et Essentia*, chap. 2. See also John F. Wippel, *The Metaphysical Thought of Thomas Aquinas: From Finite Being to Uncreated Being*, Monographs of the Society for Medieval and Renaissance Philosophy, vol. 1 (Washington, D.C.: The Catholic University of America Press, 2000), 331–332.

21. Black, 12.

22. Thomas Aquinas, *ST* I, 78, 4.

23. Etienne Gilson, *The Christian Philosophy of St. Thomas Aquinas*, trans. L. K. Shook (Notre Dame: University of Notre Dame Press, 1956), 206.

24. Thomas Aquinas, *De Anima*, 398.

25. Ibid., 397.

26. Ibid., 396.

27. Thomas Aquinas, *Summa Contra Gentiles* II, chap. 60, no. 1.

28. Thomas Aquinas, *SCG* II, chap. 73. no. 14.

29. "Applicatio cogniti ad cognoscentem, quae cognitionem facit, non est intelligenda per modum identitatis, sed per modum cuiusdam repraesentationis." Thomas Aquinas, *Quaestiones Disputatae de Veritate* 2.5 ad 7.

30. "Similitudo aliquorum duorum ad invicem potest dupliciter attendi. Uno modo secundum convenientiam in natura; . . . Alio modo quantum ad repraesentionem; et haec similitudo requiritur cognoscentis ad cognitum." Thomas Aquinas, *QDV* 2.5 ad 9.

31. Gyula Klima, "Tradition and Innovation in Medieval Theories of Mental Representation," *Proceedings of the Society for Medieval Logic and Metaphysics* 4 (2004), 4–11 at 4.

32. Gyula Klima, "Aquinas' Proof of the Immateriality of the Intellect from the Universality of Human Thought," *Proceedings of the Society for Medieval Logic and Metaphysics* 1 (2001), 19–28 at 21.

33. This position must be sharply distinguished from the claim in contemporary philosophy of mind, advanced by Donald Davidson and critiqued by Jaegwon Kim, that the *mental* supervenes on the *physical*. In the Thomistic context with a hylomorphic metaphysics, forms are taken to be real principles, and so the 'real' is not equivalent to the 'physical' in Davidson's sense. See Donald Davidson, *Essays on Actions and Events* (Oxford: Oxford University Press,

1980) and Jaegwon Kim, *Supervenience and Mind: Selected Philosophical Essays*, Cambridge Studies in Philosophy (Cambridge: Cambridge University Press, 1993).

34. Similarly, in the case of the universal intention or concept within the intellect, the accidental form represents the substantial form of the object.

35. Gyula Klima, "Is Ockham Off the Hook?," (presented at the University of Toronto Colloquium in Mediaeval Philosophy, September 24, 2005), 1–2; available at <http://www.fordham.edu/gsas/phil/klima/FILES/Toronto.pdf>.

36. Thomas Aquinas, *ST* I, 85, 2.

37. Ibid., *ST* I, 78, 3.

38. Klima, "Tradition," 5.

39. Michael R. DeWeese and Anthony Zador, "Efficiency Measures," *Nature* 439 (2006), 920–1 at 920. For example, researchers investigating the neural response to external auditory stimulus, such as speech, have recently found that there are precise neural encodings of these sounds within the brainstem region of the subcortex. "Overall, the brainstem response reflects acoustic characteristics of the speech stimulus with remarkable precision" such that the transfer of information from speaker to hearer effects a "brainstem encoding of speech." Nina Kaus and Trent Nicol, "Brainstem Origins for Cortical 'What' and 'Where' Pathways in the Auditory System," *Trends in Neurosciences* 28, no. 4 (2005), 176–181 at 178–179. "Vast amounts of information about the phonetic content of the utterance" are "reflected with remarkable precision in aggregate subcortical neural activity." Brad Wible, Trent Nicol, and Nina Kaus, "Encoding of Complex Sounds in an Animal Model: Implications for Understanding Speech Perception in Humans," in *Auditory Cortex: Towards a Synthesis of Human and Animal Research*, ed. R. Konig et al. (Oxford: Lawrence Erlbaum Associates, 2005), 241–254 at 252.

40. Haldane, 45.

41. Klima, "Tradition," 10; cf. James Ross, "Adapting Aquinas: Analogy and Forms," *Proceedings of the American Catholic Philosophical Association: Reckoning with the Tradition* 78 (2004), 41–58 at 50.

42. James F. Ross, "Together with the Body I Love," *Proceedings of the American Catholic Philosophical Association: Person, Soul, and Immortality* 75 (2001), 1–18 at 8.

43. Thomas Aquinas, *SCG* III, chap. 108, no. 4.

44. Thomas makes this point in regard to form at the level of species. In his discussion of angels in *ST* I, 50, 4, he notes that "such things as agree in species but differ in number, agree in form, but are distinguished materially."

45. Klima, "Aquinas' Proof," 22.

46. King denies that encoding needs to be an isomorphism, "since the 'code' need not reflect all the features of the 'message' in its previous environment (e.g., the size of the inscription is not preserved in an utterance of the written message)." See Peter King, "Scholasticism and the Philosophy of Mind: The Failure of Aristotelian Psychology," in *Scientific Failure* (Rowman & Littlefield, 1994), 9. Page references are to the on-line version at <http://individual.utoronto.ca/pking/articles/lastcheck/Scholasticism_and_the_Philosophy_of_Mind.pdf>. However, isomorphism as considered in the present paper does not require reflection of all such features, but rather recoverability of all information.

47. F. William Lawvere and Stephen H. Schanuel, *Conceptual Mathematics: A First Introduction to Categories* (Cambridge, UK: Cambridge University Press, 1997). The use of

the term "category" in category theory should not be confused with its use in Aristotelian metaphysics. The two usages are largely unrelated.

48. The full, technical definition of an isomorphism requires a bit more apparatus. In category theory, a "category" consists of a class of *objects* and a class of *maps* between objects. A map f from object X to object Y is written $f{:}X \rightarrow Y$. Given any two maps $f{:}X \rightarrow Y$ and $g{:}Y \rightarrow Z$, there is a third map $g^\circ f{:}X \rightarrow Z$ called the *composition* of f and g.

Maps must satisfy two axioms:

a) Identity: for every object X, there exists a map $id_X{:}X \rightarrow X$ called the identity map on X, such that for every map $f{:}A \rightarrow B$ we have $id_B {}^\circ f = f = f^\circ id_A$.

b) Associativity: for any maps $f{:}A \rightarrow B$, $g{:}B \rightarrow C$, and $h{:}C \rightarrow D$, $h^\circ(g^\circ f) = (h^\circ g)^\circ f$.

An *isomorphism* is then defined as follows. Given a map $f{:}X \rightarrow Y$, if there exists a map $g{:}Y \rightarrow X$ such that $f^\circ g = id_Y$ and $g^\circ f = id_X$, then f is an isomorphism and g is its inverse map. In this case, g will also be an isomorphism with f as its inverse.

49. Thomas Aquinas, *De Anima*, 551–553.

50. Although it is beyond the scope of this paper, the present account of sensory knowledge can be extended to intellectual knowledge along the following lines. The agent intellect defines a further map of *abstraction* from individual intentions to concepts. (The distinction between the intelligible species and the concept is here being elided). The concept is then isomorphic, not to the individual essence of the object, but only to the object's specific essence.

51. W. Norris Clarke, *The One and the Many: A Contemporary Thomistic Metaphysics* (Notre Dame, IN: University of Notre Dame Press, 2001), 157.

52. Ibid., 158.

Why We Can No Longer Rationally Believe that Our Intellective Soul Is a Substantial Form: On the Degringolade of the Simplicity Argument

Benjamin Hill

Abstract: The most pedigreed line of thought about mind is the simplicity argument: that the unity of thinking entails the simplicity, immateriality, and immortality of soul. It is widely taken to be a rationalist argument, as opposed to an empiricist or peripatetic argument (see Mijuskovic, *The Achilles of Rationalist Arguments*), which was completely destroyed by Kant in the First Critique. In this paper it is argued that there is a conceptual connection between the downfall of the Aristotelian conception of soul as substantial form and the downfall of this argument in that in the downfall of the Aristotelian conception of soul it became acceptable to view the functional unity of a material system as constituting a genuine unity per se. This then undermined all philosophical motivation for the postulation of substantial forms. As a result, there was no longer reason for rooting the unity of apperception in the simplicity of a subsistence soul as opposed to some simply emergent power of thinking.

In the Second Paralogism, Kant famously described the simplicity argument as "the Achilles of all dialectical inferences . . . ; no mere sophistical ploy . . . but an inference which appears to withstand even the keenest scrutiny." Nonetheless its "*nervus probandi*," he told us, is a "transcendent" principle, a "natural and inevitable illusion" which "incites us to tear down all boundary-fences and to seize possession of an entirely new domain which recognizes no limits of demarcation."[1] Often, this analysis is taken to be the coup de grâce for philosophical demonstrations of soul's immateriality and immortality. I wish to suggest, however, that we can better understand the collapse of the simplicity argument by reading Kant as not refuting it so much as reporting, in his delightful, critical way, its demise. I suggest that rather than taking Locke's suggestion that matter might think as a starting point for reflections on mind which, via La Metterian materialism and Humean skepticism, culminated in Kantian agnosticism, we ought to view Locke's suggestion as the first whisperings that a death has already taken place, whispers which during this period (1689–1781) grew into ecstatic rumor (La Metterie), suspicion (Hume), and finally fact (Kant). In other words, something had earlier happened that, conceptually, allowed Locke to propose his notorious suggestion and Kant to bury rationalist psychology.

What had happened, I'd like to suggest, was the collapse of the concept of substantial form. Nothing new in saying that, of course, but what I have in mind is not just *that* it collapsed but *how* it collapsed, in particular the role played therein by the problem of the *mixtions*. I mean not to lessen in any way the familiar, internal difficulties with melding the Platonic strains of substantiality and immortality with the Aristotelian notion of soul as substantial form; Pomponazzi's critique I think is quite damaging.[2] As a matter of historic fact, however, Pomponazzi's critique was not so received, and not merely because of the hegemony of an entrenched and reactionary inquisitional cabal. Pomponazzi was simply giving voice to what had already been insinuated by the Fifth Lateran Council—that rational *understanding* of the soul was in a crisis state.[3] In this crisis, however, very few saw, as of yet, any reason for rationally doubting, let alone abandoning, the belief in soul's immortality. I take it that reciprocal considerations apply to interpreting the rejection of soul as a straightforward consequence of the mechanistic philosophy: the persistence of the Cartesian reinterpretation of soul qua substantial form, especially with its status as sui generis, belies the full adequacy of such an unnuanced explanation.[4] Rather, the inability of sixteenth and early seventeenth century philosophers to let go of this doctrine of soul qua substantial form was due to there not yet being a suitably developed alternative to the Christianized Aristotelian model, a problem which was to persist until (among many other things) the development and promulgation of the mechanistic resolutions of the *mixtions* problem in the mid to late seventeenth century. What these resolutions provided were robust notions of functional unity and emergent property, thereby undercutting all motivation for positing substantial forms. As a result, philosophers increasingly found it natural to convert thinking substances into thinking powers, or more accurately, they increasingly found no compelling reason to postulate a thinking *substance* on the basis of there obtaining in us a power for thought.

I: The Simplicity Argument and Substantial Forms

I take it that the simplicity argument is quite familiar to all of us:

1. The possibility of thought requires per se unity.[5]
2. Only certain kinds of substances may be united per se, namely those which are absolutely simple.
3. Therefore, soul must be an absolutely simple substance.[6]

For Christian Aristotelians, the dilemma is generated by the competing pressures of soul as individual substance (needed for avoiding Averroism and securing natural, personal immortality) and soul as form, the *principium unum* which accords humans not simply *unum per accidens* but *unum per se*.

Were mortalism not proscribed, explaining how soul qua substantial form in-formed the human body would be relatively straightforward. Aristotle's substantial forms are *logoi*, accounts or principles, rather than things. Consequently they cannot attach to matter as parts or elements. Certainly they cannot attach as physical parts since they are not themselves physical. But neither could they attach as metaphysical parts since they fall outside of the category of things or "this-es".[7] The appeal to substantial form is intended to explain how the various elements unite to form organs and how organs unite to form individuals. Consequently it must be *somehow* different from these material elements so that it may "rule over" them. Yet it cannot be *something* different lest the non-reductive identity between the informed matter and the in-forming substantial form (central to the Aristotelian conception of *universalia in rebus*) be lost.[8] What is able to preserve the numeric identity of substantial form and informed matter despite different predicates being truly applicable to them is the distinction between adverbs and what they modify. For example, in a runner's running quickly her quickness clearly differs somehow from her running since she could be running slowly. Nevertheless, her quickness is not different in either the sense of being some special thing appended to her running or in the sense that it is an event or activity she performs in addition to her running. Her quickness simply is her running, just as it would be her awkwardness were she to run awkwardly too. But of course because of the non-reductive nature of this identity relation, it does not follow that her quickness is her awkwardness. Such an adverbial difference is sufficiently loose so as to allow appeals to substantial forms to be explanatorily significant yet is tight enough to allow for the per se unity of hylomorphic beings. For example, just as the fact that Socrates has a pug nose, rather than a porcine snout, is adequately explained by *his* partaking of Humanity (since that is the way *his* matter determinates the determinable Humanity), so too is the fact that Socrates is rational is adequately explained by *his* partaking of Humanity, since that is the way *his* soul determines the determinable Humanity. Thus Socrates' pug-nosedness is the same as his rationality despite each having radically different definitions and each being spoken of in radically different ways.[9] Requiring the substantial form to be an individual thing, and so determinate rather than determinable, severs such non-reductive identity relations since the subject of all predications regarding substantial forms must now be that underlying individual substantial form rather than the subject of the in-forming relation (i.e., the primary substance) spoken of in qualified terms.[10] In effect, this adverbial approach folds the categories of 'substantial united,' 'really united but divisible in thought,' and 'indivisible even in thought' into one another while at the same time still allowing us to speak of matter and form as if they were distinct things. Because our mental discriminations in these cases do not constitute genuine mental separation, there are no real differences between them.

Few were more sensitive to this problem of reconciling individual subsistence and substantial form than Aquinas and fewer still were more sensitive to the philosophical dangers of the contrived and ad hoc. Aquinas most certainly would have agreed that doctrinal consistency can never be achieved through retreat, withdrawal, or intellectual disassociation; he would have certainly agreed that such consistency could only be achieved through philosophical congruence. This is what makes his resolution of the two ideas so disappointing, for, as Donald Able has argued, withdrawal and disassociation seem to be all that Aquinas had to offer in his doctrine of separated substances.[11] Per se unity is the problem here. Insofar as separated substances are supposed to have "present in" them their own properties (the point of course is that they be determinate and individual), they cannot suitably saturate and merge with utterly accident free prime matter. To effect a proper hylomorphic merging, the separated substance's accidents would somehow have to also merge with prime matter to become "present in" the composite rather than just the separated substance.[12] So, if we are to take the Thomistic suggestion of separated substances seriously, we must find some room for the accidental features of separated substances qua substantial forms within the *unum per se* hylomorphic composite.[13] And, to avoid Able's charge, we must do so along principled grounds. Fortunately (or not as it will turn out), just such grounds began emerging in the sixteenth and seventeenth centuries from the problem of *mixtions*.

II: The Problem of *Mixtions*

The problem of *mixtions* was not new to the sixteenth and seventeenth centuries. Indeed it goes all the way back to Aristotle's *De generatione et corruptione* I.10: "Some things are such as to act and others such as to suffer action from them. Moreover, some things—viz. those which have the same matter—reciprocate, i.e., are such as to act upon one another and to suffer action from one another; . . . When there is a certain equilibrium between the powers [of reciprocating things], then each of them changes, *out of its own nature towards the dominant*; yet [in such mixtions] neither becomes the other, but both become an intermediate with properties common to both. . . . [In general,] some things *are potentially* while others *are actually*; the constituents [in a true mixtion] can be in a sense and yet not-be. The compound may *be actually* other than the constituents from which it has resulted; nevertheless, each of them may still *be potentially* what it was before they were combined, and both of them may survive undestroyed."[14] In the sixteenth and seventeenth centuries, however, this problem, for a variety of reasons, took on a new urgency and increase in scope.[15] Francisco Suárez (*Disputationes metaphysica* XV—On the Formal Cause of Substance) presented the problem as follows:

> the substantial form is a thing distinct from matter. Therefore either it is something before its generation or it is nothing. If it is something, it is, therefore, a substantial form [what else would it be?] before it comes to be since substantial forms are indivisible. . . . This, however, is impossible because there would then be no substantial generation. . . . But if the other alternative is chosen, namely, that before generation the form is nothing, it follows that a form comes to be out of nothing, which is contrary to the axiom of the philosophers: *Nothing comes to be out of nothing*. Nor is it satisfactory to respond that it is not the form which comes to be but the composite, while the composite comes to be from matter, and

> thus there is nothing that comes to be out of nothing. This is, I say, not satisfactory because this reply consists more in words and in a manner of speaking than in reality. For the form really did not exist before generation, and afterwards it does exist because the composite does not come to be except insofar as it is composed out of matter and form; it is not, however, composed except out of real entities. Therefore, the substantial form came to be. Finally, this reply does not suffice because when the whole composite is corrupted, the form truly ceased to exist and passes into nothing; for it was something before and afterwards it is nothing. Therefore, when the whole begins to be, the form also comes to be.[16]

The problem is pretty straight-forward. As a matter of fact, we can recognize different levels of combination. In some, like Heraclitus's *kykeon* (the posset of barley, wine, and cheese) or jars of sand, each element of the mixture retains its own nature and the mixture itself does not take on any new nature of its own. In others however, like the mixture of water and wine, the two elements so thoroughly intermingle that there is no way of phenomenologically picking out each elementary particle, but nonetheless each retains its proper nature and the mixture itself does not take on any new nature. Finally, in yet others, like metal alloys, there is such a thorough intermingling of the elements that the whole assumes "an intermediary state with properties common to both" because each element "changes out of its own nature." Anything combined to such a degree as this is a *mixtion* and the philosophical problem concerns the disappearance of the elemental substantial forms and the emergence *ex nihilo* of a new one to govern the *mixtion*. These new, "intermediate" properties are quite clearly internal properties of the *mixtion*—thcy flow from the *mixtion* itself—and cannot be reduced down to the properties of either of its elements. Thus, where or whence do they emerge? If not from some newly emergent substantial form, then from what; and if from some newly emergence substantial form, whence did it come?

There seem to be few good options for resolving this. First, it cannot be maintained that the *mixtion's* new properties are produced by either of the elemental substantial forms in their original state since each has been changed "*out of its own nature*."[17] Nor can it be maintained that that these new properties are traceable to the corruption of the elemental substantial forms since substantial forms are necessarily incorruptible. (Indeed, that is one of the great benefits of identifying intellective soul as a substantial form—securing natural immortality follows easily.) Nor finally can it be maintained that the new properties trace back to a substantial form that itself naturally emerges *ex nihilo* because it is a general, logical principle that natural processes are continuous and the boundary between being and non-being is rigidly discrete—hence, *ex nihilo nihil fit*.[18] The only viable candidate seems to be to characterize the new properties as the products of a new substantial form that itself is the natural product of the interaction of the elemental substantial forms. Such, it seems to me, is Suárez's account of the eduction of substantial form from the pre-existing, mixed matter: Because the *mixtion's* substantial form is not something "that properly is, which subsists and has being," but rather is something "which inheres in another . . . , it comes to be out of a presupposed matter of which it is composed, and thus it does not come to be according to its entirety, but according to some part of itself." (Thus, there is no violation of the Law of Non-being.) This eduction, however, is governed by the natures of the material elements involved: "even though these forms are contained in the potency of matter and come to be by an action of an agent outside, as it were, that potency [i.e., the other material elements], this does not mean . . . that they do not actualize the potency of matter and inhere in it. It only means that, since, before they come to be they are only contained in potency and in their cause and after they come to be they are actually and outside their cause, they are, therefore, made from the potential being of matter in which they were contained and they are educed into act by the power of the agent."[19]

"Ok fine," you might be thinking, "what's the problem?" Notice that in the eduction of a *mixtion's* substantial form, the agents, which as efficient causes actualize the potency of the mixed matter, can be nothing other than the elemental substantial forms themselves. Thus, they themselves must be contained in the *mixtion* in such a way that they could physically interact. They must be "juxtaposed" such that "*any and every part* of each constituent" is interspersed with "the parts of the other." And note: the parts we are speaking of are not the material parts of the original mixables, but the parts of the substantial forms themselves since they are—indeed only they can be—the agents involved in the natural change of the *mixtion's* internal properties. This is the trend toward the "spatialization" (Norma Emerton's term) or "concretization" (Robert Pasnau's term) of substantial form.[20] The elemental *substantial forms* have to be actual parts of the *mixtion* so that they may then physically interact so that an entirely new substantial form may itself be educed from the *mixtion's* underlying matter.

Two themes are converging here. First, the substantial form must be identified with the set of essential properties in order to be entities appropriate for physically interacting with one another. They can no longer be an underlying principle comprising the formal cause of an element; they must exert some sort of natural efficient causality, which requires that they exhibit some kind of physical subsistence. As incomplete substances they cannot subsist as independent substances, but they can perhaps subsist as the determinate physical properties of their substances. The problem with this, however, is that it obliterates the distinction between accidental forms and substantial forms by eliding the distinction between determinable and determinate properties. Essential properties have to be determinables if they are to retain sufficient generality to be applicable to many individuals. For instance, reason as an essential property of man manifests in actual people in a variety degrees—not only are some people plainly much smarter than others, people are smarter or denser in different ways: one might be a deeper thinker, another might be quicker, yet another more original and creative, and yet another more analytical. It is equally true to say of any one of us, no matter how smart or slow she may be, that she is rational and that she currently possesses reason; indeed it is still true to say that of her even when she is currently sleeping, unconscious, vegetative, or mentally retarded. When the truth-making grounds for the assertion are the possession of a nature underlying its exemplification or material manifestation, there is no problem.

When, however, its truth-making grounds become the material manifestation of that determinate property—i.e., that specific degree of reasonableness exemplified—there are problems. There are sorities-style problems with demarking the level of reasonableness for grounding its truthful predication and there are problems with attributing the property to those not currently exhibiting it, such as a man sleeping or making an inferential mistake.[21] Now, determinate properties, by virtue of their specific nature, fall within the realms of fate and the accidental. It might be essential to us that we are rational, but it most certainly is an accident that all of us reading this journal have had the good fortune to attend such wonderful schools that we might develop, however far we may have, our capacities for intelligence and wisdom. This basic analysis was what underlay the semantics of Aristotle's distinction between said-of predicative relations and present-in ones. By reifying substantial forms in this way, the "is" of said-of predications becomes obscured with and slides into the "is" of present-in ones. Or as Dennis Des Chene put it, the "is" of *informatio* has dissolved into the "is" of inherence.[22] Throughout the seventeenth century, this elision hardened and became philosophical orthodoxy. If one reflects on the early modern critiques of substantial forms, one can readily perceive this. Locke's attacks against Aristotelian essentialism, for example—those based on the existence of monsters as well as those based on the alleged continuity of the Great Chain of Being—illustrate this quite nicely. So too does Locke's claim that "particular Beings, considered barely in themselves, will be found to have all their Qualities equally *essential*; and every thing, in each Individual, will be *essential* to it, or, which is more true, nothing at all [will be essential to it]."[23]

This elision, in turn, precipitated the collapse of hylomorphism by undermining the original motivation for postulating substantial forms. They were supposed to explain why certain sets of properties, rather than others, were compossible by being the unique source of the compossibility of that set of properties. But if substantial forms simply are those sets of compossible properties, appeal to their being that set's principle or source of unity is vacuous. By rendering it trivially true, the appeal is sapped of any genuine explanatory force. By reifying substantial forms, in other words, we are prevented from seeing any deeper (metaphysically) into objects than simply *that* they are in-formed; and by being unable to see any deeper, no appeals to substantial forms can provide any explanatory gain or intellectual satisfaction.

Consider what happened to Suárez's battery of arguments for the reality of substantial forms.[24] Within one generation they were gone, ignored and forgotten. As far as I can tell, Suárez's analyses and arguments were never refuted; indeed the surprising thing is that they seem not to have been really engaged. The point I am trying to make here, however, is that they really didn't need to be refuted or engaged because something akin to a collective gestalt-shift was unfolding: Suárez's arguments vanished simply out of irrelevance. In the early seventeenth century the drive toward the physicalization of form met up with a complementary drive in the metaphysicalization of classical atomism and produced a more seductive rival for the *mixtion* problem. In response to the "first reason for doubting the reality of substantial forms," Suárez argued "that an aggregate of many accidental faculties or forms in a simple substantial subject is not enough to constitute a natural thing," because "in addition to these accidental forms there is required a form to rule, as it were, over all those faculties and accidents and to be the source of all actions and natural changes . . . and [to serves as] the subject in which the whole variety of powers and accidents is rooted and unified in a certain way. Therefore, . . . there is needed a substantial form distinct from the accidents and more intimate and perfect than they are."[25] This very distinctness was what was being lost because, as Suárez himself admitted in a much later disputation, "we can never explicate the essences of things, as they are in themselves, but only through their being ordered to [i.e., superordinate to] some property."[26] All that one was compelled to postulate was some superordinate *property* serving as the basis for the primary substance's unity, a point the "new scientists" of the seventeenth century were coming to realize. Without property-independent access to the underlying substantial form, its postulation could not be seen as anything other than gratuitous and question-begging once a suitably vigorous rival account of unity appeared, which was just what happened with the development of the mechanistic philosophy and functionalist accounts of per se unity.[27]

The shift was from requiring that the relevant properties *be structured by something* unitary to *their being structured* (in certain ways) constituting unity. In countenancing mechanistic causality, the conceptual logjam engendered by the ancient Principle of Causal Synonymy was broken.[28] No longer were philosophers required to disinter some underlying thing exemplifying or containing the emergent property itself (whether virtually, eminently, or formally) in order to have an adequate understanding of its exemplification. (Notice how the concepts of eminence and virtualness simply vanished during the course of the seventeenth century; this is yet another a sign of the collapse of the Principle of Causal Synonymy and the acceptance of emergence as a metaphysically legitimate phenomena.) Philosophers were able to fully satisfy their understandings without "bridging the gap," as it might be put nowadays, simply because the emergence of the property was itself now viewed as a bridge.[29]

We must be very careful to distinguish between what is being said here and what is not. What is not being said is that an emergent property may be treated as primitive or properly basic. That would be just as vacuous and unsatisfying as the Aristotelian postulations of underlying substantial form. What is being said in stating that a property is genuinely emergent is that it correlates with an underlying complex interaction, i.e., that it correlates with a particular pattern of properties, or with matter properly organized and disposed. It is that—our connecting the emergent property with an underlying pattern of interactions—which undergirds the explanatory force of any appeal to a property's emergence and sanctions the focus on the properties themselves rather than on an underlying substantial form extruding them. Because of its centrality for understanding phenomena, the task of fitting phenomena to maximally consistent and extensive, yet detailed and specific, patterns is ineliminable from the drive to understand. And it is only from this task of fitting phenomena to patterns that any insights into *how* a phenomena obtains may be gleaned. The challenge, then, for the "new scientists" of the seventeenth century was to develop models of, and explanations for, these complex interactions of elements as well as developing analyses of the kinds of and limits to such material organizations that still allowed for the emergence of the properties in question and the proper functioning of the organisms or systems on which they supervene.

III: Conclusion

To late seventeenth and eighteenth century eyes, then, the attempt to reify substantial forms and transform them into entities capable of self-subsisting is self-defeating rather than demonstratively false. It was self-defeating because of the conceptual pressures it placed on the powers and properties exemplified by a primary substance. In effect, the attempt interposed an opaque veil between a thing's having characteristic properties and the underlying causes of those properties by virtue of characterizing the identity conditions for substantial forms solely in terms of those *exemplified* powers and properties rather than in the natures underlying those exemplifications.[30] There are good reasons for these identity conditions of course: the underlying natures are mysterious, utterly so in fact. Mechanical explanations in terms of the relationships between physical entities and their manifest physical properties are much more intellectually satisfying precisely because they allow us to recognize connections and patterns in principle unobservable within the hylomorphic system. And when the focus is exclusively on these physical patterns and connection, there is no basis for, and indeed no need for, going beyond the patterns.

This was in essence what underlay Kant's charge that the inference to the subsistence of simple soul was based on a transcendent principle. There is no basis for going beyond the experienced patterns and connections between thoughts and our experience of ourselves as phenomenal thinkers. The early modern shift to the acceptability of mechanistically emergent properties undermined philosophy's most significant and plausible claim for thinking that intellective soul is a simple, subsistence, immaterial and immortal substantial form—the per se unity of thought. Once the general idea that per se unity might wholly and non-reductively emerge from a complex comprising literally many interacting parts was sanctioned for use in other areas of natural explanations, its application to thought and mind was simply a matter of time.

The University of Western Ontario

Notes

1. Kant, *Critique of Pure Reason*, trans. Norman Kemp Smith (London: MacMillan, 1950) A351, 335 and A296/B353, 299.

2. Pietro Pomponazzi, *On the Immortality of the Soul*, trans. William Hay, in *The Renaissance Philosophy of Man*, ed. Ernst Cassirer, Paul Kristeller, and John Randall (Chicago: University of Chicago Press, 1948), 280–381. Notice in chapter fifteen that he characterized this as a "neutral problem" akin to the possible eternality of the created world. In *De*

immortalitate even Pomponazzi was committed to the belief in the immortality of soul, and indeed to its rationality (in some sense of rationality); what he doubted was the possibility of demonstrating that belief. *Cf.* this, however, with the more radical *Apologia* (Bologna, 1518) and *Defensorium* (Bologna, 1519) in which he characterized the thesis as actually contrary to reason.

3. Fifth Lateran Council, Session 8, December 19, 1513: "The sower of cockle . . . has dared to scatter . . . some extremely pernicious errors . . . on the nature of the rational soul, with the claim that it is mortal, or only one among all human beings, and since some, playing the philosopher without due care, assert that this proposition is true at least according to philosophy, it is our desire to apply suitable remedies against this infection and . . . condemn and reject all those who insist that the intellectual soul is mortal, or that it is only one among all human beings, and those who suggest doubts on this topic. For the soul not only truly exists of itself and essentially as the form of the human body, . . . but it is also immortal; and further, for the enormous number of bodies into which it is infused individually, it can and ought to be and is multiplied. And since truth cannot contradict truth, we define that every statement contrary to the enlightened truth of the faith is totally false and we strictly forbid teaching otherwise to be permitted. We decree that all those who cling to erroneous statements of this kind . . . should be avoided in every way and punished as detestable and odious heretics and infidels who are undermining the catholic faith. Moreover we strictly enjoin on each and every philosopher who teaches publicly in the universities or elsewhere, that when they explain or address to their audience the principles or conclusions of philosophers, where these are known to deviate from the true faith—as in the assertion of the soul's mortality or of there being only one soul or of the eternity of the world and other topics of this kind—they are obliged to devote their every effort to clarify for their listeners the truth of the christian religion, to teach it by convincing arguments, so far as this is possible, and to apply themselves to the full extent of their energies to refuting and disposing of the philosophers' opposing arguments," (All Catholic Church Ecumenical Councils—All the Decrees, http://www.piar.hu/councils, text taken from *Decrees of Ecumenical Councils*, ed. Norman Tanner).

4. At least one philosopher, Justin Skirry, sees the Cartesian doctrine of soul as less of a reinterpretation and more of an annexation of the Aristotelian doctrine, indeed so much so that Skirry conceives of the Cartesian substantial union of mind and body as just the hylomorphic uniting of matter and form. (See his "A Hylomorphic Interpretation of Descartes's Theory of Mind-Body Union," *Proceedings of the American Catholic Philosophical Association* 75 (2001): 267–284; "Does Descartes's Real Distinction Argument Prove Too Much?" *American Catholic Philosophical Quarterly* (78 (2004): 399–424; and "Descartes's Conceptual Distinction and Its Ontological Import," *Journal of the History of Philosophy* 42 (2004): 121–144. Within the intellectual halls of the Church, the Cartesian reinterpretation lingers still. See Alfred Freddoso, "Good News, Your Soul Hasn't Died Quite Yet," *Proceedings of the American Catholic Philosophical Association* 75 (2001): 79–96 and Christopher Gilbert, "Catholic Cartesian Dualism: A Reply to Freddoso," *American Catholic Philosophical Quarterly* 79 (2005): 233–249.

5. As Kant put it: "the manifold representations, which are given in an intuition, would not one and all be *my* representations, if they did not all belong to one self-consciousness. As my representations (even if I am not conscious of them as such), they must conform to the condition under which alone they *can* stand together in one universal self-consciousness [i.e., the conditions for the transcendental unity of apperception], because otherwise they would not all without exception belong to me," (Kant, *Critique of Pure Reason*, B132, 153).

6. Of course directly following from this are two key conclusions, the immateriality and immortality of soul:

4. Material substances are per se divisible.
5. Therefore, material substances cannot be absolutely simple.
6. Therefore, soul must be an immaterial substance.
7. Absolutely simple substances cannot be naturally corrupted or destroyed.
8. Therefore, soul must be an immortal substance.

7. For discussion of adverbial interpretations of Aristotelian substantial forms see Theodore Scaltsas, "Substratum, Subject, and Substance," *Ancient Philosophy* 5 (1985): 215–240 and Charlotte Witt, "Hylomorphism in Aristotle," *Aperion* 22 (1989): 141–158.

8. Suppose that the in-forming relation is understood in a reified manner as obtaining between a thing and another thing. Insofar as the things are typologically similar, the ruling-over relation which happens to obtain between substantial form and informed matter will be, at least in principle, convertible, thus rendering substantial form's ruling over informed matter merely accidental. By simply investing the reified substantial form with an intrinsic power for ruling over matter the problem is not solved so much as merely pushed back with the threat of infinite regress now looming—what in-forms the substantial form with this power; what nature in-forms this nature such that it necessarily has the power to rule over matter?

9. The non-identity of Plato and Socrates despite the identity of explanations for their distinctively human features is preserved in the same way: Plato's nose being aquiline is adequately explained by *his* partaking of Humanity but Socratic pug-nosedness is not the same as Platonic hook-nosedness.

10. E.g., Socrates qua animal and Socrates qua rational.

11. "It is difficult to avoid the impression that Aquinas is simply creating an ad hoc hypothesis simply to defend his theory that the human soul is both a substance and the form of the body," (Donald Able, "Intellectual Substance as Form of the Body in Aquinas," *Proceedings of the American Catholic Philosophical Association* 69 [1995]: 233). See also: "The plausibility of Aquinas' theory is lessened by the fact that it requires apparently ad hoc modifications of both Aristotle's and his own metaphysics, and produces an intellectualist [i.e., Platonic] view of human nature," (234). See St. Thomas Aquinas, *Summa theologiae*, 1a, q.75, a.2, res: "Respondeo dicendum quod necesse est dicere id quod est principium intellectualis operationis, quod dicimus animam hominis, esse quoddam principium incorporeum et subsistens. . . . Ipsum igitur intellectuale principium, quod dicitur mens vel intellectus, habet operationem per se, cui non communicat corpus. Nihil autem potest per se operari, nisi quod per se subsistit. Non enim est operari nisi entis in actu, unde eo modo aliquid operatur, quo est. Propter quod non dicimus quod calor calefacit, sed calidum. Relinquitur igitur animam humanam, quae dicitur intellectus vel mens, esse aliquid incorporeum et subsistens." For discussion consider J. Obi Oguejiofor, *The Philosophical Significance of Immortality in Thomas Aquinas* (Lanham, MD: University Press of America, 2001) and Robert Pasnau, *Thomas Aquinas on Human Nature: A Philosophical Study of Summa theologiae 1a 75–89* (Cambridge: Cambridge University Press, 2002).

12. If it helps: Those familiar with Paul Spade's pin cushion analogy in "The Warp and Woof of Metaphysic: How to get Started on Some Big Themes" (http://www.pvspade.com/Logic/docs/WarpWoof.pdf) can perhaps visualize the problem by visualizing how the two pin cushions on p. 18 could merge. The separated substance pin cushion—pins and all!—must be fitted to the pinless upper hemisphere of the physical being pin cushion. If the

pins are driven out to the level of the physical substance's pins, then there is per se unity but no longer any determinacy within the substantial form. If, however, the pins remain encased in the substantial form's assigned hemisphere (representing a different level at which accidental predication occurs and, necessarily, a different metaphysical subject of such predications), then there is no basis for ascribing per se unity to this kind of composition.

13. The lines suggested in *De ente et essentia*—that a thing's substantial form becomes determinate via the in-forming relation and, as individuated and determinate, takes over from matter the task of individuating the particular in-formed substance—are, more or less, the lines adopted by the natural philosophers in the *mixtion* literature. And as I argue below, these lines are precisely what generate the problems with conceiving intellective soul as substantial form. For discussion of Aquinas's doctrine see Robert Pasnau and Christopher Shields, *The Philosophy of Aquinas* (Boulder: Westview Press, 2004), 54–59.

14. Aristotle, *De generatione et corruptione*, in *The Complete Works of Aristotle*, ed. Jonathan Barnes (Princeton: Princeton University Press, 1984), I.10, 328a19–31 and 327b23–26, 1:536–537

15. Robert Pasnau has recently suggested as much: see Robert Pasnau, "Form, Substance, and Mechanism," *The Philosophical Review* 113 (2004): 31–88.

16. Francisco Suárez, *On the Formal Cause of Substance: Metaphysical Disputation XV*, trans. John Kronen and Jeremiah Reedy (Milwaukee: Marquette University Press, 2000), 44 (my emendations). Suárez calls this issue a "specialis difficultas" at the end of the first section and devotes the entire second section to its resolution. In the words of Kronen, "never before or since has there been so thorough a treatment of the Aristotelian notion of form," (Introduction to *On the Formal Cause of Substance*, 9). See also Dorothea Frede: "*mixis* is not easily classified as a kind of change within one of the ten categories. . . . [I]t is a change that involves different substances and their properties in a complex way. It is neither the result of simple substantial change in the sense of generation proper, nor a straightforward case of alteration, nor a change in quantity, nor is it locomotion," ("*On Generation and Corruption* I.10: On Mixture and Mixables," in *Aristotle: On Generation and Corruption, Book I: Symposium Aristotelicum*, ed. Frans de Haas and Jaap Mansfeld [Oxford: Clarendon Press, 2004], 290).

17. The elemental substantial forms are supposed to be potentially in the *mixtion* in the sense that they could be separated out from the *mixtion* and revert back to their actual existence. The puzzle, of course, is how that is compatible with the per se unity of the *mixtion*.

18. Creation *ex nihilo*, by the crossing of the rigid boundary between non-being and being, violates the law of non-contradiction—before any object can become anything, it must first be a something, since any change of state entails the existence of the thing to undergo the change. Consequently it can only be performed directly by God; Nature could never cross such a threshold. Moses Mendelssohn nicely expressed this point in the *Phädon*: "Die Sätze, sprach Sokrates, deren Richtigkeit wir nicht mehr in Zweifel ziehen, sind diese: Zu einer jeden natürlichen Veränderung wird dreyerley erfodert: 1) Ein Zustand eines veränderlichen Dinges, der aufhören, 2) ein anderer, der seine Stelle vertreten soll, und 3) die mittlern Zustände, oder der Uebergang, damit die Veränderung nicht plötzlich, sondern allmählig geschehe. Was veränderlich ist, bleibet keinen Augenblick, ohne wirklich verändert zu werden. Die Folge der Zeit gehet in einem fort, und es giebt keine zween Augenblicke, die sich einander die nächsten sind. Die Folge der Veränderungen kömmt mit der Folge der Zeit überein, und ist ebenfalls so stätig, so unzertrennlich, daß man keine Zustände angeben kann, die sich einander die nächsten wären, oder zwischen welchen nicht ein Uebergang

Statt finden sollte. Sind wir nicht über diese Punkte einig worden? . . . Das Verderben nimmt durch unmerkliche Grade allmählig zu. Endlich zerfällt das Gebäude, und löset sich in seine kleinsten Theile auf. Aber was geschieht? Hören diese Theile auf, Veränderungen zu leiden? gehen sie ganz verloren? Es scheinet nicht, versetzte Cebes. Unmöglich, mein Werthester! erwiederte Sokrates, wenn das wahr ist, worüber wir einig geworden: denn giebt es wohl ein Mittel zwischen Seyn und Nichtseyn? Keineswegs. Seyn und Nichtseyn wären also zween Zustände, die unmittelbar aufeinander folgen, die sich einander die nächsten seyn müßten: wir haben aber gesehen, daß die Natur keine solche Veränderungen, die plötzlich und ohne Uebergang geschehen, hervorbringen kann. Erinnerst du dich wohl noch dieses Satzes? Sehr wohl, sprach Cebes. Also kann die Natur weder ein Daseyn noch eine Zernichtung hervorbringen?" (Mendelssohn, *Phädon* [Projek Gutenberg—DE], http://gutenberg.spiegel.de/mendelss/phaedon/ phaed14.htm).

19. Suárez, *Formal Cause of Substance*, 53–55 passim.

20. Norma Emerton, *The Scientific Reinterpretation of Form* (Ithaca: Cornell University Press, 1984), 48–75 and Pasnau, "Form, Substance, and Mechanism," 31–88.

21. "What's the problem," you might ask: either we contradict the definition of man as a rational animal or we must (momentarily!) exclude that "man" from the class of men, neither of which are very attractive consequences.

22. Dennis Des Chene, *Physiologia: Natural Philosophy in Late Aristotelian and Cartesian Thought* (Ithaca: Cornell University Press, 1996), 53–80.

23. John Locke, *An Essay concerning Human Understanding*, ed. Peter Nidditch (Oxford: Clarendon Press, 1975), III.vi.5, 441–442.

24. To be found in sect. 1 of *On the Formal Cause of Substance.*

25. Suárez, *On the Formal Cause of Substance*, sect. 1, 21 (with my emendations).

26. Francisco Suárez, *Disputationes metaphysica*, dis. 40, sect. 4. Quoted in Des Chene, *Physiologia*, 75.

27. Supplemented, generally, with a collocation constraint to avoid such problems as the functional unity of the solar system (or a naval armada or government bureaucracy or etc.) constituting by itself a genuine per se unity.

28. "Causal Synonymy" is R. J. Hankinson's term—"The idea that an agent which produces some particular property must itself exhibit the property in question: if an agent *A* is causally responsible for some property *F* holding of *B*, then *A* must itself possess *F*, and make *B F* in virtue of its *F*-ness," (R. J. Hankinson, appendix to *Cause and Explanation in Ancient Greek Thought* [Oxford: Clarendon Press, 1998], 449).

29. To ask how or demand that an "explanatory gap" be bridged is, it seems to me, a very misleading way of expressing a worry about the current understanding of the model for the underlying pattern of interactions; even when we reach the point at which most of us judge that the demand has been satisfied, if we were to carefully consider it, we would see that the gap itself is still there but that we no longer "feel" the insufficiency, the disjointedness, between the model and the property's emergence.

30. To stick with the underlying natures is to lapse into either Averroism or a Third Man regress, to say nothing of the following point.

The Separate Minds of Church and State: Collective Mental States and Their Unsettling Implications

H. M. Giebel

Abstract: Claims regarding collective or group mental states are fairly commonplace: we speak of things like the belief of the Church, the will of the faculty, and the opinion of the Supreme Court, often without considering what such claims really mean and whether they are true in any interesting sense. In this paper I take a threefold approach: first, I articulate several ways in which a group might be said to have beliefs and other mental states. Second, I explore the implications, positive and negative, of these accounts of collective mental states. Third, I give a brief defense of my own view despite its somewhat disturbing implications for our membership in Church, State, and other groups.

The *Catechism of the Catholic Church* starts by noting, "We begin our profession of faith by saying: 'I believe' or 'We believe.'"[1] Later in Part One, it elaborates:

> "I believe" (*Apostles' Creed*) is the faith of the Church professed personally by each believer, principally during Baptism. "We believe" (*Niceno-Constantinopolitan Creed*) is the faith of the Church confessed by the bishops assembled in council or more generally by the liturgical assembly of believers. "I believe" is also the Church, our mother, responding to God by faith as she teaches us to say both "I believe" and "We believe."[2]

While claims of collective belief are perhaps to be expected in religious communities, we find them in more secular settings as well. For example, the U.S. Declaration of Independence asserts that we Americans hold some famous propositions to be self-evident. The rulings of the U. S. Supreme Court routinely begin, "Justice N. delivered the opinion of the Court," which clearly implies that the Court has at least one opinion. Various organizations, both secular and religious, have mission statements that include key beliefs, desires, and other mental states of their groups.

The big question is whether, and in what sense(s), claims about the existence of collective mental states can be true. In this paper I shall attempt to answer the big question by taking a threefold approach: first, I shall articulate several ways in which a group might be said to have beliefs and other mental states. Second, I shall explore the implications, positive and negative, of these accounts of collective mental states. Third, I shall give a brief defense of my own view despite its somewhat disturbing implications for our membership in Church, State, and other groups. The first two parts are meant to give something like an aerial view of the logical terrain; the third is meant to suggest which parts of that terrain might be most habitable.

I. Some Possibilities for Collective Mental States

It seems to me that there are several obvious possibilities regarding what we mean when we say that a group has some mental state (and whether our claim is true). For convenience, I'll label them with both names and numbers:

1. The Nonexistence View: There is no such thing as a collective or group mental state; there are only mental states of individuals. Persons saying things like "Americans value baseball, hot dogs, apple pie, and Chevrolet" either spout nonsense or refer to the coincidence of many people's similar but individual mental states. Both Searle and Bratman seem to endorse views in this area: although both speak of collective or shared mental states, the states they describe are those of individuals (such as "I intend that we J").[3]

2. The Additive View: A group has a given mental state if and only if at least one of its members has that mental state. If I say, "My family was offended by the graphic violence on that television program," I mean that at least one member of my family felt offended, and my statement is true just in case at least one of us actually did feel offended.

3. The Critical-Mass View: A group has a given mental state if and only if at least *n*% of its members, where *n* is some number greater than 0 and less than or equal to 50, have that mental state. The statement, "My students want a five-minute break in the middle of our two-hour class" is true in virtue of there being a critical mass of students (in this case, about 40%) who want such a break (as indicated by their visible fidgeting and/or drowsiness after about an hour).

4. The Majority-Rules View: A group has a given mental state if and only if more than 50% of its members have that mental state. For instance, "The Harvard faculty believes that its president should step down," means that a majority of the faculty members hold this belief and is true if and only if the majority actually does hold the belief. Something like this view has been endorsed by Anthony Quinton and attacked by Margaret Gilbert, among others.[4]

5. The Near-Consensus (or Majority-Plus) View: A group has a given mental state if and only if at least *n*% of its members, where *n* is some number greater than 50 and less than 100, have that mental state. So "Catholics believe that active euthanasia is morally wrong" is true just in case a strong (specified) majority of members of the Catholic Church does believe that it is wrong.

6. The Consensus View: A group has a given mental state if and only if all of its members have that mental state. On this view, "We believe in God the Father

Almighty" means that *all* of us believe in God the Father Almighty; if it turns out that one of the utterers of this statement does not so believe, then either the statement is false or the nonbeliever is not a member of the group indicated by "we."

7. The Strong Leader View: A group has a given mental state if and only if its leader—the person, or perhaps persons, with the group's decision-making power—has that mental state. For example, the claim, "The United States Army intends to attack Baghdad" is true just in case it is true that the U. S. Army's commander-in-chief intends to (order the) attack.

8. The Externalist View(s): A group has a given mental state not in virtue of any or all of its members' having that state but in virtue of appropriate external features or actions such as votes, rules, or constitutions. Such external features or actions will involve some or all of the group's members, of course, but the idea is that these members' features or actions (or products of their features or actions), not their mental states, determine the mental states of the group. One might say, for example, that the statement, "The South African people wanted Nelson Mandela to be their president" is true if and only if they voted him into office; or that the claim, "The International Society of Atheists believes that God does not exist" is true if and only if such a claim is stipulated in the group's constitution, rules, or other defining statement. Margaret Gilbert appears to endorse an externalist view when she argues that a group is the subject of a belief or psychological attribute if and only if its members form a *joint commitment* to have that belief or attribute.[5]

Astute observers will notice that all of the approaches to collective mental states except the nonexistence view and perhaps the externalist view seem to have the strange implication that a group may have collective mental states that are wholly irrelevant to the group's nature, activities, or interests. For example, if each member of the ACPA intends to brush his or her teeth before bed tonight, accounts 2–7 appear to commit us to the view that the ACPA intends to brush its teeth tonight. I suggest that we avoid this odd result by adding a qualification to each of these accounts of collective mental states:

A. The Relevance Qualification: A group has a given mental state—belief, desire, intention, etc.—if and only if the appropriate condition (expressed in whichever of views 2–7 is correct) is met *and* that state is relevant to the group's nature, activities, or interests. (I conveniently assume that there is some coherent sense in which a group can be said to have a nature, activities, or interests. If this is not the case, my qualification should of course be ignored.) With this qualification, a pact by the members of the Oral Hygiene Society to brush their teeth might qualify as indicative of a collective intention even on non-externalist accounts, but the coincidentally similar intentions of ACPA members to perform the same action would not. Although the relevance qualification is somewhat vague, it is intuitively attractive and may help us avoid blatant commissions of the fallacy of composition. I turn in the next section to the implications of each particular account of collective mental states.

II. Implications of the Accounts

In the explanations of the competing views, I tried to include examples that would enjoy at least some initial plausibility. It seems that there is something to be said for each of the accounts; each also has its peculiar drawbacks and counter-intuitive results. In this section I outline the main positive and negative implications of each account.

The nonexistence view (that there are no collective mental states) appears to be the simplest of the eight candidates and may be seen as the default position. After all, groups are composed of individuals, and it may seem natural to conclude that "group mental states" can be reduced to the mental states of the individuals composing the group. Further, for many groups and situations it seems downright bizarre to say that the group in question has mental states: for example, what are Congress's desires? Caucasian-Americans' intentions? Microsoft's feelings? Besides all that, the fact that groups apparently don't have their own minds or brains (above and beyond the minds or brains of their members) suggests that they have nowhere to house their own mental states.

Despite its merits, the argument that there are no collective mental states is bound to make some people a little nervous, especially when they start applying its conclusion to things like business ethics and just war theory. The fear, of course, is that if the group in question has no mental states then it does not perform any voluntary actions (which require willingness and the relevant beliefs) and therefore is not morally responsible for anything it does. But we want to hold the Nazis responsible for war crimes and Exxon responsible for the *Valdez* oil spill and Al-Qaida responsible for terrorism. The apparent inability of the nonexistence view to provide a coherent framework for doing so may send some in search of greener pastures.

The additive view is in one sense the direct opposite of the nonexistence view. While the nonexistence view includes *none* of the group members' mental states in those of the group, the additive view includes *all* of their mental states, or at least all of the relevant ones. The critical-mass view is similar to the additive view in that the mental states of a non-majority subset of the group are the mental states of the group as a whole. For the sake of brevity, I shall treat the critical-mass view along with the additive view first, then suggest a modification to the additive view that doesn't apply as neatly to the critical-mass approach.

The additive and critical-mass views of collective mental states may be workable for relatively small and relatively homogeneous groups like (some) families, but they force their adherents (if they have any) to the strange conclusion that most groups have many contradictory beliefs, desires, feelings, and intentions. For example, on the additive and critical-mass accounts the American people believe that George W. Bush is a good president and that he's a lousy one; they intend to support the war in Iraq and to protest it; they are pleased and also horrified by South Dakota's law banning most abortions; they hope that Hillary Clinton will be the next president and that she will not.

One might suggest that at least the additive view could be made more palatable by taking into account things like the intensity of mental states and the number of group members who have them. Perhaps it could be further developed into an additive-subtractive view of collective mental states whereby we would use something akin to a utilitarian calculus to arrive at a collective mental state that might bear some resemblance to Rousseau's notion of the general will. We'd add the number of instances of a particular mental state in the group, accounting for its intensity in each case, and subtract the instances of the opposite state, again accounting for intensity. On the new additive-subtractive view, then, we could conclude that at the time of the 2004 presidential election the American people weakly believed that George W. Bush should remain president for a second term, which may be a more attractive conclusion than the additive view's implication that the American people believed both that he should remain president and that he should not.

It will soon be noticed that the "improved" additive-subtractive view of collective mental states is not without problems of its own. Perhaps most obviously, any approach using a utilitarian-like calculus will inherit many of utilitarianism's difficulties, including enormous logistical difficulties in recording and adding or subtracting all of the relevant states of all group members, the possible tyranny of those with especially intense beliefs and desires, and the incommensurability of various mental states. The incommensurability problem looms especially large: we're not just tallying pleasures and pains as with utilitarianism, but also beliefs, desires, emotions, and intentions, many of which have no clear opposite. In addition to the problems borrowed from utilitarianism, the additive-subtractive view looks suspiciously similar to the majority-rules view but adds complexities that some may see as unnecessary. I now turn to the relative merits and demerits of the majority-rules view.

The democratic flavor of the majority-rules view may lend it some appeal, especially among democratically-minded folks (as Americans tend to be). It seems to work particularly well in groups that are themselves democratic in nature, such as voting U.S. citizens and members of the faculty senate. A clear advantage of the majority-rules view is that it solves the problem of contradictory mental states that arose with the additive and critical-mass views.

Just as the additive-subtractive approach to collective mental states borrowed utilitarianism's difficulties, the majority-rules view may inherit at least one criticism of democracy: tyranny of the majority. Can it really be right to say that 51% of the group believes, intends, and desires on behalf of the group as a whole (including the dissenting 49%)? Does that imply that a member of the minority can have one belief *qua* individual and a contradictory belief *qua* member of the group? If so, we seem to have relocated the contradictory-mental-state problem rather than solved it. Another apparent difficulty with the majority-rules approach, in some ways the opposite of the first problem, arises in non-democratic groups in which a minority holds most or all of the decision-making power. In such cases, the majority-rules view commits us to the claim that the group has certain mental states (those of the majority) but consistently acts on mental states it does not have (those of the minority), even when the mental states on which it acts are in direct conflict with those it actually has. The counterintuitive implications of determining group mental states according to those of some subset of the group, whether majority or minority, may leave the nonexistence view of collective mental states looking not so bad after all. We do have a few more views to consider, though; perhaps one of them will be an improvement over the choices thus far.

The near-consensus view avoids the problem of counterintuitive ascriptions of mental states in cases of nearly-even split among group members. It does not avoid the problem of tyranny of the majority, though: the majority must be larger in this case but can still tyrannize. Further, it shares the second problem of the majority-rules view: the tyranny of the minority in non-democratic groups. As if these problems weren't enough, the near-consensus view borrows to some extent the major problem of the consensus view, to which I now turn.

The consensus view has the advantage of being the most clear-cut of the options (with the possible exception of the nonexistence view): if it ever is true that a group has some mental state, surely it is true when every one of the group's members has that state. For example, if it is possible for the U.S. Conference of Catholic Bishops to hold beliefs, then surely the fact (and it seems safe to assume that it *is* a fact) that each of its members believes that God exists is sufficient to show that the USCCB as a group believes that God exists.

The major problem with the consensus view is that groups without complete consensus (or, in the case of the near-consensus view, groups without a sufficiently strong majority) have no mental states. It may be somewhat surprising to discover that the consensus view, and in some cases even the near-consensus view, can yield the same conclusion as the nonexistence view: for any given group, there may be no group mental states. The potential problem with *that*, as we have seen, is that a group with no mental states performs no voluntary actions and thus is not morally responsible for anything it does.

Views 2–6 (the additive, critical-mass, majority-rules, near-consensus, and consensus views) might be called quantitative approaches to collective mental states: whether a group has a particular mental state depends on whether the specified number or percentage of group members has it. The strong leader view is more qualitative in nature: it emphasizes the authority of group leaders rather than quantities of group members. This view seems to fit rather naturally in discussions of collective intention; that is, it seems natural that one who chooses for the group also intends for the group (as with the earlier example of the army commander). It fits less well in accounts of other states such as emotions (as we can see again with the army commander: the army isn't happy about attacking Baghdad just in virtue of its commander's being happy about it). To an even greater extent than some of the quantitative views, the strong leader view raises concerns about tyranny of the minority. It is also important to note that many groups have more than one leader, in which case it seems we have to supplement the strong-leader view with one of the quantitative views or a second-order application of the strong-leader view in order to determine the mental states of the sub-group of leaders.

An externalist approach to collective mental states adds an element of verifiability that the other views lack: it may be an advantage that on such an account it is fairly clear what would count as evidence for a claim that a group has a particular mental state, and that such evidence is directly observable by those outside the group. However, empirical verifiability may come at the price of plausibility as an account of real mental states. It is difficult to see how something like the majority of votes cast or a constitutional amendment literally could be a desire or belief. More likely, it may seem, votes and amendments are signs or perhaps models of collective mental states.

It may be possible to combine the strong-leader and externalist approaches not only with one of the quantitative views but also with each other. For example, Raimo Tuomela argues that a group believes some proposition *p* if and only if its leaders "positionally believe" or accept *p* as the view of the group in their exercise of their group responsibilities in the relevant social circumstances.[6] On Tuomela's account, the leaders' having a positional belief that p does not imply that any of them personally believes that *p*, but it does imply that each of them believes that the group's view is *p*. The relevant social circumstances to which Tuomela refers involve members' tasks and social roles as well as the group's formal rules and informal agreements; this addition moves his account into the externalist camp in addition to the strong leader camp.

We have seen in this section that each of the proposed views of collective mental states has some counterintuitive implications. While the quantitative possibilities are meant to be exhaustive, there may be qualitative or externalist approaches that I have overlooked and that avoid the problems with the accounts I've discussed. Since none come to mind, I proceed to propose my own tentative view of collective mental states, knowing that its implications are bound to be unsettling.

III. A Tentative Account of Collective Mental States (or, Is this Group Really the ACPA?)

As I mentioned at the beginning of this paper, the aim of the first two sections was to give a fly-over of the logical landscape. In this section, I take a closer look at some areas that look habitable to me, although even these have their share of rocky terrain.

A natural beginning for such a tour may be the observation that the definition of "group mental state" must depend in large part upon the definition of "group". If it turns out (as I believe it does) that there are several types of group, then it may not be surprising if there turn out to be several types of group mental state. For my purposes, a "group" in the broadest sense of the term is simply any combination of multiple individuals. The class of groups initially may be divided into "cohesive groups" and "non-cohesive groups". Non-cohesive groups are mere aggregates of individuals: for example, President Bush, Britney Spears, my friend Bill, and my aunt Suzy form a non-cohesive group (we might call them the BS group for short). Cohesive groups are composed of individuals who come together for some reason or purpose and/or who are bound by social ties. There may, of course, be varying types and degrees of cohesion among cohesive groups; one type of cohesion will be of particular interest soon.

The non-existence view of group mental states is clearly a strong candidate for the correct assessment of the mental states of non-cohesive groups. Not only do such groups share with other groups the obvious lack of a group mind or brain, their very lack of cohesion suggests that any mental states that happen to be similar among the group members are simply the individual members' mental states. So the fact, if it is a fact, that each member of the BS group wants pizza for lunch, does not imply that the BS group wants pizza for lunch. In non-cohesive groups, the objection to the non-existence view regarding group responsibility does not arise, since a non-cohesive group does not perform joint actions.

Because of its intuitive attractiveness and inapplicability of the most obvious objection, I believe the non-existence view of non-cohesive group mental states is correct. However, it is interesting to note that the application of any of the other views could yield the result that a non-cohesive group has no group mental states: a quantitative view accompanied by the relevance qualification would yield no group mental states if there were none relevant to the group's nature, interests, or activities (and, of course, that would be the case if the group had no nature, interests, or activities); a strong-leader view would yield no group mental states given that the group had no leader; and an externalist view would yield no group mental states given that the group had no rules, commitments, votes, or other relevant external features. So if there were reason to prefer parallel accounts of group mental states for the different group-types or to think there were no group-types, any of the views would do.

Regarding cohesive groups, it seems to me that although we may use any or all of the quantitative approaches (perhaps especially the near-consensus view) in everyday speech, they aren't capable of showing that there are collective mental states that have anything especially *collective* about them. That is, on the quantitative accounts, "collective" mental states are just aggregates of individual mental states. So while a majority-rules or near-consensus version of a group mental state may be a helpful shorthand way of referring to the mental states of group *members*, it doesn't tell us anything of interest about the group as a whole.

It seems that to capture the notion of a collective or group mental state, we need something that makes reference to the unique qualities of groups: we need a qualitative approach like the strong-leader view or an externalist view (or a combination of the two). A purely strong-leader approach is too inclusive: a group's leader may have mental states that are relevant to the group but that do not have the status of group mental states, such as private plans for or attitudes toward the group and its activities. Even a condition that group mental states include only those that are known won't solve the problem, since it could be well-known that a group's leader has group-related yet personal opinions, desires, or intentions. An obvious example would be the leader's desire to resign: clearly, the group doesn't desire to resign in virtue of its leader's desire.

A purely externalist approach seems to have a difficulty akin to that of the quantitative approaches: while the quantitative views couldn't capture anything truly *collective* about collective mental states, an externalist approach can't capture anything truly *mental*. As I noted earlier, external group features such as rules or votes look more like models or signs of collective mental states than like mental states themselves. Perhaps that's simply the way things are: given that there are no group minds, perhaps there are no group mental states in the literal sense of "mental." It may be that an interesting and helpful model of group mental states is the best we can do; it may be that such a model can support voluntary group action, or at least a useful model of group action. My preference, though, is for a combination approach akin to Tuomela's for cohesive groups: such an approach captures the collectivity of collective mental states by referring to the group's relevant externalities such as rules and agreements, and it captures the mentality of collective mental states by requiring that the group's leaders believe that the mental state in question is that of the group. In some groups, though, even this combination approach isn't enough.

To demonstrate the shortcomings of the combination strong-leader-externalist approach to collective mental states, I'll need to propose a further division of group-types. We'll say a group is "mental-state-defined" if and only if, to be a member of the group, one must have some specified mental state; all other groups are non-mental-state-defined. There can be non-cohesive mental-state-defined groups, such as all of the depressed people in the Midwest. Non-cohesive mental-state-defined groups at first appear to be the exception to the rule that non-cohesive groups have no mental states, but any mental states even this type of non-cohesive group has are only "group" mental states in the non-literal, shorthand sense: if I say, "Here is a really depressed group," what I really mean is, "Here are a bunch of really depressed individuals."

Things get more interesting when we look at mental-state-defined cohesive groups: groups that come together, at least in part, for purposes related to their members' shared mental states. Typical examples include religious groups, which come together to affirm shared beliefs about and attitudes toward God, and political groups, which form to affirm shared beliefs about political systems and intentions to act on those beliefs. It is necessary but not sufficient that the group's leaders, in the relevant social circumstances (including the group's formal and informal declarations), believe that the group has a particular mental state (call it *M*); they, and the group's other mentally competent and informed members, must actually have *M*. Those who do not have mental state *M* are not members of the mental-state-defined group, perhaps despite outward appearances to the contrary: those who appear to be members but do not have *M* are pseudo-members (or, perhaps more kindly, formal or social "members"). So, for example, one who formally joins the Republican party under pressure from her family or for the purpose of sabotaging it, but does not believe the claims in the party's platform, would be a pseudo-Republican (or a formal or social "Republican"); she would not, strictly speaking, actually be a member of the Republican party.

If I am correct in suggesting that there are cohesive mental-state-defined groups, and that these include religious and political groups, we arrive at some interesting and unsettling implications for our own group membership (or pseudo-membership). Given that the Catholic Church is a mental-state-defined group with many group beliefs, and given that we have sufficient information and mental competence to know what those beliefs are, those of us who disagree with any of those beliefs are not Catholics—we're mere pseudo-Catholics. Further, if it is true that our country was founded for the purpose of affirming certain beliefs and attitudes (for example, beliefs about inalienable rights and attitudes toward government and equality), then many of us are pseudo-Americans. In fact, it may turn out that most of us in the American Catholic Philosophical Association are neither Americans nor Catholics.

University of St. Thomas (St. Paul, MN)

Notes

1. *Catechism of the Catholic Church*, 1994, paragraph 26.

2. Ibid., paragraph 167.

3. See John Searle, *The Construction of Social Reality*, (New York: Free Press, 1995); and Michael Bratman, *Faces of Intention*, especially the essay "I intend that we J," (Cambridge: Cambridge University Press, 1999).

4. See Anthony Quinton, "Social Objects," *Proceedings of the Aristotelian Society* 75 (1975), 67–87; Margaret Gilbert, "Modelling Collective Belief," reprinted in *Living Together*, (Rowman & Littlefield, 1996).

5. See Gilbert, *op. cit.*

6. Raimo Tuomela, "Group Beliefs," *Synthese* 91 (1992), 285–318; see also his *The Importance of Us*, (Stanford: Stanford University Press, 1995).

Abstraction in al-Fârâbî

Richard C. Taylor

Abstract: Al-Fârâbî's thought on intellect was known to the Latin West through the translation of his *Letter on the Intellect*, through the *Long Commentary on the De Anima* by Averroes and through some other works. Al-Fârâbî identified the active power of intellect in Aristotle's *De Anima* 3.5 as the unique and separately existing Agent Intellect, but the role of the Agent Intellect in forming intelligibles in act in the human soul is by no means unequivocally clear. Further, the apprehension of intelligibles by human beings and the intellectual development of the soul, oftentimes described as an activity of abstracting (*intaza`a*), seems to be a genuine abstraction from experience, yet it somehow involves the emanative power of the Agent Intellect. This paper works to provide a coherent explanation of the nature of abstraction and the role of Agent Intellect in that activity.

For those who study Medieval philosophy in the Latin West with particular interest in the teachings of Aquinas and other thinkers of the thirteenth century, the importance of the philosophical thought of al-Fârâbî (d.950–951) is perhaps easily overlooked. There are few mentions of the name of al-Fârâbî in Aquinas and the work of al-Fârâbî is seldom cited, though he is sometimes mentioned together with Avicenna and Averroes as one of the Arab philosophers.[1] His teaching on the nature of abstraction, however, had a significant impact on the Latin West and together with the teachings of Averroes in the *Long Commentary on the De Anima* played a central role in the development of a genuine theory of abstraction. Indeed, the epistemological accounts of the formation of intelligibles in the human mind by these two philosophers from the Arabic tradition can be said to be the *sine quibus non* of the development of the epistemological teachings of Thomas Aquinas, in spite of the fact that Aquinas was deeply critical of both of them.[2] Still, those accounts can also be said to be foundational influences in what Carlos Bazán has considered the Thomistic culmination of a genuinely novel philosophical synthesis of Augustinian, Aristotelian and Neoplatonic thinking on the part of Latin thinkers of the thirteenth century.[3] In the case of Aquinas, even his new conception of Aristotelian hylomorphism and his teaching that the human soul is fully form of the body while also being "subsistent-substantial-form"[4] can be traced to the influence of philosophical principles in Averroes and al-Fârâbî.[5]

Al-Fârâbî's thought on intellect was known to the Latin West through the translation of his *Treatise on the Intellect* (*Risalah fî-l-'aql* or *De intellectu* in the Latin version)[6] and also through the *Long Commentary on the De Anima* by Averroes. In what follows here my focus is for the most part on the teaching of al-Fârâbî in this work on the way in which human beings apprehend intelligibles and become knowers per se. I will briefly set out the account of al-Fârâbî in the *Treatise on the Intellect*, show the partial transmission of his views by Averroes, indicate three key notions found in Aquinas which can be traced to al-Fârâbî and to Averroes's critique of al-Fârâbî, and conclude with remarks on the importance of al- Fârâbî's conception of intentional transference or abstraction.

I

In his *Principles of the Opinions of the People of the Virtuous City* (*Mabâdi' ârâ' ahl al-madîna al-fâḍilah*) translated by Richard Walzer in *al-Fârâbî on the Perfect State*,[7] and also in his *Political Regime* (*as-Siyâsa al-Madaniyya*),[8] al-Fârâbî provides an emanative account of cosmos. At the top of this hierarchy rests "The First Existent which is the First Cause for the existence of all the rest of the beings [of the universe] and which is free of every kind of deficiency."[9] At the bottom of the series of emanated intellects and body-and-soul complexes corresponding to the heavenly cosmology, the emanated intellects come to an end with the Agent or Active Intellect (*al-'aql al-fa''âl*) which is associated with the sphere of the moon. In this work al-Fârâbî attributes "to the heavens, and not to the active intellect, the production of both characteristics of the sublunar world that are invariable and those that vary."[10] In his *Treatise on the Intellect*, however, the forms of the natural world are described as emanated from the Agent Intellect.[11] Still, in both of these works, this last of the emanated intellects or intelligences is intimately involved in human intellectual understanding.

Claiming to follow the Aristotelian account found in the *De Anima* of Aristotle,[12] al-Fârâbî remarks that Aristotle speaks of intellect in four senses: intellect in potentiality (*'aql bi-l-quwah*), intellect in act (*'aql bi-l-fi'l*), acquired intellect (*'aql mustafâḍ*), and the Agent Intellect (*al-'aql al-fa''âl*). The intellect in potentiality, located in some way in the soul,[13] functions as "something the essence of which is ready and disposed for abstracting (*tantazi'u*) the essences (*mâhiyât*) and forms (*ṣuwar-hâ*) of all existents from their matters so as to make all of them a form or forms for it."[14] Once abstracted, the forms come to belong to the intellect which was in potentiality such that this intellect becomes those forms. Even Aristotle's image of the wax and signet ring of *De Anima* 2.12 is inadequate for conceiving this identity, he insists, because there is no distinction of the recipient intellect and the form which it receives: "this essence itself becomes these forms (*hadhihi adh-dhâtu nafsu-hu taṣîru tilka aṣ-ṣuwar*)." These received forms, he remarks, are appropriately denominated "intelligibles" (*al-ma'qûlât*), a name which he says is derived from "the name of this essence which abstracted the forms of the existents,"[15] namely the intellect which is in potentiality and which is then after abstraction in actuality. Prior to abstraction, the term "intelligibles in potentiality" (*ma'qûlât bi-l-quwa*) was suitably used of the forms existing in matters "outside the soul" (*khârij an-nafs*),[16] while subsequent to abstraction they are rightly called "intelligibles in act" (*ma'qûlât bi-l-fi'l*).

The intellect in potentiality becomes "an intellect in actuality" (*'aql bi-l-fi'l*) when the abstracted forms come to be in the soul. At that moment, intelligibles in potency or forms in matters in the world become intelligibles in actuality realized in the soul. Here al-Fârâbî emphasizes the ontological difference between the intelligibles in potency existing in the things of the world and the intelligibles in act which come to exist in the soul by stating that categories such as place which apply to things of the world do not apply with the same meaning when used of intelligibles in act:

> [T]he meanings of these categories or many of them must be understood in some other senses, different from those senses, for example, place when it is considered in regard to the intelligible in actuality. For if you consider the meaning of place in regard to it, either you will not find in it any of the meanings of place at all, or, if you should apply the term "place" it must be understood by you in regard to it in a different meaning, and this meaning according to a different sense.[17]

This illustrates for al-Fârâbî that what come to be in the soul's intellect in actuality are forms or intelligibles which at once have an intentional or formal identity with their source in enmattered intelligibles and at the same time have an ontological reality or status quite different from those enmattered forms.

> When they become intelligibles in actuality, then their existence (*wujûdu-hâ*), insofar as they are intelligibles in actuality, is not the same as their existence insofar as they are forms in matters (*ṣuwar fî mawâdda*). And their existence in themselves is not the same as their existence insofar as they are intelligibles in actuality.[18]

This emphasis on the ontological status of intelligibles is important for al-Fârâbî since it focuses on the subject in which the intelligibles exist. When the individual attains the intelligibles in act, this level is that of the intellect in actuality. If that individual goes on to acquire intelligible after intelligible, so that eventually the individual has come to have all the intelligibles abstracted from the world,[19] the individual's intellect becomes something of a different ontological status, namely, the acquired intellect (*al-'aql al-mustafâḍ*). As al-Fârâbî puts it,

> And when it has come to be (*ḥaṣala*) an intellect in actuality (*'aqlan bi-l-fi'l*) in relation to all intelligibles and it has become one of the existing things (*ṣâra aḥada al-maujûdât*)[20] because it became the intelligibles in actuality (*al-ma'qûlât bi-l-fi'l*), then, when it thinks that existent thing

> which is an intellect in actuality, it does not think an existing thing outside of itself but rather it only thinks itself.[21]

That is, the apprehension of intelligibles in actuality on the part of the soul by abstraction led to the origination of a new existence in the soul, namely the existence of the intellect in actuality as the realization of a power of the soul.[22] Subsequent to this, when it has its own self as subject for all the intelligibles, it no longer needs to look to the world and to perform abstraction of forms existing in things where those forms are in matter as intelligibles in potency. Further, when it has all the intelligibles in itself as subject, thinking no longer requires an external object. At this point, the human knower is substantially transformed in nature from the existence of a transitory and perishable entity into an entity with an immaterial activity of its own with the intelligibles in itself as its objects.[23] This new entity is the acquired intellect (*al-'aql al-mustafâḍ*).

> [I]t thinks (*'aqalat*) in actuality, insofar as its existence in itself is an intellect in actuality and an intelligible in actuality, which is different from the way in which these things in themselves are thought at first. For they were first thought according as they were abstracted (*intaza'at*) from their matters in which their existence is and according as they are intelligibles in potentiality (*ma'qûlât bi-l-fi'l*). They are thought a second time in such a way that their existence is not that previous existence, but their existence is separate from their matters, according as they are forms which are not in their matters and according as they are intelligibles in actuality. *For when the intellect in actuality thinks the intelligibles which are forms belonging to it* (*ṣuwar la-hu*) *insofar as they are intelligible in actuality, then the intellect which, as we first said, is the intellect in actuality, becomes now the acquired intellect* (*al-an al-'aql al-mustafâḍ*).[24]

This status of being the acquired intellect is the realization of a substantial existence of a different sort, not merely the exercise or actualization of a power of the soul existing in the body. This new existence is that of an immaterial substance now existing as an eternal entity. As such it comes to exist nearer to the level of the ever eternal and fully actual Agent Intellect which contains all intelligibles in act.[25]

Thus far in al-Fârâbî's account in the *Treatise on the Intellect*, little mention has been made of the role of the Agent Intellect in the process of abstraction. As noted earlier, al-Fârâbî in this work holds that the Agent Intellect provides forms to things of the sublunar realm. Does it likewise provide intelligibles to the human intellect?[26] No, rather than being what provides the intelligibles themselves directly to the human intellect—something which would render abstraction based on experience of forms in the world superfluous—the Agent Intellect in this work by al-Fârâbî is conceived as providing to the human soul the intellectual power by way of a communicated principle to carry out abstraction. He writes,

> The Agent Intellect which Aristotle mentioned in the third treatise of the *De Anima* is a separate form which never existed in matter nor ever

> will exist in it, and it is in a certain manner an intellect in actuality close in likeness to the acquired intellect. The Agent Intellect is that principle which makes (*ja'ala*) that essence which was an intellect in potentiality into an intellect in actuality and which makes (*ja'ala*) the intelligibles which are intelligibles in potentiality into intelligibles in actuality.[27]

This is reiterated by al-Fârâbî in the course of an analogical explanation of abstraction by way of the images of the sun and light in which the light produced by the sun is a cooperating cause providing actuality of transparency thereby providing a necessary condition for sight and the actuality of colors to be perceived. Drawing the analogy, al-Fârâbî writes that the Agent Intellect provides the principle for abstraction or intentional transference[28] to the soul.

> And in a similar manner there comes to be (*taḥṣulu*) in that essence (*adh-dhât*) which is an intellect in potentiality something whose relation to it is as the relation of transparency in actuality to sight. But the Agent Intellect provides it (*yu'tî-hi*) this thing so by it it becomes a principle for which the intelligibles which were in potentiality become intelligibles in actuality for [the intellect]. Just as the sun is that which makes the eye to be sight in actuality and visible things to be visible in actuality, insofar as it provides it illumination, so likewise the Agent Intellect is that which makes (*ja'ala*) the intellect which is in potentiality into an intellect in actuality insofar as it provides it that principle, and through this very same thing the intelligibles become intelligibles in actuality.[29]

In al-Fârâbî, then, the Agent Intellect supplies to the human intellect the principle by which there takes place a genuine abstraction of forms coming from the world where they exist as the forms of things external to the soul. Further, in this work the intelligibles in the Agent Intellect do not emanate upon the receptive human potential intellect. Rather, a genuine abstraction brings about intelligibles in act in the individual human intellect as subject which is then termed intellect in actuality and, when all intelligibles have been apprehended, there comes to be the self-sufficient and eternal acquired intellect. That abstraction comes about when the Agent Intellect provides a necessary condition so that those intelligibles come to be in the potential intellect transforming it into the intellect in actuality. And it does this by giving to the human intellect the principle of intellectual transference by which abstraction takes place, a principle described as being like light.

This understanding of al-Fârâbî's teaching on abstraction in the *Treatise on the Intellect* can be confirmed by consideration of his views set out in *The Perfect State*. In this work he describes the 'making' of the intellect in potentiality into an intellect in actuality in different and more illuminating language repeatedly using the verb *naqala*, "to transfer."

> Neither in the rational power nor in what nature provides (*a'ṭî*) is there something sufficient to become by itself an intellect in actuality. Rather,

> to become an intellect in actuality it needs something else *to transfer it* (*yanqulu-hâ*) from potentiality to actuality. However, it becomes an intellect in actuality when the intelligibles arise in it. The intelligibles which are in potentiality become intelligibles in actuality when they come to be understood by the intellect in actuality. But they need something else *to transfer* them from potentiality to make them come to be in actuality. The agent which *transfers* them from potentiality to actuality is a certain essence the substance of which is a certain intellect in actuality and separate from matter. For this intellect provides (*yu'ṭî*) something like light to the material intellect which is in potentiality an intellect. . . .[30]

After recounting the image of the sun, he explains,

> When there comes to be (*ḥaṣala*) in the rational power from the Agent Intellect that thing the relation of which to it is like the light for sight, intelligibles in the rational power then come to be (*ḥaṣalat*) from the sensibles which are preserved in the imaginative power (*al-quwa al-mutakhayila*).[31]

The activity of imagination with its special mimetic or representative powers is central to the account of abstraction for al-Fârâbî though he does not discuss it in his *Treatise on the Intellect*. This is perhaps simply because his chief focus in this work is on the power of intellect and not lower powers which aid intellect. However, in *The Perfect State* the imaginative power appears repeatedly to contribute to the explanation of the preintellectual formation of images for abstraction and to explain the use of known intelligibles in the realm of worldly sensible things.[32] As a faculty of the soul, it functions as a power for retaining "the imprints of the sensibles in the soul when these sensibles are no longer perceived."[33] Said to be located in the heart, it stands in judgment of sensibles and "separates them from each other and connects them with each other in various ways"[34] and functions as being "matter for the faculty of reason."[35] As "a disposition and a form in the body"[36] intermediate between the powers of sense and reason, it apparently plays a preparatory role for the abstraction which can only properly belong to intellect insofar as it will turn "to those imprints of sensibles which are preserved in it and have remained, and will act upon them by associating and dis-associating them with one."[37] In its imitative function depicting the higher at a lower level, it imitates intelligibles on the level of sensibles or other lower levels since "it receives from the agent in the way in which it is able to receive this in accord with its substance and disposition (*isti'dâdi-hâ*)."[38] The power of the Agent Intellect, however, is required for abstraction which is much more than the association of ideas.

These texts are central to the explication of al-Fârâbî on abstraction since they indicate that the Agent Intellect provides for human understanding not in its giving intelligible content by way of some sort of emanation but in its providing the soul with an intellectual power to transfer an intelligible in potency in the soul derived from experience of the world to the level of intelligible in actuality in the intellect. The formal content of knowledge, then, will be constituted from the potentially intelligible form existing in the thing experienced.

In the account of the *Treatise on the Intellect*, then, the cooperating causality of the Agent Intellect is required for the abstraction of the formal content intelligible in potentiality in the things of the world experienced by human beings. The power of intellectuality sufficient to form intelligibles in the soul is not present in human beings per se but rather must be provided to the soul from an external source, the Agent Intellect, which acts in a way analogous to light as understood in Aristotelian natural philosophy.[39] By this power it is possible for human beings to attain ultimate happiness, writes al-Fârâbî, for that is constituted in intellectual understanding at the level of the immaterial acquired intellect.

> But one must not understand by our saying 'in potentiality' here that the Agent Intellect is in potentiality in such a way that it receives these forms, so that they come to be in it insofar as they are received; but we intend that it has a potentiality for producing them (*yaj'alu-hâ*) in matter as forms and this is the potentiality insofar as it acts in something else and it is that which produces forms in the matters. Afterwards, it undertakes to bring them [the forms in matter] closer to that which is immaterial little by little until there comes to be the acquired intellect and with that the substance of man or man, insofar as he becomes a substance through it (*yatajauhiru bi-hi*), becomes something closer to the Agent Intellect. This is the ultimate happiness and the afterlife, namely that there comes to man some other thing through which he becomes a substance. And there comes to him his final perfection, namely that there acts some other thing through which he becomes a substance with some other action through which he becomes a substance, and this is the meaning of the afterlife.[40]

On this account it is possible for a plurality of individual human beings to attain to the level of acquired intellect such that each of them would contain its own set of intelligibles in actuality acquired from experience, intelligibles in actuality the veridical nature of which may be guaranteed by the abstractive power of the Agent Intellect[41] which is also cause of the natural forms of things, that is, of the intelligibles in potentiality.[42] And it is this Agent Intellect which contains within itself the primary set of intelligibles in actuality, not abstracted from experience, but rather eternally present and eternally in actuality while also originative of the forms of the world. In this way the Agent Intellect appears to ground the ultimate unity of intelligible discourse and science and perhaps to regulate the transference of intelligibles in potency into the individual intellect as intelligibles in act so that the intelligibles in all human intellects are in accord with the true intelligibles in the Agent Intellect itself.

II

In his *Long Commentary on the De Anima*, Averroes attacked al-Fârâbî's conception of the Agent Intellect as an extrinsic cause efficient of human intellectual abstraction on the grounds that on al-Fârâbî's account the activity of intellectual understanding cannot properly belong to human beings. Instead, Averroes insisted that the Agent Intellect must be understood as both efficient cause of abstraction and also as intrinsic formal cause acting within each human being. As I have explained elsewhere, Averroes held in all three of his *Commentaries* on the *De Anima* that the Agent Intellect must be understood as "form for us."[43] This is clearly stated repeatedly in the *Long Commentary on the De Anima of Aristotle*.

> For, because that in virtue of which something carries out its proper activity is the form, while we carry out our proper activity in virtue of the agent intellect, it is necessary that the agent intellect be form in us. . . . [I]t is necessary that a human being understand all the intelligibles through the intellect proper to him and that he carry out the activity proper to him in regard to all beings, just as he understands by his proper intellection all the beings through the intellect in a positive disposition (*intellectus in habitu*), when it has been conjoined with forms of the imagination.[44]

In his mature *Long Commentary on the De Anima*, Averroes declined to follow the emanationist accounts of the origin of the world found in al-Fârâbî and Avicenna. He also rejected Avicenna's notion that intellectual understanding required some sort of linking with or emanative reception from the separate Agent Intellect which contained all the forms of things of the sublunar world.[45] And Averroes likewise rejected the idea of a post mortem existence for the rational soul (Avicenna) or for select individuals who attained the rank of acquired intellect (al-Fârâbî). However, Averroes took from al-Fârâbî the notion of a genuine abstraction of the intelligible content of intellectual understanding from experience of the world. And, in spite of his criticism of al-Fârâbî for neglecting to have the Agent Intellect as intrinsic "form for us," Averroes followed al-Fârâbî in conceiving the Agent Intellect as the source not of intelligible content of human abstraction emanated into the human intellect, but rather as the source for the abstractive power by which intelligibles in potency are transferred from one level of existence in the human internal powers of the soul subsequent to sensation to another level of existence as intelligbles in act in the receptive power of human intellect.

> It was necessary to ascribe these two activities to the soul in us, namely, to receive the intelligible and to make it, although the agent and the recipient are eternal substances, on account of the fact that these two activities are reduced to our will, namely, to abstract intelligibles and to understand them. For to abstract is nothing other than to make imagined intentions intelligible in act after they were [intelligible] in potency. But to understand is nothing other than to receive these intentions. For when we found the same thing, namely, the imagined intentions, is *transferred in its being from one order into another*, we said that this must be from an agent cause and a recipient cause. The recipient, however, is the material [intellect] and the agent is [the intellect] which brings [this] about.[46]

III

Three notions derived directly or indirectly from al-Fârâbî and Averroes's critique of al-Fârâbî were adopted and adapted by Thomas Aquinas as key elements for his own account of intellectual understanding.

First, in accord with al-Fârâbî and Averroes, Aquinas held that the basis of intellectual cognition is first and foremost to be found in the forms of things of the world of human experience understood as intelligibles in potency received into the internal powers of the soul through sensation. All three of these thinkers held that this intellectual understanding on the part of individuals required that the forms of things of the world are apprehended intellectually by a transference of intelligible content (*ma'ânin, intentiones, rationes*) from the level of being of the sensible to the level of being of the intelligible. Aquinas writes in his *Commentary on the Sentences*,

> [W]hen the intellect understands some quiddity, it is necessary that the likeness of its *ratio* in species come to be in it, although perhaps the mode of being for each is not the same. For the form existing in intellect or in sense is not the principle of knowing according to the mode of being it has in each, but according to the *ratio* in which it shares with the exterior thing.[47]

Second, each of these thinkers held that transference of intelligibles in potency in things of the world into the intellect as intelligibles in act in the mind is to be attributed to the Agent Intellect which is the source of the principle or power employed in abstraction. For al-Fârâbî and Averroes, following the Greek and Arabic traditions, the Agent Intellect was a single separately existing entity available to all human beings in philosophical understanding.[48] However, for Aquinas the agent intellect is a power of the human soul multiplied individually in each and every human being simply. In his *Summa Theologiae*, Aquinas appeals to experience to confirm this.

> We know this by experience, when we perceive ourselves to abstract universal forms from particular conditions, which is to make intelligibles in act. However, no action belongs to some thing except through some principle formally inhering in it, as it was said earlier, when the potential intellect was treated. Therefore, it is necessary that the power which is the principle of this action be something in the soul. And for this reason Aristotle compared the agent intellect to light which is something received in air. However, Plato compared the separate intellect impressing upon our souls to the sun, as Themistius says in his commentary on *De Anima* book 3.[49]

However, for the mature Aquinas those intelligibles in act in the individual human mind are properly called intelligible species and are *rationes* and representations of the natures of things in the world.[50] For al-Fârâbî, the intelligibles in act existed (1) in each individual human actual intellect which has as its ultimate goal its highest completion and perfection as a fully intellectual and immaterial acquired intellect existing at or near the level of the Agent Intellect, and (2) in the Agent Intellect which originally emanated forms to the natural world. For Averroes the single Agent Intellect provides not the quidditative content but rather the principle or power for transference of intelligibles in potency to the separate Material Intellect where they exist as intelligibles in act as a unitary thesaurus of intelligibles for human science and discourse.[51]

Third, the notion used in the text of Aquinas cited immediately above draws on Averroes's own principle of the Agent Intellect as "form for us" and as our intrinsic formal cause. This is all the more explicit when Aquinas writes,

> [I]n any given thing acting, there must be some formal principle by which it formally acts. For something cannot formally act in virtue of what is separate in being from it. Even if what is separate is a moving principle for acting, still there must be something intrinsic by which it formally acts, whether that [principle] be a form or some sort of impression. Therefore there must be in us some formal principle by which we receive intelligibles and another by which we abstract them.[52]

As I have explained elsewhere, for Aquinas this principle is intrinsic and multiplied in accord with the number of human beings conforming with the Aristotelian requirements of it being an intrinsic form.[53] In contrast, for Averroes the argument meant that the Agent Intellect must indeed be intrinsic while also existing as a transcendent entity which is a single principle shared by each human being. The reasoning for this can be traced to Averroes's third reading of the *Paraphrase of the De Anima* by Themistius in connection with inadequacies in his doctrine of intellect in his *Middle Commentary on the De Anima*.[54]

IV Conclusion

The teachings of al-Fârâbî on intellect played a profound role in the formation of the views of Averroes and Aquinas, yet each of these thinkers had deeply differing doctrines regarding the nature and activity of abstraction and regarding the nature of the Agent Intellect and its role in this process. For al-Fârâbî, the human activity of abstraction or intentional transference was a genuine apprehending of the intelligible natures of things of the world, with the Agent Intellect not providing the intelligible content by way of emanation. It did so by being what "provides" (*yu'ṭî*) a principle like light as a power which makes (*ja'ala*) intelligibles in potentiality into intelligibles in act in the human potential intellect when it transfers them (*yanqulu-hâ*) from potentiality into actuality. It seems that for al-Fârâbî the single Agent Intellect may have additionally played the role of guaranteeing the veridical nature of abstraction and the unity of all intelligibles in individual intellects with primal forms in the Agent Intellect by this principle of transference. In this way the Agent Intellect functioned as a thesaurus of forms for the world directly and for the human intellect indirectly without emanating those forms into the human intellect.

Al-Fârâbî's Aristotelian realist doctrine of intentional transference or abstraction of forms from the world was adopted by both Averroes and Aquinas. Averroes and Aquinas both embraced the Agent Intellect as principle of transference of intelligibles making the human intellect to exist at a higher level of intellectual understanding. But Averroes insisted that the Agent Intellect must be not only efficient cause of transference but also intrinsic formal cause as "form for us" since we employ it by our will. He also moved away from al-Fârâbî by insisting that there be one shared Material Intellect as receptive of the transferred or abstracted intelligibles. Aquinas, as we have seen, agreed with the principle that the agent intellect must be "form for us" but seemingly did not understand and certainly did not accept Averroes's use of it.[55] Instead, he used it to undergird his view that each human being must have an individual power of the soul called agent intellect exercised at will and also a receptive individual material intellect. Aquinas further rejected the notion of a unity of intelligibles in act in a single transcendent intellect as the foundation for human intersubjective discourse and scientific understanding which was common to al-Fârâbî (the Agent Intellect) and Averroes (the Material Intellect). Instead, Aquinas reconceived the very nature of the intelligibles in act in his doctrine of intelligible species. Nevertheless, foundations for that doctrine as well as foundations for the teachings of Averroes are to be traced to al-Fârâbî who set forth a doctrine of abstraction or transference of the forms of things of the world to human intellect.

Marquette University

Notes

1. Aquinas refers to all these thinkers as *arabes* regularly in his *De unitate intellectus contra averroistas*. See, e.g., *De unitate intellectus, Sancti Thomae de Aquino, Opera omnia*, v. 43 (Rome 1976), 302a–b and 314a–b. Etienne Gilson recognized the importance of al-Fârâbî in his "Les sources greco-arabes de l'augustinisme avicennisant," *Archive d'histoire doctrinale et littéraire du moyen âge* 4 (1929) 5–149 and published a Latin text of the *De intellectu* (115–126). Al-Fârâbî's influence is also discussed by Alain de Libera in *La querelle des universaux. De Platon à la fin du Moyen Âge* (Paris: Editions du Seuil, 1996) 110–124. Herbert Davidson's chapter "Alfarabi on Emanation, the Active Intellect, and Human Intellect" in his *Alfarabi, Avicenna, and Averroes, on Intellect. Their Cosmologies, Theories of the Active Intellect, and Theories of Human Intellect* (Oxford: Oxford University Press, 1992), 44–73, remains the most comprehensive account of intellect in al-Fârâbî. Among recent literature the most challenging and controversial is Philippe Valat's *Farabi et l'École d'Alexandrie. Des prémisses de la connaissance à la philosophie politique* (Librairie Philosophique J. Vrin: Paris, 2004). Vallat's commissioned contribution on al-Fârâbî to the current CNRS Project in Paris, "Noétique et théorie de la connaissance dans la philosophie arabe des IXe–XVIIe siècles," directed by Meryem Sebti and Daniel de Smet, will likely be the most comprehensive account when the Project volume is published.

2. Aquinas is critical of al-Fârâbî's conception of intellect in his discussion of seeing God face-to-face in the next life in his *Commentary on the Sentences of Peter Lombard*. See *In 4 Sent*, d.49, q.2, a.1, Resp. http://www.corpusthomisticum.org/snp40492.html (Textum Parmae 1858 editum ac automato translatum a Roberto Busa SJ in taenias magneticas denuo recognovit Enrique Alarcón atque instruxit). Of course, Aquinas is famously critical of Averroes in his *De unitate intellectus*.

3. See B. Carlos Bazán, "The Human Soul: Form *and* Substance? Thomas Aquinas's Critique of Eclectic Aristotelianism," *Archives d'histoire doctrinale et littéraire du moyen âge* 64 (1997) 95–126; "Was There Ever a 'First Averroism'?" in *Geistesleben im 13. Jahrhundert*, ed. Jan A. Aertsen and Andreas Speer (Miscellanea Mediaevalia 27) (Berlin: W. de Gruyter, 2000) 31–53, ; "13th Century Commentaries on *De Anima*: From Peter of Spain to Thomas Aquinas," in *In Commento Filosofico nell'Occidente Latino (secoli XIII–XV)*, ed. Gianfranco Fioravanti, Claudio Leonardi and Stephano Perfetti (Turnhout: Brepols, 2002) 119–184; and "Radical Aristotelianism in the Faculties of Arts. The case of Siger of Brabant," in *Albertus Magnus und die Anfänge der Aristoteles-Rezeption im lateinischen Mittelalter : von Richardus Rufus bis zu Franciscus de Mayronis. Albertus Magnus and the beginnings of the medieval reception of Aristotle in the Latin West : from Richardus Rufus to Franciscus de Mayronis*, ed. Ludger Honnefelder, Rega Wood, Mechthild Dreyer and Marc-Aeilko Aris (Münster: Aschendorff Verlag, 2005) 585–629.

4. Bazán 2002, 181.

5. Bazán describes the teachings of Aquinas in his *Commentary on the De Anima of Aristotle* as "a synthesis of previous methods and the deepest effort to understand Aristotle in such a way that the principles of hylomorphism are respected (though transcended) and the requirements of the Latin vision of man and the world are satisfied." Bazán 2002, 175. As will be indicated below, the teaching of Aquinas that the content of natural human knowledge must be garnered only through abstraction working with images arising from sense perception of the world can be traced to al-Fârâbî and Averroes. The notion that Aquinas perhaps took this understanding solely from his reading of Aristotle would entail inexcusable ignorance of the historical context of the study of Aristotle's *De Anima* in the thirteenth century. Prior to availability of Averroes's translated works, Augustinian, Avicennian and Neoplatonic (via the *Liber de causis*, Boethius, and other sources) views of the human soul as a rational substance or *hoc aliquid* were dominant rather than the notion of the soul as properly *forma corporis*. The ca. 1225 Latin translation of the *Long Commentary on the De Anima of Aristotle* by Averroes—which carried within it a complete text of the Arabic *De Anima* as well as references to a second translation, quotations from Alexander of Aphrodisias, and detailed argumentative discussions of the teachings of Theophrastus, Alexander, Themistius, al-Fârâbî, Ibn Bajja/Avempace, and others, together with a critical analysis of the *De Anima*—was an indispensable tool and guide for Latins seeking to understand the difficult text of Aristotle. The Arabic of this work is not extant except for fragments. The Latin is edited in *Averrois Cordubensis Commentarium Magnum in Aristotelis De Anima Libros*, ed. F. Stuart Crawford (Cambridge: Mediaeval Academy of America, 1953).

6. At the beginning of this work al-Fârâbî explains that "The word intellect (*al-ʿaql*) is said in many ways." His treatise starts with an explanation of the ways in which the term intellect (*ʿaql*) is used in common speech, in theological contexts, and then in various works by Aristotle. The great bulk of this work is devoted to his understanding of its use by Aristotle in the *De Anima*. See note 12 below on the question of whether al-Fârâbî had read the *De Anima* directly. The text of this work was edited by Maurice Bouyges, S.J., in *Alfarabi. Risalah fi al-ʿaql*, (Beyrouth: Dar el-Machreq Sarl, 1983, 2nd edition). Hereafter, I refer to this work as *Treatise*. There is a partial English translation by Arthur Hyman in *Philosophy in the Middle Ages*, ed. Arthur Hyman and James J. Walsh (Indianapolis: Hackett Publishing Co., 1973, 2nd edition) 215–221. Here I follow this translation for the most part though with some significant modifications. For a complete French translation, see *L'épître sur l'intellect. al-Risâla fi-l-ʿaql. Abû Nasr Al-Fârâbî*, traduit de l'arabe, annoté et présenté par Dyala Hamza

(Paris: Harmattan, 2001). One of the most valuable studies devoted to the *Treatise* itself is that of Francesca Lucchetta in her *Farabi. Epistola sull' intelletto. Traduzione, introduzione e note* (Padova: Editrice Antenore, 1974), a work I discovered after presenting this paper. Much of what I write here is in full accord with Lucchetta's insightful views, though the issues and the orientation with the work of Averroes and Aquinas are not all the same.

7. al-Fârâbî, *al-Fârâbî on the Perfect State. Abû Naṣr al-Fârâbî's Mabâdi' ârâ' ahl al-madîna al-fâḍila*, ed. and trans. Richard Walzer (Oxford: Clarendon Press, 1985). Hereafter I refer to this as *The Perfect State.*

8. *Al-Fârâbî's The Political Regime (al-Siyâsa al-Madaniyya also known as the Treatise on the Principles of Beings)* ed. Fauzi M. Najjar with introduction and notes (Beirut: Imprimerie Catholicque, 1964). Hereafter I refer to this as *The Political Regime.* The teachings in *The Perfect State* and *The Political Regime* are quite similar for the most part.

9. *The Perfect State*, 56–57.

10. Davidson, *Alfarabi, Avicenna, and Averroes on Intellect*, 47.

11. In the sublunar realm matters "have been given in actuality the forms which are in the Agent Intellect." *Treatise*, 29.2; Hyman trans., 219. Translation slightly modified. And it is the celestial bodies which provide the Agent Intellect with "the matters and substrata in which it acts." *Treatise*, 34.2–3; Hyman trans., 221.

12. Note, however, that Marc Geoffroy has argued persuasively that it may well be the case that al-Fârâbî never read the text of Aristotle's *De Anima* but rather relied on works by Alexander of Aphrodisias and on the pseudo-Aristotelian *Theology of Aristotle* (based on the *Enneads* of Plotinus but significantly modified under Aristotelian influences) for his 'Aristotelian' understanding. See Marc Geoffroy, "La tradition arabe du *Peri nou* d'Alexandre d'Aphrodise et les origines de la théorie farabienne des quatre degrés de l'intellect," in *Aristotele e Alessandro di Afrodisia nella Tradizione Araba*, ed. Cristina D'Ancona and Giuseppe Serra 191–231. (Subsidia Mediaevalia Patavina 3). Padova: Il Poligrafo casa edirice s.r.l., 2002. Also see Vallat (2004) and Alaine de Libera, *La querelle des universaux*, (Paris: Seuil, 1996), who provide valuable discussions of Neoplatonic thought underlying the teachings of al-Fârâbî. Detailed consideration of these issues is beyond the scope of this paper. Regarding the *Theology of Aristotle* and the *Plotiniana Arabica*, see Peter Adamson, *The Arabic Plotinus: a Philosophical Study of the 'Theology of Aristotle'* (London: Duckworth, 2002).

13. Al-Fârâbî chooses to be imprecise and describes it as "a certain soul, or part of a soul, or one of the powers of the soul" and then explains it in terms of its function. *Treatise*, 12.6–7; Hyman trans., 215.

14. *Treatise,* 12.7–9; Hyman trans., 215.

15. Ibid., 13.3–4; Hyman trans., 215.

16. Ibid., 16.5; Hyman trans., 216.

17. Ibid., 17.7–8; Hyman trans., 216.

18. Ibid., 16.6–8; Hyman trans. 216. Translation slightly modified.

19. Cf. Aristotle, De Anima 429b6–10.

20. Regarding this phraseology, cf. Aristotle, *De Anima* 429a24. The sense is that a new existence and substance comes about now.

21. *Treatise*, 18.9–19.1; Hyman trans., 216. Translation slightly modified.

22. While the intellectual understanding of intelligibles in actuality must involve an immaterial reception in the material intellect of the individual knower, al-Fârâbî does not provide an account of the nature of this intellect and its reception sufficient to indicate whether it is anything more than an immaterial yet perishable power belonging to a perishable human soul in accord with the teachings of Alexander of Aphrodisias. Regarding Alexander's views and the available Arabic translations of his works, see Davidson (1992) 30–41.

23. As will be seen below, al-Fârâbî describes this ontological change with an Arabic verb meaning "to become a substance," *yatajauhiru*. This is both the perfection and completion of human nature and at the same time the "substantification," a making into a substance, of a generable and perishable entity which comes to be eternal in nature. Here al-Fârâbî perhaps has in mind the Platonic or Neoplatonic understanding that transitory sublunar entities are not properly denominated *ousiai* or substances, a term properly reserved for imperishable and eternal transcendent entities. In this sense a human being as an Aristotelian hylomorphic *ousia* or substance could be said to attain its fulfillment and ultimate happiness only when its intellect becomes a transcendent and immaterial (Platonic or Neoplatonic) *ousia* or substance in its own right. As al-Fârâbî remarks later in the *Treatise*, this latter existence is "the ultimate happiness and the afterlife." *Treatise*, 31.6; Hyman trans., 220.

24. *Treatise*, 19.6–20.3; Hyman trans., 217. Emphasis added; translation modified.

25. Ibid., 31.5; Hyman trans., 220. Averroes critically remarks that this entails that "something generated receives something eternal and is made like it, and in this way what is generated will become eternal, which is impossible." *Averrois Cordubensis Commentarium Magnum in Aristotelis De Anima Libros*, 485.

26. See note 30 on four sorts of emanation in al-Fârâbî.

27. *Treatise*, 24.6–25.3; Hyman trans., 218. Translation slightly modified. In *The Political Regime* al-Fârâbî writes that the Agent Intellect "makes (*yajʿalu*) the things which are not in their essences intelligible to be intelligible." It raises (*yarfaʿu-hâ*) things which are not per se intelligibles to a rank of existence higher than they possessed naturally so that they are intelligibles for the human intellect in act. In this way the Agent Intellect causes them to become intelligibles in act for the human rational power, assisting it to reach the rank of the Agent Intellect which is the end of human beings in their perfection and happiness. *The Political Regime*, 34–35.

28. On this, see Richard C. Taylor and Max Herrera, "Aquinas's Naturalized Epistemology," *Proceedings of the American Catholic Philosophical Association* 79 (2005) 83–102.

29. *Treatise*, 26.9–27.7; Hyman trans., 218. Translation modified. The image of the sun is used in both *The Political Regime* and *The Perfect State*. In the former he writes that "the Agent Intellect emanates (*yufîdu*) upon human beings a thing which it impresses in its rational power which is such that the relation of this thing to the rational soul is like the relation of light to sight. For by means of this thing, the rational soul has understanding of the Agent Intellect and by it the things which are intelligible in potency become intelligible in act." *The Political Regime*, 35–36. Note that here the Agent Intellect provides something to the rational soul by emanation which is not the intelligibles in the Agent Intellect itself but rather a power or means by which the human soul is able to abstract intelligibles in potency and thereby to have in itself intelligibles in act.

30. *The Perfect State*, 198–200. Translation substantially modified. Emphasis added. In *The Political Regime*, al-Fârâbî writes that, "In regard to what the Agent Intellect provides (*yuʿṭî-hi*) to human beings there is similarity with what is the case for the heavenly bodies.

For it provides (*yuʿṭî*) to human beings first a power and a principle by which it achieves or by which human beings are able by means of their souls to achieve the rest of what remains of perfection for them. This principle is the first sciences and first intelligibles which come about in the rational part of the soul. For [the Agent Intellect] provides it these notions and intelligibles after it came to be present in human beings and made to come about in them first the sensing part of the soul and the desiderative part by which the two natures of desire and aversion belong to the soul" (*The Political Regime*, 71–72). On 73 of the same work he explains that the Agent Intellect provides the principles and primary notions which the human rational power employs in the intellectual understanding which is itself happiness. These are called "first intelligibles which are common to all human beings" in *The Perfect State*, 202–3. At 204–207, he writes, "The presence of the first intelligibles in man is his first perfection, but these intelligibles are supplied to him only in order to be used by him to reach his ultimate perfection, i.e. felicity. Felicity means that the human soul reaches a degree of perfection in existence where it is in no need of matter for its support, since it becomes one of the incorporeal things and one of the immaterial substances and remains in that state continuously for ever." Translation slightly modified. As I understand al-Fârâbî, there are at least four sorts of emanations from the Agent Intellect. The first is that of the forms of natural things in the world. The second is that of the power of abstraction or intentional transference into the human rational power. The third is that discussed in these passages from the latter part of *The Political Regime*, namely, the common principles of human thought, such as the notion that the whole is greater than the part, and the like. The fourth is a special emanation of intelligibles upon the intellect of the prophet or religious ruler, something quite different from the second sort of emanation which provides a principle of abstraction for natural knowing. Regarding this fourth sort of emanation, see *The Perfect State*, 220–225 , and 245 ff. Phillip Vallat discusses the historical development of these 'common notions' through the Greek tradition and in al-Fârâbî in his *Farabi et l'École d'Alexandrie*, 207–238. His discussion focuses for the most part on the third type of emanation seemingly to the extent that the power for abstraction or intentional transference, the second sort of emanation, is argued to be reduced to what I call the third type. See *Farabi et l'École d'Alexandrie*, 226 ff. However, it is difficult to understand how these principles and common notions are themselves alone sufficient to enable human beings to transfer particular intentions intelligible in potency in the soul's internal powers to the level of immaterial intelligibles in act in the material intellect when human beings have intellectual understanding. Thérèse-Anne Druart has studied the issue of first intelligibles in "Al-Fârâbî, Ethics and First Intelligibles," *Documenti e Studi sulla tradizione filosofica medievale*, 8 (1997), 403–423; and the issue of emanation in al-Fârâbî in two articles: "Al-Fârâbî and Emanationism," in Studies in Medieval Philosophy, ed. John Wippel (Washington, D.C.: The Catholic University of America Press, 1987) 23–43; and "Al-Fârâbî, Emanation, and Metaphysics," in *Neoplatonism and Islamic Thought*, ed. Parviz Morewedge, (Albany: SUNY Press, 1992) 127–148. More detailed discussion of emanation in al-Fârâbî is beyond the parameters of this paper.

31. *The Perfect State*, 202. My translation. On the important role of the imaginative power in thinkers of the Arabic tradition, see Deborah L. Black, *Logic and Aristotle's Rhetoric and Poetics in Medieval Arabic Philosophy* (Leiden: Brill, 1990). Also see her, "Imagination and Estimation: Arabic Pradigms and Western Transformations," *Topoi* 10 (2000) 59–75.

32. Regarding the latter, see *The Perfect State*, 172–173.

33. Ibid., 164–165.

34. Ibid.

35. Ibid., 174–175.

36. Ibid., 212–213.

37. Ibid., 210–211. Translation slightly modified.

38. Ibid., 214–215. The imaginative faculty plays an important role in prophecy and is discussed in *The Perfect State* in the pages which follow.

39. Cf. Alexander of Aphrodisias, *De Anima Liber Cum Mantissa*, ed. Ivo Bruns (Berlin: Typis et Impensis Georgii Reimer, 1887). [Commentaria in Aristotelem Graeca, Suppl. II, pt. 90.23–91.4], where intellect is said to be from outside and not part of the soul per se. Also see the article by Geoffroy cited above at note 12.

40. Treatise, 30.9–31.9; Hyman trans., 220. Translation slightly modified. In *The Political Regime* the Agent Intellect is described as charged with providential concern over the rational animal to make "it reach the highest of the ranks of the perfection which man can attain, which is ultimate happiness. This comes to pass when man comes at the rank of the Agent Intellect." In this way the Agent Intellect is "said to be the Guardian Spirit and the Holy Spirit" (*The Political Regime*, 32).

41. Precisely the question of whether abstraction is done by the human soul with a power granted to it or by the Agent Intellect's own power present in the human soul is an issue on which Averroes criticizes al-Fârâbî. The mature Averroes in his *Long Commentary on the De Anima of Aristotle* rejects the notion of there being multiple human material intellects (which he accepted in his *Short* and *Middle Commentaries* on the *De Anima*) each with its own set of intelligibles in act, in favor of there being a single shared Material Intellect containing the unique set of abstracted human intelligibles in act. On this see, Richard C. Taylor, "Intelligibles in act in Averroes," in *Averroès et les averroïsmes juif et latin. Actes du colloque tenu à Paris, 16–18 juin 2005*, ed. J. -B. Brenet (Turnhout: Brepols, 2007) 16–18. Also see the discussion below in section II. My thanks to Therese-Anne Druart for her comment on the ambiguity of this notion. In her valuable comments at the oral presentation of this paper, Deborah Black stressed that the reception of intelligibles in act is described as taking place in the human material intellect when the intellectual "light" of the Agent Intellect has transferred or abstracted the particular intentions from experience of the world. There appears to be no need for an additional activity of impressing intelligibles in act upon the material intellect since the nature of the material intellect is such as to receive intelligibles in act as soon as they are available as such to it.

42. For Themistius, whose *Paraphase of the De Anima of Aristotle* was available in Arabic translation, individual human actual intellects are responsible for abstraction from human experience but they are guided in that activity by the "light" of the Productive/Agent Intellect which precontains all the forms. In this way there is intersubjective understanding and science: "For we would not understand one another unless there were a single intellect that we all shared." Themistius, *In Libros Aristotelis De Anima Paraphrasis*, ed. R. Heinze, (Berlin: G. Reimeri, 1899), [Commentaria in Aristotelem Graeca, 5.3], 104; *Themistius, On Aristotle's On the Soul*, trans. Robert B.Todd, (Ithaca, NY: Cornell University Press, 1996), 129. The corresponding Arabic has "For it is right that, if we do not have one intellect in which we all share, then we also do not have understanding of one another." *An Arabic Translation of Themistius' Commentary on Aristotle's De Anima*, ed. Lyons, 189. Themistius indicates the presence of all forms in the Productive/Agent Intellect when he asks, "From what source will the potential intellect also come to think all objects, if the intellect that advances it to activity does not think all objects prior to it?" *In Libros Aristotelis De Anima Paraphrasis*, 103; Todd

trans., 128. The corresponding Arabic has, "Whence does the intellect which is in potency come to understand all the things if what leads it to act is not first understanding all the things?" Lyons ed., 188.

43. For a discussion of the Agent Intellect acting in the soul in the process of abstraction according to Averroes, see Richard C. Taylor, "The Agent Intellect as 'form for us' and Averroes's Critique of al-Fârâbî," *Topicos* (Universidad Panamericana, Mexico City) 29 (2005) 29–51. Reprint in *Proceedings of the Society for Medieval Logic and Metaphysics* 5 (2005)18–32 http://www.fordham.edu/gsas/phil/klima/SMLM/PSMLM5/PSMLM5.pdf.

44. *Averrois Cordubensis Commentarium Magnum in Aristotelis De Anima Libros*, 499–500.

45. This is a common view of Avicenna's thought found in Herbert Davidson's *Alfarabi, Avicenna, and Averroes, on Intellect* and in the work of a number of other modern scholars. Recently Davidson's view has been challenged. See Dimitri Gutas, "Intuition and Thinking: The Evolving Structure of Avicenna's Epistemology," in *Aspects of Avicenna*, ed. Robert Wisnovsky (Princeton: Markus Wiener Publishers, 2001) (reprinted from *Princeton Papers: Interdisciplinary Journal of Middle Eastern Studies*, Vol. IX) 1–38; and Dag Nikolaus Hasse, "Avicenna on Abstraction," ibid., 39–72. For an account which seeks to reconcile the differences between these views through careful reconsideration of relevant texts in Avicenna, see Jon McGinnis, "Making Abstraction Less Abstract: The Logical, Psychological and Metaphysical Dimensions of Avicenna's Theory of Abstraction," in the present volume of *Proceedings*.

46. *Et fuit necesse attribuere has duas actiones anime in nobis, scilicet recipere intellectum et facere eum, quamvis agens et recipiens sint substantie eterne, propter hoc quia hee due actions reducte sunt ad nostram voluntatem, scilicet abstrahere intellecta et intelligere ea. Abstrahere enim nichil est aliud quam facere intentiones ymaginatas intellectas in actu postquam erant in potentia; intelligere autem nichil aliud est quam recipere has intentiones. Cum enim invenimus idem* transferri in suo esse de ordine in ordinem, *scilicet intentiones ymaginatas, diximus quod necesse est ut hoc sit a causa agenti et recipienti. Recipiens igitur est materialis, et agens est efficiens. Averrois Cordubensis Commentarium Magnum in Aristotelis De Anima Libros*, 439. Emphasis added.

47. "*. . . et similiter ad hoc quod intellectus intelligat aliquam quidditatem, oportet quod in eo fiat similitudo ejusdem rationis secundum speciem, quamvis forte non sit idem modus essendi utrobique. Non enim forma existens in intellectu vel sensu, est principium cognitionis secundum modum essendi quem habet utrobique, sed secundum rationem in qua communicat cum re exteriori.*" *In 4 Sent*, d.49, q.2, a.1, Resp. http://www.corpusthomisticum.org/snp40492 .html (Textum Parmae 1858 editum ac automato translatum a Roberto Busa SJ in taenias magneticas denuo recognovit Enrique Alarcón atque instruxit). Aquinas surely has in mind the text of Averroes cited in note 46 above.

48. Note that the level of the acquired intellect which constitutes human perfection, the end of human beings and the very meaning of the afterlife, is something achieved only by a small number for al-Fârâbî. Much the same is said by Averroes in his *Epistle 1 On Conjunction*. See *Averroès. La Béatitude de l'Âme. Éditions, traductions et études*, ed. and trans. Marc Geoffroy and Carlos Steel (Paris: Librairie Philosophique J. Vrin, 2001) 218.

49. *Et hoc experimento cognoscimus, dum percipimus nos abstrahere formas universales a conditionibus particularibus, quod est facere actu intelligibilia. Nulla autem actio convenit alicui rei, nisi per aliquod principium formaliter ei inhaerens; ut supra dictum est, cum de intellectu possibili ageretur. Ergo oportet virtutem quae est principium huius actionis, esse aliquid in anima. Et ideo Aristoteles comparavit intellectum agentem lumini, quod est aliquid receptum in aere.*

Plato autem intellectum separatum imprimentem in animas nostras, comparavit soli; ut Themistius dicit in commentario tertii de anima. Summa theologiae, Prima Pars, 1, 79, 4 resp.

50. *[L]icet species intelligibilis qua intellectus formaliter intelligit sit in intellectu possibili istius uel illius hominis, ex quo intellectus possibiles sunt plures, id tamen quod intelligitur per huiusmodi species est unum, si consideremus habito respectu ad rem intellectam, quia uniuersale quod intelligitur ab utroque est idem in omnibus. Et quod per species multiplicatas in diuersis id quod est unum in omnibus possit intelligi, contingit ex immaterialitate specierum, que representant rem absque materialibus conditionibus indiuiduantibus, ex quibus una natura secundum speciem multiplicatur numero in diuersis.* Thomas Aquinas, *Quaestiones disputatae De anima*, Q.5, A.3, ad 7.

51. Regarding the Material Intellect, see Richard C. Taylor, "Separate Material Intellect in Averroes's Mature Philosophy," in *Words, Texts and Concepts Cruising the Mediterranean Sea. Studies on the sources, contents and influences of Islamic civilization and Arabic philosophy and science, dedicated to Gerhard Endress on his sixty-fifth birthday*, ed. Ruediger Arnzen and Joern Thielmann [Orientalia Lovaniensia Analecta series] (Leuven: Peeters, 2004) 289–309. Regarding the Agent Intellect, see my article cited in note 43 above.

52. *Oportet autem in unoquoque operante esse aliquod formale principium quo formaliter operetur. Non enim potest aliquid formaliter operari per id quod est secundum esse separatum ab ipso, set etsi id quod est separatum sit principium motiuum ad operandum, nichilominus oportet esse aliquod intrinsecum quo formaliter operetur, siue illud sit forma siue qualiscumque impressio. Oportet igitur esse in nobis aliquod principium formale quo recipiamus intelligibilia et aliud quo abstrahamus ea.* Aquinas, *Quaestiones Disputatae De Anima* q. 5, resp. *Thomas Aquinas, Quaestiones de anima in Opera Omnia*, v. 24.1. ed. B. -C. Bazán (Roma: Commissio Leonina; Les Éditions du Cerf, 1996). At *Summa Contra Gentiles*, Book II, chap. 76 n. 18 he writes, "nothing carries out an activity except through some power which is formally in itself. . . . Therefore, it is necessary that the principles in virtue of which these actions are attributed [to human beings], namely the possible intellect and the agent intellect, be certain powers existing formally in us." *Nihil operatur nisi per aliquam virtutem quae formaliter in ipso est: unde Aristoteles, in II de anima, ostendit quod quo vivimus et sentimus, est forma et actus. Sed utraque actio, scilicet intellectus possibilis et intellectus agentis, convenit homini: homo enim abstrahit a phantasmatibus, et recipit mente intelligibilia in actu; non enim aliter in notitiam harum actionum venissemus nisi eas in nobis experiremur. Oportet igitur quod principia quibus attribuuntur hae actiones, scilicet intellectus possibilis et agens, sint virtutes quaedam in nobis formaliter existentes. Corpus Thomisticum, Sancti Thomae de Aquino, Summa contra Gentiles, Textum Leoninum emendatum ex plagulis de prelo Taurini 1961 editum ac automato translatum a Roberto Busa SJ in taenias magneticas denuo recognovit Enrique Alarcon atque instruxit.*

53. See my forthcoming article cited in note 41 above

54. This is a complex doctrine which I will explicate at length elsewhere. On the importance of the *Paraphrase of the De Anima* by Themistius for the development of this principle in Averroes, see my forthcoming article "Intelligibles in act in Averroes" cited in note 41. For the *Middle Commentary*, see *Averroes. Middle Commentary on Aristotle's De Anima. A Critical Edition of the Arabic Text with English Translation, Notes and Introduction*, by Alfred L. Ivry. (Provo, Utah: Brigham Young University Press, 2002).

55. However, Aquinas does seem to understand it when he cites al-Fârâbî, Avicenna and Averroes in discussing knowledge of separate substances and the promised afterlife reward of seeing God face-to-face in his *Commentary on the Sentences*. See *In 4 Sent*, d.49, q.2, a.1, Resp. Cf. note 47 above.

Making Abstraction Less Abstract: The Logical, Psychological, and Metaphysical Dimensions of Avicenna's Theory of Abstraction

Jon McGinnis

Abstract: A debated topic in Avicennan psychology is whether for Avicenna abstraction is a metaphor for emanation or to be taken literally. This issue stems from the deeper philosophical question of whether humans acquire intelligibles *externally* from an emanation by the Active Intellect, which is a separate substance, or *internally* from an inherently human cognitive process, which prepares us for an emanation from the Active Intellect. I argue that the tension between these doctrines is only apparent. In his logical works Avicenna limns an account where through the internal human process of abstraction accidents accruing to an essence existing in matter are extracted, thus preparing the essence for new accidents emanating externally from the Active Intellect, which make the essence something conceptualized in the intellect. This study, then, outlines the epistemological and metaphysical framework presented in the logical works that underpins Avicenna's theory of abstraction presented in his psychological works.

In his 2001 article "Avicenna on Abstraction" Dag Hasse submits Avicenna's doctrine of *tajrīd*, abstraction, to close scrutiny. He focuses on a cluster of concepts that appear in Avicenna's earliest treatment of abstraction and then follows their evolution throughout Avicenna's corpus. In opposition to a well-received view that makes Avicenna's notion of abstraction a metaphor for an emanation from the Active Intellect, and thus an operation that is external to the human soul, Hasse concludes that for Avicenna abstraction refers to an internal cognitive operation proper to the human soul itself. Hasse's approach is self-avowedly a 'developmental approach,' which he glosses as "an explanation that does not consider [Avicenna's] philosophy a system but follows the formation of the theory from the writings of his youth to that of his age."[1]

Although I think that Hasse's conclusions concerning Avicenna's theory of abstraction are on the whole correct, the approach by which he arrives at those conclusions, I believe, is potentially dangerous; for, in the words of Wordsworth, "we murder to dissect." *Pace* Hasse, Avicenna himself thought he had a philosophical system and yet Hasse's account leaves unclear how abstraction fits into that system and more specifically what role, if any, the Active Intellect plays in Avicenna's noetic. Moreover, if Hasse is correct in that abstraction refers to an operation internal to the human soul and not to the activity of a separate Intellect (and again I believe that he is correct), then certain serious philosophical puzzles arise. Richard Taylor, following in the footsteps of Averroes, has noted perhaps the most pressing problem, namely, "How is one to explain the inter-subjective unity of scientific discourse?"[2] The problem as I understand it is this: if abstraction were an operation internal and proper to each human intellect, then the product of such an operation, namely, the intelligible concepts, would be as numerous and diverse as the human intellects that produce them; however, when there is scientific knowledge, what is known is not unique to the various intellects, but is universal and is at least potentially common to all intellects. Thus, if abstraction is an internal human operation, whose product is something *particular* to the individual performing the act of abstraction, what is it that explains the *universal* nature of scientific knowledge as it exists in different intellects?

Again, on the whole I agree with Hasse's conclusions, even if not always his approach. Thus what I want to undertake here is a *synthetic approach*: an explanation that considers how abstraction fits in with other elements in Avicenna's philosophical system, such as the Active Intellect, as well as showing how Avicenna could have responded to the charge that his theory of abstraction precludes the unity of scientific knowledge.

In order to see how Avicenna's theory of abstraction fits into his overall system, however, we must begin with a topic that initially may seem unrelated to Avicenna's psychology, namely, his doctrine of essences (*māhīyāt*).[3] For our purposes there are three important things to note about Avicenna's account of essences.[4] First, essences are significant for Avicenna's general theory of knowledge because there is a close relation between essences and conceptualization (*taṣawwur*), where conceptualization for Avicenna is one aspect of scientific knowledge (*'ilm*) and is closely linked with concept acquisition and mastery.[5] Indeed for Avicenna all knowledge begins with conceptualization, and what is conceptualized are essences.

Second, and more substantively, although for Avicenna essences exist only either in a concrete particulars or in conceptualization, he also believed that they could be considered in *three*, not just two, respects: they can be considered as they exist in concrete particulars and in conceptualization *as well as in themselves*. Avicenna has been criticized for his doctrine of the three respects on the grounds that if, as he maintained, essences exist *only* as concrete particulars or conceptualized, then there is no way left that they could exist in themselves.[6] Of course the objection only works if one assumes that when something can be considered in one way, it must be able to exist in that exact way, an assumption that just seems to be false. Consider natural or counting numbers. Any instance of such a number can only ever exist as either odd or even, but certainly natural numbers can be considered just as natural numbers independent of any features that follow upon being odd or even. In similar fashion, I maintain that for Avicenna essences in themselves *do exist*, even though they only exist *as* a concrete particular or *as* something conceptualized, just as natural numbers exist only *as* odd or *as* even, even though they can be considered in themselves.

The third point concerns how one should understand, first, the *particularized* existence of essences both in concrete particulars and in conceptualization and, second, the relation of these modes of existence to essences considered in themselves. Inasmuch as essences exist, whether in concrete particulars or in conceptualization, one or another set of accidents follows upon that given mode of existence. The accidents that follow upon being in concrete particulars are owing to the matter in which the essences occur and include such things as a determinate magnitude, position, place as well as certain qualities such as color, external appearance, ordering of the bodily parts and the like. These accidents are in effect the features that make something sensible or perceptible.[7] As for the accidents that follow upon conceptualization, Avicenna listed such things as being a logical subject and predicate, universality and particularity as well as essentiality and accidentality in predication. In effect these are the features that give our thinking a logical component and allow us to use logic in scientific inquiry.[8] For Avicenna it is the presence of one or the other set of these accidents that particularize (*yakhuṣṣu*) the essences so that they exist either as a concrete particular or as something conceptualized.

What is implicit in Avicenna's point about the essences' being particularized by these accidents is that essences in themselves are a common element in both concrete particulars and objects of conceptualization.[9] The same essences exist in both, albeit particularized by different sets of accidents. This point is suggested forcefully in the *Najāt*, where Avicenna writes about 'thingness' (*shay'īya*); for there he seems to take thingness as closely related to, if not identical with, essences considered in themselves. Thus he writes:

> There is a difference between the thingness and the existence in concrete particulars; for the account [of what something is] has an existence in concrete particulars and in the soul [i.e., as conceptualized] and is something common [to both]. That common thing, then, is the thingness.[10]

In short, on the interpretation I am suggesting concrete particulars and objects of conceptualization have one factor that is identical to both, namely, the essence considered in itself, and another factor that makes them different from one another, namely, the set of accidents that follows on whether the essence exists as material or as conceptual.

This long digression concerning essences was needed if we are to understand fully Avicenna's psychological theory of abstraction to which I now turn. The first thing to note about Avicenna's conception of abstraction is that there are different kinds of abstraction depending upon the type of perception (*idrāk*) involved, whether sensible perception, imaginative perception, intelligible perception or the like.[11] Avicenna identifies the kinds of abstraction by the degree to which the essences are extracted or removed from the material accidents.[12] Thus in sensation the sensible object is not wholly abstracted from the matter itself; for as long as one is sensibly perceiving a given material object sensible perception requires the very presence of that object, whereas once the object is removed from the sensory field, the correlative sensation ceases. Between sensation and imagination there is a higher degree of abstraction, since the imagined object is wholly abstracted from the matter itself and so can be perceived even in the absence of the material object. Still the imagined object is not abstracted from the accidents of matter, "since the form that is in the imagery faculty depends upon the sensible form and on a certain quantification, qualification and position."[13] The degree of abstraction is even greater between the imagery faculty and the estimative faculty, since the estimative faculty perceives the non-sensible aspects of material things, as for example good and evil as well as motion, space and time. The final degree of abstraction, when all associations with matter and its accidents are removed, occurs in the case of intellectual perception, upon which I shall now focus.

In *Kitāb al-Burhān*, III.5, Avicenna limned his theory of intellectual abstraction, adding quickly that the specific details would need to await his discussion in his psychological works.[14] Although we shall turn to those details shortly, the substantive outline presented in this logical work is important, since in it Avicenna drew attention to what he believed were the essential elements of his theory of intellectual abstraction. In what follows I consider the various points that Avicenna mentioned as occurring during the process of abstraction as they appear in this logical work.[15] I in turn develop those points in light of comments that he made in his psychological writings.

First, Avicenna was emphatic that knowledge—or more exactly the conceptualizing aspect of knowledge—requires sensation. That is because through sensation the imagery faculty acquires the sensible forms and, when in the imagery faculty, these forms or essences are the potential intelligibles.[16] The sensible forms presented to the imagery faculty are the likenesses of essences as those essences exist in concrete particulars or sensible objects.[17] As we have seen, however, the forms or essences in the imagery faculty, although abstracted from the very matter itself of the sensible object, have not been abstracted from the material accidents or concomitants that follow on the essences' being in the concrete particulars. It is precisely because they have not been abstracted from these material concomitants that the forms in the imagery faculty are only potentially intelligible. In order that they become actually intelligible, they must be abstracted completely or perfectly from all the material accidents.

Second, in the outline from *Kitāb al-Burhān*, Avicenna notes that it is the human's own speculative intellect (*'aql naẓarī*) that carries out this final process of abstraction whereby the essence in itself is extracted from all the material accidents or concomitants. Far from being anything mysterious, however, abstraction as it is characterized in this logical work turns out to be just like 'setting [the accidents] to one side' (*yaṭraḥuhā min jānib*) and 'isolating' (*yufridu*) what belongs to the essence itself. In other places, Avicenna likewise describes the process of abstraction in deflationary terms, such as 'focusing on' (*yata'ammalu*)[18] or 'reviewing in order to familiarize oneself with something' (*yaṭṭali'u*).[19] In short, abstraction for Avicenna simply seems to be a process of selectively attending to certain essential features of the sensible object, as that object appears in the imagery faculty, to the exclusion of other accidental features.

What is conspicuous by its absence from Avicenna's outline of the process of abstraction in the passage from *Kitāb al-Burhān* is any mention of the Active Intellect (although he would mention It later in the same chapter when discussing methods of acquiring assent (*taṣdīq*)). I do not think that the absence of the Active Intellect in Avicenna's account of abstraction in this logical work is because he has a different view here than the one he will present in his psychological works; rather, it is because the Active Intellect simply plays no role in the process of abstraction itself, although, as I shall argue, It does play a vital role in conceptualization inasmuch as It illuminates that which the human intellect has abstracted. In other words, although abstraction and the illumination from the Active Intellect are closely related, nonetheless, they are really distinct activities, each which with its own unique role in Avicenna's noetic.

In order to appreciate the close relation and yet distinct natures of Avicenna's theories of abstraction and illumination we must return to the doctrine of essences and then next consider how Avicenna understood the model upon which he based thinking, namely, seeing. I have argued that for Avicenna abstraction involves the intellect's selectively attending to certain essential features of the essence of a thing as that essence exists in the imagery faculty, in which case the essence is in a particular image belonging to a particular individual and as such is a concrete particular. In this respect the intellect sets to one side those accidental features that belong to the essence as a result of its existence in matter. Again those things that particularize the existence of an essence as a concrete particular simply are the accidents that follow upon the matter, and so once the human intellect is no longer attending to any of the accidents and concomitants that follow upon the matter what exists in the intellect cannot be considered as something existing as a concrete particular; for all the accidents that particularize its existing as a concrete particular have been removed. Consequently, since, as we have seen earlier, essences for Avicenna always and only exist either as concrete particulars or as conceptualized, what the human intellect is considering when all the material accidents have been set to one side must have an existence as something conceptualized. Moreover, as conceptualized the essence must have those intelligible accidents that particularize its existing as such, as for example universality and particularity in predication as well as essentiality and accidentality in predication. These accidents that particularize the essence as existing in conceptualization (or what Avicenna would call the 'intellectual forms' (*ṣuwar 'aqlīya*) as opposed to the material forms)[20] do not come to be *ex nihilo*; rather, they are, I maintain, what emanate from the Active Intellect when it illuminates the *abstracta* of essences in the human intellect.

In order to justify my suggestion, we must consider Avicenna's explanation of how illumination takes place. His account, which is rich, is an extended comparison between the interaction among the Active Intellect, the abstracted essences and the human intellect and the interaction among the Sun, sensible objects and the faculty of sensation.[21] What is clear from Avicenna's discussion about the Active Intellect is that he thought that the act of thinking is similar to the act of seeing. The question is whether he intended this comparison to be only a colorful metaphor, which simply sparks our imagination, or he intended this comparison more robustly, namely, that vision is the model upon which one should understand cognition. I assume he intended the model in the more robust sense, and thus getting a grip on how Avicenna understood the act of seeing will shed light on how he understood the act of thinking.

In *Kitāb an-Nafs* III.7, Avicenna defended his own preferred intromission theory of vision against certain objections.[22] What is important for our purposes about his discussion there is that he was quite explicit about what does *not* happen in the case of vision as well as summarizing what does happen. He was adamant that vision is not "*only* by extracting (*naz'*)[23] the form from the matter, that is, taking the form itself from the matter and transferring it to the sensing power."[24] In other words, vision is not simply an act of abstraction such that the visible object is stripped of its material and then impressed on the sensing faculty. In fact, he went on to say that nobody believes that. By parity of reasoning, then, thinking cannot simply be either a mere act of abstraction or the Active Intellect's impressing the abstract intelligibles into the human intellect, at least not if thinking takes place in the way that seeing does.

Instead, Avicenna insisted that vision is a type of affection (*infi'āl*). "Now we say that sight in itself receives from the object of sight a form common to the form that is in [the object of sight], not [the object of sight's] very own form . . . and so the one sensing that [form] does not lose its [own] form, but rather there is found in it only the likeness of [the object of sight's] form."[25] It is worth noting that in this description it is the sensible object—not the Sun, which has not even been mentioned at this point—that acts on the sensing faculty so that it sees. Avicenna next immediately qualified this account of vision and said that unlike such sense modalities as touch and smell, which occur by direct contact with the object of sensation, vision requires a certain minimal distance between the visual apparatus and the object of vision in order that what has the sensible form may project a ray (*shu'ā'*) that conveys a sensible image (*shabaḥ*) of itself to whatever is turned towards it (*mā yuqābiluhū*); however, in order for the object of vision to project this ray the intervening distance must be transparent, and it is the Sun that causes the transparency of the medium.

This is Avicenna's theory of vision in a nutshell. Let us now see if we can map on the various features of vision mentioned here with the various features of human cognition that appear in Avicenna's discussion of the Active Intellect. Three points of comparison are obvious: the forms or essences in the imagery faculty function like the objects of vision; the rational soul or human intellect, which will be impressed by the forms or essences, is comparable to the faculty of vision itself; and finally the Active Intellect plays the role of the Sun. Despite these obvious points of comparison, there are two other factors required for vision that have not been assigned their cognitive counterparts, namely, one, the perceiver's facing the object of vision and, two, the transparent medium. If we take Avicenna's language describing abstraction literally, that is, as a type of 'attending to' and 'reviewing,' then abstraction corresponds with the perceiver's turning towards and facing the object of vision. In fact, during Avicenna's discussion of the Active Intellect's role in cognition, he explicitly likens the perceiver's facing (*muqābil*) the visible object to the rational soul's reviewing (*ṭālaʿat*) the form in the imagery faculty, where again 'reviewing' was one of Avicenna's preferred explanations for abstraction.[26]

Thus we are left only with assigning the cognitive counterpart corresponding with the transparent medium. Again, in vision it is the light emanated from the Sun that causes the medium to be transparent, and above I claimed that it is the intelligible accidents emanated from the Active Intellect that cause the *abstracta* to be intelligible, or we might say, to be transparent to the intellect. Now at *Kitāb an-Nafs* III.1, Avicenna maintained that there is one sense in which light is the transparency of the medium.[27] Thus if light can be considered the transparency of the medium in vision, so analogously the intelligible accidents or intellectual forms that emanate from the Active Intellect into the rational soul can play the role of the transparency of the medium in cognition.

We now have all the pieces to see the parallels between vision and cognition in Avicenna's philosophical system. Through sensation the imagery faculty is supplied with a number of forms or essences of things, which exist in particular images, and so exist together with certain material accidents or concomitants. These images correspond with the colored bodies in the world, which are potentially visible. These partially material images in the imagery faculty project an intelligible 'image' or likeness of themselves that is analogous to the projected visible images of the visible objects. It is these intelligible likenesses that are impressed on and affect the rational soul such that there is thought. However, in order for these intelligible images to be efficacious the rational soul must be turned towards them, which occurs as a result of the human intellect's act of abstraction. In addition, the Active Intellect must illuminate these intelligible images, which occurs as a result of its emanating intelligible accidents so that the essences exist as something conceptualized. The parallelism between Avicenna's theories of vision and cognition turn out to be almost exact, which is what we wanted.

The above completes the psychological aspect of the role that Avicenna assigned to the Active Intellect. There is, however, another role related to the generation and corruption of material things that Avicenna assigned to the Active Intellect, but now under the guise of the 'Giver of Forms' (*wāhib aṣ-ṣuwar*). Although the relation of the Active Intellect's role in generation and corruption to his overall theory of cognition may not be immediately apparent, it is, I believe, essential to explaining how Avicenna might have accounted for the puzzle concerning the inter-subjective unity of scientific discourse.

Since our concern is with the role of the Active Intellect in cognition, we need only briefly consider its role in generation and corruption.[28] According to Avicenna every material substance has an elemental configuration suitable to the essence informing it. Moreover, elemental configurations are constantly undergoing alterations as a result of the motions of the heavenly bodies. When in a given material substance these alterations in its elemental configuration are significant enough, the matter no longer is suitable to the essence informing it, and so the matter receives a new essence that is suitable to its new elemental configuration. Again it is the motions of the heavenly bodies that are the causes for the changes in a material substance's elemental configurations; however, as such the heavenly bodies are only preparatory or auxiliary causes for the occurrence of the new essence. The cause that imparts the new essence, that is, the new form, is 'The Giver of Forms,' which Avicenna identified with the last of the separate substances or Intellects, and indeed is the Active Intellect mentioned in his psychological work. The Giver of Forms, then, causes the suitable elemental configuration to receive the new form by emanating the appropriate form into the prepared matter.

The parallelism between the Giver of Forms' emanating forms into the matter and the Active Intellect's emanating intelligible accidents into the rational soul is significant in explaining how Avicenna might account for the inter-subjective unity of scientific discourse. A general principle of Avicenna's philosophical system is that whatever is received is received according to the mode of the receiver. Now given that the Giver of Forms and the Active Intellect are one and the same it seems reasonable to assume that what it emanates are essences of things in themselves together with the intelligible accidents. Now when these emanated essences encounter suitable elemental configurations, the matter is suitably disposed to receive only the essences or forms themselves, not the intelligible accidents. The intelligible accidents, then, are not received when essences inform the matter in the generation of new substances; for the reception of the intelligible accidents occurs only in the case where the recipient is immaterial. Humans in the act of sensibly perceiving in turn receive these essences together with the accompanying material accidents and concomitants that have become associated with them through their existence in matter. It is precisely because humans do receive the essences together with the material accidents and concomitants that the process of abstraction is required. When the material accidents and concomitants are stripped away, however, the essences are then themselves prepared to re-receive the intelligible accidents that are again being emanated by the Active Intellect. Consequently, when the intelligible accidents are rejoined with the essences, the essences' existing as something conceptualized in various human intellects truly are the very likenesses of those essences existing in the Active Intellect. Thus, despite the fact that the intelligibles are in *this* human intellect or *that* human intellect, it is the very same likenesses in both. It is this fact that accounts for the inter-subjective unity of scientific discourse in Avicenna's philosophical system, or so I contend.

To conclude briefly, abstraction is not a mere metaphor for emanation from the Active Intellect, but neither is it some dangling feature in Avicenna's philosophical system. Abstraction understood as a process internal to the human intellect is a systematically, well-integrated element not only in Avicenna's psychology, but also his logic, natural philosophy and metaphysics. In fact, it is in understanding the intertwined operations of both the human speculative intellect and the Active intellect, namely, abstraction and emanation respectively, as they play out in Avicenna's philosophical system as a whole that one comes to understand their irreducibly distinct and yet affiliated roles in that system.

University of Missouri at St. Louis

Appendix: Translations of Relevant Texts

Text 1: *Introduction* (ed. al-Hudayri), I.2, 15.1–8:

Essences' Three Respects

The essences of things might be in the concrete particulars of the things or in conceptualization, and so they can be considered in three respects. [One] is the consideration of the essence inasmuch as it is that essence without being related to one of the two [ways] of existence [i.e., either in the concrete particulars or conceptualization] and whatever follows upon it insofar as it is such. [Two] it can be considered insofar as it is in concrete particulars, in which case certain accidents that particularize its existing as that follow upon it. [Three] it can be considered insofar as it is with respect to conceptualization, in which case certain accidents that particularize its existing as that follow upon it, as, for example, being a subject and predicate, and also, for example, universality and particularity in predication, as well as essentiality and accidentality in predication; for being essential and being accidental are not in things existing in the external [world] by way of predication, nor is something a logical subject (*mubtada'*) and a logical predicate (*khabar*), nor [is something] a premise and a syllogism and the like.

Text 2: *The Soul,* (ed. Rahman), II.2, 58–61:

Investigation of the Kinds of Perception That Belong to Us

[58] Let us now discuss the sensory and perceptible powers and do so comprehensively. So we say: it seems that all perceiving is only to take in the form of the perceptible in one way or another. So if the perception is of something material, it takes its form abstracted from matter in a certain way. The kinds of abstraction, however, are different and their degrees are dissimilar; for owing to the matter, the material form happens to have certain states and factors that do not belong to it essentially from the perspective of what that form is. So sometimes the extraction (*naz'*) from matter is together with either all or some of those associations, whereas at other times the extraction is perfect, that is, in that the formal aspect (*ma'ná*) is abstracted from the matter and from the concomitants that it has on account of the matter. An example of it is that the human form and essence (*māhīya*) is a nature with respect to which all the individuals of the species are without doubt equally common. In its definition it is a single thing, whereas it is accidental to it that it existed in this and that individual and so was multiple, where that [i.e., existing in this and that individual] does not belong to it on the part of its human nature. If the human nature were to have in it what requires multiplicity, then human would not be predicated of something one in number, whereas if humanity belonged to Zayd so that it is his humanity, then it would not belong to Amr. Hence one of the accidents that happens to belong to humanity owing to [59] the matter is this species of multiplicity and divisibility. Accidents other than this also belong to it, for instance, when it is in a given matter, it occurs with a certain

degree of quantity, quality, place, position and all of those things foreign to its nature. That is because if humanity were according to this or some other degree of quantity, quality, place and position so that it is humanity, then every human would necessarily be common to another in those accounts, while if it is so that humanity is according to some other degree and manner of quantity, quality, place and position, then every human would necessarily be in common with respect to it. Hence the human form essentially is not something deserving that any of these concomitants, which are accidental to it, attach to it; rather, [they] are due to the matter because the matter to which [the human form] is joined had these concomitant attached to it. So sensation takes the form from the matter together with these concomitants and together with an occurrence of a relation between [the form] and matter which when that relation ceases, that taking [of the form from the matter] stops. That is because [sensation] does not thoroughly extract the form from matter, but rather it needs the existence of the matter too, in that that form belongs to it.

The imagery faculty and imagination free the form extracted from matter even more so. That is because [the imagery faculty] takes [the form] from the matter inasmuch as [the form] does not need the existence of its matter for its existence in [the imagery faculty and imagination], because even if the matter were to vanish or cease, the form is something whose existence remains in the imagery faculty. So [the imagery faculty's] taking [the form] destroys the association [60] between [the form] and matter; nevertheless, the imagery faculty has not abstracted it from the material concomitants. So sensation neither abstracts it completely from the matter nor abstracts it from the concomitants of matter, whereas the imagery faculty has abstracted it completely from matter, but it did not abstract it altogether from the concomitants of matter, since the form that is in the imagery depends upon the sensible form and on a certain quantification, qualification and position. Also in the imagery faculty it is wholly impossible to imagine in any way a form in which all the individuals of that species are common, whereas it is possible that there are existing and imaginable people who are not in the way that the imagery faculty imagines that human.

The act of the estimative faculty exceeds this level a little in abstraction because it grasps the formal aspects that are not in themselves material, although they happen to be in some matter. That is because shape, color, position and the like are things that cannot but belong to corporeal matters. As for good, evil, harmony, strife and the like, they in themselves are not material things, but sometimes are accidentally material. An indication that these things are not essentially material is that if they were, then good, evil, harmony and strife would not be intellected save as some accident of a body, whereas that [i.e., that good, evil, harmony and strife are not intellected as some accident of a body] is frequently intellected and in fact exists. So it is clear that these things in themselves are immaterial and their being material is accidental to them. Estimation grasps and perceives only the likenesses of these things, and hence estimation frequently perceives certain immaterial things and takes them from the matter just as it [61] likewise perceives insensible accounts, even though they are material. So then this extraction is more thorough and closer to simplicity than the first two [kinds of] extraction. Still despite that it does not abstract this form from the concomitants of matter, it takes it as a singular and according to one matter after another and in relation to it and as something associated with a sensible form that is surrounded by the concomitants of matter and by whatever is common in it in the imagery faculty.

As for the faculty in which there are the permanent forms—whether forms of existents that are not at all material and being material is not accidental to them or forms of material existents but which are in every way free of the associations of matter—clearly [that faculty] perceives the forms in that it takes them as something wholly abstracted from matter. [This] is obvious with respect to what it essentially separated (*mujarrad*) from matter. As for what belongs to matter—either because of its material existence or [because] that [existence] is accidental to it—[the faculty] abstracts it from the matter and from the concomitants of matter together with it, taking it as something abstracted until there is the likeness of the human that is said of many and until the many has been taken to be a single nature, and it isolates it from every material quantity, quality, place and position. Were it not to abstract it from that, it would not turn out that it is said of all. So by means of this the perception of judging based on sensing, imagining, estimating and intellecting are distinguished. We have now urged the discussion in this chapter to this account.

Text 3: *Book of Demonstration* (ed. Badawi), III.5, 160.7–17: Outline of Avicenna's theory of abstraction

Essences perceptible in existence are not in themselves intelligible, but perceptible; however, the intellect makes them so as to be intelligible, because it abstracts their true nature from the concomitants of matter. Still, conceptualizing the intelligibles is acquired only by means of sensory perception in one way, namely that sensory perception takes the perceptible forms and presents them to the imagery faculty, and so those forms become subjects of our speculative intellect's activity, and thus there are numerous forms there taken from [for example] perceptible humans. The intellect, then, finds them varying in accidents such as it finds Zayd particularized by a certain color, external appearance, ordering of the limbs and the like, while it finds Amr particularized by other [accidents] different from those. Thus [the speculative intellect] receives these accidents, but then it extracts them, as if it is peeling away these accidents and setting them to one side, until it arrives at the formal aspect (*ma'nā*) in which [humans] are common and in which there is no variation and so acquires knowledge of them and conceptualizes them. The first thing that [the intellect] inquires into is the confused mixture in the imagery faculty; for it finds accidental and essential features, and among the accidents those which are necessary and those which are not. It then isolates one formal aspect after another of the numerous ones mixed together in the imagery faculty, following them along to the essence [of human].

Text 4: *The Soul* (ed. Rahman), V.5, 234–236:

The Active Intellect and emanation

[234] The human soul is at one time something intellecting potentially and thereafter becomes something intellecting actually. Now whatever emerges from potency to act does so only by means of a cause in act that causes it to emerge, and so in this case there is a cause that causes our souls to emerge from potency to act with respect to the objects of intellection. Since it is the cause with respect to providing the intellectual forms (*ṣuwar ʿaqlīya*), it is nothing but an actual intellect in whom the principles of the intelligible forms are separate (*mujarrada*) [from matter], and whose relation to our souls is the relation of the Sun to our vision. Just as the Sun is actually visible in itself [235] and through its light it makes actually visible what is not actually visible, so likewise is the state of this intellect vis-à-vis our souls; for when the intellectual faculty reviews the particulars that are in the imagery faculty and the light of the aforementioned Active Intellect shines into us [and] upon them, the things abstracted (*mujarrada*) from matter and its concomitants are altered (*istiḥālat*)[29] and impressed upon the rational soul . . . in the sense that reviewing them prepares the soul in order that the thing separate (*mujarrad*) from matter [coming] from the Active Intellect [i.e., the intellectual forms or intelligible accidents] emanates upon them. . . . So when a certain relation to this form befalls the rational soul by means of the Active Intellect's illumination, then from [the form] there comes to be in [the soul] something that in one way is of its genus and in another way is not. It is just like when light falls on colored objects; it produces an effect in seeing them that is not in every way [reduced] to their sum. So the images that are potentially intelligible become actually intelligible—not themselves but what is acquired from them. In fact, just as the effect resulting from the sensible forms by means of the light is not itself those forms, but rather something related to them that is engendered by means of the light in the recipient facing [the light], so likewise when the rational soul reviews those forms in the imagery faculty and the light of the Active Intellect comes into a type of contact with them, then they are prepared [236] so that from the light of the Active Intellect they come to be the abstract version of those forms free from [material] taints within [the rational soul].

Text 5: *The Soul* (ed. Rahman), III.7, 141–142:

Outline of Avicenna's theory of vision

[141] Let us now resolve the aforementioned sophism. That to which they adhere, namely that proximity precludes seeing and that it is impossible to derive colors and shapes from their matters, would turn out to be true for them only if it were said that seeing, or any of the [other] sensations, is *only* by extracting the form from the matter, that is, taking the form itself from the matter and transferring it to the sensing power. Now this is something that no one affirms; rather, they said that is by way of being acted upon, where being acted on is not that what is acted on strips away the power or quality of the agent. Quite the contrary, [what is acted upon] receives from [the agent]

either the likeness (*mithal*) of [the agent's power or quality] or something generically different from [that power] (*jinsan ghayrahā*). Now we say that sight in itself receives from the object of sight a form *common* to the form that is in [the object of sight], not [the object of sight's] very own form (and equally that which is sensed by immediate proximity such as what is smelled and touched), and so the one sensing that does not loose its form, [142] but rather there is found in it only the likeness of its form. Some things, however, can be acted upon by [the agent] through direct contact (*mulāqa*), whereas when others are in direct contact, then something that is required (so that [the agent's] impression has an effect) is suspended [from acting]. In this context, it is the ray (*shu'ā'*) whose being connected with the visible form that is required in order that what possesses the form might from its form project into another a sensible image (*shabaḥ*) corresponding with what we see [as a result] of its projecting its corroborative sensible image when the light is intensely upon it so that it colors whatever is in front of it with its color. So [the ray] conveys [the image] accurately when what is in front of it is receptive to that (even through the intermediacy of a mirror as well) assuming that that visible object is duly illuminated. Furthermore it needs some intermediary, such as the tool to assist it in it, namely, the transparent, and that its magnitude has a delimited limit with respect to which nothing smaller than it occurs.

Notes

1. Dag Nikolaus Hasse, "Avicenna on Abstraction" in *Aspects of Avicenna*, ed. R. Wisnovsky (Princeton, NJ: Markus Wiener Publishers, 2001), 39–72, 40.

2. *Middle East Studies Association Bulletin* 39 (2005): 180–182, esp. 182.

3. Hasse notes the importance of essences to Avicenna's theory of abstraction and briefly discusses them as well; see "Avicenna on Abstraction", 49–51.

4. See text 1 of the appendix, which is taken from *Madkhal*, ed. al-Hudayri, al-Ahwani and Anawati (Cairo: The General Egyptian Book Organization, 1952), I.2, 15.1–8.

5. See *Madkhal*, 1.3, 17.7–17.

6. See E. Gilson, *Being and Some Philosophers* (Toronto: Pontifical Institute of Medieval Studies, 1952), 75–76.

7. See *Kitāb al-Burhān*, ed. Badawi (Cairo: Dār an-Nahḍa l-'arabīya, 1966), III.5, 159.8–9; 160.12–13; *Kitāb an-Nafs* ed. F. Rahman (London: Oxford University Press, 1959), II.2, 59.2–4.

8. See *Madkhal*, I.2, 15.5–8.

9. A similar point has been made by Meryem Sebti, "Le statut ontologique de l'image dans la doctrine avicennienne de la perception," *Arabic Sciences and Philosophy* 15 (2005): 109–140. Sebti further observes that the essences in themselves are common also to the representations in the faculties of sensation, imagination and estimation. As for the significance of this point for understanding how Avicenna understood the relation between logic and the sciences see my "Logic and Science: The Role of Genus and Difference in Avicenna's Logic, Science and Natural Philosophy," *Documenti e Studi sulla tradizione filosofica medievale* 18 (2007): 165–186.

10. *Najāt*, ed. M. T. Dānishpazhūh (Tehran: Dānishgāh-yi Tihrān, 1985), 519–520.

11. See *K. an-Nafs*, II.2. 58.

12. See Text 2 of the appendix.

13. See *K. an-Nafs*, II.2. 60.

14. *K. al-Burhān*, III.5, 160.7–17.

15. See Text 3 of the appendix.

16. *K. an-Nafs*, V.7, 235.

17. Thus Avicenna says about the visible form, although the point can generalized to all sensible forms: "Now we say that sight in itself receives from the object of sight a form *common* to the form that is in [the object of sight], not [the object of sight's] very own form (and equally that which is sensed by immediate proximity such as what is smelled and touched), and so the one sensing that does not lose its form, but rather there is found in it *only the likeness* (*mithal*) *of its form*" (*K. an-Nafs*, III.5, 141–142).

18. See *K. an-Nafs*, III.5, 235, where he speaks of 'focusing on' as being preparatory for illumination by the Active Intellect; and again *K. aṭ-Ṭabī'īyāt*, ed. Zayed (Cairo: The General Egyptian Book Organization, 1983), II.9, 142.4–6, and although the topic of discussion there is 'analysis' (*taḥlīl*), since in its proper technical sense analysis for Avicenna involves a breaking down of a thing into its constitutive parts for the purposes of defining or definition, at the very least it would seem that Avicenna conceives of abstraction as related to analysis inasmuch as abstraction is the primary cognitive process by which one acquires definitions.

19. Throughout *K. an-Nafs*, III.5, where Avicenna discusses abstraction and the Active Intellect, especially 235.

20. *K. an-Nafs*, V.5, 234. It may be worth noting that Avicenna most frequently used the past participial adjective, *ma'qūla*, to modify form, and thus the sense is 'intellected form'. The use of the nisba adjective, *'aqlī*, is rare in *K. an-Nafs* and the only other occurrences of it in this text of which I am aware are at V.6, 243, 245 and 250, where all the references either explicitly or implicitly seem to refer to what emanates from the Active Intellect or exists only in an intellect; it might also be worth noting that this adjective would appear frequently in Suhrawardī's *Ḥikmat al-ishrāq* (The Wisdom of Illumination), where it always refers to what exists only in an intellect. In light of these considerations, I suggest the phrase *ṣuwar 'aqlīya* is indicating a special kind of form, an 'intellegizing form' or even 'intentional form' (if you will), namely, the accidental forms that make the abstracted forms in the human intellect to be 'intellected forms.'

21. See Text 4 of the appendix.

22. See Text 5 of the appendix.

23. *Naz'* is a common term that Avicenna used when discussing abstraction and indeed he may have considered the two terms mere synonyms, although more research would be needed before such a conclusive identification could be made.

24. *K. an-Nafs*, III.7, 141.

25. Ibid, 141–142.

26. *K. an-Nafs*, V.5, 235.19–20.

27. *K. an-Nafs*, III.1, 92.

28. See Avicenna, *K. al-kawn wa-l-fasād,* XIV and *Ilāhīyāt,* IX.5 for discussions of the role of the 'Giver of Forms' (*wāhib aṣ-ṣuwar*) in the processes of generation and corruption.

29. *Istiḥāla* is Avicenna's preferred term for change with the respect to *qualitative accidents*, or alteration. Throughout Avicenna's *Physics* and *K. an-Nafs* when Avicenna uses *istiḥāla* alone without an additional preposition, he takes it intransitively, and so should simply be translated as 'is altered'. When he intends it transitively he adds the preposition *ilá*; see, for example, II.1, 52, II.2, 66 and III.5, 127. Hasse misses this point when he translates this sentence "[the particulars] are transformed into something ABSTRACTED" ("Avicenna on Abstraction," 54), which ironically gives the impression that that Active Intellect transforms the images in the human intellect into *abstracta*, the very position that Hasse rejects.

Evidentialism and Faith: Believing in Order to Know

John Zeis

Abstract: Evidentialism is generally taken to be a position which is not friendly to a religious epistemology. However, in this paper, I will argue for a religious epistemology which is compatible with fundamental tenets of an evidentialist position on epistemic justification. It is a position which entails both a "will to believe" which goes beyond the standard evidentialist principles governing the appropriate doxastic attitude towards a proposition, but nonetheless satisfies epistemic principles at the basis of an evidentialist position on justification. If my argument is successful, a proponent of a conception of religious faith may be able to have her cake and eat it too: namely, she may be able to fundamentally accept both the evidentialist demand that epistemically rational belief fit, or be supported by evidence as well as the position that rational faith is willing belief beyond what one's evidence strictly demands.

The Cue from Augustine

I will argue for a conception of faith which is compatible with fundamental tenets of an evidentialist position on epistemic justification. It is a position which entails both a "will to believe" which goes beyond the standard evidentialist principles governing the appropriate doxastic attitude towards a proposition, but nonetheless satisfies epistemic principles at the basis of an evidentialist position on justification.[1] If my argument is successful, a proponent of a conception of religious faith may be able to have her cake and eat it too: namely, she may be able to fundamentally accept both the evidentialist demand that epistemically rational belief fit, or be supported by evidence as well as the position that rational faith is willing belief beyond what one's evidence strictly demands.

My cue for the position offered here is taken from Augustine's *Epistula,* where he states:

> The true reasoning by means of which we understand what we believe is to be preferred to false reasoning, but that very faith in things not yet understood is undoubtedly to be preferred too, since it is better to believe

> in what is true but not yet seen than to think that you see something true which is really false. (*Epistula* CXX ii 8; 711.11–16)[2]

My aim here is not textual analysis, but rather the construction of a reasonable conception of the relation between faith and reason compatible with the quoted passage regardless of whether or not it is an accurate interpretation of Augustine's own position on the issue. Given that *caveat*, I take the following to be a plausible derivation from the above quote from Augustine. Although the notion would be foreign to him, I will assume that we may take Augustine to be recommending a position on epistemic justification for faith and so will couch my derivation within that context. The first assertion, namely that "true reasoning by means of which we understand what we believe is to be preferred to false reasoning," seems unproblematic. Having a true justified belief is epistemically preferable to having a false justified belief. Cogent inferences involving false beliefs, unlike cogent inferences involving only true beliefs, cannot produce positive knowledge. This I take to be non-controversial. But the claims implied by the remaining statement in the quote are another story. The statement is that "faith in things not yet understood is undoubtedly to be preferred too, since it is better to believe in what is true but not yet seen than to think that you see something true which is really false." As I take it, the first part of this statement implies that having a belief on the basis of faith which is not yet known is also to be preferred to having rationally justified false beliefs. And since he takes it to be "better to believe in what is true *but not yet seen*" than to believe in something false, I take it that this also implies that he does not take it that withholding assent is preferable in all cases where evidence is insufficient, at least not in all cases where the proposition in question is true. This is all quite controversial and surely any self-respecting evidentialist would have to reject these implications! However, as I will argue, there is a way of understanding this position on faith in such a way as to yield a position which, even given fundamental evidentialist principles, is reasonable.

The Position Derived from Augustine and Evidentialism

What does such a position derived from Augustine (I'll henceforth refer to it as the "DA" position) entail and what is the argument for such a position?[3] Here is DA in a nutshell. The epistemic end of belief is knowledge and this implies at least that it is epistemically better to know what is true than it is to believe what is false or not know what is true. According to DA, what should be one's cognitive posture if there is sufficient evidence for a proposition? Well, just what constitutes "sufficient" evidence may be vague, so let's consider *conclusive* evidence, for conclusive evidence would surely be sufficient. Evidence for a proposition is evidence for the truth of that proposition, and where one then has conclusive evidence for the truth of the proposition, one ought to believe it. However, if the evidence for a proposition, say not-*p*, is inconclusive, then not-*p* may very well be false. If not-*p* fits the evidence that I have better than *p*, but the evidence for not-*p* is inconclusive and if not-*p* is *in fact* false, then in certain cases, it is epistemically better for me to believe *p* than it is for me either to believe not-*p* or not believe *p*. Since it is epistemically better for me to know the truth than it is to believe what is false or not know the truth, when the evidence for not-*p* is inconclusive and *p* is in fact true, my believing *p* rather than either believing not-*p* or withholding belief in *p* and in not-*p* in certain cases puts me in the best position to come to know the truth. Hence, in such cases it is epistemically better for me to believe *p*. Whatever it is epistemically better for an agent to believe is what it is epistemically justified or rational for an agent to believe. Hence, even if not-*p* fits the evidence I have better than *p* does, then as long as the evidence for not-*p* is inconclusive, then if I will to believe *p* and *p* is in fact true and puts me in a better position to *know* the truth, I am epistemically rational in believing *p* rather than not-*p* or withholding belief in *p*. The non-controversial truth of evidentialism is that if I will to believe *p*, even if *p* is in fact true, if I then encounter *conclusive* evidence for not-*p*, I ought to reject *p* and believe not-*p*. However, if *p* is in fact true, then I will never encounter evidence which is conclusive for the truth of not-*p*; and if *p* is true, and if I am persistent and evidentially conscientious, it is very likely that I will encounter mounting evidence for *p* and shrinking evidence for not-*p*. And if I then encounter evidence sufficient to support *p* (and if I am not in a Gettier-type situation in respect to *p*), I will then know *p*.

This is the outline of the position which I wish to defend here, but how is this position consistent with a fundamentally evidentialist position on justification? In order to answer this question, I will examine and critique the position in light of the evidentialist position of Earl Conee and Richard Feldman, the current authoritative expositors and defenders of evidentialism.[4] As they conceive it, evidentialism entails the following principle concerning epistemic justification.

> EC. Believing is the justified attitude when the person's evidence on balance supports a proposition, disbelieving is the justified attitude when the person's evidence on balance supports the negation of a proposition, and suspension of judgment is the justified attitude when the person's evidence on balance supports neither a proposition nor its negation.[5]

EC is clearly inconsistent with DA. What is clearly objectionable to the evidentialist in DA is that according to EC, believing a proposition is epistemically justified for a person only if it fits or is supported by the evidence the person has; and as I have inferred from the quote from Augustine, a belief may be justified *even if its negation "fits the evidence" better*. Given EC, it would be bad enough if DA entailed that faith can be rationally justified "when the person's evidence on balance supports neither a proposition nor its negation."[6] If that were the position, it would still conflict with evidentialism, but not because DA and evidentialism would imply *contrary* beliefs, just contrary doxastic attitudes, for in this case EC would just imply a suspension of belief either way. But if DA goes as far as I think it does, it implies that belief in a proposition can be rationally justified in conditions under which evidentialism implies that the only rational attitude is believing the negation of that proposition.

So it is clear: DA contradicts the demands of evidentialist principle EC. According to this evidentialist principle, epistemic justification supervenes solely upon evidential conditions, but DA implies that faith beliefs can be justified in the absence of such evidential conditions. Of course the discrepancy between the implications of DA and evidentialism could easily be resolved if the sort of justification by faith implied by DA was not *epistemic* justification but rather another sort of justification, say prudential, moral, or religious justification abstracted from considerations of epistemic justification.[7] This however is not an option; for epistemic justification is characterized by its aim of the acquisition of knowledge, and that's precisely what I am arguing that the justification for belief in position DA has as its aim. So the conflict between DA and the evidentialist position cannot be resolved by appealing to distinct sorts of justification.

So how is the conflict to be resolved? I think that the way to the resolution of the problem can be found by starting with Earl Conee's discussion in "The Truth Connection." In that discussion, Conee confirms what we take to be the end of rational inquiry:

> [I]n rational inquiry we do seek to believe the truth. But not for its own sake. It is sought as a constituent of our goal—the goal of knowing the truth.[8]

And he continues by tying the epistemic aim of knowing the truth to the demands of evidentialism:

> Any plausible view accommodates the fact that ordinarily the rational way to believe in pursuit of knowledge is to believe in accordance with one's evidence as to the truth of the matter. If one's epistemic goal is to know whether or not a given proposition is true, ordinarily it is rational to believe the proposition just when one's evidence supports the proposition sufficiently strongly to provide the justification needed for knowledge of the proposition. If one's epistemic goal is to maximize one's total stock of knowledge, then again it is ordinarily rational to pursue this goal by believing exactly those propositions that are sufficiently supported by one's evidence. These considerations suggest a certain hypothesis concerning the nature of the truth connection. Believing a proposition is epistemically justified exactly when the person's evidence sufficiently supports the truth of the proposition.[9]

This is exactly what one would expect from an evidentialist position: evidence is that which provides the truth connection necessary for knowledge.

Nonetheless, as Conee shows, this is only "ordinarily" so, and that "[t]here are unusual circumstances which refute the hypothesis."[10] He presents a number of cases as counterarguments to the hypothesis,[11] a number of cases which show that evidential support is *not* a necessary condition for epistemic justification or rationality: cases which he thinks apparently show that it is not the case that "positive epistemic value is possessed by all and only instances of having an attitude toward a proposition that is supported by one's evidence at the time."[12] The counter-example which he gives that is epistemically closest in kind to the faith beliefs in DA is his second genie example. In this case there is a genie who will prevent you from ever having a view supported by the evidence again unless you have an unsupported attitude now, and if you do have an unsupported attitude now, you will have many supported attitudes later. In this case, it seems that one's evidential support is not necessary for positive epistemic value. Hence, if epistemic justification is that which serves the aim of acquiring knowledge, then here we have a clear case where the aim is best satisfied by adopting belief in the absence of *any* evidential support. It also shows that even if evidence is what provides the truth connection necessary for knowledge, and hence adequate evidential support is a necessary constituent of knowledge, there are going to be cases where in order to acquire the necessary evidence, a person will be epistemically justified or rational only if she violates evidential principle of justification EC. This in itself may be taken to imply that evidentialism is an inadequate theory of epistemic justification, but that is not what I am taking it to imply (and, of course, neither does Conee). In this unusual case, what is crucial is that the reason why the evidentialist principle EC is to be set aside in the short haul is that this is the only way to satisfy the aim of the principle in the long haul. Principle EC is the default principle of epistemic justification, but satisfaction of principles of justification does not guarantee satisfaction of the aim of such principles; and in cases where this is so, it will be justified to set aside such principles. In such a position, evidence is still that which provides the truth connection necessary for knowledge, and as such, the fundamental insight of evidentialism can still be salvaged even in the face of such cases where strict evidential implications are not necessary for the epistemic justification for believing a proposition.

> This shows that the epistemic sort of justification that believing can have does not consist entirely in evidence that the belief is true. Epistemic justification for believing therefore does not have the hypothesized connection to truth. It is not a kind of justification which is provided only by evidence for the truth of the belief.[13]

But if Conee concedes that being epistemically justified in believing a proposition "does not consist entirely in evidence that the belief is true," how then can he salvage evidentialism? He salvages evidentialism by distinguishing the epistemic justification for *believing* a proposition from the epistemic justification for a *proposition* itself.

> What must be epistemically justified in order to know is not "the belief" in the sense of: the believing of the proposition. It is "the belief" in the sense of: the proposition believed. What gets justified by the answer to the

> question—How do you know?—is the known proposition, not believing it. This is the justification that is the topic of the truth connection. Hence, it is the propositional sort of epistemic justification that enters into the truth connection.[14]

The distinction between epistemic justification for belief and epistemic justification for a proposition, according to Conee, is that it is only epistemic justification for a proposition which is evidence for the truth of a proposition, and it is the relation of evidential support which provides epistemic justification with its truth connection. This relation is necessary for epistemic justification for a proposition, but not for epistemic justification for *believing* a proposition. In the genie case above, there is epistemic justification for believing in the absence of any evidential support. Hence believing a proposition can be epistemically justified, because it serves the aim of acquiring knowledge, even in cases where the proper evidentialist truth connection is not present.

In defending the evidentialist position against the genie cases, Conee introduces the notion of "maximal intrinsic epistemic value." He claims that with this notion, an evidentialist position regarding positive epistemic value can be salvaged.[15] Conee holds that an evidentialist position is not subject to counterexamples such as the ones he constructed if *intrinsic* epistemic value is what is at issue. This is so because in the cases where evidence is not necessary for epistemic rationality, the effects of the belief contribute to the total epistemic value that the belief produces but do not have a constitutive role in yielding epistemic value—it does not have *intrinsic* epistemic value. This is *not* the case for beliefs which are supported by one's evidence, and hence Conee contends that it is plausible that only beliefs which have adequate evidential support are the sorts of beliefs which have maximal intrinsic epistemic value.

It is not entirely clear to me just how, in general, to distinguish between beliefs which have a constitutive role in yielding epistemic value from ones which do not have such a role. But if we examine the genie case we may be able to better understand how to draw the necessary distinction between such cases and cases where evidence is the determinate factor constituting belief. What seems clear in the genie case is that the belief is merely instrumental in producing maximal epistemic value. In the genie case, there is no intrinsic epistemic value accruing to the belief adopted, it is that the situation is engineered in such a way that the belief adopted is extrinsic to the resultant epistemic value produced by adopting the belief. What we need to consider now is whether faith beliefs in the DA position are more comparable to the kind of belief in Conee's genie example, or more comparable to beliefs which are adequately supported by evidence. Perhaps then we will be able to determine whether or not faith beliefs of the sort defended in the DA position have maximal intrinsic epistemic value or not; and furthermore even if not, whether or not they should be considered epistemically rational.

First off, in the position derived from Augustine, the presumption is that, necessarily, the faith beliefs in question are true.[16] DA is a plausible position only given that presumption. The position DA will *not* justify faith beliefs which are false—only faith beliefs which are true can be justified. If one asks, "Well, how do we *know* that these beliefs are true?" the response would be that, if it is a matter of faith, you are putting the cart before the horse. This implies, of course, that if someone adopts what *appears* to her to be a faith belief, she may, in fact, be dead wrong; and if she *is* wrong, all bets are off! Not only that, but also, if someone adopts what appears to her to be a faith belief and it is true, but it is only true by lucky happenstance, this also does not constitute the kind of faith belief necessary for the plausibility of DA. Augustine's slogan taken from Isaiah 7:9, *credo ut intelligam*, suggests that he himself does not see mere faith or belief in the truth as sufficient in itself: faith is justified when it leads one to knowledge or understanding. In other words, in certain cases, faith (in the absence of sufficient evidential support) is necessary as a means of coming to knowledge. In order for DA to be plausible, this condition must be a constituent of the position.

Some views on the justification of faith beliefs may entail that false faith beliefs may be justified, analogous to the way ordinary beliefs which are well supported by evidence but in fact are false are justified. But this is not an option in DA; and the basis for this is that if DA is a position derived from Augustine, then only true faith beliefs can be justified.

Conee's second genie case is definitely pretty close in kind to a faith belief adopted according to the conditions for an epistemically justified belief entailed by DA, but we'll need to adapt it to insure that it fits the truth condition for faith beliefs in DA. Recall that in Conee's case there is a genie who will prevent you from ever having a supported view again unless you have an unsupported attitude now, and if you do have an unsupported attitude now, you will have many supported attitudes later. Conee does not say whether or not the belief which is unsupported in this second genie case must be true, but let's say that it is a true belief. This now does seem to be a case which is very close to the kind of faith belief justified according to DA. However, the fact that the unsupported belief is true is not sufficient if the positive epistemic value which results from the belief (i.e., the support of many beliefs later) is connected merely instrumentally or by mere happenstance. In DA, a faith belief is not merely instrumental or connected by mere happenstance to the resultant epistemic value; the resultant epistemic value must be connected *intrinsically* to the adopted faith belief.

Foundherentism and Faith

But how can a faith belief be of *intrinsic* epistemic value? In order to answer that question, I will adopt an analogy from Susan Haack's *Evidence and Inquiry*.[17] Haack's picture of epistemic justification is what she calls "foundherentist." She calls it such because in such a position, there is no clear distinction between a foundationally justified belief and a belief justified by its coherence with other beliefs. She illustrates the relation of justification in a foundherentist position with the use of a crossword puzzle analogy. I think that Haack's foundherentist view of justification best captures the position of justification in a position derived from Augustine; in fact when modified to accommodate a doxastic system which includes faith beliefs, I think it best captures the merits of a position wherein the rationality of faith is based upon the *credo ut intelligam* dictum.[18] As in Haack's use of the metaphor, the clues are the pieces of evidence, and in this case the given clues as the evidence (whatever you think that that is) which we appeal to in any inquiry which reason can discover in its natural deployment without reliance upon faith. Think of the entire crossword puzzle as the whole of knowledge, and this section of the puzzle to be a section where some of the answers (beliefs) from reason butts-up against some of the answers (beliefs) of the faith. The entries based on the five clues below will represent our non-theological knowledge, and to the extent that the clues and the answers are the same will be the extent to which there is a common body of knowledge accessible without the aid of faith. Here then, is the puzzle.

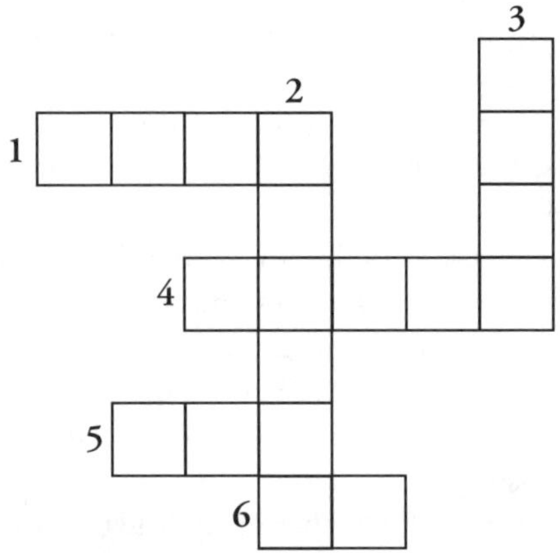

Across:

1.
4. The skeleton of the head
5. A writing instrument or a small enclosure for animals
6. The opposite of stop

Down:

2. A good form of outdoor exercise for cardiovascular health and strength of the legs
3. Who hath said in his heart that there is no God

As can be seen, there is a clue missing from the puzzle; and because of that, there is no determinate solution to the puzzle; and in particular, no determinate solution for #2 down: it is indeterminate whether *hiking* or *biking* should be the entry. The missing clue is not accessible to all and is available only to those who have faith; but if you have faith, this part of the puzzle is then determinately resolvable. The missing clue is:

1. A cartoon image of a good idea is a light ________.

With the addition of this clue, the puzzle is determinately resolvable: the entry for #1 across is *bulb* and therefore #2 down is clearly *biking*, not *hiking*.

However the puzzle is merely indeterminate before this clue is given, it is not the case that *hiking* is positively supported by the evidence. And as I see it, DA entails the stronger position: that faith can trump reason even when one's evidence unaided by faith supports the contrary belief. Can the puzzle analogy be adjusted to illustrate a case parallel to that? I think it easily can. Imagine that the clue for #2 down in the original puzzle is this:

2. A good form of outdoor exercise for cardiovascular health and strength of the legs which Uncle Harry most often engages in.

And also imagine that Uncle Harry takes you hiking every Sunday but that he has never taken you bike riding, and you have no other evidence that Uncle Harry rides a bike. In this case, your evidence, in accordance with Principle EC, now positively supports *hiking* as the entry for #2 down. However, once again you are offered and you again take the missing clue. Would *biking* still be the correct answer even in this case? Well, it surely would be if the following were so. Unbeknownst to you, Harry is a closet bicyclist. He has a dream of competing in the *Tour de France*, and trains for it by riding on mountain roads twenty hours a week, whereas he only hikes three hours a week. You don't know all this however because he is embarrassed to tell anyone—he is 55 and thinks everyone would think he is being ridiculous!

If we use the analogy of this crossword puzzle for the relation between faith and reason, we get that both faith and reason—or what one can know on the basis of what evidence is available in the absence of faith—are insufficient sources of knowledge. Not only is it the case that neither faith nor reason are sufficient sources of knowledge, but faith and reason are complementary. Faith perfects reason and reason perfects faith. Reason is autonomous in the sense that it considers distinctive evidence (has its own clues). The same should be said of faith. However, neither faith nor reason can constitute a complete science or body of knowledge (crossword puzzle) and there are no absolutely clear boundaries as to where reason ends and faith begins. There is also no clear distinction between empirical, scientific, or philosophical propositions and propositions based upon faith (which entries are *solely* dependent on faith versus which entries are *solely* dependent upon reason). Another feature of note of the analogy regarding the relation between faith and reason is that a clue (evidence) is given for faith, *not* a dictated answer; and hence the believer or community of believers, using other evidence and beliefs from faith and reason, must figure out or interpret the meaning of the evidence provided by faith. What Scripture and the Tradition entail itself requires the use of unrestricted reason.

From my adaptation of Haack's crossword puzzle analogy, we get a view of the relation between faith and reason and a conception of justified belief which has the kinds of features which I think we are looking for in a position derived from Augustine. Such a view is coherentist in the sense that the entirety of knowledge, including that from both faith and reason, is viewed as a network of beliefs. No belief is wholly justified on its own, but is in some respects justified because of its relations to other beliefs. For example, part of the justification of my answer (belief) that #4 across is *skull* is its relation to my answer (belief) for #2 down, which of course in turn depends on my answers for #1 and #5 across. Even for #1 across, which represents a faith belief, although its clue (evidence) is unique in being from a source distinct from reason and common beliefs, or the data of ordinary experience, part of its justification will depend upon its relation to my other beliefs. The coherentist aspects of the picture of justification capture nicely the implications of the dictum *credo ut intelligam* as I conceive of it in DA. As I noted above, in the DA position, the dictum implies that faith is justified because it is a means to knowledge or understanding. If we project this in the way suggested by the crossword puzzle analogy, faith is a means to acquiring and enhancing knowledge not just for propositions of the faith, but for one's entire network of beliefs or body of knowledge.

However, the view is not strictly coherentist because it provides for the kind of input from outside of our network of beliefs as evidence as well as the network of beliefs. Each of the answers (beliefs) has some clue (evidence) from outside of the network of beliefs (other answers in the puzzle). The advantage of a foundationalist view over a coherentist view of justification is that it allows for non-propositional evidence.[19] And non-propositional evidence may be of many different sorts. DA implies no theory about the general criteria for evidence. There is room for the evidence of the senses, introspective evidence, testimonial evidence, and even the evidence of mystical experience. Obviously, in DA, the evidence of faith (i.e., the clue for #1 across) is something distinctive from the more common modes of evidence, such as evidence from the senses, introspective evidence, or human testimonial evidence. Some of the plausible candidates for viewing the clue or the evidence for #1 across are divine testimony or mystical experience. The reason why the clue for #1 is not included with the other clues however is that the evidence of divine testimony and mystical experience, even granted that there are such types of evidence, is *not* the sort of evidence which all have access to, and in fact perhaps just a few have access to. And why would this be so? Why is it that not all have the evidence of the faith? Well this is just where the will to believe implied by DA comes into the picture.

As I expressed it in my outline of DA, there are certain cases where even if not-*p* fits the evidence that I have better than *p*, it is epistemically better for me to believe *p*. Since it is better for me to know the truth than it is to believe what is false or not know the truth, when the evidence for not-*p* is inconclusive (and *p* is in fact true) my believing *p* rather than either believing not-*p* or withholding belief in p and in not-*p* in certain cases puts me in the best position to come to know the truth. And in such cases it is epistemically better for me to believe *p*. The case of faith is just such a case.

Viewed strictly from the point of view of the evidentialist principle EC, the clue for #1 across does *not* meet the standards of evidence. In other words, higher-level epistemic questions can be raised about just what one's evidence is.[20] One can ask whether or not believing that *X* is part of my evidence is something for which I have sufficient evidence. In the crossword puzzle analogy, *if* the clue for #1 across *is* considered part of my evidence for the solution of the puzzle, then my evidence *does sufficiently justify* my belief that the answer for #1 across is *bulb*. But since there is not sufficient evidence for the clue for #1 across being considered part of my stock of evidence, it requires an act of faith on my part in order for me to take the clue for #1 across as evidence. So the situation is something like this. Prior to making an act of faith in accepting the clue for #1 across as part of my evidence, that clue is not part of my evidence; and so there is no entry for #1 across. So my accepting the clue for #1 across as evidence is a belief which is not supported by my evidence. And so prior to accepting the clue for #1 across, that *biking* is the correct entry for #2 down is *not* adequately supported by my evidence. However, if I will to accept the clue for #1 across as evidence without supporting evidence for its being such, the evidence from the clue for #1 across then supports the entry for #1 across being *bulb*, which in turn supports the entry for #2 down being *biking*. This is very much like Conee's second genie case, wherein which if, but *only if*, you have an unsupported belief now, you will have many supported beliefs later on down the road.

Back to Augustine: credo ut intelligam

But does this picture adequately capture the relation between faith and reason, and more specifically between faith and evidence? Is it plausible to conceive of an act of faith being something that involves what amounts to a second order volition to believe?[21] What I mean by a second order volition to believe is that it is an attitude structurally similar to Frankfurt's second order volitions. A first order volition is an effective will to *do X*, whereas a second order desire or volition is the desire or effective will to *desire or will to do X*. As I am conceiving of it, an act of faith involves a second order volition to believe that something constitutes revelatory evidence. Since DA is a position derived from Augustine, perhaps the most appropriate source to consider is Augustine's own account of his conversion in the *Confessions*. Augustine is struggling with his inability to completely commit himself to Christ and forsake his "unclean" desires. He prays and pleads that he will be released and cleansed now! And this is his account of what follows.

> 29. I was saying these things and weeping in the most bitter contrition of my heart, when suddenly I heard the voice of a boy or a girl I know not which—coming from the neighboring house, chanting over and over again, "Pick it up, read it; pick it up, read it." [*260*] Immediately I ceased weeping and began most earnestly to think whether it was usual for children in some kind of game to sing such a song, but I could not remember ever having heard the like. So, damming the torrent of my tears, I got to my feet, for I could not but think that this was a divine command to open the Bible and read the first passage I should light upon. For I had heard [*261*]

> how Anthony, accidentally coming into church while the gospel was being read, received the admonition as if what was read had been addressed to him: "Go and sell what you have and give it to the poor, and you shall have treasure in heaven; and come and follow me." [*262*] By such an oracle he was forthwith converted to thee.
>
> So I quickly returned to the bench where Alypius was sitting, for there I had put down the apostle's book when I had left there. I snatched it up, opened it, and in silence read the paragraph on which my eyes first fell: "Not in rioting and drunkenness, not in chambering and wantonness, not in strife and envying, but put on the Lord Jesus Christ, and make no provision for the flesh to fulfill the lusts thereof."[*263*] I wanted to read no further, nor did I need to. For instantly, as the sentence ended, there was infused in my heart something like the light of full certainty and all the gloom of doubt vanished away. [*264*][22]

What are the salient features of this conversion for the purpose of understanding its epistemically relevant properties? First, Augustine is praying and pleading for a way to conquer his lust—he has a desire or will to be saved, but is too weak to effect it. Second, he is distraught and weeping, but he then hears an unknown child's voice commanding "Pick it up; read it." Third, and most critically, he takes this as a divine command. As he says: "I could not but think that this was a divine command." Fourth, recalling the account that he had heard of Anthony's conversion being effected by an accident of his hearing of a gospel, Augustine interprets the command to pick up and read to mean that he is to arbitrarily take the first text he sees as the answer to his prayer. And last, but not least, he takes the text he encounters to so perfectly answer his prayer that he is infused with "something like the light of pure certainty."

The third stage of Augustine's conversion process, i.e., his taking the voice of the child to be the expression of a divine command, functions analogously to the way in which the clue for #1 across functions in the crossword puzzle. Unlike the other clues, it is not a given that the clue for #1 across is evidence. The clue functions as evidence only for those who choose to accept it as such; and that it is to be taken as such is not itself something which is sufficiently supported by the evidence. Augustine does not point to any evidence (except perhaps just the impulsion to believe) that supports his taking the child's voice saying "Pick it up, read it" as a divine revelation, and I can't imagine what kind of evidence *would* sufficiently support his taking it as such. But similarly, as with the person solving the crossword puzzle who chooses to accept the clue for #1 across, once Augustine accepts the child's voice to be divine revelation, this leads him to knowledge or understanding. However, this is all just hooey if what Augustine heard was *not* a divine revelation. The plausibility of DA rests crucially upon the premise that whatever is accepted as evidence of divine revelation is *in fact* divinely revealed.

Augustine's conversion is an extraordinary passage of faith, but it is not by any means unique. Many believers testify to similar extraordinary experiences of revelation[23] and even more ordinary passages of faith seem to share with Augustine's conversion a point, or more commonly points, when the person accepts something as evidence for a divine revelation. What is it for someone to accept Scripture as divinely revealed, or to accept that the Magisterium of the Church is the authentic interpreter of Scripture? Can this be plausibly construed as a person's consideration of whether or not this is the case by an application of an evidentialist standard like EC? I don't see how. It seems to me much more plausible to consider the act of faith to be a decision or choice or acceptance to take the bible as divinely revealed in the absence of sufficient support by one's body of evidence. The same could be said for taking some event as miraculous. Although he didn't get the picture entirely correct, there is something fundamentally right about Hume's attack on the rationality of belief in miracles—and what he has right is that it is implausible to think that taking something as a miraculous event is something that "fits the evidence" or "on balance is supported by the evidence."

But then, what distinguishes this sort of act of faith from mere wishful thinking? The key is found in a full appreciation of Augustine's *credo ut intelligam*. First, the act of faith is an act which has as an intrinsic result—understanding or knowledge. Second, and most simply, an act of faith is necessarily belief in what is true. Third, wishful thinking is belief aimed at some end or other, like peace of mind, or hope; but not at the epistemic end—the acquisition of knowledge. And finally, and perhaps most importantly, according to DA, the knowledge and understanding which proceeds from an act of faith is persistent and conscientious in searching for and assessing evidence—in fact, this evidential sensitivity is itself a large part of what constitutes the resultant understanding. It is true that a strong faith belief may more doggedly resist defeaters, and superficially, this may appear to another as mere wishful thinking. But the epistemic principle justifying stronger resistance to defeaters when an act of faith is at stake, is perfectly rational.[24] If the faith belief *is* true, then there is no more certain basis for belief; for if the faith belief is true, it is either directly or indirectly revealed by God, the author of all truth, and therefore is less likely to be mistaken. There is, of course, the danger of a stubborn and inflexible dogmatism, but only if the believer presumes an infallibility regarding his belief. But that would amount to presuming one's infallibility regarding the interpretation of the clue or evidence which prompts the belief. There is no presumption of such infallibility in DA.

It seems clear that if faith has the epistemic properties entailed by DA, then it is rationally justified. But the subsequent question is whether faith's epistemic justification is merely what Conee considers to be epistemic justification for *believing* a proposition or, rather, might it be epistemic justification for a *proposition* itself. Well, it surely satisfies the conditions for epistemic justification for belief; and whether it satisfies the conditions for epistemic justification for a proposition will depend upon whether the belief itself is constitutive of knowledge. Looking back once more to the crossword puzzle analogy, what we have is that if one makes an act of faith in accepting the clue for #1 across as evidence, then the clue justifies the proposition itself, i.e. that *A cartoon image of a good idea is a light bulb*, for it is constitutive, and not merely instrumental, in producing knowledge. So the act of faith has two epistemic tiers: the second or higher order tier which is the acceptance, without sufficient evidence, of something's constituting considerable evidence. At this tier, there is just epistemic justification *for belief.* But the first order tier, which involves the interpretation and assessment of the evidence provided by the clue for #1 across, we have epistemic justification for the *proposition*. If that is the case, then it is reasonable to believe that the kind of truth connection which is necessary for knowledge is attributable to acts of faith as well. So that is why, for the person of faith, in reflection upon the person who lacks faith, it appears to be the case that "there but for the grace of God go I."

Canisius College

Notes

1. James F. Ross has defended the position of cognitive voluntarism in many articles. See, e.g., his "Cognitive Finality" in *Rational Faith: Catholic Responses to Reformed Epistemology,* ed. Linda Zagzebski (Notre Dame: University of Notre Dame Press, (1993), 226–255. See also John Zeis, "Volitionalism and the Virtue of Faith" in *American Catholic Philosophical Quarterly* Vol. LXVIII, No. 1, (1994), 57–71. Whether cognitive voluntarism is a viable position is an issue that is beyond the scope of the discussion in this paper. Nonetheless, it is clear that a position on faith which is derived from Augustine, which is the sort of position which I attempt to articulate here, must be one which includes a cognitive voluntarist perspective. See Eugene TeSelle's entry on "Faith" in the *Encylopedia on Ausgustine*, 347–350.

2. Translated by Norman Kretzmann in, "Faith Seeks, Understanding Finds," *Christian Philosophy*, ed. Thomas P. Flint (Notre Dame: ND Press, 1990), 25.

3. I will assume that the rational aim of belief is knowledge and that epistemic justification of a belief or a proposition is justification which is based solely and intrinsically on the aim of acquiring knowledge. Even granting that premise, the evidentialist will argue that one ought always to base one's beliefs merely on one's evidence, and this is what being epistemically rational entails. See Richard Feldman, "The Ethics of Belief," in *Philosophy and Phenomenological Research* May 2000, 60 (3), 667–695. The evidentialist can admit other sorts of rationality; say pragmatic or moral, but *epistemic* rationality is a property which always supervenes on evidence that is available to a person. See Earl Conee and Richard Feldman, *Evidentialism* (Oxford: OUP, 2004), 101.

4. I wish to thank Earl Conee and Rich Feldman for their generosity in discussing with me an earlier draft of this paper. I also wish to thank Trent Dougherty for extensive comments which he sent me on an earlier draft of this paper.

5. Conee and Feldman, 102. EC is the revised version of principle EJ (83), which is that a "Doxastic attitude D toward proposition p is epistemically justified for S at t if and only if having D at t toward p fits the evidence that S has at t." Feldman and Conee revised EJ to the notion of "fit" in EJ. They claim that this is the sort of justification which is characteristically epistemic and basic to an evidentialist epistemology (254).

6. Ibid.

7. Conee distinguishes between epistemic justification and on other sorts of justification, e.g., moral or prudential, on the basis that epistemic justification always has some bearing on the truth of the belief. See "The Truth Connection," in *Evidentialism*, 243.

8. Conee, "The Truth Connection," 248.

9. Ibid, 249.

10. Ibid.

11. See 249ff.

12. Ibid., 257.

13. Ibid, 250.

14. Ibid, 252.

15. See V3*, 258.

16. As TeSelle puts it in *op. cit.*, for Augustine "...belief is without error or ignorance." 348. It is clear that TeSelle uses "belief" here as a synonym for "faith".

17. Susan Haack, *Evidence and Inquiry* (Oxford UK and Cambridge USA: Blackwell, 1993), 19. Since Haack introduced foundherentism, other philosophers have followed her lead in taking a middle way through the standard dichotomies of foundationalism/coherentism and internalism/externalism. In fact, Earl Conee himself is sympathetic to this view. See his "The Basic Nature of Epistemic Justification," *The Monist* 71, 389–404 (1988).

18. I think that my modification of Haack's foundherentist position clearly incorporates the implications which Augustine draws from the *credo ut intelligam* dictum. These implications are the following: (1) The attempt to gain knowledge or understanding without faith is futile. (2) Faith is a stage on the way to knowledge. Faith is not yet understanding, but it seeks understanding. (3) The quest for knowledge prompted by faith is not only legitimate, but gains an independent validity and moves beyond mere faith. See TeSelle, *op. cit.*, 347–348.

19. Haack, 27.

20. William P. Alston, "Epistemic Desiderata," *Philosophy and Phenomenogical Research*, 53, no.3 (September 1993): 527–551. In this article, Alston identifies "higher level requirements" as one of four prominent candidates of "putatively necessary conditions of justification" (528–529).

21. The distinction between first and second order desires and volitions is developed by Harry Frankfurt in his "The Freedom of the Will and the Concept of a Person," *Journal of Philosophy*, lxviii, no. 1 (Jan. 1971): 5–20.

22. *Confessions* Book 8, Chapter 12.

23. Although I do not think that I have had such experiences, several trustworthy people of faith close to me have testified to such experiences.

24. In his "Heeding Misleading Evidence" in *Evidentialism*, 267, Conee argues that "...any alleged knowledge that could survive the acquisition of defeating contrary evidence against its basis would have the tenacity of dogma, not knowledge." The distinction between the position which I argue for here and Conee's position in this article is, I think, this: If someone assents to a proposition on the basis of what he takes to be faith, he would have to take such a basis to be true and well-founded. However, since one can be *wrong* about it

being actually grounded in faith, the mere fact that *if* it is grounded by faith it must be true does not justify his dismissing all defeating contrary evidence and resorting to blind dogmatic adherence. I think such an attitude would be contrary to the faith which seeks understanding. Nonetheless, if he does take his belief to be grounded in faith, the fact that if it is then it must be true will justify a more critical attitude toward defeating contrary evidence than if he takes his belief to be grounded by some source other than faith.

Cognitive Faculties and Evolutionary Naturalism

Bernardo Cantens

Abstract: In *Warrant and Proper Function* Plantinga argues that his natural view of warrant is best understood within a supernatural ontology. A central reason why a naturalistic ontology cannot accommodate his version of natural epistemology is that it cannot explain the reliability of cognitive functions. He presents arguments for the following two conclusions: (1) that naturalism is probably false; and (2) that naturalism is irrational. He considers the latter to be his main argument. The objective of this paper is to refute Plantinga's arguments for the conclusion that naturalism is irrational. I will demonstrate that given naturalistic evolution, we have reason to believe that it is likely that we would develop reliable cognitive *theoretical* faculties. As a result, a naturalist has sufficient epistemic ground to maintain the reasonableness of the view that her theoretical cognitive faculties are reliable and her theoretical beliefs true. It is, therefore, not irrational to be a naturalist.

In *Warrant and Proper Function* Plantinga argues that his natural view of warrant is best understood within a supernatural ontology. A central reason why a naturalistic ontology cannot accommodate his version of natural epistemology is that it cannot explain the reliability of cognitive functions. He presents arguments for the following two conclusions: (1) that naturalism is probably false; and (2) that naturalism is irrational. He considers the latter to be his main argument. The objective of this paper is to refute Plantinga's arguments for the conclusion that naturalism is irrational. The paper is divided into two parts. In the first part, I will explain Plantinga's arguments. In the second part, I will demonstrate that, given naturalistic evolution, we have reason to believe that it is likely that we would develop reliable cognitive *theoretical* faculties, and thus that a naturalist has sufficient epistemic ground to maintain the reasonableness of the view that her theoretical cognitive faculties are reliable and her theoretical beliefs true.

1. Plantinga's Argument against Naturalism

Plantinga begins by claiming that a common belief, one that seems highly attractive to most people (not just theists), is that our cognitive faculties have the *function* of providing us with true belief.[1] This means that our cognitive faculties were designed with this intended purpose. He argues that from a theistic perspective, this view is not problematic, since the idea that God has created us with cognitive faculties with the purpose of acquiring true beliefs coheres well with most other common and central theistic beliefs. This is precisely what one would expect from a good, omniscient, and omnipotent supernatural being.[2] On the other hand, from a metaphysical naturalistic perspective, this view is not at all likely. Thus, from a naturalistic perspective, the view that the proper function of our cognitive faculties is the production of true beliefs is problematic. Why does Plantinga think that, given naturalism, reliable cognitive faculties are unlikely?

Metaphysical naturalists believe that we are the product of evolution by natural selection. Naturalism, therefore, implies Darwinian evolutionary theory. Plantinga points out that, if any purpose or proper function can be attributed to our cognitive faculties from the naturalistic perspective, it would have to be something like survival and not true belief. He argues: "If our cognitive faculties have originated as Dawkins thinks, then their ultimate purpose or function (if they have a purpose or function) will be something like *survival*; but then it seems initially doubtful that among their functions—ultimate, proximate, or otherwise—would be the production of true beliefs."[3] He then goes on to argue (using Patricia Churchland's arguments) that the combination of metaphysical naturalism and Darwin's evolutionary theory, a view he refers to as *naturalistic evolution* (henceforth NE), leads us to doubt two things: "(a) that the purpose of our cognitive systems is that of serving us with true beliefs, and (b) that they do in fact service us with true belief."[4]

Plantinga interprets Quine and Popper as defending the view that it is highly probable that evolution by natural selection alone could produce cognitive faculties that are reliable. He interprets Darwin and Churchland as holding the opposite view, namely, that it is improbable that evolution by natural selection alone could produce cognitive faculties that are reliable. He refers to this latter view as "Darwin's Doubt."[5] What Plantinga calls Darwin's Doubt, therefore, seems to be the key issue in his argument for the falsity of naturalism. Plantinga's argument in defense of Darwin's Doubt considers creatures similar to us living on a planet similar to ours. We are then to consider the likelihood that these creatures would develop reliable cognitive faculties through NE. He discusses five distinct possible ways in which these creatures' beliefs may be connected to their behavior. Of the five, only one would be connected in the right way to tend towards true beliefs under NE.[6] Such a belief structure would require two things: 1) that the beliefs be causally connected to behavior, and (2) that the behavior be adaptive. He explains: "A fifth (and final) possibility is that the beliefs of our hypothetical creatures are indeed both *causally connected with their behavior* [my emphasis] and also *adaptive* [my emphasis]."[7] If Plantinga's hypothetical creatures had such a belief structure, the probability that their cognitive faculties would be reliable, given NE, would be high. However, even with causally connected and adaptive belief systems there is no guarantee that this will lead to true belief. Plantinga argues: "So perhaps their behavior has been adaptive, and those beliefs could nonetheless be wildly wrong. There are indefinitely many belief-desire systems that fit adaptive behavior, but where the beliefs involved are not for the most part true. A share of probability has to be reserved for these as well."[8] Once these probabilities are equally distributed, it is evident that the likelihood that these creatures would develop reliable cognitive faculties through NE is low.[9] At a minimum, Plantinga argues, we should remain *agnostic* about the reliability of our cognitive faculties.

1.1 Argument for the Irrationality of NE

Plantinga argues that NE is irrational because agnosticism about the reliability of our cognitive faculties leads to skepticism about the reliability of our belief-producing cognitive faculties, and thus is an undercutting defeater for all our theoretical beliefs. (Notice that the conclusion that NE is irrational is different from the claim that it is probably false.) Plantinga claims that the there are only two possible ways out of this path to radical skepticism: (1) that one introduce a defeater for the defeater , or (2) that one introduce another source of evidence for the truth of the reliability of the theoretical-belief-producing cognitive faculties. If the naturalist can neither produce (1) nor (2), then the right attitude is to remain, at a minimum, *agnostic* towards all our theoretical beliefs. Notice that since NE is a theoretical belief, a naturalist should also come to doubt the truth of NE, and thus defeat his defeater. This opens the way to start over the belief process, which will continue in an endless loop. Thus, for a naturalist to accomplish (1), she must introduce a non-circular defeater. According to Plantinga, this undercutting defeater is an undefeatable defeater, and thus naturalism leads to skepticism about theoretical beliefs.

2. A Response to Plantinga's Argument against Naturalism

I want to refute Plantinga's conclusion for the irrationality of NE. To refute the claim that naturalism is irrational, I will demonstrate that given NE, we have reason to believe that we would develop reliable cognitive *theoretical* faculties. My argument complements two existing arguments.[10]

2.1 Reliability of Our Theoretical-Belief-Producing Cognitive Faculties

Plantinga distinguishes between cognitive mechanisms producing beliefs relevant to survival and reproduction, and cognitive mechanisms producing theoretical beliefs which are not relevant to survival and reproduction. I will refer to the former as *survival cognitive faculties* and to the latter as *theoretical cognitive faculties.* In essence, Plantinga concludes that from a naturalistic perspective it may be plausible to argue that cognitive faculties that are reliable-for-survival can be held to be reliable-for-truth. (Since my interest hereafter lies in the notion of reliable-for-truth and we have already made the distinction between survival cognitive faculties and theoretical cognitive faculties, I will use the term "reliable" as synonymous with reliable-for-truth). However, even if one were to concede that the probability that we develop reliable survival cognitive faculties (SR) given naturalistic evolution [i.e., P(SR/NE)] is high, the probability that we develop reliable theoretical cognitive faculties (TR) given naturalistic evolution [i.e., P(TR/NE)] remains low. Plantinga may be willing to consider the Darwinian principle that the development of faculties is connected to the survival needs of an organism as potential evidence for the view that survival cognitive faculties are reliable.[11] However, he argues that even if one could show that the reliability of our cognitive faculties can be justified by naturalistic evolution to the extent that they produce survival related *true* beliefs, they cannot be justified further. Since theoretical beliefs are not survival related, we have no reason to believe that our cognitive faculties are reliable-theoretical-belief-producing faculties.

Does one give up too much ground if one concedes that cognitive faculties producing beliefs relevant to survival and reproduction will tend to produce true belief given naturalistic evolution? Plantinga's strongest argument is against the reliability of cognitive faculties that produce theoretical beliefs: since theoretical beliefs are in no way relevant to an organism's survival, it is difficult to defend the thesis that they are probably reliable.

> So even if you think Darwinian selection would make it probable that certain belief-producing mechanisms—those involved in the production of beliefs relevant to survival—are reliable, that would not hold for the mechanisms involved in the production of the theoretical claims of science, such beliefs, for example as E, the evolutionary story itself. And of course the same would go for N.[12]

Plantinga claims that given the imprecision of probability arguments a more appropriate view to adopt with respect the reliability of theoretical cognitive faculties is agnosticism.[13] So the conclusion is not that our theoretical cognitive faculties are probably defective, but rather that we do not know (i.e., we have no reason to believe) that they are reliable. From this central idea of agnosticism about the reliability of one's theoretical cognitive faculties he constructs his main argument for the irrationality of naturalism. Since we cannot trust our theoretical cognitive faculties, we cannot trust any of the content of the beliefs that result from their theoretical processes. Once the process has been corrupted its results are called into question, producing a radical form of skepticism about our theoretical beliefs. According to Plantinga, this does not demonstrate the falsity of NE, but it does make it irrational for one to sustain such a view.

2.2 Evolutionary Darwinian Response

An evolutionary response to Plantinga's argument requires that we show that the probability of reliable theoretical cognitive faculties (TR), given naturalistic evolution [i.e., P(TR/NE)] is high. But it seems that such an argument is precluded because theoretical beliefs are not relevant to an organism's survival and reproduction. However, if the probability of reliable survival cognitive faculties (SR), given naturalistic evolution [i.e., P(SR/NE)], is high, and thus faculties and cognitive mechanisms producing beliefs relevant to survival and reproduction tend to produce true beliefs, what needs to be considered is the relationship between survival cognitive faculties and theoretical cognitive faculties. In what follows, I want to argue that there is an important and relevant relationship between these two cognitive faculties that neither Plantinga nor his critics consider. I want to show that in the arsenal of Darwinism there are numerous doctrinal weapons to defend the view that if P(SR/NE) is high, then there is good reason to believe that P(TR/NE) is also high, *even if theoretical beliefs are not directly related to an organism's survival and reproduction.*

Earlier, I questioned whether one gives up too much ground to naturalists, if one concedes that it may be likely that P(SR/NE) is high. Why? Darwin's *law of correlation of growth* claims that a consequence of the development of variations that are selected through natural selection is the development of related and associated traits that are not selected for by natural selection. This, coupled with Darwin's doctrine of *natural selection*, provides part of the required material for supporting the view that if P(SR/NE) is high, then there is good reason to believe that P(TR/NE) is also high.

The central idea of the *law of correlation of growth* is that an organism's parts are so intimately connected that, during the different stages of its development, a modification of one part cannot take place without a modification in another part. In addition, the complexity of organisms is such that these secondary effects of natural selection are extremely difficult to understand or predict. Darwin explains:

> It is, however, far more necessary to bear in mind that there are many unknown laws of correlation of growth, which, when one part of the organization is modified through variation, and the modifications are accumulated by natural selection for the good of the being, will cause other modifications, often of the most unexpected nature.[14]

What evidence does Darwin have for the law of correlation of growth? Darwin obtained part of the supportive evidence for this doctrine in his observations of domestic animals and breeders' power of accumulative selection of these animals' variations in a direction that was useful for the breeders. As one specific variation was selected for and accumulated over generations, the growth and development of the targeted variation would become obvious, but so would other variations. These secondary effects of artificial selection were widespread and documented by Darwin. However, even if Darwin's law of correlation of growth could be defended, the relations are so complex that we cannot deduce any laws concerning the regulation of these correlations. Therefore, it seems that they would not be very helpful for the naturalist's argument.

While Darwin noted the infinite complexity of organisms and the complexity involved in associating the diverse, indirect consequences of artificial and natural selection, he also noted certain regulative doctrines—the law of correlation of growth being one of them. Darwin also associated certain regulative laws governing the outward manifestations of the law of correlation of growth. For instance, Darwin explains: "The several parts of the body which are homologous, and which, at an early embryonic period, are alike, seem liable to vary in an allied manner."[15] Homologous parts or faculties share a similar or related structure, function, or origin. So when natural selection, through the accumulation of a given variation, modifies an organism's part or faculty, we should expect changes in homologous parts and faculties. Thus, we should expect changes in parts or faculties that are either similar or related in structure, function, or origin to that which is modified. Let us refer to this as the *law of homologous relations*. Notice that the obscurity of the law of correlation of growth concerns the mysterious homologous relations that exist in organisms and not in the truth of the *law of homologous relations*. Therefore, in cases when homologous relations are perspicuous, there is no reason that the law of correlation of growth cannot be applied as an explanatory account of the particular modifications in question. Returning, then, to our analysis of the relationship between the theoretical cognitive faculties and survival cognitive faculties, we can argue that these faculties exhibit a homologous relationship. Why? For one thing, they share a similar physical origin, namely, the brain. Thus, it should be expected that the development of the brain as a result of natural selection's power of accumulation on survival cognitive faculties will affect the growth and development of the many other faculties related to the brain. But why should we believe that theoretical cognitive faculties should develop in the direction of reliabilism?

To answer this question, we have to appeal to Darwin's doctrine of *natural selection*. Faculties designed by natural selection will develop so that the information they provide about reality and its operations will be more accurate relative to the survival needs of the organism in question. The evidence for this is the basic Darwinian principle that natural selection always designs organisms toward those variations which will provide functions that will benefit the organism's survival chances. Whether the faculty in question is the antenna of an insect, the ears of a bat, or the eyes of a human, we would expect that, given NE, its evolutionary future (if it has a future) will develop towards a structural design that is most advantageous for the organism's survival. This is the evolutionary tendency that should be expected of all organic mechanisms that develop under a design that is guided by the forces of natural selection. Therefore, representations that provide accurate descriptions of reality and its operations relative to the organism's survival needs will be the result of a design by natural selection. But how does this help the naturalist, since, if theoretical reasoning is not survival related, there would be no tendency to use it, and thus no reason to believe that it has developed as a reliable cognitive faculty under NE?

To conclude this argument, we need to consider Plantinga's idea of theoretical reason. What are these theoretical faculties that Plantinga thinks are not related to survival? He says ". . . belief involved in logic or mathematics or set theory course."[16] Plantinga is right that these topics are in no way related to survival, for their nature is theoretical. We may add to this list the study of being *qua* being, substance, and most philosophical topics. Indeed, much of our reflective thought is not necessary for our survival. Plantinga, however, seems to be conflating the object of cognition with the process of cognition. Could we not argue that these theoretical thought processes share a neurological common origin with survival thought processes;

and, moreover, that this common neurological origin is one that has been greatly useful for our species' survival? Let us refer to this as the *neurological principle of identity.* If theoretical cognitive faculties and survival cognitive faculties are in actuality one and the same faculty, why shouldn't we expect that if the probability that survival cognitive faculties are reliable, given NE, is high, then the probability that theoretical cognitive faculties are reliable, given NE, is also high? I believe we should expect that *Homo sapiens* would manifest this correlation of growth in their reasoning power. Why? The basic reasoning involved in survival-related cognitive activities, such as tool-making, escaping from enemies, capturing enemies, avoiding predators, capturing prey, and forming primitive social groups, etc., exhibits the basic foundational qualities involved in theoretically-related cognitive activities, such as those involved in scientific investigations. We can therefore argue that if P(SR/NE) is high, then there is good reason to belief that P(TR/NE) is also high, *even if theoretical beliefs are not directly related to an organism's survival and reproduction*. If this argument is successful, then we have reason to trust our theoretical cognitive faculties, and thus we also have reason to trust any of the content of the beliefs that result from these processes. Thus, we can reject Plantinga's conclusion that accepting naturalism is irrational.

3. Conclusion

I want to clarify that in this paper I do not defend naturalism over theism, or the view that our cognitive faculties are explained better under a naturalistic hypothesis than they are under a theistic hypothesis. I have not attempted to demonstrate that our cognitive faculties are derived from Darwinian evolution or the view that, given naturalistic evolution, our theoretical cognitive faculties are reliable. Instead, I have attempted to defend the weaker claim that a naturalist has sufficient epistemic ground to maintain the reasonableness of the view that her theoretical cognitive faculties are reliable. As a consequence, she does not have to maintain an agnostic position with respect to the reliability of her theoretical cognitive faculties and theoretical beliefs. And further, the naturalist is epistemically justified in the source of her theoretical beliefs, and thus has no undefeatable defeater. It is, therefore, not irrational to be a naturalist.

Barry University

Notes

1. Plantinga says, "Most of us think (or would think on reflection) that at least a function or purpose of our cognitive faculties is to provide us with true beliefs." Alvin Plantinga, *Warrant and Proper Function* (Oxford: Oxford University Press, 1993) 216.

2. This view is questionable. Some may argue that what one should expect from God is that we have the necessary cognitive mechinisms to come to love Him. But why should we believe that true theoretical beliefs are necessary for this?

3. Alvin Plantinga, *Warrant and Proper Function*, 218.

4. Ibid.

5. I will not discuss here whether Plantinga provides an accurate exegesis of Darwin's view. However, he does not provide much evidence in the way of defending this representation of Darwin.

6. First, there is some probability that beliefs are not causally connected to behavior. Second, there is some probability that beliefs are epiphenomenal effects of causes that also cause behavior. Third, there is the probability that beliefs are "syntactically" connected and not "semantically" connected. And fourth, there is the probability that beliefs are maladaptive.

7. Alvin Plantinga, *Warrant and Proper Function*, 225.

8. Ibid., 227.

9. Plantinga uses Bayes's Theorem in his discussion of probabilities.

10. See Evan Fales, "Darwin's Doubt, Calvin's Calvary," and William Ramsey, "Naturalism Defended," in *Naturalism Defeated? Essays on Planting's Evolutionary Argument Against Naturalism*, ed. James Beilby (Ithaca & London: Cornell University Press, 2002).

11. According to this principle, for instance, we would not expect that our visual perception to develop with the purpose of acquiring the power to see microscopic images, since these images would not be immediately advantageous for our survival. Thus the development of the eye would not be expected to be so sophisticated so as to produce such images.

12. Alvin Plantinga, *Warrant and Proper Function*, 233.

13. He says, "Still, the argument for a low estimate of P([T]R/(N&E&C)) is by no means irresistible. In particular, our estimates of the various probabilities involved in estimating P([T]R/(N&E&C)) with respect to that hypothetical population were (of necessity) both extremely imprecise and also poorly grounded. You might reasonably hold, therefore, that the right course here is agnosticism: one does just not know (and has no good way of finding out) *what* P([T]R/(N&E&C)) might be." Alvin Plantinga, *Warrant and Proper Function*, 229.

14. Charles Darwin, *Origin of Species* (New York: Random House Value Publishing Inc., 1979) 134.

15. Ibid., 182–182.

16. Alvin Plantinga, *Warrant and Proper Function*, 232.

Hylomorphism and Post-Cartesian Philosophy of Mind

William Jaworski

Abstract: Descartes developed a compelling characterization of mental and physical phenomena which has remained more or less canonical for Western philosophy ever since. The greatest testament to the power of Cartesian thinking is its ubiquity. Even philosophers who are critical of post-Cartesian anthropology (philosophers, for instance, who are self-professed exponents of one or another form of hylomorphism) nevertheless *tacitly endorse Cartesian assumptions*. Part of what leads to this strange inconsistency is that by and large philosophers no longer know what a non-Cartesian anthropology looks like. I discuss some commitments characteristic of post-Cartesian philosophy of mind, and present an alternative conception of psychological phenomena more consistent with a hylomorphic framework.

1. Hylomorphism and the Post-Cartesian Tradition

Mind-body problems are a Cartesian legacy.[1] In the wake of the scientific revolution, Descartes developed a compelling characterization of mental and physical phenomena which has remained more or less canonical for Western philosophy since. Perhaps the greatest testament to the power of Cartesian thinking is its ubiquity. Even philosophers who are critical of Descartes or of post-Cartesian anthropology generally—philosophers, for instance, who are self-proclaimed exponents of some type of hylomorphism—*nevertheless tacitly endorse Cartesian assumptions*. They won't admit this *if asked*, of course; they nevertheless make their minds known in other ways: in the kinds of questions they ask, the problems they take seriously, and the solutions they find attractive. Part of what leads to this strange inconsistency is that by and large philosophers no longer know what a pre-Cartesian anthropology looks like. Imagination is limited by a dearth of alternatives, and the commitments of a specific philosophical tradition soon become general preconditions for intelligibility. I am concerned here with discussing some of the commitments characteristic of post-Cartesian philosophy of mind, and presenting an alternative more consistent with a hylomorphic psychology.

2. Two Post-Cartesian Assumptions

Post-Cartesian philosophers tend to endorse a dichotomous understanding of mental and physical concepts. I will refer to this as *The Mental-Physical Dichotomy Assumption* or simply *Dichotomy*. Dichotomy is the working hypothesis that human behavior can be described in terms of two vocabularies or conceptual frameworks, the mental and the physical, which are supposed to be logically independent of each other in the sense that a description of something in terms of one is supposed to imply nothing about it in terms of the other. Describing something in physical terms is supposed to imply nothing about its mental characteristics, and describing something in mental terms is supposed to imply nothing about its physical characteristics. The distinction is primarily conceptual not metaphysical. The mental and the physical are principally understood as two distinct types of vocabularies or conceptual frameworks which may or may not correspond to two distinct types of entities or phenomena.[2]

Dichotomy implies that it is conceivable for there to be "zombies," physical beings which are behaviorally indistinguishable from humans but which are nevertheless nonmental, and that it is conceivable for there to be "Cartesian egos," mental beings which are psychologically indistinguishable from humans but which are nevertheless nonphysical. Dichotomy does not imply, however, that the mental and physical conceptual frameworks are mutually exclusive, that something falling under a mental concept cannot also fall under a physical one. The idea, rather, is that the frameworks are *logically independent*; the application of the concepts belonging to one is *neutral* with regard to the application of concepts belonging to the other. Something's being mental does not imply that it is nonphysical, but neither does it imply that it is physical. Something which falls under a mental concept *need not* fall under a physical concept, but neither is it the case that it *must not* fall under a physical concept; the application of mental concepts is neutral with regard to physical conditions, and the same is true *mutatis mutandis* of physical concepts: Their application is neutral with regard to mental conditions.[3]

A second idea characteristic of post-Cartesian thinking is what I will call the *Mental Privacy Assumption*, or simply *Privacy*—the idea that the mental is or includes a domain of "private" subjective phenomena. Privacy is one way of formulating the mental side of Dichotomy.

The notions central to a private conception of mentality include *consciousness*, *subjectivity*, *introspectibility*, *privileged access*, and the like, whereas the notions central to a "public" or intersubjective conception of mentality are *intentionality* and *rationality*. Philosophers use the term 'consciousness' in a number of ways. In one sense, for instance, it is roughly synonymous with 'intentionality.'[4] But philosophers also use the term 'consciousness' to refer to what is supposed to be a private, "inner" domain of subjective ideas or impressions—phenomena to which supposedly I, the experiencing subject, and I alone enjoy privileged, perhaps incorrigible access. This is a fundamentally Cartesian conception of the mental.

In the *Meditations*, Descartes advanced what we might call an *inner-perception* model for psychological discourse. Psychological discourse, he suggested, is analogous to ordinary perceptual discourse; psychological predicates and terms are related to an "inner" domain of experiences in something analogous to the way talk of colors, sounds, shapes, and the like are related (or are supposed to be related) to an "outer" domain of objects. The objects in this room might not exist in fact, but they at least *seem* to exist, and we can observe and describe this domain of experiential *seemings* in a way that roughly parallels the way we take ourselves to observe and describe the objects in the room. Psychological language, our talk of various modes of thought, describes this "inner" domain of private appearances.

Privacy has been a highly influential way of characterizing the mental side of Dichotomy, and it remains at the forefront of contemporary philosophy of mind. Its principal advocates are philosophers who "take consciousness seriously" such as Thomas Nagel (1974, 1986, 1994), David Chalmers (1996, 2002b), Galen Strawson (1994), Gregg Rosenberg (2004), and (at one time at least) Frank Jackson (1982, 1994). These philosophers claim that we have direct introspective access to *qualia*: qualitative features of experiences (sounds, odors, flavors, tickles, itches, and the like), which are supposedly impossible to describe verbally or to share or cooperatively evaluate with others, but to which each of us individually has experiential access.

Together Dichotomy and Privacy underwrite various mind-body problems. Consider, for instance, the problem of other minds: If mental phenomena are private or subjective, if I alone have access to my mental states, then other people can't know what my mental states are, or whether I have any mental states at all. Conversely, I can have no access to other people's mental states—if in fact there are any other people since, for all I know, there might not be: the public, objective, physical bodies I see around me might simply be automata which act in every way *as if* they had consciousness experiences like mine, but which have no "inner" mental life at all.

The innovation of philosophers who take consciousness seriously has been to stand this skeptical worry on its head in order to support a certain kind of antireductionism (Nagel 1974; Jackson 1982, 1986). If reductive physicalism is true, they argue, and mental states are identical to physical states, then necessarily two beings which are physically indistinguishable must be mentally indistinguishable as well. And yet clearly, the argument runs, it is possible that two beings might be behaviorally—physically—indistinguishable and yet mentally distinct: the private inner experiences of one might differ from those of the other; one might be a *qualia zombie*, for instance, and lack altogether the type of inner private experiences the other has. Hence, the mental cannot be the physical, and reductive physicalism must be false.

A widespread aversion to reductionism has gained these ideas many sympathizers, and has therefore enlarged the appeal of a Cartesian conception of mentality—so much so that it is no longer confined to philosophical discussions, but has worked its way into scientific and even public discourse, as in a *New York Times* Op-Ed piece (June 20, 2005) by former governor of New York, Mario Cuomo:

> The best way to test [the] proposition . . . that human life exists as early as fertilization . . . would be . . . to consider testimony . . . describing when consciousness first appears. . . .

To many it seems obvious that there is something "inner" or "private" about our mental states. You cannot experience my pain, nor can I experience yours; you needn't make known to me your thoughts, nor need I make known to you mine. But there have long been those who have resisted the suggestion that these truisms support a Cartesian conception of mentality.[5] Following their lead, I will sketch an alternative non-Cartesian conception of psychological discourse and its relation to natural science. It claims that psychological predicates and terms are neither mentalistic nor physicalistic in the way post-Cartesian philosophy has described. I will begin by explaining how this conception fits into a broader hylomorphic framework—a *hylomorphic theory of mind.*

3. Action Descriptions and a Hylomorphic Theory of Mind

The term 'theory of mind' refers here to any philosophical psychology capable of addressing contemporary mind-body problems, and that means especially a philosophical psychology which provides an account of how psychological discourse is related to natural science. 'Hylomorphic' on the other hand refers to a metaphysic along the lines of Aristotle's. Its central idea is that particulars are composites of a structure and something structured. Organisms consist of materials or components of some empirically-specifiable sort structured in a way defined by the possession and exercise of certain capacities: developmental, metabolic, reproductive, perceptive, cognitive, and the like. Capacities of these sorts are what categorize organisms as living things of one or another kind, and the capacities which categorize *us* in particular as the kind of living things *we* are include capacities for engaging in activities expressed by psychological predicates and terms: thought, feeling, intentional action, and the like. A hylomorphic theory of mind ('HTM' henceforth) is a hylomorphic theory which is capable of addressing contemporary mind-body problems and hence capable of competing with the range of more familiar post-Cartesian alternatives. I take such a theory to consist of at least three components: first, a general ontology postulating entities of one or more generic ontological types such as substances, properties, events, facts, or the like; second, a special ontology consisting of an inventory of entities belonging to those types; and third, a philosophy of psychological language. I will focus only on the third of these components.

HTM's philosophy of psychological language is characterized by six features. It claims that psychological discourse is *action-inclusive*, *body-inclusive*, *externalistic*, *holistic*, *primitive*, and *heterologous*, as I call it; that is, the principles governing the use of its predicates and terms are structurally unique, and as a result cannot be modeled on the principles governing predicates and terms of other, non-psychological forms of discourse. Jointly these claims entail a view of psychological discourse which rejects both Dichotomy and Privacy. In what follows I will discuss only the first three of these features, and only in connection with the description of actions.

HTM rejects the idea that we can describe human behavior in terms of mental and physical concepts dichotomously understood. Instead, HTM claims that human beings are bodies, organisms, with distinctive properties expressed by *a unique vocabulary of predicates and terms which are neither mental nor physical in the post-Cartesian sense, but which share features of both*. The human body is not a mere collection of atoms or molecules, something exhaustively describable in the vocabulary of the natural sciences; nor is the human mind a collection of thoughts or impressions exhaustively describable in a mental vocabulary devoid of reference to bodily parts and conditions. Unlike post-Cartesian philosophy, HTM claims that the language we *really* use to describe human behavior is at once both psychological and bodily. Its stock of primitive predicates and terms includes the likes of 'believes,' 'desires,' and 'hopes,' but it also includes 'walks,' 'shouts,' and 'grapples,' as well as 'hand,' 'mouth,' and 'foot.' In other words, it includes not just an inventory of prototypical mental expressions, but also an inventory of expressions for the description of actions and for the description of the bodily parts and conditions involved in their performance.

According to HTM, *agency* is a psychological concept; the vocabulary we use to describe what people *do* is part of the same conceptual apparatus we use to describe what they *think* and *feel*. HTM agrees with Davidson therefore that "intentional actions are clearly included in the realm of the mental along with thoughts, hopes, and regrets. . . ." (1970, 211). It claims that psychological language is *action-inclusive*. It also claims that psychological language is *body-inclusive*; that the application of action predicates and terms requires the satisfaction of certain bodily conditions. HTM goes beyond the ontological point that the occurrence of thought and action requires the satisfaction of both psychological and bodily conditions; its point is *conceptual* as well—the very *meanings* of predicates and terms used to describe human thought and action imply the satisfaction of bodily conditions. It is not conceptually possible, for instance, to whistle or sing without a mouth, or to snap one's fingers without fingers. According to HTM, the language we use to describe human behavior is not an amalgamation of two distinct vocabularies, a mental and a physical; it is rather a vocabulary specially suited to the description of beings which are at once bodies, knowers, and agents—bodies whose knowing and acting are irreducible behaviors not expressible in a vocabulary other than an action-inclusive, body-inclusive vocabulary of this distinctive sort. According to HTM, then, the post-Cartesian distinction between the mental and the physical misrepresents the language we actually use to describe human behavior.

In addition, HTM claims that the application of psychological predicates and terms depends not just on the satisfaction of bodily conditions, or on the satisfaction of mental conditions as Cartesians would conceive of them (states in some sense "internal to" the person or the organism); they require the satisfaction of certain *environmental conditions* as well. HTM claims, in other words, that psychological discourse is *externalistic* (Putnam 1975b, Burge 1979). According to HTM, the application of psychological predicates and terms depends on the organism's social and physical environment—its relations to other organisms and its surroundings.

We can illustrate the aforementioned points by considering some examples bearing on the description of actions. The first illustrates the dependence of action ascriptions on intentions; the second illustrates their dependence on the environment:

> *Example 1*: A mad neuroscientist has planted a device in my nervous system which allows him to control the movements of my limbs remotely, the way neuroscientist Jose Delgado once dramatically halted a charging bull with the push of a button.[6] The mad neuroscientist pushes a button which initiates a certain sequence of neuronal firings and muscular contractions: my arm moves toward the glass, and my hand grasps it. I am either sedated and unconscious while this is occurring, or else am consciously struggling in vain to overcome the movements—the way someone with Tourette's syndrome might struggle in vain to master various involuntary ticks. In any event, I do not intend to reach toward and grasp the glass.
>
> *Example 2*: I am frequently subject to very vivid and long-lasting hallucinations. In an attempt to understand my condition, scientists have connected me to a host of sophisticated devices which record the states of my nervous system. On one occasion I hallucinate that I am reaching for a glass of water though no glass of water is present. I move in every way exactly as if this were the case even though it is not. My arm moves in a certain direction exactly as if I were reaching for a glass, and my fingers close exactly as if I were grasping one. The experimental apparatus shows that the state of my nervous system at the time of this occurrence was precisely what it would have been if I had really been reaching for a glass and grasping it.

In both examples the same bodily movements occur: my arm extends and my fingers close; but in neither case do I perform an act of reaching for a glass of water. This is clear in Example 1 if we consider evaluations of what I've done: Suppose that under the circumstances reaching for a glass of water would be morally or legally blameworthy. If the neuroscientist forced my limbs to move, I would not (rightly) incur moral or legal blame. My limb movements do not count as an action, and the reason, it seems, is that they are not accompanied by an intention to move them. The case of Example 2 is even clearer: I fail to perform an act of reaching for a glass of water in this case because *there is no glass of water*.

These examples illustrate that ascribing to someone the performance of an action requires that the agent intend to perform the action, and that the agent be situated in an environment suitable for its performance. For me to perform an act of reaching for a glass of water, I must intend to do so, and I must be situated in an environment with a glass of water toward which I can reach.

Further examples show that the application of action predicates requires certain social conditions as well.[7] Austin's examples concern speech acts specifically:

> The uttering of the words is, indeed, usually a, or even the, leading incident in the performance of the act . . . but it is far from being usually, even if it is ever, the sole thing necessary if the act is to be deemed to have been performed . . . it is always necessary that the circumstances in which the words are uttered should be in some way, or ways, appropriate, and it is very commonly necessary that either the speaker himself or other persons should also perform certain other actions. . . . Thus, for naming the ship, it is essential that I should be the person appointed to name her, for (Christian) marrying, it is essential that I should not be already married with a wife living, sane and undivorced, and so on. (Austin 1962, 8–9)

Wittgenstein made a similar point: Putting a crown on a man's head, he said, is a coronation only in certain social circumstances (*PI* 584).[8] (Malcolm extended Wittgenstein's point to *thoughts* as well as action in a move which anticipated the externalism of Putnam and Burge.)[9] Application conditions for action predicates, conditions which are conceptually necessary for their application to an object or objects, comprise not just bodily movements, then, but also psychological, environmental, and social conditions as well.[10]

These conditions, moreover, must be related to each other in appropriate ways. Consider another example: Suppose I believe (falsely) that saying, "Abracadabra!" will cause the death of my rival. I utter the fateful word, and it just so happens that at that very moment my rival, who is always careless when crossing busy streets, is struck by a bus and killed. We don't ascribe to me the act of killing my rival despite the fact that he *was* killed, and I *did* intend to kill him. The reason is that my intention does not *explain* the killing. The killing occurred not because of any sorcerous powers I possess, but because of my rival's careless disposition. Likewise, if the mad neuroscientist causes my hand to grasp the glass, but this time I happen to want to grasp the glass, and even form the intention to do so, I still fail to act, and for the same reason: my intention does not *explain why* my limbs are moving. They are moving not because I want a drink of water, but because the mad neuroscientist is triggering the appropriate neuromuscular events. In order for an action to occur, the intention must *cause* or *explain* the action.

And that's not all. The intention must cause or explain the action *in the right way*. Consider standard examples of deviant causal chains in which the agent is situated in the right social and physical environment to perform an action of a certain type, intends to perform an action of that type, the intention explains what the agent does, and yet fails to do so in a way that qualifies the agent's doing as an action (Bennett 1965; Chisholm 1966; Davidson 1980, Essay 4; Mele 1992). Eleanor intends to humiliate Madeleine by spilling coffee on her in a way that looks like an accident. She decides to walk across the room and feign tripping on the rug. She begins to advance, but is made so nervous by the realization that she is actually acting on her intention that she trips unintentionally out of nerve-induced clumsiness, and soils Madeleine's dress. Eleanor intended to spill coffee on Madeleine; her intention also explains why she was crossing the room, why she got nervous, and hence why she ended up spilling the coffee. The problem is that it doesn't explain the spilling *in the right way*. The availability of another explanation of the spilling in terms of nervous states and their effects on coordination disqualifies the occurrence as an action. Actions occur only when the agent's intentions are causally or explanatorily related to the action in a very particular way.[11]

So the application of action predicates comprises at least five types of conditions: bodily conditions such as movements or other bodily states of the agent; intentions, beliefs, desires, and other paradigmatic mental conditions; environmental conditions; social conditions; and relations among all of these.[12] To describe something in psychological terms, then, is not to describe occult inner phenomena, but *patterns of interaction among organisms and their environments*. The vocabulary we use to describe distinctively human behavior is a cohesive whole which integrates a range of intentional, social, environmental, and bodily conditions, all of which are conceptually necessary for the application of psychological predicates and terms. It is therefore at odds with both Dichotomy and Privacy. Mental states are not private possessions; they are not impressions on the screen of some inner theatre, not something "in the head"; they are something public, something "in the world." Psychological discourse is a way of describing the behavior of animals who relate in complex ways to other animals and their environments, and whose ways of being thus related constitute a shared, "public" domain of rational evaluation. Psychological discourse is a social language; it is *the* social language, *the* vocabulary in terms of which we describe the characteristic activities of social animals of the sort which humans are. It remains to consider how psychological discourse thus understood is related to scientific discourse.

4. Organic Composition and the Natural Science of Human Behavior

According to HTM, organisms are structured beings; more specifically, they are *multi-structure complexes*, complexes of multiple hierarchically-arranged systems and subsystems. According to HTM, psychological discourse concerns one type of structure; natural scientific discourse concerns another. The language of beliefs, desires, states of character, personality traits, and the like describes and partially constitutes those patterns of engagement with and response to other people, our physiological states, and the environment, which are bound up with rational evaluation and normative concepts such as choice and moral responsibility. This type of rational behavior includes what I will call *the natural science of human behavior*.

According to HTM, the natural scientific study of human behavior marks the attempt to answer certain kinds of questions about human activities and capacities. The natural sciences are often concerned, for instance, with answering certain types of how-questions—questions such as *How are humans able to generate a three-dimensional visual field from a pair of two-dimensional retinal images?* or *How are humans able to coordinate the movement of their limbs in the production of complex aesthetic effects as in dance or musical performance?* Questions such as these request an analysis of a certain capacity or activity in terms of a number of contributing "steps." Consider by analogy the question *How does one dance a swing*? It expects an answer which breaks down the dance into a number of components such as, "One-two-three, one-two-three, back-step." We can call how-questions of this sort *analytic how-questions*.

There are several types of analytic how-questions. Of particular interest here are *how-questions of mechanism*. Consider again the question *How does one dance a swing*? The answer, "One-two-three, one-two-three, back-step," takes the question to ask for a *method*. The answer, "First, get a good teacher; then practice, practice, practice," takes the question to ask for *means*. An answer which takes the question to ask for a mechanism is harder to imagine. Suppose, however, that an impatient student in a neuroscience class complained as follows: "Look, all semester we've been talking about how individual neurons perform simple little tasks, but what I want to know is how humans manage to perform big complicated tasks. For instance, how does one dance a swing?" In this context, the answers, "First, get a good teacher; then practice," and "One-two-three, one-two-three, back-step" are clearly out of place. What the student has in mind is an answer such as, "The primary motor cortex has a group of cells which generate actions potentials; and these in turn trigger action potentials in the adjacent cells and," etc. Such an answer aims at describing the *mechanisms* at work in dancing a swing.

How-questions of mechanism are often a point of departure for natural scientific investigation, and for a type of explanation Cummins (1975) has called 'functional analysis.' We understand how the eye contributes to vision, for instance, by analyzing its activity into a number of subactivities each of which is performed by a subsystem. This analytic methodology can be iterated with regard to the subsystems themselves. We can ask how, say, the eye's *receptor* subsystem works, and its receptive activity can be analyzed into further *sub*-subactivities performed by *sub*-subsystems: the *introduction* of light energy to the system, its *conversion* to neural energy, its *transmission* to other subsystems, etc. We use the same analytic methodology when describing how, say, the conversion subsystem works: we postulate a series of *sub-sub-sub*activities performed by *sub-sub-sub*systems: an incoming photon *strikes* a receiver molecule; this *initiates* a chemical reaction which in turn *activates* sodium channels on the cell membrane, and so on. This analytic process can be iterated until the relevant subactivities are no longer analyzable—a level at which subsystems are unanalyzable simples, presumably the level of fundamental physics.[13]

According to HTM, the structural composition of organisms is reflected in the way we study them scientifically. Analytic how-questions and Cummins-style functional analyses provide a basis for understanding the notion of an *organic part*, or *organ*. The general idea is this: An organism is capable of performing a range of activities expressed by a vocabulary of primitive predicates and terms. Each of those activities can be analyzed into a number of mechanistic subactivities performed by various subsystems. Those subsystems are the organism's functional or organic parts—its organs. Something is a part of an organism, in other words, if and only if it performs a subactivity, or sub-subactivity, or sub-sub-subactivity, or etc. which contributes to the performance of some activity of that organism.

If the notion of a mechanistic or what I sometimes call a *functional* contribution to the activity of a whole can serve as a basis for the organic part-whole relation, it can serve as a principle for organic part individuation as well: parts *x* and *y* of organism *z* are distinct just in case they contribute to the activity of *z* in different ways; they are distinct, in other words, just in case they perform different *functions* in *z*.[14]

Since parthood is a relation, something's status as an organic part depends on its relationship to an organic whole. Some things, however, such as an electron, are capable of existing independently of organisms. They stand in organic part-whole relations merely contingently. According to HTM, these entities display a dualism of organic and nonorganic properties. An mRNA molecule, for instance, has certain properties (such as mass) irrespective of its environment. Under the right conditions, however, that molecule contributes to the activities of a whole; in a living cell, it operates as a *messenger molecule*, a functional contributor to the cell's organic processes. According to HTM, atoms, molecules, electrons, and the like can be organs. Nucleic acids, hormones, and neural transmitters are perhaps the clearest examples. They are *genes*, growth *factors*, metabolic and behavioral *regulators*. A string of DNA always has certain atomic or molecular properties regardless of its environment; according to HTM, however, it *acquires new properties* when integrated into a cell; it makes a functional contribution to the activity of the whole, and gains thereby the status of an organic part. It and parts like it are literally *organ-ized* in a living thing.

HTM claims, then, that there are two irreducibly distinct types of properties: properties which characterize organic structures, and properties which certain things possess independently of their inclusion in organic structures. According to HTM, the properties and relations expressed by psychological predicates and terms are of the former, organic sort. They are complex relations involving organisms, their environments, and their bodily states, all of which have a place in a structure of rational relations. Certain questions about that structure create a context in which natural scientific investigation contributes to our understanding of psychological behavior. The natural science of human behavior aims at describing the substructures which enable humans to engage in the behaviors they do (the composition of those substructures, their states, their evolutionary origins, the conditions necessary for their maintenance, etc.).

According to HTM, then, psychological discourse and natural science are in different lines of work. Psychological discourse is descriptive and partially constitutive of human rational behavior; the natural science of human behavior, on the other hand, is a species of rational behavior which aims at describing the substructures which make that behavior possible. Both types of structures are essential to distinctively human behavior. Each conceptual framework has, therefore, the limited aim of describing and explaining a distinct type of structure—the structure of reasons in human behavior versus the substructures which enable rational behavior to occur—and for that reason, neither psychological discourse nor natural science could ever provide a complete account of human behavior. Neither has the resources to answer all the questions about human activities and capacities we are capable of asking, and which constitute our investigation of human nature.

Instead, they address different aspects of human behavior, or more precisely, different levels or types of human behavioral organization or structure in what is a multi-structural phenomenon.

A theory along these lines is at once both non-Cartesian, and yet in a certain sense post-Cartesian. It is capable of addressing the same issues as rival post-Cartesian theories, but it does so from a non-Cartesian understanding of psychological discourse and psychophysical relations. It has enough in common with its post-Cartesian competitors that it can dialogue fruitfully with them, but is sufficiently different that it is not committed to endorsing their conclusions about what humans are and what the natural sciences can or cannot reveal about them.[15]

Fordham University

Notes

1. Contemporary philosophy of mind intersects at various points the philosophy of language, philosophy of science, ethics, epistemology, and metaphysics. The metaphysical intersection deals with mind-body problems. These have two features in common: a distinction between mental and physical phenomena, and premises which make it difficult to see how the two are related. Consider, for instance, the following claims: (i) We are conscious beings; but (ii) we are composed entirely of non-conscious parts (molecules, atoms, etc.). It seems that (iii) no number of non-conscious parts could jointly produce a conscious whole, for if N atoms do not constitute a conscious whole, it is implausible to suppose $N+1$ atoms could, and yet it seems that (iv) the properties of composites are determined by the properties of their parts, the way my mass, for instance, is determined by the masses of the atoms and molecules composing me. Given reasonable assumptions, claims (i)–(iv) are jointly inconsistent, and yet each enjoys a certain *prima facie* plausibility. It is difficult to know which to reject, or how to challenge the validity of the argument which purports their inconsistency.

2. Neither dualism nor monism is supposed to be true by definition. Determining the truth or falsity of one or the other is supposed to require argument, and hence the definitions in terms of which these theories are understood must be neutral with regard to their truth or falsity. If the mental were defined not as a type of discourse or concept, however, but straightaway as a type of *property* or *thing*, a nonphysical one, dualism *would* be true by definition. The sense, therefore, that the truth or falsity of dualism or some form of monism is a live philosophical issue which cannot be settled simply by attending to definitions cannot be sustained if the mental-physical distinction is drawn metaphysically. The mental and the physical must be defined as two distinct vocabularies or conceptual frameworks which, in the absence of further arguments, may or may not describe the same domain of phenomena.

3. This point has often been misconceived. Hobbes, for instance, wrongly understood Descartes's *Meditations* this way (AT VII, 173). The text of *Meditation Two* (AT VII, 27–28), as well as Descartes's need for an argument establishing the real distinction of mind and body in *Meditation Six*, and his response to Hobbes (AT VII, 175) set the record straight. More recently, Searle has made a similar mistake when discussing what he calls "conceptual dualism": "It is customary to think of dualism as coming in two flavors, substance dualism and property dualism; but to these I want to add a third, which I will call 'conceptual dualism.' This view

consists in taking the dualistic concepts very seriously, that is, it consists in the view that in some important sense 'physical' implies 'nonmental' and 'mental' implies 'nonphysical.' Both traditional dualism and materialism presuppose conceptual dualism, so defined. I introduce this definition to make it clear why it seems to me best to think of materialism as really a form of dualism. It is that form of dualism that begins by accepting the Cartesian categories" (Searle 1992, 26). Searle wrongly takes the post-Cartesian mental-physical distinction to be founded not on the neutrality of one framework with respect to the other in the sense just described, but on the exclusion of one by the other. He claims that the traditional vocabulary of post-Cartesian philosophy takes the application conditions of physical predicates and terms to require the *non-satisfaction* of mental conditions, and the application conditions of mental predicates and terms to require the *non-satisfaction* of physical conditions. Searle claims his view rejects conceptual dualism, and he is right. That claim, however, seems rather uninteresting since no one in post-Cartesian philosophy endorses conceptual dualism as he conceives of it. What is far more interesting is the fact that Searle formulates his own theory in terms of the standard post-Cartesian mental-physical—an unfortunate tribute to the entrenchment of post-Cartesian modes of thought.

4. When phenomenologists, for instance, speak of "perceptual consciousness," of how, say, our perceptions of the objects around us are structured or "constituted," they are talking about our perceptions *of* certain things. This concerns the directionality, the "aboutness" of intentionality.

5. They include Wittgenstein and those influenced by him, as well as philosophers weaned on Greek classics such as Gilbert Ryle and J. L. Austin, and also certain American philosophers such as Wilfrid Sellars, Donald Davidson, the later Hilary Putnam, and Tyler Burge.

6. Horgan, John. 2005. "The Forgotten Era of Brain Chips." *Scientific American* 293: 66–73.

7. Anscombe (1957) too adverts to the necessity of the right environmental conditions in her account of action: " . . . moving his arm up and down with his fingers round the pump handle *is*, in these circumstances, operating the pump; and, in these circumstances, it *is* replenishing the house water-supply; and, in these circumstances, it *is* poisoning the household . . . there is one action with four descriptions, *each dependent on wider circumstances*" (46; final emphasis added).

8. "A coronation is the picture of pomp and dignity. Cut one minute of this proceeding out of its surroundings: the crown is being placed on the head of the king in coronation robes.—But in different surroundings gold is the cheapest of metals, its gleam is thought vulgar. There the fabric of the robe is cheap to produce. A crown is a parody of a respectable hat" (Wittgenstein 1953, 584).

9. "A thought requires circumstances or, in Wittgenstein's word, 'surroundings' [*Umgebung*]. Putting a crown on a man's head is a coronation only in certain circumstances. The behaviour of exclaiming 'Oh, I have not put out the milk bottles,' or the behaviour of suddenly jumping up, rushing to the kitchen, collecting the bottles and carrying them outside—such behaviour expresses the thought that one has not put out the milk bottles *only in certain circumstances*. The circumstances necessary for this simple thought are complex. They include the existence of an organised community, of a practice of collecting and distributing milk, of a rule that empty bottles will not be collected unless placed outside the door, and so on. These practices, arrangements and rules could exist only if there was

a common language; and this in turn would presuppose shared activities and agreement in the use of language. The thought about the milk bottles requires a background of mutual purpose, activity and understanding" (Malcolm 1964, 176). Twin Earth thought experiments showed that the deployment of propositional attitude expressions depended on social and environmental conditions. The considerations advanced here show that the deployment of action predicates depends on social and environmental conditions in the same way. When I say, "Eleanor checkmated Alexander by moving her queen to h7," I am saying that Eleanor is situated in a certain physical and social environment, that she and Alexander have certain intentions, desires, and beliefs, and that under such conditions, she has undertaken certain bodily movements. By contrast, someone who was moving in every way exactly as if she were checkmating an opponent would *not* be doing so if there were no opponent, or if she lacked the relevant intentions, desires, or beliefs, or inhabited a world in which there were no such game as chess.

10. Strawson (1959, 110) refers to such conditions as 'logically adequate criteria' for deploying a certain predicate or description. Wittgenstein (1953) too calls them criteria, and distinguishes them from symptoms, as Anthony Kenny explains: "Where the relation between evidence and conclusion is not something discovered by empirical investigation, but is something which must be grasped by anyone who possesses the concept of the relevant kind of thing, then the evidence is not a mere symptom, but is a criterion of the state of affairs in question. A red sky at night may be a symptom of good weather the following morning; but the absence of clouds, the shining of the sun, etc., tomorrow are not just symptoms but criteria for the good weather" (Kenny 1989, 5).

11. Searle (1983) tries to get at this by using the language of causal self-reference: The intention must include that the action be done by carrying out this very intention. Davidson, on the other hand says, "I despair of spelling out . . . the way in which attitudes must cause actions if they are to rationalize them" (Davidson 1980, 79).

12. Importantly, the bodily condition needn't specify the occurrence of certain movements, but could specify their non-occurrence as well. Consider so-called *negative actions*: refusing to sign one's name, abstaining from fatty foods, refraining from voicing a wry quip, invoking one's Fifth Amendment right, etc. These appear to be genuine actions. They can be done intentionally, willfully; one can try to do them, fail in one's attempt, merit praise or blame as a result, etc. Their performance, however, does not consist in the occurrence of any particular bodily movements; rather, they occur only if certain social and environmental conditions obtain together with certain intentions on the part of the agent, and the agent does *not*, for instance, undertake bodily movements of certain sorts.

13. The idea is similar in many respects to what homuncular functionalists have claimed as the basis of their view (Lycan 1987). The difference between HTM and homunctionalism is that the latter endorses a functionalist conception of mental properties and psychological discourse which HTM rejects. According to homunctionalism, mental properties are higher-order properties; having one amounts to having some lower-order property satisfying a certain description. It claims therefore that psychological discourse is an abstract language for the description of what are at bottom fundamental physical processes. HTM denies this understanding of mental properties and psychological discourse. It takes mental properties to be primitive first-order properties corresponding to a distinctive type of ontological structure, and it takes psychological predicates and terms to be primitive first-order predicates and terms which express those properties.

14. The result is a view of organic composition similar in many respects to the view van Inwagen (1996, 94-95) has defended. HTM's account of organic composition can be taken as a way of elaborating van Inwagen's idea of being "caught up in a life": To be caught up in the life of an organism is to make a mechanistic or functional contribution to its activity. Roughly, then, *x* is an organic part of *y* just in case *y* performs an activity which admits of a mechanical analysis, *M*, into subactivities, and *x* performs one of those subactivities. There is, then, an organic part corresponding to each of the subactivities postulated by *M*. Call the subactivity performed by organic part *p* of organism *o*, the *function of p in o relative to M*, and call the parts which perform the subactivities postulated by *M*, the *M-parts of o*. In that case, organic parts can be identified and distinguished in terms of their functions: *x* and y are the same *M*-part of *z* exactly if the function of *x* in *z* relative to *M* is identical to the function of *y* in *z* relative to *M*.

15. *Reply to Commentator*: Many thanks to Kevin Sharpe for his delightful and very incisive comments. I've found them very stimulating, and I'm gratified to hear that he's attracted to a hylomorphic view. I think he's found some very nice examples which illustrate some important points—examples which, he says, challenge first my claim that psychological discourse (including action discourse) is body-inclusive, and second, my claim that psychological discourse is externalistic. So let me say a couple words in response.

First, I'm not *too* worried about Kevin's examples. If he's right that the application conditions of some action predicates are independent of bodily conditions, I'm not sure it affects my rejection of Dichotomy all that much. Rejecting the latter would require at a minimum that, say, *a significant core* of psychological predicates imply the satisfaction of bodily conditions. ('A significant core' and not just 'at least one' because an isolated case could probably be accommodated within a post-Cartesian framework by means of some type of *ad hoc* maneuver.) I'm not sure, however, that the rejection of Dichotomy requires me to claim that the application of *all* action predicates implies the satisfaction of bodily conditions.

Second, if he's right, and not all psychological predicates contain bodily application conditions, their applicability might still depend on the applicability of psychological predicates which *do*. A predicate such as 'thinking,' for instance, might be applicable only to human organisms despite the fact that its application conditions do not advert to specific bodily parts. A fuller account of predicates of this type concerns another feature of HTM's philosophy of psychological discourse which I didn't discuss, namely, its *holism*. Davidson, for instance, among others, has argued that, say, believers must also be desirers, knowers, agents, etc., and this suggests that 'believes' might be applicable only to beings which lead more or less human lives. (The classic difficulties with behaviorism cited by Chisholm and Geach are instructive in this connection as well.) But because a full response along these lines concerns something I didn't discuss in the paper, I'm not going to say anything further about it here. The bottom line is this: If Kevin is right about the examples he cites, I'm not sure it affects my point all that much.

That said, however, I'm not sure that he *is* right; that is, I'm not sure I find his discussion of swinging a bat, reaching for a glass of water, and searching for the Fountain of Youth very convincing. In the case of swinging the bat, for instance, it's for a reason he himself suggests: 'swinging a bat' is a *determinable predicate*. (Notice I avoid his terminology of determinable *actions*; I don't think there are such things. There are only determinable *descriptions* of actions. Elsewhere I've developed an account of determinable predicates. It is highly technical and difficult to summarize because it trades on a logic of how-questions inspired by the work of Nuel Belnap, but I'd be happy to say more about it during the Q&A if you're interested.) If x swings a bat, we can always ask, "*How* did x swing it?" where we mean to request a more determinate description of the manner in which it was done—a description we often express using the instrumental "with" as in, "x swung it with his arms," or "with his feet," or as in Kevin's example, "with his mind," or "with his telekinetic powers," etc. It would never do to say, "He didn't swing it *with* anything; he just swung it." Swinging a bat (understood as an action) is always something that happens in some determinate way or other. In this sense it is no different from saying "x *did something*." The main point we can derive from this example is that we are *always free to describe our actions in indeterminate ways*. Criminals, philanderers, and teenagers do this all the time: "Where were you last night?" "Out." So too politicians: "What does your administration plan to do about Iraq?" "We are taking all necessary steps." The important point is this: *The fact that we can describe our actions in indeterminate but determinable ways does not show that the performance of those actions and fully determinate descriptions of them do not require the satisfaction of bodily conditions.*

Three points in connection with the reaching example: First, I detected a subtle equivocation in Kevin's discussion. The predicate 'reaches' behaves differently from 'reaches for x.' Kevin may be right that 'reaches' doesn't imply the existence of something toward which one reaches. But I wasn't discussing *reaching* simpliciter, but instead reaching *for something*. Second, let me say a word about the predicate 'searching for x,' and Kevin's nice example of Ponce de Leon and the Fountain of Youth. Although the surface grammar of 'searching for x' ('A-ing for x') superficially resembles that of 'reaching for x,' its depth grammar is clearly different. One expression implies that x exists; the other does not. The two have a different semantics, and are therefore different cases. So although I think Kevin is right that 'y searches for x' doesn't imply that x exists, it doesn't affect the claim that 'y *reaches* for x' *does* imply that x exists. Finally, Kevin claims he doesn't "get the intuition" that I'm not reaching for a glass of water when there is no glass of water but I hallucinate there is. So let me try to pump some of the relevant intuitions. Consider another case in which there is no glass of water; there is instead a glass of engine coolant. Is it plausible to suppose that if I mistakenly take the engine coolant for water and drink it that I have thereby succeeded in drinking water? If so, it's difficult to see how we could *ever* be mistaken in this way at all. Our ordinary discourse about mistakes of this sort seems to involve a heavy externalist component. Likewise, imagine that instead of a glass, there is a man's crotch or a woman's breast or your wallet or (worse yet!) your cocktail. At my trial for sexual harassment or theft would it do for legal counsel to say, "Judge, my client was merely reaching for a glass of water; that's not a crime"? I doubt it, and the reason again, I suspect, is that when push comes to shove our notion of what counts as an action is robustly externalistic. The way my lawyer should describe the situation parallels the way externalist theories of perception describe hallucination: Hallucinations are not perceptions, but non-perceptual states which might in certain ways superficially resemble perceptual ones. My lawyer should say not that I was reaching for a glass of water, but that I was in a state which in certain ways superficially resembled an act of reaching for a glass of water—I *took* myself (wrongly) to be reaching for a glass of water. Hallucinations are not a species of perception, and "misfired" attempts at intentional action are not a species of intentional action (although they might be reckoned "doings" of some other sort). In some ways, then, what Kevin has articulated is not so much a criticism of the externalist view, so much as an *internalist* alternative to it—something very much Cartesian in inspiration. I'll end on a note with which I began: We must never underestimate the power of Cartesian modes of thinking—even among philosophers attracted to a hylomorphic view.

Bibliography

Anscombe, G. E. M. 1957. *Intention*. Oxford: Blackwell.

Austin, J. L. 1962. *How to Do Things with Words*. Cambridge, MA: Harvard University Press.

Bennett, D. 1965. Action, Reason and Purpose. *Journal of Philosophy* 62: 85–95.

Burge, Tyler. 1979. Individualism and the Mental. *Midwest Studies in Philosophy* Vol. 4. Minneapolis: University of Minnesota Press, 73–122.

Chisholm, Roderick. 1966. Freedom and Action. In *Freedom and Determinism*, ed. K. Lehrer. New York: Random House, 28-44.

Cummins, Robert. 1975. Functional Analysis. *Journal of Philosophy* 72: 741–64.

Davidson, Donald. 1980. *Essays on Actions and Events*. Oxford: Clarendon Press.

Jackson, Frank. 1982. Epiphenomenal Qualia. *Philosophical Quarterly* 32: 127–136.

———. 1986. What Mary Didn't Know. *The Journal of Philosophy* 58: 291–95.

Kenny, Anthony. 1989. *The Metaphysics of Mind*. Oxford University Press.

Kim, Jaegwon. 1993. *Supervenience and Mind*. Cambridge University Press.

Lycan, William G. 1987. *Consciousness*. Cambridge, MA: The MIT Press/A Bradford Book.

Malcolm, Norman. 1964. Scientific Materialism and the Identity Theory. *Dialogue* 3: 115–25. Reprinted in *The Mind/Brain Identity Theory*, ed. C .V. Borst. New York: Macmillan, St. Martin's Press (1970).

Mele, Alfred R. 1992. *Springs of Action: Understanding Intentional Behavior*. New York: Oxford University Press.

Nagel, Thomas. 1974. What Is It Like to Be a Bat?. *Philosophical Review* 83: 435–50.

Putnam, Hilary. 1975. The Meaning of "Meaning." In *Mind, Language, and Reality: Philosophical Papers*, vol. 2. Cambridge University Press.

Searle, John. 1983. *Intentionality: An Essay in the Philosophy of Mind*. Cambridge University Press.

———. 1992. *The Rediscovery of the Mind*. Cambridge, MA: The MIT Press/A Bradford Book.

Strawson, P. F. 1959. *Individuals*. London: Methuen.

Wittgenstein, Ludwig. 1953. *Philosophical Investigations*, 3rd edition, trans. G. E. M. Anscombe. New York: Macmillan Publishing Co., Inc.

Shoemaker's Problem of Too Many Thinkers

David B. Hershenov

Abstract: Shoemaker maintains that when a functionalist theory of mind is combined with his belief about individuating properties and the well-known cerebrum transplant thought experiment, the resulting position will be a version of the psychological approach to personal identity that can avoid The Problem of Too Many Thinkers. I maintain that the costs of his solution—that the human animal is incapable of thought—are too high. Shoemaker also has not provided an argument against there existing a merely conscious being that is not essentially self-conscious but is spatially coincident with a person who is essentially self-conscious. Both the person and the merely sentient being will be transplanted when the cerebrum is. And another thought experiment will make it impossible for Shoemaker to identify the person and the merely conscious being.

Part I. Introduction

Psychological approaches to personal identity are distinguished from body and biological accounts of identity by the former's insistence that some kind of mind is essential for our persistence.[1] A problem arises for those psychological approaches that are committed to the person being spatially coincident with, but distinct from the human animal and body. (For the purposes of this paper, the human animal will be identified with the organic body.) If the person can think, then it would appear that the human animal can also. The person and the animal share the same brain as well as every other atom of every other organ. Given this physical identity and the fact that they both have the same causal relations to the environment and linguistic community, why then should only one of the two beings have the ability to think? Such mental duplication appears inevitable on pain of violating the supervenience of the mental on the physical, construing the latter to include causal ties to the environment as well as the physical properties of the animal. And if both can think then there arises what Olson called the "epistemic problem" of being unable to know whether one is the human animal or the person. The dilemma that both the person and the human animal can think has been labeled by Sydney Shoemaker "The Problem of Too Many Minds."[2] I prefer to call it the problem of too many thinkers since it could be that two thinkers share one mind much as conjoined twins could share one bruise.

Shoemaker maintains that when a functionalist theory of mind is combined with his belief about individuating properties and the well-known cerebrum transplant thought experiment, the resulting position will be a version of the psychological approach to personal identity that can avoid The Problem of Too Many Thinkers. I don't believe that Shoemaker's account has satisfactorily ruled out the biological account's solution to The Problem of Too Many Thinkers which identifies human persons and human animals while maintaining their persistence conditions are those characteristic of an organism.[3] The costs of Shoemakers' solution—that the human animal is incapable of thought—are too high. But even if I am wrong about how well his account can avoid the biological approach's concerns, The Problem of Too Many Thinkers does not go away. This is because Shoemaker has not provided an argument against there existing a merely sentient being (I am using "sentient" as a synonym for "conscious") that is not essentially self-conscious but is spatially coincident with a person who is essentially self-conscious. Both the person and the merely sentient being will transplanted when the cerebrum is.[4] And another thought experiment will make it impossible for Shoemaker to identity the person and the merely conscious being. Finally, there is one last too many thinkers worry that is due to the possibility of the thinking brain that results from Shoemaker abandoning his earlier belief in a brain state transfer device that allows the person to survive without his original brain.

Part II. Shoemaker's Attempt to Avoid Spatially Coincident Thinking Beings

Shoemaker tries to avoid The Problem of Too Many Thinkers by claiming that animals do not think. Since animals don't have minds and persons are not identical to animals but instead constituted by them, there is no duplication of thought problem. Shoemaker's position that the animal does not think is in part based on his notion that properties are identified and individuated by their contribution to the causal powers of the subject or substance that possesses them. The causal powers have implications about the future of their possessors. This means that what properties a thing will have will depend upon its persistence conditions. Shoemaker argues that if there are spatially coincident entities then their different persistence conditions will mean they won't share all their properties. He insists that whatever else a person is, it surely is a subject of thought, i.e., a being that thinks. The mental properties of the person are causally efficacious, bringing forth other mental property tokens and eventually actions by way of the physical properties of the cerebral cortex that instantiate them. If we assume that the functional role of certain mental properties is uninterrupted during the cerebrum transplant procedure in which a person leaves behind one animal and is placed into a new body, this suggests that those mental properties were never instantiated in either the new or the old animal. The mental properties contributed to the mental causal powers of the transplanted *person*, thus neither human animal thought even during the time it was spatially coincident with the body switching person.

To illustrate the above point, Shoemaker asks the reader to imagine a scenario in which a person appears to be calculating a complicated math problem before, during and after the entire transplantation procedure which, due to localized anesthesia, he is unaware is taking place. The person begins thinking about the problem when spatially coincident with one animal, continues his calculations despite being reduced to just a few pounds and inches when his cerebrum is removed, and completes his computation after becoming spatially coincident with a different animal into which his cerebrum has been transplanted. At the end he recounts each step of his reasoning. So described, it would seem that the mental processes involved in the search for a solution to the math problem began while the person possessed one organic body and ended when the person obtained a new organic body.[5] So neither organic body was in any sense the subject engaged in the entire mathematical calculation. And since mental properties are individuated by their complete causal/functional contributions to a subject or substance, neither human animal can be said to possess the mental properties involved in the mathematical reasoning. The mental properties possessed by the person before the transplant were not possessed by the spatially coincident animal constituting that person because they were causally connected to (post-transplant) mental states that were obviously not thoughts of the original animal. Shoemaker concludes that the human animal doesn't think in this scenario or any other. Only persons have mental properties and minds. Thus there is no Problem of Too Many Thinkers.

Part III. An Alternative Explanation of Cerebrum Transplants

I share Shoemaker's belief that there are not spatially coincident thinking entities in the above story, but don't believe that he has made a convincing case that the thinker is not a human animal, a being that is essentially alive, rather than an entity that is essentially a thinking creature and spatially coincident with the animal. Neither his causal powers account of properties, nor combining that with his functionalist account of mind has ruled this out. And more importantly, the costs of his solution are too high: animals are incapable of thought and thus there are no evolutionary pressures selecting their cognitive faculties.

Shoemaker's causal powers account won't by itself establish that the bearer of mental properties is a creature that has them essentially. In fact, the causal mental powers of one thinker may have been produced by the mental properties of another thinker. This has to be admitted because the particular instantiations of mental properties in my mind can cause certain mental states and powers in you and we obviously aren't the same substance. So causal ties between mental properties and mental powers are not enough to determine that they inhere in the same thinker. Some other independent account of the *appropriate* causal ties will determine the bearer of the mental properties since merely contributing causal powers won't suffice.

So Shoemaker is assuming that in the transplant scenario there are the *appropriate* causal connections that make mental contents the contents of the same substance. And this involves the familiar appeal of the psychological approach to personal identity to psychological continuity of memories, desires, beliefs, intentions etc. A cerebrum transplant will thus appear to preserve personal identity since wherever the recipient of the cerebrum is to be found, so will what appear to be the memories, desires, intentions and beliefs of the pre-transplant person. However, there are available some plausible arguments that people's intuitions about such brain transplant scenarios mislead them.

Although it might initially sound rather odd, the advocate of the biological approach to personal identity can claim that there is not one thinking entity calculating the entire math problem in Shoemaker's example. Instead, one being started the equation and a different individual finished it, even though neither knew of this teamwork. So even if mental properties are individuated—a la Shoemaker—by their contributions to the causal powers of the subject that has them, since they can also cause mental states in other beings as well, psychological continuity is no guarantee that only one thinker is involved. And it may be that the mental properties bestow *shorter lived* causal powers upon the animal. So while a Shoemaker-like argument might explain why an aggregate of atoms briefly constituting a person can't think because its persistence conditions don't provide for a long enough existence, the same reasoning can't extend to the animal for the period prior to the cerebrum transplant.

What the advocate of the biological approach to personal identity has to do is to explain away the appeal of the two considerations that lead most readers to maintain that the best description of the transplantation of an intact cerebrum involves a person switching bodies. The first has to do with the appearance of uninterrupted consciousness and a person's later insistence that he can remember the thoughts that he had during this transplant process and before it transpired. The second has to do with the prudential (or quasi-prudential) concern felt for the future well-being of the recipient of one's cerebrum. There are grounds for reinterpreting the phenomena that give rise to the first reason to believe body-switching is possible. The philosophy of mind literature provides us with a number of scenarios where the *alleged* recollection of certain thought content is false because there was actually no thinking going on at that earlier time. Consider Davidson's Swampman who comes into existence when lightning hits certain swamp chemicals. Let's say that the result is a being with a brain physically identical to the reader's. Swampman doesn't initially think since he lacks the requisite causal connections to objects and perhaps also because he is not a member of a linguistic community. Later, after he has obtained the causal contacts sufficient for thought, he will insist that he had thoughts back in the swamp. But he would be wrong if a certain kind of externalist about semantic content is correct.

Something similar would be true if each of us was a duplicate in a series of short-lived beings. Each of our predecessors existed but for a split second, which isn't enough time to have a thought. Each can utter a syllable before replacement.

But the replacement occurs so smoothly and quickly that observers believe that one person has persisted throughout. We, who are the last in the series differ from our short-lived predecessors in that we have existed long enough to acquire meaningful thoughts. But we will insist that we have memories of earlier events when we didn't exist but were preceded by a series of beings each existing for but a brief moment and undergoing a fraction of the physical changes that a person who persisted through the entire time would have undergone. Our "memories" are false, thus they are perhaps not memories.

The claim that a whole cerebrum transplant would not result in a person switching bodies can garner some support from the case of fissioning and transplantation. Imagine that before Adam's brain is fissioned, he is working on a mathematical problem. (Assume both hemispheres of his brain have the resources to engage in mathematical reasoning and each hemisphere has a record of the part of the calculation made possible so far by the combined hemispheres.) Then the brain is split and each hemisphere is placed in the empty skull of different beings. The cerebral hemispheres originally belonging to Adam never cease to realize conscious states during the procedure—but because of the localized anesthesia, the conscious beings supported by the removed cerebral halves, let's call them Lefty and Righty, are unaware of the surgical operation. Has the problem been continuously worked on by one person? I don't believe so. The classical logic of identity wouldn't allow us to say that Adam survives as both the resulting beings if Lefty and Righty are distinct entities. And it would be arbitrary to state that Lefty rather than Righty is Adam or vice versa. And it seems absurd to insist that Lefty and Righty are just two parts of a separated person since there is absolutely no communication between the two. It would appear that neither Adam, Lefty or Righty continuously worked on the mathematical calculation.

Since readers have just imagined a case in which a *seemingly* uninterrupted conscious thought process is actually had by more than one being, they should be more open to doubt Shoemaker's conclusion that there is continuous thought by the same person when an undivided cerebrum is transplanted. What retrospectively appears to an individual as his own earlier thinking, need not actually be so. Of course, Shoemaker's case doesn't involve fissioning. There isn't any danger of a person fissioning out of existence with the removal of a person's entire undivided cerebrum. An intact functioning cerebrum appears sufficient to realize a person and thus the same person would seem to persist through a transplant of that cerebrum into a new body. But why think that the same person survives the transplant? Why not explain away the appearance of continuous thought as we did in the fissioning scenario? Shoemaker himself admits that in a case of fission what matters in survival can be present even though identity is not preserved. The person with the whole cerebrum could be just as mistaken about his past as the two persons who each have half a cerebrum and both think that they are identical to the pre-transplant person who is the source of their psychology.

The lesson of all of this is that what appears retrospectively to people to have been their earlier thoughts may not have been thought at all. In the case of the series of individuals, there wasn't anyone who had a thought before our appearance. In the scenario of the fissioned beings, there was no continuous subject of a thought that existed before and after the fissioning. Perhaps the two persons resulting from fissioning, unlike Swampman and the longerlasting final person in the series, had thoughts from the first moment of their existence. What might distinguish the persons resulting from fission from those in the other two scenarios is that the former's cerebral hemispheres have possessed histories in which they each realized the thought of a person who had the ties to the environment and linguistic community required for mental content. The two persons resulting from cerebral fissioning may be able to inherit the requisite semantically significant causal connections from the prefissioned individual. But even if such people can think from the moment of their origins, it would still be wrong to believe they have any of the memories of the person who bequeaths them his cerebral hemispheres.

The second reason most people would (mistakenly) believe that they are each identical to the being that ends up with their functioning cerebrum is that this being would be the one whose future they care about if they pondered the possibility of a transplant before it occurred. Their concern is taken as tracking identity. But here the lessons of fission may again be relevant. Parfit, as well as Shoemaker, famously argued that there was something like prudential concern for the mental life realized by each transplanted hemisphere.[6] Even the most selfish person would probably admit to caring about what would happen to each of the persons with half of his upper brain. They would have many of his beliefs, desires, concerns, values as well as the parts of his brain that are sensitive to pain. He would certainly care if one of his cerebral hemispheres were destroyed in the removal process and the only the other was successfully transplanted for then in the absence of branching (fissioning) he would appear to survive. But it is hard to imagine him caring (much) less if both hemispheres were successfully transplanted, though as a result of this double success he would not survive as either of the two resulting persons. So the quasi-prudential concern that he would feel before the fissioning for the resulting pair of beings does not indicate anything metaphysically important about his identity because he would cease to exist with fissioning. The upshot is that prudential concern doesn't matter metaphysically. It doesn't tell us anything about our identity and probably misleads us in cases of undivided brain transplants. Shoemaker's position would be much stronger if like Unger, Baker and Velleman he claimed what mattered in survival weren't satisfied in the non-identity preserving fission scenario. Once he allows what matters to be preserved without identity in the fission case, his claim that the undivided transplant case is identity preserving is weakened.

The advocate of the biological approach to personal identity will maintain that if the lessons of Swampman, the series of short-lived duplicates, and the persons resulting from fissioning, all of whom mistakenly believe that they had thoughts before they actually did, are combined with Parfit's insight about prudential concern, we have been provided with resources to challenge Shoemaker's interpretation of a scenario of apparently uninterrupted thought during a whole cerebrum transfer.

The transplant of the cerebrum would not involve a person switching bodies, only a person who wrongly thinks he once had a different body.

If a person can't be transplanted, then Shoemaker's account of the causal individuation of properties can't support his claim that organisms don't think. The cerebrum transplant would not be a case of a chain of thought beginning as the person was constituted by one human animal and ending when it is constituted by another. The causal properties of the mental properties would *not* be possessed *only* by a person capable of thinking with the cerebrum. Thus it would be plausible to maintain that the animal's cerebrum made it possible for the animal to think and that there were two thinking animals in Shoemaker's thought experiment.

Part IV. Shoemaker's Conflict with Conventional Biological Wisdom

Now some readers might think that the result is a stalemate: they have their initial transplant intuitions, but have since been provided with an alternative account to explain away the appearance of continuous thought and body switching. Maybe they still think, as I do, that the account of the transplant offered by psychological approach to personal identity is slightly more compelling because they can't help but believe that identity is what matters and that our concern tracks identity. What is to make them favor one analysis of cerebrum transplants over the other? Perhaps the advocate of the biological approach to personal identity will maintain that this tie can be broken, or the psychological account's slightly greater appeal can be offset, if the reader considers the extent of belief revision that Shoemaker demands of biologists. Biologists are going to be quite surprised to learn that no animal can think. Shoemaker must deny thought to *any* animal, not just human animals. Shoemaker admits that removing the part of a dog's brain that is responsible for its consciousness would be the transplanting of the dog—if the dog is the sentient being that is spatially coincident with the canine animal. Shoemaker writes:

> What happens if the cerebrum from the head of one dog is transplanted into the head of another, carrying with it the psychology of the first? It sounds harsh to say that dogs are not a kind of animals. It is probably not true that "dog" relates to "canine animal" the way "person" relates to "human animal," permitting the formulation of the claim that the relation of dogs to canine animals is one of constitution rather than identity. But if not, I think we could introduce a sortal term that does so relate to "canine animal" and that the claim it would enable us to formulate would be true.[7]

This means that before such a removal, the biological entity, the canine, was not conscious. A different entity, spatially coincident with the animal, was thinking the dog thoughts and feeling the dog emotions. The entity that loses its brain in the operating room of the "mad veterinarian," has not suddenly lost its capacity for sentience, it never had such a capacity. Nor did the animal ever have the capacity for actions resulting from conscious mental states. The logic of Shoemaker's thesis would entail that spatially coincident with every crow, fish, and frog and the like, there is a merely sentient being that could be transplanted when its brain was. However, the less impressive the mind of an animal, and the less distinctive its personality, the less important the mind seems to the identity of its possessor. Because of this, readers might be more likely to resist Shoemaker's transplant thesis with "lower" animals. They may doubt that a creature with the mind of a bird is transplanted when its cerebrum is. The hope of the advocate of the biological approach to personal identity is that these readers extend such skepticism towards the transplantation of the person's cerebrum.

Any skepticism the reader harbors towards this thesis of Shoemaker's may be strengthened by considerations of ontogenetic biological development. Before and after birth the human animal, like many other animals, develops an immune system, various organs, tissues, muscles, teeth, hair etc. which enable it to survive in its environmental niche. And just as animals develop non-conscious adaptive capabilities, so it would seem that they acquire early on in their lives many conscious powers to meet the challenges of their environment.[8] But this isn't true if Shoemaker's thesis is correct. Not only is an animal incapable of thought, but it doesn't *act*. If actions occur only when there are intentions, then all actions involve mentation, and thus it is not the canine animal that acts but only the spatially coincident thinking entity for whom Shoemaker plans to introduce a new sortal name.

The advocate of the biological approach to personal identity might further undermine Shoemaker's view by showing how poorly it fits into a evolutionary perspective or even a religious inspired account of directed evolution. Imagine the first kind of organism in natural history that had the physical structures necessary to give rise to minimal conscious. Those animals, according to Shoemaker, could not use such organs to think. However, all of their other organs will fit nicely into an evolutionary perspective where they are selected because of their advantages to the animal that possessed them. But the consciousness-realizing cerebrum is the exception. It was not a useful addition to the animal. No animal evolved a thinking organ as a part. Nor did a new species come into existence when thinking beings came into existence. Not only did these new conscious creatures not evolve from an older species, replacing it or coexisting with it, but they weren't even animals.

While Shoemaker's account doesn't have animals evolve to where they can exemplify and possess personhood, it doesn't rule out that animals benefited from the emergence of consciousness. It is not hard to imagine organisms like the human animal reaping the rewards of being spatially coincident with a sentient person. But what is so odd is that the animal does so in the way some hosts benefit from parasites. It may actually be misleading to speak of conscious beings such as persons as being parasites, not because this unflattering term biases readers against Shoemaker's psychological approach to personal identity, but since they never existed separately from the animal and aren't alive. (I don't think Shoemaker can even allow persons to be contingently and derivatively alive a la Lynne Baker for then there would be pressure to make animals contingently persons and thus thinkers.) This absence of life makes sentient beings such as persons more akin to viruses than parasites.

Persons, like viruses, reproduce and spread only by making use of the living. Now this is perhaps an even less flattering description than attributing persons parasitical status, but it does seem accurate given Shoemaker's ontology.

Readers would be mistaken if they thought that I was suggesting that consciousness on Shoemaker's account is not a product of evolution. My complaint is only that it is not a property exemplified by an evolving animal. What makes the Shoemaker story so difficult to fit into an evolutionary world view is that the genotypical basis for persons is a part of the animal but the phenotypical expression is not. And yet the phenotypical expression is not like an animal artifact that comes to exist independent of the animal like a nest or dam. Rather, it comes to exist in the same place as the animal and is composed of the exact same matter.

Part V. Mere Sentience, Self-Consciousness and The Problem of Too Many Thinkers

Unbeknownst to Shoemaker, another version of The Problem of Too Many Thinkers emerges from the transplant of a dominant cerebral hemisphere. Even if both hemispheres are capable of realizing self-consciousness, imagine that one hemisphere has lost the ability to realize more than *mere* sentience prior to the transplantation of the other hemisphere that is capable of supporting not just mere sentience but also self-consciousness. The being with the impaired cerebrum would be like a newborn, an Alzheimer patient, or lower animal that was sentient but not self-consciousness and thus unable to think about its thoughts. An important question is that if the two hemispheres just mentioned belonged to the listener, where would the listener be found if the hemispheres were separated and the one capable of supporting self-consciousness transplanted into a cerebrumless body just like that of the listener? I suspect that most listeners will not see this as a case of fissioning out of existence but will identify with the individual that has the hemisphere that is capable of realizing self-consciousness. Shoemaker himself provides reasons to take this view since he relies upon Nozick's closest continuer approach in cases of asymmetrical branching.[9] The self-conscious individual will believe it is the listener and will have thoughts about its past, present and future. The other, devoid of self-consciousness, will be living in the present, unable to think of itself as having done anything in the past or future. What this identification suggests is that listeners are essentially self-conscious persons, not merely sentient thinking beings. This thought experiment, unlike the "normal" whole cerebrum transplant, can determine whether we are essentially self-conscious persons rather than essentially merely sentient beings that are only contingently self-conscious.

Now if the person is transplanted, what do we say about the thinking being left behind? Is it the human animal? Can the animal think low level thoughts that don't involve self-consciousness, contrary to what Shoemaker claims? Shoemaker would deny this for the same type of argument as before can be run to show that the merely sentient being is distinct from the animal. All we have to do is to imagine that the merely sentient being with the remaining hemisphere can also be transplanted, its thought uninterrupted in the process. Of course, these thoughts would not involve self-consciousness but that doesn't mean there can't be a chain of connected thoughts about something in the world. What this indicates is that the merely sentient being is not identical to the animal. But nor is it identical to the person. This all suggests that there is another level of constitution in between the animal and the self-conscious person. It would appear that the merely sentient being existed before the injury or the fissioning. It is not a new entity that came into existence because of injury or symmetrical fission and transplantation.

Even if one insists that the merely sentient creature is new, i.e., just budded into existence while the transplanted person is not, it still seems that there are possible scenarios in which there is a sentient being that is not a self-conscious person. Shoemaker is thus wrong to claim that whenever there is consciousness there is self-consciousness.[10] It seems that a late fetus or newborn is conscious but without being self-conscious or psychologically continuous with any later creature. And likewise for the brain zap victim reduced to an infant-like state that Shoemaker claims is not identical to the person who possessed the brain prior to zapping.[11] Moreover, the advanced Alzheimer's patient too would lack the psychological continuity, integration and self-consciousness that Shoemaker claims characterizes a person. I don't think the merely sentient individuals with the zapped or Alzheimer's riddled brains just came into existence. And it seems very implausible to maintain that a sentient baby went out of existence when the capacity for self-consciousness arose and a person emerged, and then perhaps came back into existence when an injury or disease caused the loss of self-consciousness. So if there is a thinking being that is a mere sentient being distinct from the organism and the person, there still looks like a problem of too many thinkers will arise.

We seem to be left with two spatially coincident conscious beings. Both are necessarily thinking beings but only one is a person and essentially self-conscious, the other being contingently self-conscious and able to exist without being able to reflect upon its conscious states. An Olson-like epistemic problem of being unable to determine whether one is the essentially merely sentient being or the essentially self-conscious person could only be avoided if the sentient non-person doesn't have the capacity to become even contingently self-conscious. By why shouldn't it have that capacity if the physically identical person does? It is hard to understand why different persistence conditions should prevent two thinking beings possessing the same brain from having similar mental capacities. So even if Shoemaker's response to the biological account of personal identity is adequate—and we have surveyed some reasons to doubt that animals are mindless—he is still left with one too many thinkers.

A final worry is that Shoemaker's functionalism, his theory of individuating properties by the causal powers they bestow upon their subject, and his psychological continuity account of personal identity fail to provide the means to prevent the brain, or a part of it, from being a thinking being. The cerebrum transplant thought experiment that allegedly shows persons to have different persistence conditions and thus mental properties from animals won't show that the cerebrum (or part of it) isn't a thinking substance. If Shoemaker still believed in the possibility of brain state transfer devices then he would have a scenario in which the person survived but their brain didn't.[12] But having abandoned that belief, he can only avoid the extra thinker by either identifying persons with parts of their brains or by joining with those who have confidence that they can survive their organic brains being replaced by inorganic parts.

SUNY Buffalo

Notes

1. Most philosophers of personal identity are attracted to some version of the psychological account. Besides Shoemaker's approach, very good accounts of the psychological approach are Lynne Rudder Baker's *Persons and Bodies: A Constitution Approach* (Cambridge: Cambridge University Press, 2000), Derek Parfit's *Reasons and Persons* (Oxford: Oxford University Press, 1983) and Peter Unger's *Identity, Consciousness and Value* (Oxford: Oxford University Press, 1990). Eric T. Olson provides the most thorough biological account of identity in his *The Human Animal: Identity without Psychology.*

2. Shoemaker, Sydney. "Eric Olson: The Human Animal." *Nous.* 33:3 (1999) 499. Shoemaker, S. "Self, Body and Coincidence." *Aristotelian Society Supplement.* 1999. 79. I prefer to call the puzzle "The Problem of Too Many Thinkers." This is because the problem may take the form of two thinkers sharing one mind and the same thoughts. So whether there are two minds or just one whenever there are spatially coincident thinking beings, there will always be two thinkers.

3. See Olson's defense of the biological approach against Shoemaker in his "What Does Functionalism tell us About Personal Identity?" *Nous,* 682–697.

4. By describing the entity as "merely sentient," I do not mean to imply it can't become self-conscious, only that self-conscious is not essential to it.

5. Ibid., 300–307.

6. Parfit, Derek. *Reasons and Persons.* (Oxford: Oxford University Press, 1983) 245–280. Peter Unger has responded to Parfit's claim that identity is not what matters in his *Identity, Consciousness and Value* (Oxford University Press, 1990). See David Hershenov's response to Unger in his "Countering the Appeal of the Psychological Approach to Personal Identity." *Philosophy* 79 (2004) 445–472.

7. Shoemaker. "Self, Body and Coincidence." Op. cit. 303, note 14.

8. See Antonio Damasio's *The Feeling of What Happens: Body and Mind in the Making of the Consciousness* (San Diego: Harcourt Press, 1999) for a biological account of the development of what he calls the "core" and "biographical selves" from an earlier "proto-self." This continuity could contribute to undermining Shoemaker's claim that the person is substance distinct from the organism.

9. See the discussion of a brain state device that makes a psychological duplicate without destroying wiping clean the person's original psychology. "Personal Identity: A Matertialist's Account," in Shoemaker and Swinburne's *Personal Identity* (Oxford: Basil Blackwell, 1984) 131.

10. See Shoemaker's discussion of how the unity of consciousness brings with it self-consciousness and how this fits with his functional account of mind and psychological account of personal identity. *Personal Identity*. Op. cit. 102.

11. Shoemaker. *Personal Identity*. Op. cit. 87.

12. Shoemaker. "Functionalism and Personal Identity—A Reply." *Nous*. 38:3, 2004, 525.

The Need for Explanation in the Philosophy of Mind: A Case Study

Stephen R. Grimm

Abstract: Explanatory inquiry characteristically begins with a certain puzzlement about the world. But why do certain situations elicit our puzzlement (or curiosity) while others leave us, in some epistemically relevant sense, cold? Moreover, what exactly is involved in the move from a state of puzzlement to a state where one's puzzlement is satisfied? In this paper I try to make sense of these questions by focusing on two case studies, one from the popular literature on string theory and one from recent debates in the philosophy of mind.

Explanatory inquiry characteristically begins with a certain puzzlement about the world. As Jonathan Lear, commenting on Aristotle's interest in explanatory knowledge (or *episteme*), aptly notes:

> it is a remarkable fact about us that we cannot simply observe phenomena: we want to know *why* they occur. We can imagine beings who simply watched the sun set and the moon rise in the heavens: they might come to expect regular transitions, but they would lack curiosity as to why the changes occur. We are not like that. The heavenly motions cry out (*to us*) for explanation. (1988, p. 3)

I take it that the same puzzlement that drove Aristotle's interest in explanatory knowledge continues to drive inquirers today. Not just the heavens, but the tides, the photoelectric effect, and so on, cry out (*to us*!) for explanation.

But Lear also seems right about the following point: we can, apparently, imagine beings who share many of our beliefs about the world and yet fail to be puzzled by it. So what exactly is it that accounts for *our* puzzlement? What inspires *our* explanatory inquiries? To suggest, as Lear suggests, that it is our native curiosity that inspires our inquiries helps to illuminate these questions. But in another way it only postpones them. For again we can ask: In virtue of what do certain situations elicit our *curiosity*? What is it that distinguishes those situations that elicit our curiosity from those that leave us, in some epistemically relevant sense, cold?

In this paper I will try to address these issues by focusing on two basic questions. The first question we have seen already in passing; since it will recur throughout the paper it will be helpful to refer to it simply as **Q1**, as follows:

Q1: What is it *in virtue of which* a situation stands in need of explanation for someone?[1]

The second question builds on the first. We can refer to it simply as **Q2**:

Q2: Given that a situation stands in need of explanation for someone, what does it take, from an epistemic point of view, to *satisfy* that need?

Another way to think of **Q2** is as follows: What is it that, when things go well, takes someone from having a need for explanation to having satisfied that need? Or again: what kind of epistemic gain is involved, exactly, in moving from the one state to the other?

After trying to clarify the nature of these questions in Section 1, I will suggest one promising way of answering both questions in Section 2. In Section 3, I will then consider how this proposal helps to make sense of a recent debate in the philosophy of mind concerning the nature of *qualia*.

1. Two Senses

One reason why answering **Q1** has proven difficult is because there are two quite different ways in which a situation might stand in need (or fail to stand in need) of explanation for someone. We might characterize the first of these needs as *practical* and the second as *epistemic*.

The practical need for explanation is fairly straightforward. In this sense, whether or not a situation stands in need of explanation for you will depend on whether you deem it worth the bother, in some all-things-considered sense. Thus my leaky roof will stand in need of explanation for me but not for you in virtue of the fact that although the well-being of my roof is prudentially valuable to me, this is (let's suppose) far from true for you.

But there is another sense in which a situation might seem to stand in need of explanation for someone, one that considers things from a more purely *epistemic* point of view. As Carl Hempel (1965) points out, in addition to the obvious practical incentives we have for wanting to explain our environment, we also seem to have a distinctively intellectual desire to make sense of the world, a desire rooted in our

> *sheer intellectual curiosity*, in [our] deep and persistent desire to know and to understand [ourselves] and [our] world. So strong, indeed, is this urge that in the absence of more reliable knowledge, myths are often invoked to fill the gap (p. 333; my emphasis).

Building on Hempel's appeal to curiosity, we might therefore say that the sign that a situation stands in need of explanation, *from a purely epistemic point of view*, is that it is capable of eliciting our curiosity.[2]

To say that a situation's ability to elicit our curiosity is a "sign" that it stands in need of explanation for us, of course, does not yet tell us what it is, in virtue of which, a situation stands in need of explanation. What it does do, however, is offer a new and potentially more tractable way of posing our first question, **Q1**. We might therefore think of the following "curiosity-oriented" question as a variant of our original "need for explanation" question, as follows:

Q1*: In virtue of what do certain situations elicit our curiosity?

What this variant of our first question reminds us is that some situations seem to elicit our curiosity and others fail to elicit our curiosity. What is it, then, that accounts for the difference?

2. A New Proposal

Several candidates have been proposed as answers to **Q1** and its variants; here we can only briefly review a few. For example, it is often suggested that a situation stands in need of explanation for someone (alternative, that it elicits someone's curiosity) in virtue of the fact that the situation comes across as *surprising* or *unexpected*, given the rest of what the person believes.[3] The basic problem with accounts of this sort is that there seem to be countless situations that strike as entirely *un*surprising, or that in some sense we fully expect, and yet nonetheless stand in need of explanation for us. Thus, for example, the squeaking wheel on my bicycle might be painfully familiar to me as well as entirely expected, yet for all that it will presumably be something that stands in need of explanation for me (cf. Lipton 2004, p. 26).[4]

In the remainder of this paper I would therefore like to take a fresh approach to **Q1** and its variants by mining an insight originally proposed by Robert Nozick some twenty-five years ago. According to Nozick:

> I am tempted to say that explanation locates something in actuality, showing its actual connections with other things, while *understanding* locates it in a network of possibility, showing the connections it would have to other nonactual things or processes. (Explanation increases understanding too, since the actual connections it exhibits are also possible.) Recall how illuminating it can be to place something, something actual even, in a typology or a two-by-two matrix, how salient is the insight gained through locating it in that network of alternative possibilities. (1981, p. 12)

What is particularly important here, I submit, is the connection that Nozick draws between our attempts to understand the world—to satisfy our needs for explanation—and the notion of a "network of alternative possibilities." Building on this connection, what I want to suggest in the remainder of this paper is that our attempts to explain the world are necessarily informed by the network of possibility that we bring to bear on the world. More directly, what I want to suggest is that *the need for explanation arises for us in the first place only because we view the world in terms of this network of possibility.*

Brian Skyrms, for one, has proposed a similar framework in more formal terms as follows:

> Let {Si} be an exhaustive set of mutually exclusive possible states of the system of which S* is a member. . . . Degrees of explanatory power are relevant to the force with which the explanation resolves the puzzlement: why S* rather than something else? (1980, pp. 140–41)

Although Skyrms does not explicitly make the connection to our need for explanation, it is easy enough to do some reverse engineering here. Suppose, for example, we accept Skyrms's suggestion that our "puzzlement" is resolved to the extent that we can identify the factor or factors that help to discriminate among the various possibilities that are in some sense "live" relative to S*. If so, then it is natural to think that the reason why S* stood in need of explanation for someone in the first place is in virtue of the person's sense that there were various alternatives ways that the system might have been, various alternatives states it might have assumed. If Skyrms and Nozick are right, moreover, then in many important cases where we experience a need for explanation, the need is elicited—alternatively, our curiosity is elicited–by our sense that (in some way) the situation might have been otherwise.

Before we continue with this suggestion, at this point it will help to clarify an important ambiguity: thus, I have sometimes used expressions such as "various ways the situation might have been" and sometimes (as in our discussion of Skyrms a moment ago) expressions such as "various ways the system might have been." But these expressions seem to mean different things. For example, we can easily imagine things like "systems" (or maybe "substances") being otherwise, but what does it mean for a situation to be otherwise? If a "situation" is anything like what metaphysicians think of as an "event," then at the very least it is controversial whether an event can survive a change among its constituent parts. So consider: if Lewis delivers his lecture on modality two months later than originally planned, does this qualify as the same event as the originally planned lecture, or as something altogether new? Opinions divide sharply here, and it is no easy matter to decide which view we should prefer.[5]

To my mind, however, the best way to sidestep these difficulties, as well as to shed further light on our question, is by drawing attention to the fact that the sorts of situations we have been considering all along are quite *finely structured*. Suppose, for example, we come to learn some fact: say, that A is F (perhaps, that the tides are low). The reason why this fact seems to stand in need of explanation for us, I now want to suggest, is because of our sense that the "subject" of this fact, A, in some sense might have been otherwise: in other words, because of our sense that in some way A might have been (say) G. What elicits our curiosity with respect to the fact that A is F, accordingly, is not simply our registering of the fact that A is F, but rather our registering of the fact that A is F *along with* our sense that that things might have been otherwise: here, that A might have been G. It is therefore this whole conglomerate—both our belief that A is F *and* our belief (or sense) that A might have been G—that plausibly elicits our curiosity.[6]

Borrowing from the work of Alan Garfinkel (1981) and Peter Lipton (2004), we can think of the one possibility, A is F, as *the fact*, and the other possibility, A is G, as *the foil*. On this way of looking at things, it will therefore be the combination of fact and foil that together constitute a "situation" for us. Although it will continue to be useful to talk of "situations" in what follows, however, according to the proposal on offer here the important thing to bear in mind is that the sort of situation that elicits our curiosity seems to be a composite thing—again, a thing that consists of a fact along with at least one foil.

Combining these clarifications with our previous discussion, on this proposal two preliminary answers to our questions, **Q1** and **Q2**, naturally fall out. Regarding **Q1**, we now have reason to think that what elicits our curiosity with respect to a situation is *our desire to figure out why the fact rather than the foil obtained.* This then invites the following answer with respect to **Q2**: that the way to satisfy this need is to identify what it is that the difference between the fact and the foil depends on.

By appealing to an example from recent debates in the philosophy of mind, in the next section I will try to clarify this proposal in two ways. First, by showing how the need for explanation is importantly shaped by the network of possibility we bring to bear on the world. Second, by illustrating what is typically involved in the move from a need for explanation to the apparent satisfaction of that need.

3. The Case

Consider then Michael Tye's (2002) case against qualia in the philosophy of mind. *Qualia* are typically thought to be the aspects of conscious experience that characterize *what it is like* to have the experience: e.g., what it is like to be visually conscious of the redness of a red balloon, or tactually conscious of the balloon's smoothness. Considered in one way, Tye argues, it is undeniable that there are such phenomenal aspects of conscious experience. Of course there is something that it is distinctively *like* to experience the world; and hence qualia, in a certain respectable sense, undoubtedly exist. What Tye denies, however, is that qualia can be thought of as irreducible or brute nonrepresentational aspects of conscious experience. Tye calls such allegedly brute aspects of experience "Qualia" with a capital "Q" and insists that, understood in this way, there are no Qualia.[7] They are a philosophical fiction. On his view:

> Any adequate account of the subjective or phenomenal aspects of our visual states ought to yield an understanding of why those states have those aspects. Why, for example, does having a visual experience of blue 'feel' the way it does and not some other way? It is hard to see how any satisfying answer can be given to this question if the phenomenal aspects of such experiences derive from visual Qualia.
>
> Suppose, for example, that there are visual Qualia and that such Qualia are nonphysical and irreducible. Then the 'felt' aspect of the visual experience of blue is a matter of its having a special, nonphysical property. It is the presence of this property that gives the visual experience its distinctive 'feel.' Does this really offer us any enlightenment? Apart from

> the usual concerns about the emergence and causal role of such properties we may still wonder why the visual experience that has the content blue is associated with this irreducible felt quality rather than some other—why, for example, it does not have the felt experiences that represent red. This surely is an impenetrable mystery. (p. 455)

Here again, since our concern here is not with the status of Qualia *per se* (the capital "Q," controversial kind), what we should be asking is: Why is this a good reason to worry about Qualia, if it is a good reason to worry? What is it about Tye's complaint that registers with us, and makes us think that there is something here that stands in need of explanation?

To the extent that Tye succeeds in making Qualia seem in need of explanation, I suggest that it is because he reminds that we can always ask, of any particular Qualia—blue Qualia, for example—why it is associated with one felt experience rather than another. After all, according to Qualia advocates other things of this kind—red Qualia and green Qualia, for example—are said to be associated with other felt experiences. So what accounts for the difference between these things? Why, given the various ways Qualia are apparently capable of being in virtue of the kind of thing they are, are they one way rather than the other?

Naturally, Tye claims that his view has the advantage in terms of being able to answer a question along these lines: by his lights, the thing that makes the difference to why a felt experience is one way rather than another is its representational content. The reason why you enjoy an experience of red on some occasion rather than an experience of green, for instance, is because the experience is an experience *of* something red rather than an experience *of* something green. Tye can therefore point to something that plausibly accounts for why your felt experiences are one way rather another because he can point to *a difference maker*—namely, the representational contents of these states—whereas Qualia advocates can point to nothing that makes a difference to the various ways felt experience seems capable of being.

Again, it is worth focusing on Tye's discussion for at least three reasons. First, because it helps to show in the concrete how certain situations seem to stand in need of explanation for us; what's more, it helps to clarify the central psychological mechanism—our sense of the alternative possibilities that in some sense might have obtained—that prompts our puzzlement and inspires our inquiries in the first place. Second, it suggests the sort of solution that would potentially *satisfy* our need for explanation—roughly, the identification of the factor or factors that help to determine why one possibility holds rather than another. Finally, it illustrates the way in which our network of possibility is often structured in ways that are modally quite rich—at least, richer than something like broadly logical possibility can capture.[8]

University of Montana

Notes

1. Along with Peter Menzies (1989), I will start off by using the notion of a "situation" in a fairly expansive and commonsensical way, so that it is broad enough to encompass the range of categories that are usually thought to stand in need of explanation, such as events, states of affairs, facts, and so on (cf. Menzies 2004). In Section 2, I will then refine this idea.

2. In his comments at the Denison ACPA meeting, John Michael McDermott suggested that the attitude of curiosity is not quite rich enough to capture "the practical wonder at the mystery of being" that we sometimes experience in the course of our lives. I, too, think that there is an important difference between the psychology of curiosity and the psychology of wonder, one which I hope to address in later work; for the purposes of this paper, however, it is enough to focus on the notion of curiosity.

3. See, for example, Pierce ([1908] 1968, 143) and Hempel (1965, 429).

4. As Trent Dougherty has helpfully suggested, an advocate of the "surprisingness" model might be able to reply to the squeaking bicycle example by appealing to a notion along the lines of "*ur*-surprisingness"—in other words, a notion of surprisingness which measures how likely one would have taken the situation to be *before* one first learned of the situation. Still, it is not clear to me that a fully satisfying answer to Q1 can be developed along these lines. Suppose, for example, that I am only familiar with tree leaves that are green. Then at some point I notice that they can change colors (in the autumn, e.g.), and become gold, orange, and so on. It then seems that the goldness of the leaves might elicit my curiosity—and that would fit the surprisingness model (broadly construed) quite well. Once I become aware that things might be otherwise, however, it also seems that the *greenness* of the leaves might elicit my curiosity. In the midst of summer, I might therefore ask: "Why are the leaves green (rather than gold etc.)?" It is difficult to see a way to make this latter question work on the surprisingness model, however, even with the "ur-surprisingness" refinement, for it hardly seems to be the case that there was any ur-surprisingness with respect to the greenness of the leaves.

5. For overviews of these debates, see Simons (2003) and Collins, Hall, and Paul (2004, sec. 4).

6. Presumably other beliefs would not to be added here: for example, the belief that it is not the case that A is G. It is also worth noting that "belief" might be too strong of a word here. For those reluctant to multiply the number of beliefs we currently have before our minds, we could speak instead of (say) "convictions."

7. Below I will follow Tye's lead in thus distinguishing between "qualia" and "Qualia."

8. Thanks to Michael DePaul, Trent Dougherty, John Greco, John Michael McDermott, and Fritz Warfield for helpful comments on earlier versions of this essay.

Works Cited

Collins, John, Ned Hall, and L. A. Paul. 2004. "Introduction," in *Causation and Counterfactuals*. Ed. John Collins, Ned Hall, and L. A. Paul. Cambridge: MIT Press.

Garfinkel, Alan. 1981. *Forms of Explanation*. New Haven: Yale University Press.

Greene, Brian. 1999. *The Elegant Universe*. New York: Vintage.

Hempel, Carl. 1965. "Aspects of Scientific Explanation," in his *Aspects of Scientific Explanation and other Essays in the Philosophy of Science*. New York: Free Press.

Hume, David. [1748] 1963. *Enquiry Concerning Human Understanding*. 2nd edition. Ed. and intro. L. A. Selby-Bigge. Oxford: Clarendon Press.

Lear, Jonathan. 1988. *Aristotle: The Desire to Understand*. New York: Cambridge University Press.

Lipton, Peter. 2004. *Inference to the Best Explanation*. 2nd. edition. New York: Routledge.

Menzies, Peter. 1989. "A Unified Account of Causal Relata," in *Australasian Journal of Philosophy* 67: 59–83.

———. 2004. "Difference Making in Context," in *Causation and Counterfactuals*. Ed. J. Collins, N. Hall, L. Paul. Cambridge: MIT Press.

Nozick, Robert. 1981. *Philosophical Explanations*. Cambridge: Harvard University Press.

Peirce, Charles. [1908] 1968. "Retroduction and Genius," in *Science: Men, Methods, Goals*. Ed. B. Brody and N. Capaldi. New York: W. A. Benjamin.

Simons, Peter. 2003. "Events," in *The Oxford Handbook of Metaphysics*. Ed. Michael Loux and Dean Zimmerman. New York: Oxford University Press.

Skyrms, Brian. 1980. *Causal Necessity*. New Haven: Yale University Press.

Tye, Michael. 2002. "Visual Qualia and Visual Content Revisited," in *Philosophy of Mind: Classical and Contemporary Readings*. Ed. David Chalmers. New York: Oxford University Press.

Vagueness and Pointless Evil

By Michael Schrynemakers

Abstract: Many theists and atheists believe that God would not permit an evil unless God's allowing it (or an evil at least as bad) is required for a greater good. In "The Argument from Particular Horrendous Evils" (and elsewhere) Peter van Inwagen has argued against this belief by appealing to his "No Minimum Claim" (NMC), namely, that it is reasonable to believe there is no minimum amount of evil required for God's purposes. In this paper I distinguish different formulations of NMC, and, by drawing an instructive parallel to traditional sorites paradoxes, refute Jeff Jordan's criticism that because morally significant suffering is finitely diminishable, NMC must be false.

Many theists and atheists believe that God would not permit any pointless evil. In William Rowe's much discussed "The Problem of Evil and Some Varieties of Atheism" this belief is expressed as: "An omniscient, wholly good being would prevent the occurrence of any intense suffering it could, unless it could not do so without thereby losing some greater good or permitting some evil equally bad or worse."[1] Peter van Inwagen has argued against this "Standard Claim" (SC) by appealing to his "No Minimum Claim" (NMC), namely, that it is reasonable to believe there is no minimum amount of evil required for God's purposes. In this essay I distinguish different formulations of NMC, and, by drawing an instructive parallel to traditional sorites paradoxes, refute Jeff Jordan's criticism that because morally significant suffering is finitely diminishable, NMC must be false.[2]

1. Van Inwagen's Criticism of SC

Van Inwagen argues against SC as follows. There are various situations in which some evil must be permitted for an end it is morally permissible to pursue, but in which there is no *minimum* amount of evil that must be permitted for that purpose. For example, some, but no minimum, fine must be imposed to deter illegal parking. Some, but no minimum, jail sentence must be enforced to deter certain crimes. In these situations, one can prevent an evil (one hour of a jail sentence, say) without forfeiting any greater good or permitting an equal or worse evil (without loss of deterrent effect, for example), and one does nothing wrong in not doing so.[3] Since there is no precise minimum effective jail sentence for a specific crime, the selection of a jail sentence must be somewhat arbitrary. Because God may be in an analogous situation with respect to the evils of this world, there may be evils that God allows that he could prevent without losing any greater good. In fact, it is likely that God is in such a situation, and therefore we have reason to think SC is false.[4]

Van Inwagen thinks that just as it is not plausible to suppose there is a jail term that is maximally effective, such that any lesser term is less effective, it is not very plausible to suppose that:

> [T]here is a way in which evil could be distributed such that (i) that distribution of evil would serve God' s purposes as well as any distribution could and (ii) God's purposes would be less well served by any distribution involving less evil.[5]

So van Inwagen thinks it is not plausible to suppose:

> (E) There is a *specific* amount of permitted evil that is necessary and sufficient for God's purposes.

The rejection of E is one version of van Inwagen's No Minimum Claim. In "The Problems of Evil, Air, and Silence" van Inwagen provides an illustration of his NMC by considering instances of natural evil, such as William Rowe's famous case of a fawn's suffering burn pains in a forest fire, and the good of nature's laws not failing on a large scale, of nature's not being "massively irregular":

> [God] could have prevented any one of them [natural evils], or any two of them, or any three of them . . . without thwarting any significant good or permitting any significant evil. But could he have prevented all of them? No—not without causing the world to be massively irregular. And, of course, there is no sharp cut-off point between a world that is massively irregular and a world that is not. . . . There is therefore, no minimum number of cases of intense suffering that God could allow without forfeiting the good of a world that is not massively irregular.[6]

Here the No Minimum Claim may also be formulated as the rejection of:

> (E') There is a sharp cutoff between amounts of permitted evil sufficient for God's purposes and amounts of permitted evil not sufficient for God's purposes.

Van Inwagen finds E and E' as implausible as supposing that if an impressively tall prophet is required for God's purposes, there is a minimum height such a prophet must have.[7] In "The Argument from Particular Horrendous Evils," he compares the necessity of permitted evils for God's purposes to the necessity of raindrops for the fertility of nineteenth century England.[8] Just as there is no specific number of raindrops required for the latter, no one raindrop cutoff between a fertile England and an infertile England, so we should not suppose there must be a specific number of permitted evils required for God's purposes.

The implicit reasoning involved here may be abstracted from the use of the concept of a minimum amount: if there is no *specific* amount of permitted evil necessary and sufficient for purpose G, and it is morally permissible to allow *some* evil for G, then (because every instance of some amount of evil is a specific amount of evil) there are specific amounts of evil it is morally permissible to allow for G that are not necessary for G. And if that's the case, there are some evils or quantities of evil God is justified in permitting for G that are not necessary for G, contra SC.[9]

2. Van Inwagen's Misformulation

In different places, van Inwagen treats the denial of E and E' as equivalent to:

(P) For any amount of evil that would have served God's purposes, slightly less evil would have served His purposes just as well.[10]

He then makes his case against SC based on P. For example, he argues: It follows from P and (b) God should have got by with less evil, if less would have served, that (c) God should have got by with no evil at all. Since (c) is false, and P highly plausible (especially upon consideration of the above examples), (b) must be rejected.[11]

This argument may be understood two ways and is mistaken on either interpretation. "Getting by with no evil" in (ex hypothesi false) (c) means either (c1) God should have obtained purpose G with no evil, or (c2) God should have foregone G (which requires evil) altogether. For the former it seems P must be construed as:

(P*) For any [positive] amount n of evil which serves divine purpose G, there is an amount n – 1 which also accomplishes G.[12]

But clearly (c1)'s following from P* and (b) does not indicate (b) is false. (c1) 'God should have obtained purpose G with no evil' follows from P* and (b) (translated here as: God should obtain G with the least amount of evil possible), only via ex hypothesi false, (2) 'God could have obtained G with no evil.' (2) follows from P* and the ex hypothesi true (1) 'God could have obtained G with some evil' by universal instantiation and modus ponens. So clearly P*, despite its initial plausibility, must be rejected, and the fact that false (c1) follows from P*, (1), (2) and (b) does not cast doubt on (b). Since P* may be replaced by as many of its instantiations as one wishes, the rejection of P* is as warranted as (1) and modus ponens.

Perhaps van Inwagen only means by (c), (c2) 'God should have foregone G (which requires evil) altogether,' and is reasoning as follows: if every amount of evil sufficient for God's purposes, G, is such that slightly less would do as well, and it is wrong to allow any amount of evil that has this property, then it is wrong to allow any evil for G. But this last clause contradicts the assumption that God may be justified in allowing some evil for good purpose G. Therefore it is not always wrong to allow an amount of evil even if less evil would do as well.

P* is not required for this argument, so P may be understood as the more general: 'For any amount of evil which serves divine purpose G, there is a smaller amount which also accomplishes G'. But this is unacceptable also. Ex hypothesi false (2) 'God could have obtained G with no evil' does not follow from P only if evil is claimed to be infinitely diminishable (whether infinitely divisible into smaller units or not measurable by discrete units at all). But it is implausible that *pain* or *suffering* is infinitely diminishable (and SC may be revised by substituting 'pain and suffering' for 'evil'); and, since *morally significant* pain and suffering must be detectable, it is additionally implausible that pain and suffering is infinitely diminishable by morally significant amounts. Both versions fail.

In "Evil and van Inwagen" Jeff Jordan presents similar arguments. Let's call what I have phrased as a response to (c2) the "Diminishability" argument. Now, if morally significant pain is not infinitely diminishable, then P may be interpreted as P*.[13] Let's call what I have phrased in response to (c1), namely, P* (and universal instantiation) implies (2), so P* must be rejected), the "Sorites Redux" argument. Jordan thinks the Sorites Redux argument in combination with the Diminishability argument refutes van Inwagen's NMC and therefore his challenge to SC.

3. The Vagueness Response to SC

I will argue that Jordan is mistaken. Van Inwagen's objection to SC, properly formulated, does not depend on the truth of P and is in no way impugned by Jordan's remarks. In the context of the kinds of moral situations and analogies adduced by van Inwagen, P should not be treated as equivalent to the denial of E or E', and the Sorites Redux argument and the Diminishability argument do not make it unreasonable to deny E or E'. Understanding why van Inwagen himself might have conflated the denial of E (and E') with P will illuminate the nature of his challenge to SC and why Jordan fails to engage it.

Why does van Inwagen confidently shift the discussion from E and E' to P? Let's look at the example of the jail sentence and its deterrent effect. Why would someone think that for any jail sentence having some deterrent effect, that sentence minus one hour would have exactly the same deterrent effect? Well, it is difficult to see how one hour could make any difference to deterrent effect. (In fact one might reasonably claim it seems that a difference of one hour could *not* make any difference to deterrent effect.) Another way to put it is: it is difficult to see how there could be an amount of time specified to the hour *required* for deterrent effect x. How could there be a specific amount of time sufficient for x such that that particular amount minus one hour would not be sufficient for x? Why would there be such a precise one hour cutoff? It seems plausible that there is none. It also seems plausible that if there is no such cut-off then there is no amount n such that n hours is sufficient for x and n – 1 hours is not sufficient for x. And it also seems that if there is no such n, then (P*) for *any* n sufficient for x, n – 1 is also sufficient for x. So we begin from what seems obvious—that one hour could not make any difference to deterrent effect—and deduce by what seems tight reasoning, P*. What better reason could one have? Van Inwagen's shift from the denial of E and E' to P is understandable. Yet we also have this very strong independent argument against P*: repeated applications of P* to any given jail term entail the false 'No jail time is required for x.' This is parallel to what Jordan invokes.

Well of course this dilemma is just the sorites paradox, applied to jail time, and evidently both Jordan and van Inwagen fell into its trap (despite van Inwagen's alluding to it). The distinctive feature of the kinds of cases van Inwagen adduces is they involve *vague concepts*. The amount of jail time required to deter a certain crime is vague (perhaps because that deterrent effect is vague, perhaps not). Likewise, the concept of nature's being "highly regular" and the concept 'tall,' given for purposes of illustration, are vague concepts. For this essay, we may consider a concept vague if there are cases to which it clearly applies, cases to which it clearly does not apply, and "borderline" cases about which it is unclear as to whether it applies, where there seems to be no sharp boundary between borderline and non-borderline cases. For each of these terms, it seems implausible that there is a unique specific amount to which the term applies such that the term does not apply to *any* lesser amount (or any amount lesser by an appropriately small magnitude). This would deny the indeterminate range of borderline cases these terms seem to have.

So we may take van Inwagen to claim it plausible that the amount of permitted evil required for God's purposes is vague, where vagueness is understood in this way. This might be because God's purpose itself is vague, as suggested by the example of nature's being highly regular, or because His purpose depends on a vague circumstance, as in the tall prophet analogy. We can extract from van Inwagen's work a more focused challenge to SC that we may call the "Vagueness Response":

1. The analogies and examples given (in section 1) make it reasonable to believe the amount of evil required for God's purposes may be vague and hence that E is open to reasonable doubt.[14]
2. These reasons for doubting E are of roughly comparable force to, and are not undermined by (because independent of), the motivation for believing SC.
3. SC entails E.

Therefore,

4. SC is open to reasonable doubt.

4. Reply to Jordan

The Vagueness Response is immune to Jordan's criticism. If the denial of E is understood in terms of a contrast between specific and vague amounts of evil, then P and the denial of E are not equivalent and an argument for the rejection of P is not necessarily an argument for E.[15] P may be rejected for the reasons presented above in section 2 and in Jordan's essay, but this does not refute van Inwagen's NMC, properly construed.

I now make my case. To take van Inwagen's example, suppose God refrains from preventing some natural evil for the sake of G "nature's being highly regular." It seems that there is no minimum number of such allowings of natural evil whereby nature remains highly regular such that one less would make nature not highly regular. This is just because "nature's being highly regular" is a vague concept. To notice that *some* permission of natural evil is required for G and by P* we can deduce that *no* permission of natural evil is required for G, so P* cannot be true, does not make it unreasonable to continue to hold there is no minimum number of such allowings required for G. But doesn't P*'s not being true *seem* equivalent to E and E'? If one believes that it's *not true* that for *any* amount of evil sufficient for God's purposes, slightly less evil would be sufficient as well, isn't that good reason to believe there is an amount of evil sufficient for God's purposes such that slightly less is *not* sufficient, and therefore a specific necessary and sufficient amount? It does indeed seem so, as I've described in section 3 above. My reply is that we have here three propositions that I claim constitute a *paradox*:

X. P is false.

Y. X implies E.

Z. E is false.

X, Y, and Z are each plausible, and each retain some plausibility, even in the light of the others. This makes it not at all obvious which one should be given up. The intuition backing Z is not obviously weaker than arguments that can be given for X and Y; so to simply deny Z on the basis of X and Y does not resolve this puzzle. An equally strong argument may be made by appealing to X and Z to deny Y. And Y and Z may plausibly be invoked to deny X. Assuming Y and pointing out the Sorites Redux, as Jordan does, does not make belief in Z unreasonable.[16]

To illustrate, consider the following very strong argument against either X or Y. Let G stand for 'being tall,' and n stand for being some height, specified to the millimeter. From the truth of (a') being 2500 mm is tall, and the falsehood of (c') being 0 mm is tall, it seems that we should conclude X: that P* (translated here: for any n, if being n is tall, being n – 1 is tall) is false. If X is true and X implies E' (translated here: there is a one millimeter cut off between being tall and not being tall), then E'. But even after one has considered (a'), P* and (c'), (and even the fact that P* may be replaced by as many of its instantiations as one wishes), one may reasonably deny there is such a cut off and therefore the conjunction of X and (X implies E'). Precisely because G involves a vague term, the denial of E' (and E) is not obviously undermined by the plausibility of X and Y.[17]

Again, to bridge the familiar with the present context, suppose a great good G depends on (S) Samson's becoming bald via extraction. N hairs are extracted, corresponding to n evils. One may argue that (a) some number of extractions is necessary for S (and hence G), and if P (instanced here as: for any number of extractions sufficient for S, slightly less would be sufficient for S), then (c) no extractions are necessary for S, so P is not true.[18] But clearly it is reasonable to think there is no number of hairs n, such that if Samson has n hairs extracted he is bald, and if he has n – 1 hairs extracted he is not bald, even after one has considered this argument (and that P may be replaced by as many of its instantiations as one wishes). So Jordan has not shown it unreasonable to think G requires only a vague and not a specific amount of evil.[19]

For the combined Sorites Redux and Diminishability argument to refute NMC, the following is required, where G stands for God's purposes, and n stands for an amount of permitted evil:

(A) P* 'For any n, if n is sufficient for G, then n – 1 is sufficient for G' is not true.

(B) If A, then P* is false.

(C) If P* is false, then (q) there is an n such that n is sufficient for G and (n – 1) is not sufficient for G.

(D) If (q), then :

(E) There is a specific amount of permitted evil that is necessary and sufficient for God's purposes; and

(E') There is a sharp cutoff between amounts of permitted evil sufficient for God's purposes and amounts of permitted evil not sufficient for God's purposes.

B, C, and D are all prima facie highly plausible. However, G's involving vague concepts makes the falsehood of E and E' at least as plausible as the truth of B–D. For there seeming to be no sharp cut-off just is the distinctive feature of vague concepts. This seeming is not mitigated by consideration of B–D, and this is just why philosophers have called the sorites paradox a paradox. The paradox is that although it seems we cannot accept P* is true (because of the Sorites Redux), it also seems we cannot accept what that seems to entail (by B–D), namely E. In other words, E is open to reasonable doubt, even in the light of A and consideration of B–D. If it weren't, the sorites paradox wouldn't be a paradox. To make this vivid, consider that though E and the rejection of P seem equivalent, we have the very significant conflicting consideration that this equivalence implies that if we substitute 'bald' for G (and some number of hair extractions for n), then there is a one-hair cut-off between being bald and not being bald. Jordan is not justified in taking this equivalence for granted.

P should be interpreted as P* because pain is finitely divisible.[20] The Sorites Redux shows P* cannot be true.[21] Whether or not the Sorites Redux indicates P* is *false* or that E is true when G represents a vague term is what requires argument. Many philosophers have attempted to supply such arguments. Those who deny bivalence for vague sentences reject B; Intuitionists reject C; and Supervaluationists have rejected D. Ignorance theorists and Deflationists have felt it necessary to mount sophisticated arguments for (the generalized version of) E. Only the denial of A is not considered a live option. In the current climate (despite Timothy Williamson's arguments for E) few would claim E's following from A cannot be reasonably doubted, and that is what Jordan must argue for to counter van Inwagen's challenge. To bypass treatment of B–D and present only A against the Vagueness Response is just to ignore the argument.[22]

St. John's University

Notes

1. William Rowe, "The Problem of Evil and Some Varieties of Atheism" *American Philosophical Quarterly* 16 (1979): 335–341. More exactly, this proposition, generalized to include all types of evils (together with the idea that an omnipotent being could eliminate any evil), expresses the commonly held belief we may call the Standard Claim. A "greater good" is a good that does not have less value than the related evil has disvalue.

2. Van Inwagen's challenge is most fully described in "The Argument from Particular Horrendous Evils," *American Catholic Philosophical Association, ACPA Proceedings*, vol. 74 (2001): 65–80. Jordan's reply appears in "Evil and van Inwagen," *Faith and Philosophy* 20 (2003), 236–239.

3. One might wish to expand this sentence as follows: 'In these situations, one can prevent an evil *and has the right to* without forfeiting any greater good (or permitting an equal or worse evil) *and without significant cost to oneself*, and one does nothing wrong in not doing so.'

4. "The Argument from Particular Horrendous Evils," *American Catholic Philosophical Association, ACPA Proceedings*, vol. 74 (2001): 65–80. "The Magnitude, Duration, and Distribution of Evil: A Theodicy," *Philosophical Topics* 16/2 (1988): 161–187. "The Problem of Evil, the Problem of Air, and the Problem of Silence," *Philosophical Perspectives* 5, Philosophy of Religion, ed. J. Tomberlin, (1991).

5. "The Magnitude, Duration, and Distribution of Evil: A Theodicy," 167–168.

6. "The Problem of Evil, the Problem of Air, and the Problem of Silence," 64, n.11.

7. "The Magnitude, Duration, and Distribution of Evil" 168.

8. "The Argument from Particular Horrendous Evils," 76–77.

9. Note, however, that although the evil is not necessary for G, God is justified in permitting those evils *for the sake of G*.

10. "The Magnitude, Duration, and Distribution of Evil: A Theodicy," 168. "The Argument from Particular Horrendous Evils," 76. To be faithful to these sources and for the sake of fluidity, in this section I omit the explicit qualification of evil as *permitted* evil that is required by SC.

11. On 168 of "The Magnitude, Duration, and Distribution of Evil: A Theodicy," he writes:

> It is obvious that if, for any amount of evil that would have served God's purposes,

slightly less evil would have served his purposes just as well—a very plausible assumption—then the principle that God should have got by with less evil if less would have served, entails the (ex hypothesi false) conclusion that God should have got by with no evil at all.

12. More exactly, taking into account the possibility that pain and suffering cannot be measured in discrete units, P may also be construed here as 'For any [positive] amount of evil which serves divine purpose G, there is an amount smaller by no less than some finite amount which also accomplishes G'.

13. More accurately, taking into account the possibility that pain and suffering cannot be measured in discrete units, as Jordan does, the diminishability constraint forces P into P**: 'For any [positive] amount n of evil which serves divine purpose G, there is an amount smaller by no less than what is humanly detectable.' Since subtracting an amount greater than some minimum detectable amount (or some clearly undetectable amount, if possible) from a finite amount indefinitely (granting that's possible) will result in no pain and suffering, we have the same, though less tidy, rebuttal to P** as to P*.

14. Van Inwagen finds the denial of E and E' plausible and hence thinks we have good reason to believe SC false. All that is needed to challenge atheist arguments based on SC is to show that SC is open to reasonable doubt. If SC entails E and E', all van Inwagen needs then is to show E or E' may reasonably be doubted. So that weaker claim is what I have involved. (I do not think SC entails E without significant and difficult reformulation, but that is a topic for another paper.)

15. That a quantity is infinitely divisible is one reason to think it implausible that a precise amount of it is required for something. It is one reason for thinking that a specific minimum height requirement for God's prophet is implausible, for example. But it is not the only reason.

16. Moreover, Jordan's reasoning does not show P is false, only that it is not true. That distinction is significant in the present context as shown below. Jordan asserts Y on page 237. He writes, "[I]f there are whole numbers with which [P*] is false, then there is some minimum amount necessary to accomplish [G]."

17. Note that the infinite divisibility of any millimeter of height is not relevant to this.

18. The number of evils here can be measured by the whole numbers, so this can be translated as an instance of P*.

19. Jordan's reasoning leads to the conclusion that the actual number of hairs extracted must be necessary for G because it is necessary for S. This is a mistake even if one supplements his argumentation with consideration of SC. Thinking God would not permit any unnecessary evil is not a good reason for thinking there is a specific number of hairs such that if Samson has that number he is bald and if he has one more he is not bald, even if one accepts P is not true. What one should say is either that SC is false: God can be morally justified in permitting evils whose permission is not necessary for a greater good (as van Inwagen holds); or that if G is a specific good, it cannot depend solely on S (and those additional necessary factors to pick out a specific number of extractions). Also, the fact that pain is finitely diminishable does not show that a good cannot require a vague rather than a specific amount of pain, just as the fact that hair comes in discrete units does not show that a person's becoming bald requires the removal of a specific number of them.

20. See note 13 for a minor qualification.

21. Perhaps more cautiously: the Sorites Redux shows P* should be rejected. See Hartry Field's "No Fact of the Matter" in *Australasian Journal of Philosophy*, 2003, 457–480.

22. Jordan's rebuttal is persuasive only because it ignores the distinctive feature of vague concepts, namely, their seeming to have an indeterminate range of borderline cases between clear-cut cases of applicability and clear-cut cases of inapplicability, which is just what van Inwagen employs to counter the Standard Claim. (Moreover, even if arguments for E are correct, what the Vagueness Response, if successful, indicates is that SC depends on them.)

Aquinas and Themistius on Intellect

Lorelle Lamascus

Abstract: Aquinas puts forward two different, and conflicting, interpretations of Themistius's account of the intellect. In his earlier interpretation of Themistius, Aquinas understands him to hold the position that both the possible and agent intellect are separate and incorruptible, existing apart from individual human souls but shared in by individual souls in the process of knowing. In *De unitate intellectus contra averroistas*, however, Aquinas radically departs from this reading, hailing Themistius as a genuine interpreter of the Peripatetic position, while decrying Averroes's perversion of both Themistius and Aristotle. This paper examines these competing interpretations of Themistius's account of the intellect in his *Commentary on the De anima* of Aristotle, focusing on two issues central to its interpretation: (1) the nature of intellect insofar as it is separate, impassive, and unmixed, and (2) whether the productive intellect is one or many.

Introduction

In the short treatise *De unitate intellectus contra averroistas*, Aquinas cites Themistius at length and with great enthusiasm.[1] Themistius, here, is hailed as a genuine interpreter of the Peripatetic position on the intellect and its relationship to the human soul. Indeed after 1267, Themistius appears in Aquinas's work as articulating the authentic Peripatetic position, one that is in accord with Aquinas's own. This enthusiastic embracing of the Themistian position is a significant departure from Aquinas's earlier assessment of Themistius, however, as among those who hold views contrary to both "the truths of the faith" and the position of Aristotle.[2] This radical change in Aquinas's position is no doubt a consequence of a change in sources available to Aquinas. It was in 1267 that William of Moerbeke completed his Latin translation of Themistius's *Commentary on the De anima* of Aristotle.[3]

Prior to this time, Aquinas's knowledge of Themistius would have relied heavily upon the recapitulation of his thought present in Averroes's *Long Commentary on the De Anima*. His latter interpretation is quite clearly a result of access to the

Latin translation of Themistius, which, he argues, reveals Averroes's account of Themistius to be inaccurate.[4] Clearly, Aquinas thinks there are grounds for rejecting Averroes's interpretation of Themistius that can only be discovered in the text of Themistius. Nonetheless, the Latin West owed much of its knowledge of both Aristotle and the method by which to read him to Averroes, who was neither obtuse nor unskilled in philosophy. Is it truly the case, as Aquinas claims, that Averroes has perverted Peripatetic philosophy, or is Aquinas's later reading a misconstrual of the Themistian text?

In what follows, I will consider Aquinas's two interpretations of Themistius, and argue that Themistius's position differs from both of these. I will first present Aquinas's early interpretation, which presents Themistius as in agreement with Averroes and a generally Neo-Platonic understanding of the intellect. Subsequent to this, I will present Aquinas's later position, which argues against such a Neo-Platonic understanding of Themistius. Finally, I will consider Themistius's text, which I will argue lends itself to two different interpretations, neither of which is strictly Neo-Platonic. The first of these views the passive and active intellects as forming one compound productive intellect, which is part of the human soul. The second of these distinguishes between a plurality of individual productive intellects in human souls, one productive intellect over and above these, and an intermediate or medium between that is the *energeia* of the one productive intellect.

I. Aquinas's Early Position

In the *Disputed Questions on Truth*, Aquinas criticizes Themistius for holding the view that both the possible and agent intellects are separated and incorruptible.[5] In this particular question, Aquinas is considering whether or not human beings can know separate substances. He recounts the positions of Alexander of Aphrodisias, Averroes, and Themistius in his consideration of this question, attributing to all of them the positions that the agent intellect is itself one of the separate substances. The position that the agent intellect is a separate substance is based upon the description of *nous* in *De anima* as both separate and incorruptible.[6] An interpretive problem arises from this position, however, since positing an agent intellect that is a separate substance still leaves a chasm between an inseparable and corruptible possible intellect and separate substances, which are entirely beyond its nature. The agent intellect must be united to the possible intellect in order for the individual human being to know; and the possible intellect is, on Alexander's view, corruptible and material since it is of the body. This, Aquinas contends, results in Themistius's view that both the possible and the agent intellect are separate and incorruptible.

> However, since it does not seem possible for something which is incorruptible and separated, as the agent intellect, to be united as the form for the possible intellect, which, for Alexander, is corruptible and material, it has seemed to others that the possible intellect itself is separated and incorruptible. Hence, Themistius says that the possible intellect, too, is separated, and that it is natural to it to understand not only material things

> but also separated substances. He adds that its intelligible objects are not temporal, but eternal, things, and that the speculative intellect, by which we understand, is made up of the agent and the possible intellects.[7]

To summarize, Aquinas understands Themistius to hold that both the possible and agent intellects are separate and incorruptible. As such, the composite of the two forms the 'speculative intellect' and this composite is responsible for our understanding separate substances. As Aquinas notes, this places Themistius among those who "could find no way for us to understand separate substances except by understanding through some separated substance."[8] In this, he accepts Averroes's reading of Themistius as presented in the *Long Commentary on the De Anima*.[9]

Before proceeding to Aquinas's later understanding of Themistius, I would like to turn briefly to a consideration of Neo-Platonism and the nature of participation. This is of moment to the current discussion insofar as the more recent discussion of Themistius has viewed him as exhibiting some Neo-Platonic influence, but also because Averroes's influential interpretation of Themistius is bound up with Neo-Platonic influences in the Arabic tradition. Let me begin by noting that Themistius and Aristotle frequently use language that indicates sharing or participation in their discussions of intellect and other powers of the soul. Any consideration of Neo-Platonic tendencies in Themistius's own thought will need to distinguish between different senses of these terms in order to determine whether they are resonant with Neo-Platonic teachings. If we are to understand Themistius to adhere to Neo-Platonic philosophy, we will need to understand the relationship of individual *nous* to the hypostasis *nous*. To cast this in terms of our current discussion, this would mean understanding the hypostasis *nous* as a single agent intellect, which is in some way related to a multiplicity of individual intellects. Given the distinction between possible and agent intellect, this might result in understanding the possible intellect as belonging to the individual, while understanding the agent intellect to correspond to the hypostasis *nous*. Intelligibles would be known in this scenario when the individual possible intellect "participated in" the one agent intellect. But there is a significant problem with this reading. The hypostasis *nous* of Plotinus contains not only the universal intelligibles, but also every individual that exists as image of *nous* in the lower hypostases. This means that the individual intellect always already exists in *nous* as a unity of the possible and agent intellects. Consequently, even if Themistius is positing a single agent intellect of one sort or another, there is no reason to understand this as coincident with the hypostatic *nous* of the Neo-Platonists. I would also like to stress here the relationship between participation and emanation in the works of Plotinus. The emanative activity on the part of the hypostases and the participative movement on the part of the lower realms of being are a continuous motion; one does not have Neo-Platonic participation without a corresponding Neo-Platonic emanation. Thus, if it is to be argued that Themistius's interpretation of intellect bears the mark of Neo-Platonism, it is necessary to show not only that Neo-Platonic participation is present, but also that Neo-Platonic emanation is present. I will now turn to Aquinas's later interpretation of Themistius.

II. Themistius in the *De unitate intellectus contra averroistas*

Aquinas arrives at a new understanding of Themistius once he has access to his text. In an attempt to combat the Averroism of his time, Aquinas writes a short treatise on the intellect, drawing heavily on Themistius's paraphrases of the *De Anima* to counter the generally accepted Themistian interpretation that had been transmitted through Averroes to the Latin West. In this treatise, *De unitate intellectus contra averroistas*, Aquinas cites Themistius as supporting his own view, namely that:

> not only the possible intellect but also the agent [intellect] is part of the human soul, and he [Themistius] asserts that Aristotle thought this; and, further, that man is what he is, not by reason of the sensitive soul, as some falsely say, but from the more principal and intellective part.[10]

In saying this, Aquinas attributes to Themistius the position that the intellect is part of the soul, part of the human being composed of body and soul, and that the intellect is part of the soul that is joined to the body as its form. As such, the intellect must retain its incorruptible and separable qualities while being part of the soul that is the form of the body. Aquinas sees this as a tenable position insofar as some entelechies do not need bodies through which to act, and the intellect that is described as separable, having no organ, is one such entelechy.

Aquinas has two primary concerns in *De unitate intellectus contra averroistas*: (1) whether the intellect is a separate substance from the body, and (2) whether the intellect is one for all men. In addressing the issue of whether the intellect is a separate substance from the body, Aquinas begins with an examination of Aristotelian texts. He focuses primarily on Aristotle's definition of the soul as "the first act of a physical organic body" and Aristotle's various statements about the intellect, its nature, and its relationship to the body. In particular, Aquinas is concerned to explain the description of the intellect as "separable, impassive and unmixed."[11] It is Aquinas's task here to reconcile these two Aristotelian positions in such a way that the intellect is included as part of the soul that is the form of the body.

Aquinas argues that Aristotle's definition of the soul holds in such a way that the intellect can be included within it, and that the description of the intellect as separate is not at variance with this. The first evidence Aquinas gives for his position appeals to Aristotle's assertion that the intellect designates another *kind* (or genus) of soul, because it has a power that other forms of life do not. Consequently, the Averroist interpretation that "intellect is used equivocally of soul" and that the definition of soul as the form of a physical organic body "cannot be applied to it [soul]" should be rejected. Such a reading would lead to the position that intellect and soul are two different and independent substances, and that the intellect is in no way soul. Aquinas argues instead that the description of the intellect as a distinct "genus of soul" must be understood with Aristotle's subsequent remark that "it belongs to this [intellect] alone to be separated as the eternal from the corruptible."[12] Not only is the intellect a genus of soul, then, but the description of the intellect as separate and eternal is consistent with the definition of the soul as the actuality of the body. Thus, insofar as it is separable, the intellect does not have to be a separate substance.

Appealing to the description of the intellect as a power of the soul, Aquinas holds that it is a part of the soul, just as the power of sensation, and so a part of the soul that is the actuality of the body. These parts of the soul are separable by reason, not by location.[13] Aquinas is thus able to conclude that the intellect is part of the individual human soul, united to body as form.

> [C]learly therefore, that which he [Aristotle] had said above, that the soul is the act of a physical body, he here concludes not only of the vegetative, sensitive and motive [powers], but also of the intellective [power]. Therefore what Aristotle meant was that that by which we understand is the form of a physical body.[14]

Aquinas further notes that "that by which we understand" clearly refers to the possible intellect.[15]

Within the first chapter of *De unitate intellectus contra averroistas*, Aquinas references Themistius only once, though parallels with the Themistian text suggest that he is following Themistius closely. Aquinas devotes substantial space to Themistius in the second chapter, however, citing several passages from the *Commentary* in order to show that his own view is in accord with that of Themistius and other prominent Peripatetics. The Themistian passages he selects focus on the following key issues: matter-form relationship, potency-act, distinction between 'this' and 'to be', and whether humans are potential or actual intellect. Aquinas asserts here that the passages cited, taken together, show that Themistius holds the possible and agent intellect to be part of the human soul, and further that this unified intellectual part of man is that by which he is man.[16] I will consider these Themistian passages themselves in the third part of this paper. For now, I will simply note that there is nothing in these passages from Themistius to support Aquinas's claims that the description of the intellect as "separable, impassible, and unmixed" poses no problems for the position that man is active intellect, and that it is joined to him as his form. Aquinas has, however, disposed of this issue in the first chapter of his treatise. Aquinas presents the chapter two citations as positive proof that Themistius holds that man is active intellect, and that this intellective soul, through which he gets his being, is joined to the body as its form.

In chapter four, Aquinas turns to his second concern, that the Averroists hold that the possible intellect is one for all men. In discussing this issue, Aquinas utilizes two passages from Themistius that had also been used by Averroes in his argument against a plurality of potential intellects. The first considers the place of intelligibles in the transference of knowledge from teacher to learner. The second, drawn from the account of the intellect in *De anima* III. 5, describes the relationship between that which illuminates and that which is illuminated with respect to the intellect.

One reason that the Averroists hold that the intellect is one for all men is because the object of understanding is the same for all men, thus it seems that the intellect that *is understanding* is also the same for all men. Furthermore, because the agent intellect has its essence in its activity, there is no means by which to differentiate one intellect from another if they are knowing the same things. This raises three issues: (1) whether the intelligible is numerically identical because it must be the same in the teacher and the pupil, (2) whether the intelligible can exist universally in a particular intellect, and (3) how knowledge is caused in the pupil by the knowledge of the teacher, i.e., how the intelligible is transferred from one to the other. The second reason for holding the Averroist position arises from Themistius's interpretation of the intellect described in terms of light, which appears in III. 5 of Aristotle's *De anima*. In the text of Themistius, these two problems are presented as related to one another, and taken together these issues seem to form the foundation for the position that there is, in some way or another, one active intellect in which all men share.

In chapter five, Aquinas addresses the first of these issues: that if the object of knowledge is one, then the intellect directed toward it must also be one. The problem created by intelligibles, or objects of knowledge is that in order for two people to be able to understand the same thing, there must be something common between them, namely the intelligible. In what way can the intelligible be said to exist then? If it is posited as universal and shared, then it will not be possible to account for "this man" understanding. And again, if the intelligibles are to be shared, they might require some common foundation, an existence independent of individuals, but to which all individuals have access.

In response to this problem, Aquinas distinguishes between the object that is known and the understanding of that object in each of the knowers. Each knower understands the object of the intellect by means of its own act. "Whence," Aquinas writes, "Aristotle says in the *Categories* that some knowledge is singular with reference to its subject 'as a certain grammatical [point] is indeed in a subject, that is, in the soul, but is not said of any subject.'"[17] Thus Aquinas distinguishes between a singular act of understanding proper to the individual and an act of understanding absolutely considered that grasps the universal.[18] The act is singular; what is understood, however, is universal. Intelligibles are not, Aquinas argues, restricted to a universal existence, but may exist as immaterial singulars.[19] Aquinas explains that the knowledge in the pupil and in the teacher "is the same in relation to the thing known, but not, however, in relation to the intelligible species by which each one knows. For in this respect knowledge is individuated in me and in him."[20]

Aquinas cites Themistius once more, when refuting the position that the intellect can be moved by the action of something else imposed upon it.[21] In such a way would a single agent intellect move individual souls. Aquinas, however, noting that "the act of the agents is in the recipient or thing disposed" and citing Themistius, holds "that when a moved thing moves and has the action of a mover, there must be within it some act from the mover from which it has this kind of action. And this is the first principle by which it acts. It is its act and form; just as if something is made hot, it heats by reason of the heat that is in it from whatever made it hot."[22] Thus, even though knowledge is obtained from another, e.g., a teacher, it does not come to be in the student without an intellective act on the part of the student.

The student knows in one sense by knowledge, but in another by the soul, which is capable of knowing.

Citing Themistius, Aquinas quotes from the passage that investigates whether the agent intellect is one or many.

> For when he [Themistius] had inquired whether the agent intellect is one or many, he added by way of solution: "Or indeed the first illuminator is one, but those illuminated and illuminating are many. For the sun indeed is one, yet you will say that the light is shared in some way with regard to sight. For on this account, Aristotle did not posit the sun but light in his example, whereas Plato [posited] the sun."[23]

Aquinas interprets Themistius here to be describing the existence of one primary agent intellect that is the repository of all of the forms and foundations of knowledge. This agent intellect is identified with the "illuminator". Additionally, there are many individual agent intellects that exist as parts of human souls; these are the "illuminated and illuminating". Thus the primary agent intellect actualizes the many agent intellects, which in turn actualize the possible intellects which are their counterparts. Aquinas identifies the primary agent intellect as "the principle of illumination . . . some separate substance—either God, according to Catholics, or the last intelligence, according to Avicenna."[24] Aquinas further notes that Themistius uses the example of the student and teacher understanding the same object to support the claim that this primary agent intellect is indeed one.[25]

In summary, Aquinas's position is that there is one "illuminating principle", a separate substance, which actualizes the plurality of individual agent intellects. These individual agent intellects are part of the human soul, since "that by which we first understand is the species and the form."[26] Thus, the first principle through which we are and through which we understand, is the intellective soul, joined to the body as its form.

III. Themistius

It appears that Themistius's position is closer to Aquinas's second reading than to his first. For Themistius does indeed hold that both potential and actual intellects are separable, unmixed, and impassive, while maintaining that the compound of potential and actual intellect is a part or faculty of the soul. Themistius's understanding rests partly on the meanings of those terms used to describe intellect, i.e., separable, unmixed, and impassive, which do not preclude the intellect from being a part of the soul.[27] Furthermore, Themistius notes that the eternal nature of intellect does not absolutely determine its relation to the soul, i.e., it does not necessitate the conclusion that there is only one agent intellect in which all individual souls participate. It is in part because both active and potential intellect are described as separate, impassive and unmixed that Themistius understands them to be a compound, related to one another as form to matter. Taken together, the descriptors of intellect and the relationship between active and potential intellect, provide the foundation for the position that the intellect is a part of the soul. Although these two points bear upon the question of the unity or plurality of productive intellects, there are two other, more significant, texts that are central to the positions of Themistius and Aquinas in this matter. The first of these concerns the comparison of the productive intellect to light; the second concerns the conditions for the possibility of understanding among humans. Proceeding then, in the same order as we have with the texts of Aquinas, we will first examine Themistius's position regarding the relationship of intellect to the soul, and then proceed to the issue of whether the productive or active intellect is one or many.

A. The Intellect as Separate, Impassive, and Unmixed

Themistius distinguishes between a passive intellect, a potential intellect, and an actual intellect. It is the passive intellect that is perishable and of the body. The potential and actual intellects form a compound, and thus a unity; both are described as separate, impassive and unmixed.

At the beginning of III.4, Themistius wonders whether the intellect, if separable, is separable in thought or in place.[28] Earlier in his commentary, Themistius has considered the separability of the various powers of the soul, concluding that the powers belonging to the animal soul, such as sense-perception and locomotion, are separable in definition (*logos*), but not in space (*topos*). What is most notable in this early passage, however, is that Themistius marks out the intellect or "capacity for contemplation" as what "alone can be a distinct kind (*genos*) of soul, as what is eternal [is distinct] from what is perishable."[29] From this discussion, Themistius establishes that the various capacities are powers belonging to the soul. Some powers seem to be inseparable spatially because they are distributed throughout the entire organism. Nonetheless, these powers can be distinguished according to their definitions.

Most powers of soul, i.e., the vegetative, sensitive, appetitive, and motive, are distinct only in thought, since they need to be united to a body in order to function; thus they are separable in thought, but not in place. The intellect, however, having no organ by which it carries out its function, appears to be separable from the body, and not merely separable in thought.[30] The intellect cannot be separated in place since it is not a body and does not act through a body; its relation to the body is different from that of other powers of soul, since it does not need to act through an organ. This is supported by Themistius's words later in the same chapter:

> And those who say that the soul is a place of forms are quite correct, even if they misuse the term "place," not allowing that it is neither the whole soul but just the two faculties by which we think and by which we perceive, nor is it place that can surround, rather than in some way become, what it thinks and what it perceives.[31]

From this, it is apparent that the intellect can only be described in "place" in an analogical sense. Not being a body itself, the intellect does not fill space. In an analogical way, the intellect might be seen as a place because it is the receptacle of forms. In a more proper sense, however, its place is in its actualization; for while the potential intellect becomes all things, the intellect itself is not actual until acted on by the productive intellect.

Following Aristotle, Themistius states also that the intellect is unaffected, or impervious to affection.[32] In the primary sense of affection, neither sensation nor intellection is affected; rather such terminology is used in an analogous way. Themistius writes that "what is affected in a strict sense becomes the matter for what produces the affection, just as something that is being burnt, compressed, or cut [becomes the matter] for what causes the burning, compression or cutting."[33] The form of fire, for instance, imposes itself on a particular stick and so initiates a material change, i.e., a movement from one essence to another. This movement is an affection distinct from the "movements" of sensation and intellect. Themistius draws this distinction with reference to another kind of motion, i.e., activity.

> But the person who says this seems ignorant of the distinction between movement (*kinēsis*) and activity (*energeia*), i.e. that being active in respect of essence can preserve the nature of what is active, as seeing can for sight, whereas being moved in respect of essence always involves a loss of that essence from which it is moved. Also, while activity is perfect in respect of each part of the time in which it occurs, as with both seeing and thinking, movement is an imperfect entelechy and is continually adding on successively different things: place if [movement] in respect of place, size if [movement] in respect of size, and essence if [movement] in respect of essence, as with rivers and winds.[34]

The "movement" of intellect, then, is the activity of the intellect, this "being active in respect of essence." And, insofar as no substantial change occurs in the actualization of its potentiality, it is said to be unaffected. Themistius describes both the potential intellect and the power of perception as unaffected, insofar as the primary sense of affection is concerned.[35] In both cases, it is necessary that the power or potentiality be such that it is not changed (with respect to its essence) into something else by the actualization of its power. The movement involved in both perception and intellection is that of activity, i.e., the potentiality of the power is moved to activity, and completes itself through its operation. As Themistius writes, "It is, in other words, more appropriate to say that [the intellect] would be 'completed' to the fullest extent by being advanced from potentiality to actuality."[36] The actuality and potentiality of a power, then, must be understood in terms of a *hexis*, or disposition. The activity of perceiving and the activity of intellection constitute the state of actuality for each.

The description of the intellect as unmixed further distinguishes it from other powers of the soul. As Themistius explicitly states, "mixture involves a body in relation to a body."[37] In order for the intellect to be mixed, then, it would have to be both a separate substance and a corporeal one. As the intellect has no organ, and acts through itself, it is unmixed with body.[38] The intellect may also be described as unmixed in another way, insofar as it is not mixed with anything that it encounters. Such a mixture would prevent the intellect from becoming identical to its object. In order for the intellect to become identical to its object, it must be "of a nature different from everything it becomes acquainted with."[39] The description of the intellect as unmixed, then, also reveals the nature of the intellect:

> An intellect of this sort must, therefore, have no nature or form of its own except its capacity to comprehend the natures and forms that belong to other things and, through being naturally disposed to grasp all things, have no determinate form.[40]

Its nature as unmixed allows the intellect to receive all forms while being determined by none of them.

The intellect described as separate, unmixed, and impassive contributes to the understanding of the essence of the intellect. Each descriptor reveals what the intellect is not; in each of these ways it is radically other than body. In this sense, it seems unlikely that the intellect can be part of the soul that is joined to the body, or that of itself it can cause our individual being. Themistius, however, continues to hold that the intellect is a power of the soul that is the form of the body.[41] He even troubles to explain how it is possible for the intellect to be joined to it by affections, i.e., by virtue of what he terms rational affections or the passive intellect.[42] It is clear from the consideration given to the descriptors of the intellect—unmixed, impassive, separate—that these descriptors do not lead to the conclusion that the intellect is a substance separate from the human soul. Rather, as Themistius notes early in his commentary, "We know first 'by knowledge', for in respect of this, as well as 'by the soul', we are said to know. . . . Therefore it is 'by the soul' in a primary sense that we are alive, and 'by the soul' that we have sense-perception."[43]

The characterization of intellect as unmixed, impassive, and separate emphasizes its immateriality, its distinction from matter and material change. It is, as we have seen in Aquinas's texts, these very characteristics that determine whether any particular commentator understands the intellect to exist as part of an individual soul or as some separate substance participated in by many souls. Themistius clearly holds the former position rather than the latter, and interprets the description of the intellect as separate, unmixed, and impassive as distinguishing the intellective power of the soul from others. I will now turn to the question of whether the productive intellect is one or many.

B. Is the Productive Intellect One or Many?

According to Themistius, neither the possible nor agent intellect is one for all men. A great deal of discussion and dispute of this issue arises from the *De anima* passage in which Aristotle compares the active intellect to light.[44] Indeed, Mahoney points to this text as the "occasion of sharply divergent interpretations of his [Themistius's] doctrine on the agent intellect."[45] Aquinas himself uses this passage to argue for a plurality of active or productive intellects, all of which are illuminated by one higher productive intellect. This is, perhaps, not far from Themistius's own position. Themistius interprets the passage as follows:

> This is because, based on the light with which it [productive intellect] is compared [at 430a15] it is one. For light too, of course, is one, as even more is the [entity that] supplies the light, [the one] through which all sight among animals is advanced from potentiality to activity. So [on this analogy], the imperishability of the light shared [by everyone with sight] has no more relation to each organ of sight than does the eternity of the productive intellect to each [one] of us.[46]

Themistius's point in this passage seems to be that the eternal nature of the productive intellect is an issue separate from the nature of its unity and its relation to individual potential intellects. It is important to note that this passage immediately follows Themistius's arguments against those who identify the productive intellect with the first god. His emphasis on the irrelevance of the eternality of the intellect in determining whether it is one or many is clearly directed to those who interpret this to mean that the productive intellect must be one and divine, thus a god. This passage, then, appears to be a continuation of Themistius's refutation of such an interpretation of productive intellect.[47]

Themistius begins by considering how best to interpret the comparison of the intellect with light. The productive intellect is said to be one in the same way that light is one. Since both the light that illuminates and the source of the light are held in common among all who see, it follows that both the source and the medium are shared by many, though the medium must act on individual organs. From this distinction between source and medium, Themistius derives an explanation of the unity of productive intellect that provides for a plurality of individual intellects.

Themistius proceeds to consider the problems inherent in the position that there are many productive intellects. The two primary problems are (1) how to account for differentiation among individual intellects that are formally identical and (2) how to account for the common foundations of thought that make communication between humans possible. The first would not pose a problem if it were not for the fact that all productive intellects "have their essence identical with their activity, and all think the same objects."[48] If productive intellects thought different objects, then their activities, identical to both their objects and their essences, might reasonably be said to be divided; this would, however, fail to account for mutual understanding between people. Themistius resolves this issue by distinguishing between the source of light in Aristotle's analogy and the light itself.

> Now [the solution is that] the intellect that illuminates (*ellampôn*) in a primary sense is one, while those that are illuminated (*ellampomenoi*) and that illuminate (*ellampontes*) are, just like light, more than one. For while the sun is one, you could speak of light as in a sense divided among the organs of sight. That is why Aristotle introduced as a comparison not the

> sun but [its derivative] light, whereas Plato [introduced] the sun [itself], in that he makes it analogous to the good.[49]

It is this passage in particular that commentators interpret as positing one productive intellect that is responsible for "illuminating" or actualizing the plurality of individual productive intellects.[50] It is, in point of fact, quite easy to interpret the passage in such a fashion. It is difficult, however, to determine just what sort of thing this one productive intellect, responsible for illuminating all other productive intellects, might be. Themistius has clearly stated that it cannot be identified with the first god. This leaves open the possibility that it may be identified with one of the separate substances. It is difficult, however, to reconcile the nature of the separate substances as utterly uninterested in what exists below them with the idea that they in some way illuminate the minds of humans. If we concede Neo-Platonic influences are present, Themistius could mean that humans share or participate in one separate substance called *nous*. Such a reading would allow for the locating of the axioms and principles of knowledge in a single productive intellect; these intelligible entities could then serve as the condition and foundation of "common notions" and mutual understanding between men. Given Themistius's recent insistence in the text, however, on remaining true to Aristotelian doctrine, it seems implausible to attribute to him such a position.[51] There is, further, another possible interpretation of the passage, which depends upon Themistius's earlier comments regarding substance, form and matter, and the sense in which intellective soul is said to be primary.

In the above passage, Themistius speaks of the intellect that illuminates in a "primary sense". This is typically interpreted to mean that there is some primary instance of intellect that is the condition for the actuality of all other intellects. Todd notes, however, that Themistius uses "primary" in two distinct senses when speaking of the soul: logical and ontological.[52] If the first sense is meant here, then the primary productive intellect would be the condition for knowing. If the second is meant, however, the primary productive intellect might refer to the intellect insofar as it has its being through itself,[53] reaches its ultimate perfection,[54] and makes us what we are. In this latter sense, the intellectual soul is viewed as "last in terms of coming into existence, but first in terms of potentiality."[55]

Themistius has identified the productive intellect as the compound of potential and actual intellect. Rather than assume that the "primary" sense of intellect is in one separate substance, it is possible to view the individual productive intellect as this primary sense of intellect. Themistius has earlier considered the nature of substance: "Now among the things that exist we speak of one kind (the primary and most strictly meant) as substance, and speak of one [aspect] of this as matter, another as form, and a third as what comes from both."[56] In similar vein, the intellect is spoken of insofar as it is potential (matter), actual (form), and productive (the compound of the two). Themistius's further discussion of these senses of substance provides for some development of this notion. The potential intellect would thus aptly be described as "a substance in potentiality only, and not yet in itself a particular thing, but like a natural disposition for it, and a preparation for becoming a particular thing."[57] The actual intellect, being form, perfects and completes the potential intellect. "What is, as it were, combined from these is a third [thing], to which both matter and structure belong, and this is the compound (*to sunolon*) . . . [the compound] is said to be perfect, and in a perfect state (*entelos ekhein*), only when it acquires its own structure for which it had been striving."[58] This third thing corresponds to the productive intellect, since both matter and form are proper to it. It is in this sense that it is considered an 'entelechy' understood as "the *hexis* of the state of perfection (*teliotes*)."[59] This third thing, then, is the intellect in its primary sense. Potential and actual intellects, on the other hand, are different aspects of the one productive intellect, each considered with respect to its disposition or *hexis*.

Similarly, in his discussion of the relationship of actual to potential intellect as it corresponds to that of form and matter, the intellect moves toward its own perfection.

> [A]nd while one intellect must be potential, the other must be actual, i.e. perfect and not at all potential or due to natural adaptation, but an intellect and advancing it to actuality, brings to completion the intellect as a *hexis*, in which the universal objects of thought and bodies of knowledge exist.[60]

This description not only emphasizes the completion of the intellect, but explains that it is in this completion that the principles and axioms of knowledge have their being. Furthermore, the condition that makes possible common knowledge is explained here, since every completed intellect will have the "universal objects of thought and bodies of knowledge". Thus, the student and teacher have the same thoughts insofar as each completed intellect contains these universal objects of knowledge; and though knowledge is in one sense caused by the teacher, it depends equally upon the act of the student who must come to knowledge by virtue of the soul.

Themistius holds the view that there is a plurality of productive intellects; indeed this is what makes each human being to be. The soul, as the form of the body, is this productive intellect. While Themistius, in accord with the Aristotelian text, describes both potential and active intellects as separate, he does not conclude from this that there is a single compound of potential and active intellect outside of individual human souls in which all share. Rather, the potential and active intellects are composite within each individual human soul. Aquinas, in his later interpretation of Themistius, represents his thought more accurately, though his identification of the primary agent intellect with the Catholic God seems to stray a bit from an orthodox interpretation. It is clear from Themistius's own views, and from Aquinas's presentation of them, that Aquinas's first understanding of Themistius was flawed.

IV. Themistius and Neo-Platonism

I would now like to return to the question of the presence of Neo-Platonic elements in Themistius's thought. The passage in which Themistius considers whether the productive intellect is one or many tends to be read with a somewhat

Neo-Platonic eye. Todd notes that Themistius, significantly, is the first to articulate the problem of whether the active or productive intellect exists individually as part of each human being or as one for all human beings.[61] As Themistius refers explicitly to "those who think there is one soul", it is reasonable to conclude that his consideration of this issue arises out of his familiarity with Neo-Platonic thinkers. This provides evidence that Themistius is distinguishing the Peripatetic account from the Neo-Platonic one, as Blumenthal suggests,[62] and perhaps even attempting to show the Peripatetic account as superior. Further evidence of this may be seen at 48.34, where he writes, "The soul has, then, been described in outline, to the extent that it is possible to speak universally of something that does not exist universally."

Various positions are held regarding the influence of Neo-Platonism on Themistius. It is clear, as mentioned above, that he is aware of this tradition as he explicitly addresses their doctrines at points. Mahoney reads Themistius as having been influenced by Neo-Platonism.[63] Blumenthal, however, contends that, although Themistius is certainly aware of this tradition, he carefully avoids including its influences in his paraphrases of Aristotle. Although Themistius may be interpreted in a rather Neo-Platonic fashion if select passages are chosen, these same passages taken in the context of his work as a whole reveal a much different meaning. Given also his expressed outrage at those who misinterpret Aristotle, it is difficult to accept that he was unwittingly corrupted by Neo-Platonic influences. It is undeniable that Themistius makes ample use of Plato when it supports his argument, but this is not sufficient evidence for accepting a Neo-Platonic reading of Themistius.

Though, as I mentioned above, it is evident that Aquinas does deviate somewhat from Themistius's position, I think it is also evident that Themistius cannot be understood in strict Neo-Platonic terms. I would like to suggest an alternative that is perhaps midway between these two positions, and which I will call the 'Eastern' position. Recent work by David Bradshaw has emphasized the distinction between the activity or *energeia* of a thing and its essence or *ousia*.[64] Applying this distinction to the problem of the intellect, the one productive intellect may be understood as an essence, the light it emits as its activity or energy, and the many possible intellects as *dunameis*; this yields a significantly different picture of the Aristotelian doctrine of the intellect. I think this yields two possible interpretations. In the first, taking the light analogy seriously, the source of the light is an essence or *ousia*, whose activity (or *energeia*) yields the light that it emits. It is this light, according to Themistius, that illuminates individual intellects while being shared by all. A second, and I think more viable interpretation, is to apply this same relationship between *ousia* and *energeia* to the interpretation I have been suggesting in the third part of this paper. Intellect is a *dunamis* in an individual soul, but only fully realizes its essence (or *ousia*) in its actuality (or *energeia*). In this scenario the active intellect merely designates the activity or *energeia* of the intellect, and the productive intellect as a compound of passive and active corresponds to its essence, since in moving from actual to potential, the potential becomes actual.[6]

Marquette University

Notes

1. With respect to this enthusiasm, Beatrice Zeller writes, "Keeler notes that one reason why St. Thomas makes so much of Themistius in the *De Unitate Intellectus* is that in his previous works he had followed the interpretation of Themistius handed down by Averroes. This he considers to be erroneous, now that he has read the version recently translated by William of Moerbeke" (1968, 43, n. 1).

2. Thomas Aquinas *Quaestiones disputatae de veritate* 2, q.18, a.5, resp. 8.

3. Torrell 1996, 175.

4. "He then singles out Themistius among the Greeks (*Graeci*). . . . Thomas concludes that it is obvious that Averroes erroneously recounted the thought (*peverse refert sententiam*) of Themistius regarding the possible intellect and the agent intellect" (Mahoney 1994, 104).

5. Averroes, Aquinas, and Themistius distinguish several distinct kinds of intellect. I will be adhering to Themistius's usage as closely as possible. Thus, the agent intellect is also referred to as the productive or active intellect; the passive or common intellect is that which is corruptible, mixed with the body, and perishes with the body; potential intellect is the intellect in its pure receptivity, sometimes designated as possible or material. For a discussion of these and other kinds of intellect in the Arabic tradition, see Black 2005.

6. Aristotle *De anima* 3.4–5.

7. Aquinas *Quaestiones disputatae de veritate* 2, q.18, a.5, resp. 8.

8. Ibid.

9. As Mahoney notes, this is the position of Averroes, though he attributes it to Themistius. "As has already been noted, Averroes (b. 1126) takes Themistius to hold that the intellect is one for all men. In Averroes's reading of the late ancient commentator, both the potential and the agent intellects are completely separate from the body as a substance which can neither be generated nor corrupted. Averroes uses Themistius in arguing that the potential intellect is one for all men, that it contains the first principles of knowledge which all men require to think, and that the human species is eternal" (Mahoney 1973, 431).

10. Aquinas *De unitate intellectus contra averroistas* 53.

11. *De an.* 430a18.

12. "In this respect, therefore, it is another genus because the intellect seems to be something eternal, whereas other parts of the soul are corruptible. And because the corruptible and eternal do not seem able to come together into one substance, it seems that of the parts of the soul, it belongs to this part alone (namely the intellect) to be separated not indeed from the body, as the Commentator wrongly explains, but from the other parts of the soul, so that they [the eternal and the corruptible] may not come together into one substance of soul" (*De unitate intellectus* 8).

13. Ibid. 9.

14. *De unitate intellectus* 11; cf. Themistius *On Aristotle's On the Soul* 46.12–25.

15. "But lest anyone say that that by which we understand does not mean here the possible intellect, but something different, clearly this is excluded by what Aristotle says in *III De Anima*, when speaking of the possible intellect: 'I speak moreover of the intellect by which the soul thinks and understands'" (*De unitate intellectus* 11).

16. Cf. Mahoney, who writes: "From three separate passages which he quotes, Thomas concludes that Themistius holds that according to Aristotle not only the possible intellect but also the agent intellect are parts of the human soul and that man is man through his intellectual part" (1973, 435).

17. *De unitate intellectus* 112.

18. "It is therefore one thing which is understood both by me and by you. But it is understood by me in one way and by you in another, that is, by another intelligible species. And my understanding is one thing, and yours, another; and my intellect is one thing, and yours, another" (*De unitate intellectus* 112).

19. Ibid. 112.

20. Ibid. 113.

21. Ibid. 74.

22. Ibid.

23. Ibid. 120.

24. Ibid.

25. Ibid.

26. Ibid. 79.

27. The same descriptors are applied to potential and actual intellect, which is why Themistius comes to understand these as a compound, and possibly also why Averroes comes to the conclusion that the two together form a substance separate from the soul.

28. Themistius *On Aristotle's On the Soul* 93.32.

29. "Now with regard to some it is not difficult to see that they are separated in definition, but not spatially. . . . Indeed, each of the parts [of an animal] has sense-perception and movement in respect of place; and if they have sense-perception, they also have some discrimination regarding what is compatible and incompatible, and thereby have pain and pleasure, and thereby [46] desire, so that, as I said, it is easy to separate all these capacities in definition (things whose ways of functioning are manifestly distinct are also obviously themselves distinct), but impossible to do so spatially. Concerning the intellect, however, (i.e., the capacity for contemplation), nothing is yet clear, but it seems that this alone can be a distinct kind (*genos*) of soul, as what is eternal [is distinct] from what is perishable" (ibid. 45.19).

30. Interestingly, Aquinas cites the same passage from the *De anima* as does Themistius. This indicates how closely he was following Themistius in his interpretation of Aristotle's words. Cf. Themistius *On Aristotle's On the Soul* 94.34, and Aquinas *De unitate intellectus* 24–25.

31. *On Aristotle's On the Soul* 95.5.

32. The intellect is described as *apathēs* translated variously as unaffected, impassive, or impassible.

33. *On Aristotle's On the Soul* 78.5.

34. Ibid. 18.20.

35 Cf. *On Aristotle's On the Soul* 79.26ff. and 78.7–10.

36. Ibid. 94.5.

37. Ibid. 94.28.

38. "That [part] of the soul called the intellect (by 'intellect' I mean that by which the soul reasons and holds beliefs, not that [intellect] that we often mistakenly apply to the imagination too) is in actuality, therefore, none of the things that exist before it thinks one [of them]. So it is reasonable that it also not be mixed with the body, as mixture involves a body in relation to a body. And what exists as a body must exist in actuality and have a shape of its own. But the intellect could not, like perception, use the body even as an organ; indeed it would in that way share in the organ's quality, and as that quality would always coexist with its activities it would exclude the other forms." Ibid. 94.27.

39. Ibid. 94.21.

40. Ibid. 94.20–24.

41. "[I]t is clear that Plato too believes that while the [productive] intellect is 'alone immortal' (430a23), though also itself some [aspect] of the soul, the affections and the reason present in them (which Aristotle calls 'passive intellect') are perishable." Ibid. 107.4–5.

42. Ibid. 107.18–21.

43. Ibid. 46.18–21; Todd notes: "Aristotle at 414a12–13 says that the soul is 'that by which we live, perceive, and think in a primary way (*prôtôs*)'. Themistius has interpreted this 'way' as ontological, and goes on in the next sentence to introduce his own phrase 'first cause' as a prelude to restating 414a13–14. Robinson (9–11) has the interesting suggestion that there is an ambiguity in *prôtôs* between ontological and definitional priority" (1996, 171, n. 16).

44. "Since in every class of objects, just as in the whole of nature, there is something which is their matter, i.e., which is potentially all the individuals, and something else which is their cause or agent in that it makes them all—the two being related as an art to its material—these distinct elements must be present in the soul also. Mind in the passive sense is such because it becomes all things; this is a kind of positive state like light; for in a sense light makes potential into actual colours. Mind in this sense is separable impassive and unmixed, since it is essentially an activity; for the agent is always superior to the patient, and the originating cause to the matter. Actual knowledge is identical with its object. Potential is prior in time to actual knowledge in the individual, but in general it is not prior in time. Mind does not think intermittently. When isolated it is its true self and nothing more, and this alone is immortal and everlasting (we do not remember because, while mind in this sense cannot be acted upon, mind in the passive sense is perishable), and without this nothing thinks" (*De anima* 3.5).

45. Mahoney 1973, 430.

46. *On Aristotle's On the Soul* 103.21–27.

47. Aquinas himself fails to make adequate note of this, in the end concluding that there are a plurality of productive intellects in human beings, but that there is one primary productive intellect (which he identifies with God) that makes the faculty of the productive intellect in human beings able to function.

48. *On Aristotle's On the Soul* 103.29.

49. Ibid. 103.32.

50. Mahoney interprets the passage in this way, and cites both Aquinas and Siger of Brabant as interpreting the passage in similar vein (1973, 436–440).

51. *On Aristotle's On the Soul* 102.30–103.1.

52. Todd notes: "Themistius needs this qualification since 'primary' ([illegible]) is sometimes applied to the vegetative (or nutritive) soul, as at DA 416b25; for the same usage see Themistius below at 53,18 (*bis*) and 54,1. This is logical priority; this soul is a necessary condition for the existence of any other capacity of the soul, whereas the intellect is ontologically prior, since it is separate and can function independently" (1996, 155, n. 10); see *On Aristotle's On the Soul* 49.3–4.

53. *On Aristotle's On the Soul* 100.16–20.

54. "Thus he clearly believes that both intellects are separate, but that the productive intellect is more separate, more unaffected, and more unmixed, and that while the potential intellect is prior in time in its presence to us, the actual intellect is prior in nature, i.e. in completeness. Indeed he believes that the potential intellect does not even have priority in time, but that while it may be prior in its presence in me or you, it is not prior without qualification, as neither is the forerunner to the king, nor the [sun's] ray to the daylight, nor the flower to the fruit" (ibid. 106.7).

55. Ibid. 49.3–4. It is important to note, however, that Themistius distinguishes here between the soul that has the power of reasoning and "the contemplative intellect", which "is neither a capacity, nor a part of the soul described above, but a distinct substance that comes to exist as a superior in an inferior."

56. Ibid. 39.3–4.

57. Ibid. 39.

58. Ibid.

59. Ibid.

60. Ibid. 98.20–24.

61. Todd notes that "this section offers the first statement of this issue in the exegetical tradition" (1996, 103, n. 118).

62. Blumenthal 1979.

63. Mahoney 1973, 428, n. 25.

64. Bradshaw 2004, 57.

65. I would like to thank Richard C. Taylor for his useful comments on and conversations about this paper, which have contributed to my thinking and writing on its subject.

Bibliography

Aquinas, Thomas. 1968. *On the Unity of the Intellect Against the Averroists*. Translated with introduction by Beatrice Zeller. Milwaukee, Wisconsin: Marquette University Press.

———. 1993. *Disputed Questions on Truth*. Vol 2. Trans. James V. McGlynn, SJ. Chicago: Henry Regnery Co. 1953.

Aristotle. 1995. *De anima*. Loeb Classical Library. With a translation by W. S. Hett. Cambridge: Harvard University Press.

Black, Deborah. 2005. "Psychology: Soul and Intellect." In *The Cambridge Companion to Arabic Philosophy*, ed. Peter Adamson and Richard C. Taylor. Cambridge: Cambridge University Press.

Blumenthal, H. J. . 1979. "Themistius, the last Peripatetic Commentator on Aristotle?" In *Arktouros: Hellenic studies presented to Bernard M. W. Knox on the occasion of his 65th birthday*. Ed. G. W. Bowersock, W. Burkert, M. C. J. Putnam. Berlin and New York: W. De Gruyter.

———1996. *Aristotle and Neoplatonism in Late Antiquity: Interpretations of the De Anima*. Ithaca, New York: Cornell University Press.

Bradshaw, David. 2004. *Aristotle East and West: Metaphysics and the Division of Christendom*. Cambridge: Cambridge University Press.

Mahoney, Edward P. 1973. "Themistius and the Agent Intellect in James of Viterbo and Other Thirteenth Century Philosophers (Saint Thomas, Siger of Brabant and Henry Bate)." *Augustiniana*. 23: 422–467.

———. 1994. "Aquinas's Critique of Averroes's Doctrine of the Unity of the Intellect." In *Thomas Aquinas and His Legacy*. Ed. David M. Gallagher. Washington, DC: CUA Press.

Martin, Stuart B. 1966. "The Nature of the Human Intellect as it is Expounded in Themistius' *Paraphrasis in Libros Aristotelis De Anima*." *Boston College Studies in Philosophy*: 1–21.

Themistius. 1990. *Themistius' Paraphrase of Aristotle*. In *Two Greek Aristotelian Commentators on the Intellect*. Translated, with introduction, commentary and notes by Frederic M. Schroeder and Robert B. Todd. Toronto: Pontifical Institute of Mediaeval Studies.

———. 1996. *On Aristotle's On the Soul*. Translated with commentary by Robert B. Todd. Ithaca, New York: Cornell University Press.

Torrell, Jean-Pierre. 1996. *Saint Thomas Aquinas: The Person and his Work*. Volume 1. Translated by Robert Royal. Washington, DC: The Catholic University of America Press.

Aquinas on Intentions in the Medium and in the Mind

Jörg Alejandro Tellkamp

Abstract: In his philosophical works, Aquinas spends some effort establishing why cognitive beings differ from those that are not able to have a cognitive, i.e., intentional, grasp of the exterior world. Prima facie, the matter is clear, since only those beings acquire knowledge that have the proper powers to do so. One remark, however, while discussing the nature of change in the process of visual perception, strikes the reader as particularly odd, since Aquinas states that "a 'spiritual alteration' occurs in virtue of a species' being received in a sense organ or in the medium in the manner of an intention." Whereas it is not problematic to think that perceptions and thoughts are intentional, it seems peculiar to talk of the species in the medium as being received "in the manner of an intention." While current interpretations propose that Aquinas's account is either erroneous or in need of rectification, I would like to argue that the notion of mind-independent or non-cognitive intentions, which follows the Avicennian tradition, is rooted in a peculiar theory of sensible form. Given that the intentions in the medium make sense, it is, however, important to show that they differ from those intentions that are apprehended by cognitive powers. For this purpose, I will try to trace the underlying physics for cognitive change, showing that an account in terms of qualitative change leads one to posit a proper recipient of sensible forms, i.e., the sense powers.

In recent years much has been written about Aquinas's stance on intentionality, sense knowledge and its causal conditions. The spectrum of interpretations ranges from stating that his theory of the intentional being of the species is a wrong rendering of the original Aristotelian position to those who think that it is exactly the opposite.[1] Others see in it a way to account for the difference between cognitive and non-cognitive states, but with different results. One reading of Aquinas's theory of intentions states that "the difference between air or water and the power of sight or hearing is merely quantitative rather than qualitative"[2]; another, however, holds the contrary view saying that the difference between knowing the intentional aspects of sensible species and not knowing them is rooted in Aquinas's theory of formal identity and in the need to explain the role of the proper recipient, i.e., cognitive powers.[3] I should say that I am inclined to think that this latter interpretation is correct, but that it is necessary to give a more thorough account of it.

A starting point for my remarks is Aquinas's statement that "a 'spiritual alteration' . . . occurs in virtue of a species' being received in a sense organ or the medium in the manner of an intention. . . ."[4] By saying that the species are being received in the medium *per modum intentionis*, he broadens the scope of intentionality, placing it outside the mind. In doing so he seems to follow mainly Avicenna's theory of the *intentio*. If there are intentional features outside the mind and intentions in the mind, there is a somewhat obvious question as to the relationship between the two. In other words: how do the intentional features of an object actually become the content of cognition? How does the visible species of a material object in the medium differ from the one in the mind? Is there an adequate explanation to mark that difference?

If there is one, it most likely has to do with Aquinas's theory of sensible species, on the one side, and with the nature of the cognitive powers on the other. I will try to show that his theory of intentionality is based upon his physics of form and qualitative change, all of which should enlighten why sense knowledge is not in itself a physical event, even though it always has a physical event that co-occurs with it. A proper explanation of how the sense powers grasp the intentional being of a form instead of its natural being depends largely on the theory of the powers of the soul and on their relationship with the body.

The key attribute of everything intentional consists in having the intrinsic property to direct itself toward something else; it is its directionality that makes an intention an intention. Thus characterized, it is commonly held that intentions are the product of mental activities, and there is also textual evidence in Aquinas's work for such a reading. In fact, he thinks that the most salient feature of *intentio* is the fact that it is about something: "From the name 'intentio' itself you can recognize to which power it belongs. It is said that 'intendere' is like a reaching out toward something else."[5] This definition is certainly meager, since it applies to a large set of mental states and processes that operate on the basis of mental representations like, for instance, seeing an object *X* as a car or to judging an apple to be delicious. This understanding of intentionality as having basically a mind-world relation, seems to be confirmed by the Aquinas's causal explanation of sense knowledge, which establishes a link between the material objects and the cognitive powers that have a natural function to produce knowledge:

> Now, for the operation of the senses, a spiritual change is required, whereby an intention of the sensible form (*intentio formae sensibilis*) is produced in the sense organ. Otherwise, if a natural change alone were sufficient for the sense's action, all natural bodies would feel when they undergo alteration.[6]

Of course, different forms of causality have to be distinguished, because if any cause were sufficient to produce knowledge, then any given material object should have knowledge of the thing that acts on it. In order to avoid this conclusion, the intentional representation of a form is what distinguishes sentient beings from those that do not have the ability to acquire sense knowledge. Again, by stressing the functions of the senses, Aquinas seems to corroborate the fact that intentions are brought about by the mind alone.

This, however, is not his view, because he argues that intentions do not only exist in the mind, i.e., that they only exist due to the mind's activity, but rather that they also have a mind-independent existence of their own. By saying that the species in the medium have an intentional being, he does not think that intentionality falls exclusively into the realm of the mental. For modern readers this may seem puzzling, if not absurd, but not only was Aquinas already following an established tradition stemming from Avicenna and Averroes, but he may also have philosophical reasons to hold that intentions exist outside the mind.

Aquinas tells us that there is a close relationship between the species' intentional mode of existence and a causal account of perception. Now, in order to understand properly the status of intentions in the medium and its difference with known intentions in the process of sensory change (*immutatio*), it seems natural to take a look into Aquinas's Arabic sources, mainly Avicenna and Averroes.

Avicenna's *De anima* was one of the main sources for thirteenth-century psychology in general, and, of course, for Aquinas himself. In his theory of the powers of the soul, Avicenna distinguishes two types of cognitive powers that a being has in virtue of possessing an *anima vitalis*: one has an external grasp of objects (*a foris*), the other grasps them from within (*ab intus*).[7] The external apprehension is achieved by the outer senses, which are physically involved in this process meaning that the organs and the nervous system are being used. While the external grasp renders basic distinctions regarding the qualitative features of material objects (smoothness, weight, etc.), the inner senses go beyond this stage. It is their function to seize sensible forms as well as sensible intentions, which are by no means identical. Avicenna says:

> The following is the difference between grasping a form and grasping an intention: the form is what the inner sense and the outer sense grasp simultaneously. . . . By contrast, the intention is what the soul grasps of a sensible object, although it has not been previously grasped by the outer sense. . . . What the outer sense grasps first of a wolf and the inner sense afterwards is properly called form. What the hidden powers grasp without the senses is here properly called intention.[8]

Even though the form of a thing seems to be coextensive with its intention, the latter contains "information" the former does not. Following a suggestion made by Dag N. Hasse, it seems that the intentions are in themselves immaterial, like the forms, and that they too reside in the material object as inseparable attributes.[9] A wolf is not only a 'thing' with certain essential and accidental properties; it also contains meaningful information the sheep can grasp. The fact that it perceives the wolf as a natural enemy is due to the fact that wolves do eat sheep.[10] Hence, the sheep grasps in a meaningful way that the wolf is its natural enemy, establishing a species-specific objective correlation between agent (wolf) and patient (sheep)

In Hasse's terms, intentions have to be understood as "connotational attributes." Despite the objective character of the intention, being a real meaningful correlation, it is only grasped as such when adequate cognitive powers get involved. Since the outer senses only grasp those features that causally activate them, and since intentions differ in this respect from the sensible forms, it has to be a *vis occulta*, namely the *virtus aestimativa*, which "grasps the material intentions that are not in their material substrate, although it happens that they exist in matter."[11] Even though the intentions are immaterial, they always occur in a material environment and it is the role of *aestimatio* to grasp them.[12]

It has been noted that Averroes's stance on intentionality differs from that of Avicenna.[13] In his *Long Commentary on De anima* he discusses briefly Aristotle's metaphor of the ring's impression into a piece of wax in order to explain that perception has a cause and that it differs from other processes in that only the form is transmitted, but not the matter.[14] Averroes seems to have been aware of an underlying ambiguity in Aristotle's text, since it could describe cognitive as well as non-cognitive processes. Averroes's commentary on *De anima* 421b8–12, where the properties of smell and sight are discussed, is crucial:

> Just as color has a twofold being, namely, being in the colored body (this is corporeal being) and being in the transparent (this is spiritual being), so too smell has twofold being, namely, being in the body which is odorous and being in the medium. The former is corporeal being and the latter spiritual, the former natural and the latter extrinsic.[15]

In order to distinguish both types of processes, Averroes introduces the notion of a form's spiritual being, which points to the perceptible properties of material objects.[16] This spiritual being is the opposite of the mere natural being of a form.[17] In fact, Averroes also uses it in his *Commentary on De sensu et sensato* where he distinguishes three ways of understanding the sensible form.[18] There he states (1) that it can have a merely physical being (*purum esse corporale*) in material objects, (2) but it also can have a spiritual being insofar it is grasped by the soul. (3) The third modality it can exist in is in the medium, where the form's existence is a special case, because it consists in some sort of mixture of bodily and spiritual properties. While the spiritual being of the form may lead to knowledge, its natural being does not. But in order to explain the transition from the bodily existence of a form in a material thing into its spiritual being in the mind, Averroes seems to be compelled to say that the form in the medium has to have both properties.[19]

Clearly Averroes identifies the spiritual mode of existence of sensible forms with cognition, which, as he says, is due to the abstraction of form from matter.[20] Although he associates the presence of sense knowledge with the spiritual being of the species, there still remains the question about the role of the intentions. While the theory of the spiritual being of a form accounts for the difference between cognitive and non-cognitive beings, Averroes sees in the concept of intention a means to explain what cognition is about, namely that it is either about individuals in the case of sensation or about universals in the case of intellection.[21]

His commentary on *De anima* 424a17ss completes this image. The difference between forms known and forms not known lies in the fact that the first have no matter and that they are "intentiones et comprehensiones" that exist in the soul. By contrast, outside the mind there are no intentions, "but material things not known at all."[22] By saying this, Averroes seems to disagree with Avicenna regarding the mind-independent status of the intentions, giving an alternative account for cognition: the form's spiritual being. Curiously enough, Aquinas felt he could use both theories for his own version, which can best be seen when he talks about an *immutatio spiritualis seu intentionalis*. The combination of the Avicennian notion of *intentio* with the Averroistic stance on spiritual being, is therefore a salient feature of Aquinas's own commentary on *De anima* 424a17ss which I shall consider later.

All this suggests that his reading of Avicenna and Averroes is not a smooth one. Thus Hasse rightly points out that Aquinas "is not a reliable guide to Avicenna's psychology."[23] Even if this is true, it is also true that his psychology relies heavily on the Avicennian terminology. But it also is accurate to say that Aquinas has almost no use for physiology, which however is very present in Avicenna's work. Yet, following D. Black's assessment, Aquinas's theory of the inner senses and intentionality reflects a sort of syncretism that blends parts of Avicennian and Averroistic origin, so that Avicenna's impact is not as powerful as in other authors, like John of la Rochelle or even Albert the Great.[24]

It is, however, clear that Aquinas was a keen reader of Avicenna's *De anima*, which, for instance, can be seen in the *sed contra* of *Summa theologiae* I q. 78 a. 4 where he quotes him as an authority, which is highly unusual. The reason behind the importance Aquinas gives Avicenna lies in the conviction, shared by both, that the faculties of the soul are the driving force behind the theory of knowledge. They also share the view that the intentional being of the species has a mind independent existence in the medium and that it has to be distinguished from the natural being of those species, which corresponds to Avicenna's distinction of *forma* and *intentio*.

This distinction is, in fact, central to Aquinas's own theory, but he gives it an Averroistic spin. While the natural being of a species produces effects such that it manifests itself according to the same mode of existence it had in the cause, its spiritual or intentional being is not a physical event.[25] The sun, e.g., heats a stone through the form of heat, which means that this form has the same mode of existence in the sun as in the stone, because in both it is a form intrinsically linked to the presence of matter. The intentional being of a species, however, produces non-physical effects, which is the reason why the color 'red' does not cause the eye to become physically red.[26] The natural existence of sensible forms seems to indicate that, e.g., a sound has a physical component insofar as it is transmitted through sound waves. Yet at the same time the sound transmits some sort of 'information' that points to relevant features of the physical object it stems from. Thus, when a person hears someone speak, those two aspects, the merely physical and the intentional, are involved. While the physical aspects lead to a corresponding change in the sense organ, it is only the intentional being of the species that leads to a cognitive grasp of what is being said. At this point it should be clear that the physical change, which co-occurs in any process that leads to sense knowledge, only qualifies as a necessary, but not as a sufficient condition for sense knowledge.

Here the mode of reception of forms and a proper account of the physics behind it comes into play. The natural as well as the intentional being of a sensible form have a corresponding effect on a patient, but only if it is able to actually receive those forms. When a material thing receives a form according to its natural mode of being, a natural, i.e., physical change is the consequence. When something receives a form according to its intentional being, an intentional change is the consequence. Both, natural and intentional being, bring about natural and intentional change in the patient respectively.

The different modes of reception have to be underscored. According to Robert Pasnau's reading, however, "the difference between air or water and the power of sight or hearing is merely quantitative rather than qualitative."[27] Although he correctly assumes that the species have an intentional being in the medium and that the medium itself is not cognitive, he challenges the view that the difference between cognitive and non-cognitive beings is rooted in a proper theory of the powers of the soul.[28] Hence, in an almost Humean fashion the difference between the species in the medium and in the senses would be just a matter of degree and intensity.[29]

If the intentional being of sensible forms were necessary *and* sufficient for cognition, as Pasnau suggests, every object in the path of those species should be able to receive those intentions regardless of their physical and psychological constitution. Pasnau himself recognizes the absurdity of this conclusion, but gives no compelling alternative account. His view is not only counterintuitive; it also disregards the textual evidence at hand that explains the central role of the proper recipient, i.e., the cognitive powers. A comprehensive account of Aquinas's theory would include (1) the causal role of the sensible forms and its underlying physics, and (2) the ontological presuppositions that answer the question as to why the cognitive powers are the proper recipients that grasp intentions.

The Causality of Sensible Forms

Based on Aquinas's physics of the sensible qualities, I will argue that the difference between intentions in cognitive and non-cognitive beings cannot be reduced to the quantitative features of the sensible forms. It rather can be traced to his theory of the sensible qualities and to his view that the difference between the intentional being of the species in the medium and in the mind is based upon the correspondence of patient and agent and the aptitude of the first to be affected by the latter.

Following Averroes, Aquinas makes use of the notion that every agent produces something similar to it (*omne agens agit sibi simile*).[30] By this token, the function of the sense powers is defined by their correlation with a proper object.[31] A being is cognitive if and only if it can receive the intentional being of a form without the matter and when it possesses a corresponding functioning cognitive power.[32] Inversely, a specific cognitive power is able to grasp one and only one qualitative feature. This reciprocity of sensible species and cognitive power implies that patient and agent have to have common formal and material features in order to produce a change (*alteratio, immutatio*).

The difference between the intentional forms in the medium and the intentional forms in the senses depends largely on what it means for a being to be affected by such forms. Therefore the underlying physics has to be scrutinized and attention has to be called upon the fact that any type of causality is rooted in the formal identity of patient and agent. It is always a form as act that produces a change in a patient.[33] The form alone, however, is not sufficient to bring about change in a material object.[34] Hence, change is the result of an agent's form acting upon a passive substrate; but this might apply to cognitive as well as non-cognitive processes. At the beginning of this issue stands Aristotle's *De anima* 424a17ss:

> Generally, about all perception, we can say that a sense is what has the power of receiving into itself the sensible forms of things without the matter, in the way in which a piece of wax takes on the impress[ion] of a signet ring without the iron or gold; what produces the impression is a sign (*semeion*) of bronze or gold, but not qua bronze or gold.[35]

By emphasizing the reception of a form without the matter, it is obvious that any change in the senses is the result of a form's causality. Aquinas, however, thought that Aristotle's account is incomplete, because the principle of change, i.e., a form being received by something in potency would apply to any kind of change.[36] The consequence would be that the causal conditions for sense knowledge could not be explained: "Therefore it does not seem to be special (*proprium*) to sense that it can take on species without matter."[37] The reception of a form without matter is, then, common to all passive processes.

Although the reception of a form without matter is the general principle of change, it is the mode of reception, which marks the difference between cognitive and non-cognitive states.[38] Aquinas distinguishes two types of modes of reception according to the two modes of being a form can have in a material substrate: (a) one insofar the form of the patient has the same mode of existence (*modus essendi*) as the one of the agent; (b) the other insofar as the agent's form has a mode of existence that differs from that of the patient.

It seems that the mode of existence refers to the way a form manifests itself in a composite substance. According to Aquinas this means that it may exist in a thing naturally or intentionally. When an alteration occurs according to the same mode of being, the patient receives the agent's form in such a way that the form received manifests itself in exactly the same way as it does in the agent. The reason for this identity is to be found in the fact that both, agent and patient, have the same physical disposition (*dispositio*) of receiving and containing one and the same form. For example, when the air suffers a change because of the fire's heat, it acquires physically the same form of heat that already exists in the fire.[39]

The reception of a form according to another mode of being (*secundum alium modum essendi*), by contrast, does not depend on identical physical dispositions; it rather points to the fact that a form may exist in a patient in such a way that it does not alter it physically. In this respect it is worth noting that a change that originates in an agent, is completed by the mode of existence of the thing that receives it (*per modum recipientis*).

The notion of spiritual or intentional change is central to Aquinas's theory of how knowledge of intentions is acquired. It quite naturally is rooted in the distinction of act and potency and, therefore, of form and matter. Every change is thus characterized as a type of movement of something that is being actualized regarding place, quantity and quality.[40] I will focus on qualitative change alone, because it helps to understand how an object is able to obtain new features without losing the ones it already has. Technically speaking this kind of change is called *alteratio*, which denotes a change of accidents[41] or, in other words, of the qualities of the third species.[42]

The interesting point here is that Aquinas assumes that the accidental features that produce change in another object, can actually produce an effect on the sense organs and, hence, be grasped by the proper senses.[43] Those features form part of the inner structure of objects (*in profundum*) and only they can produce change in sense powers, while the quantitative attributes of the same objects cannot. Since those attributes can produce change in the senses, they are identical with the proper sense objects (*sensibilia propria*), i.e., colors, sound, smell, etc.; they are real and existing properties of material objects.[44]

In book VII, 5, of his *Commentary on Physics* Aquinas explicitly states that sensation is such a kind of change, since sensory processes correspond to qualitative changes.[45] Interestingly enough, he also finds a close relationship between that kind of cognitive change and the fact that it occurs within the sense powers.

> According to those qualities, 'change' corresponds to all sensible bodies, animate as well as inanimate. Since in animate bodies some parts are animate, i.e., sensible, like the hand or the eye, and since other parts are inanimate, like hair and bones, both are changed according to those qualities, because the senses are changed when they perceive. The activities of the senses, like hearing and seeing, are certain bodily movements together with a certain change of the senses. The senses are only active through a bodily organ: it is for bodies to be moved and changed.[46]

The significance of the qualities of the third species is obvious, because they highlight how sense knowledge is produced. Since sense knowledge has two aspects, one physical and one cognitive, it should be clear that every cognitive event is co-occurrent with a physical event, and this means that there can be no sense knowledge if there is no bodily change. Although the reception of an accidental form, i.e., a quality, co-occurs with a certain physical change, this change does not by itself cause knowledge.

Cognitive Powers as the Proper Recipients

All this bears significance regarding cognitive and non-cognitive intentions, because Aquinas can show that the principle of formal identity is valid, even though the form shared by an agent and a patient differs with respect to its mode of reception and its immateriality. The difference between known and unknown forms is basically due to the role that the receiving part, i.e., the patient plays. There are some receptive beings that have a greater "amplitude and extension" than others, and to this kind of patients belong the powers of the soul.

The advantage of such a theory consists in providing an account for *intentiones* and still showing that within the framework of Aristotelian physics the substantial and accidental forms of cognitive beings remain intact. In opposition to natural processes in which one form succeeds another (e.g., the form of heat in water replaces the form of coldness), the cognition of a sensible form does not entail that it "takes over" the form of the cognitive power, because the cognitive power already exceeds the limitations imposed by matter. For example, the power of sight grasps the color 'red', when it receives the accidental form 'red' in such a way that it exists in the eye in a different mode than in a red object.[47] 'Red' in a tomato and 'red' in the eye is formally identical, but it differs in the way it manifests itself in the tomato as well as in the eye, because its form has a natural being in the tomato and an intentional being in the sense power.[48]

Although agent and patient can contain one sensible form *X* in different modes of existence, they in fact contain the same form.[49] This is due to the principle of formal identity. The difference, however, lies in their physical disposition of receiving and containing a form, and this implies that the form *X* an agent has differs from the form *X* the patient has, but not in virtue of it being form *X*, but because of its different relation to the material substrate. This means that while a natural change involves the loss of one form and the reception of another, intentional change does not imply the patient to lose its own natural form by receiving another intentionally. This is, again, the reason why the eye does not turn red by seeing a red object. This, too, is the reason why in *Summa theologiae* I q. 14 a. 1 c. Aquinas states that:

> Cognitive beings are distinguished from non-cognitive beings in that the latter possess only its own form; whereas the cognitive being is naturally apt to have also the form of some other thing; for the species of the thing known is in the knower. Hence it is manifest that the nature of a non-cognitive being is more contracted and limited; whereas the nature of cognitive beings has a greater amplitude and extension. . . . Therefore it is clear that the immateriality of a thing is the reason why it is cognitive; and according to the mode of immateriality is the mode of knowledge.[50]

This much discussed text not only shows that immateriality is a necessary condition for knowledge; it also seems to presuppose that there are different degrees of immateriality, because of the *coarctatio formae per materiam*. This has been taken to mean that the form known literally contains matter to a greater or lesser extent, and that, therefore, it is known in a more or less abstract fashion.[51] To say this, however, is misleading, since every form qua form is immaterial and it has an intrinsic relationship to matter insofar as it is the form of a composite substance or a form contained in such a substance. Hence, by stating that forms differ according to various degrees of immateriality, Aquinas is not saying that forms qua form have such degrees; he is rather saying that forms can show those degrees to the extent that they relate to an individual matter to a greater or lesser extent.[52] He says:

> Again, a form is made finite by matter, inasmuch as form, considered in itself, is common to many; but when received in matter, the form is determined to this one particular thing. Now, matter is perfected by the form by which it is made finite.[53]

This is, of course, an important idea with repercussions on the knowledge of intentions. Now, any natural object can receive forms, but due the role of the cognitive powers forms are grasped insofar they have an intentional being, which differs from the mere natural being of forms. Here it will prove central to establish that only those powers are capable of grasping intentions. The characteristic receptivity of the cognitive powers would provide an "intentionality criterion," because the sensible forms correspond ontologically to them. Because those forms are taken to be immaterial and intentional, they can only be grasped by a cognitive power, which is immaterial.

In opposition to plants, which have powers of the soul, but no cognitive powers, animals are able to obtain knowledge, because they receive forms through their cognitive powers and they do it in such a way that the organs are not altered materially; hence it is said that the condition for sensible and intellectual knowledge is immateriality, which varies regarding its relation to matter.[54] Whereas the senses need organs to become active, the intellect has no such need. The cognitive powers in general, however, to a lesser or greater extent, go beyond the determinations of physical objects, which is why they become the proper recipients for intentions. Here the dictum *omne agens agit sibi simile* is decisive in the sense that, ontologically speaking, the intentional being of immaterial sensible forms relates to the immateriality of cognitive powers.

Of course this last point still requires further research. Yet relating the knowledge of intentions with the constitution of the cognitive powers may prove promising in order to understand better Aquinas's stance on sense knowledge and the nature of intentionality. Even if one assumes, from the viewpoint of modern philosophy, that his reliance on Aristotelian physics and its presuppositions weakens his point of view, it is unavoidable to take it into account to appreciate his theory of the intention properly.

Universidad Autónoma Metropolitana, Mexico City

Notes

1. The first view has been defended by Martin Tweedale, "Origins of the Medieval Theory that Sensation Is an Immaterial Reception of a Form," *Philosophical Topics* 20 (1992), 215–231. The second has recently been expressed by Myles Burnyeat, "Aquinas on 'Spiritual Change' in Perception," in *Ancient and Medieval Theories of Intentionality*, ed. Dominik Perler, (Leiden: Brill, 2001), 129–153.

2. Robert Pasnau, "What is Cognition? A Reply to Some Critics," *American Catholic Philosophical Quarterly* 76 (2002), 483–490, here 486.

3. Dominik Perler, *Theorien der Intentionalität im Mittelalter* (Frankfurt: Klostermann, 2002), 40.

4. Thomas Aquinas, *Sentencia libri de anima*, Opera Omnia, t. XLV,1, Commissio Leonina/Vrin, Rome/Paris 1984, II, 14, 128, 268–271: "Inmutatio uero spiritualis est secundum quod species recipitur in organo sensus aut in medio per modum intentionis. . . ." I am following Pasnau's translation *Thomas Aquinas, A Commentary on Aristotle's De Anima* (New Haven/London: Yale University Press, 1999).

5. Thomas Aquinas, *In Sent. II* d. 38 q. 1 a. 3 c.: "[...] Ex ipso nomine intentionis potest accipi ad quam potentiam pertineat. Intendere enim dicitur, quasi in aliud tendere." See also Thomas Aquinas, *ST I–II* q. 12 a. 5 c.: "Intendere est in aliud tendere. . . ."

6. Thomas Aquinas, *ST I* 78, 3 c.: "Ad operationem autem sensus requiritur immutatio spiritualis, per quam intentio formae sensibilis fiat in organo sensus. Alioquin, si sola immutatio naturalis sufficeret ad sentiendum, omnia corpora naturalia sentirent dum alterantur."

7. Avicenna, *Liber De anima seu Sextus De Naturalibus*, vol. 1, ed. S. van Riet (Louvain/Leiden: Éditions Orientalistes/Brill, 1972), 83, 56s.

8. Avicenna, *De anima* I, 5 86, 93–106: "Differentia autem inter apprehendere formam et apprehendere intentionem est haec: quod forma est illa quam apprehendit sensus interior et sensus exterior simul . . . ; intentio autem est id quod apprehendit anima de sensibili, quamvis non prius apprehendat illud sensus exterior. . . . Id autem quod de lupo primo apprehendit sensus exterior et postea interior, vocatur hic proprie nomine formae; quod autem apprehendunt vires occultae absque sensu, vocatur in hoc loco proprie nomine intentionis."

9. Dag N. Hasse, *Avicenna's De anima in the Latin West, The Formation of a Peripatetic Philosophy of the Soul 1160–1300* (London/Turin: Warburg Institute-Nino Aragno Editore, 2000), 131. See also Deborah Black, "Imagination and Estimation: Arabic Paradigms and Western Transformations," *Topoi* 19 (2000), 59–62.

10. Hasse, *Avicenna's De anima*, 130s: "The 'intention' is not in the perceiver but in the object. . . . It is therefore not correct to say that an 'intention' is a certain knowledge which the internal sense has. It is rather an indicator pointing to the significance or meaning of an image with which this indicator is connected." See also Black, *Imagination and Estimation*, 60: "Avicenna's underlying rationale for positing the existence of intentions as distinct objects from sensible forms is that since each of the external senses is correlated with a single sensible quality—vision with color, hearing with sound, and so on—external sensation as a whole can only perceive the five proper sensibles and the other physical qualities that are directly manifested by them, the latter being the common sensibles of motion, shape, and magnitude. Hence the sheep cannot literally be said to 'smell danger' in the scent of the wolf or 'see hostility' in the wolf's eyes, because smell only perceives odors

and vision colors and shapes. Rather, concomitant with its seeing and smelling the wolf, the sheep must perceive these 'intentions' of hostility and danger directly through another faculty, its estimative faculty."

11. Avicenna, *De anima* II, 2 118, 7s: "[Aestimatio] apprehendit intentiones materiis quae non sunt in suis materiis, quamvis accidat illis esse in materia. . . ."

12. Avicenna, *De anima* II, 2 119, 15s: "Constat ergo quod hae [intentiones] in se sunt non materiales, sed accidit eis esse materiatas."

13. See Deborah Black, "Models of the Mind: Metaphysical Presuppositions of the Averroist and Thomistic Accounts of Intellection," *Documenti e studi sulla tradizione filosofica medievale* 15 (2004), 319–352; also Richard Taylor, "Cogitatio, Cogitativus and Cogitare: Remarks on the Cogitative Power in Averroes," in *L'élaboration du vocabulaire philosophique au Moyen Âge*, ed. J. Hamesse and C. Steel (Turnhout: Brepols, 2000), 111–146.

14. Averroes, *Commentarium Magnum In Aristotelis De Anima Libros*, ed. F. Stuart Crawford (Cambridge: Medieval Academy, 1953), see here II, 121, 316s.

15. Averroes, *De Anima* II, 97, 276s, 22–33: "Sicut color habet duplex esse, scilicet esse in corpore colorato (et hoc est esse corporale) et esse in diaffono (et hoc est esse spirituale), ita odor habet duplex esse, scilicet esse in corpore odorabili et esse in medio; et illud est esse corporale et hoc spirituale, et illud naturale et hoc extraneum." Richard Taylor was so kind to give me a draft of his translation of Averroes's text.

16. See the introduction in "Le traité *De Anima et de potentiis eius* d'un maître ès arts (vers 1225). Introduction et texte critique," in *Revue des sciences philosophiques et théologiques* 66 (1982), ed. R. -A. Gauthier, 3–55.

17. Gauthier has rightly stated that this distinction, recurrent in Aquinas's work, is typically Averroistic. Gauthier, R. -A., "Préface," Thomas de Aquino, *Sentencia libri de anima*, Opera Omnia, t. XLV,1 (Rome/Paris: Commissio Leonina/Vrin, 1984), 225*: "On peut en dire autant d'une autre doctrine typiquement averroïste . . . : c'est la doctrine de l'*esse spirituale* ou de l'*esse intentionale*."

18. Averroes, *Compendium Libri Aristotelis De Sensu et Sensato, Compendia Librorum Aristotelis Qui Parva Naturalia Vocantur*, ed. Aemilia L. Shields (Cambridge: Medieval Academy, 1949), 31s.

19. Averroes, *In sensu et sens.*, 32: "In medio habent [formas] esse medium inter purum corporale et purum spirituale: sic enim oportet esse, quoniam natura non transit de opposito ad oppositum nisi per medium. Et propter hoc impossibile est ut spirituale acquiratur a corporali nisi per medium, quod, quanto subtilius fuerit, tanto verior et certior erit comprehensio."

20. Averroes, *In De anima* II, 121, 317, 13ss: "Et opinandum est quod receptio formarum sensibilium ab unoquoque sensu est receptio abstracta a materia."

21. Averroes, *In De anima* II, 65, 228, 47ss.

22. Averroes, *In De anima* II, 121, 317, 17–20: "Et ideo in anima sunt intentiones et comprehensiones, et extra animam non sunt neque intentiones neque comprehensiones, sed res materiales non comprehense omnino." See also Black, *Models of the Mind*, 342–345.

23. Dag N. Hasse, "Das Lehrstück von den vier Intellekten in der Scholastik: von den arabischen Quellen bis zu Albertus Magnus," in *Recherches de Théologie et Philosophie médiévales* 66 (1999), 73.

24. Black, *Imagination and Estimation*, 66–68.

25. For the sake of simplicity, I will talk only of intentional change, tacitly assuming that it is spiritual as well.

26. Thomas Aquinas, *ST I–II* q. 22 a. 2 ad 3: "Dupliciter organum animae potest transmutari. Uno modo, transmutatione spirituali, secundum quod recipit intentionem rei. Et hoc per se invenitur in actu apprehensivae virtutis sensitivae, sicut oculus immutatur a visibili, non ita quod coloretur, sed ita quod recipiat intentionem coloris. Est autem alia naturalis transmutatio organi, prout organum transmutatur quantum ad suam naturalem dispositionem, puta quod calefit aut infrigidatur, vel alio simili modo transmutatur." Contrary to this view, and regarding Aristotle, Richard Sorabji famously held that "the organ of sight . . . takes on the colour of the object seen, without taking on any material particles from the object. . . ."; see Richard Sorabji, "Body and Soul in Aristotle," in *Aristotle's De Anima in Focus*, ed. Durrant, Michael (London: Routledge, 1993), 172.

27. Pasnau, *What is Cognition?* 486.

28. Robert Pasnau, *Theories of Cognition in the Later Middle Ages* (Cambridge: Cambridge University Press, 1997), 47ss.

29. It is worth considering that the quantitative approach cannot explain the fact that different animal species do grasp different intentions of the same object. If the psychological framework of the powers of the soul was insignificant, as Pasnau suggests, then there would be no reason to suppose that the grasp one sheep has of another sheep differs from the grasp a wolf has of the very same sheep. Also, his account does not explain why human beings know identical objects under different intentional aspects.

30. Similar expressions are "simile agit sibi simile" (*In Sent.* I 36, 2, 3 c.) or "omne passivum recipit actionem agentis secundum suum modum" (*In IV Sent.* Q. 44 q. 2 a. 1 c. ad 2). See also Thomas Aquinas, *In De anima II*, 30, 198, 35. Also Gauthier, *Préface*, 223*.

31. Thomas Aquinas, *In De anima III*, 8 240, 124ss: "[...] Potencie distinguuntur secundum rationes obiectorum. . . ."

32. Perler, *Intentionalitätstheorien*, 40.

33. Thomas Aquinas, *In De anima II*, 14, 130s, 363–366: "[...] Omnis forma in quantum huiusmodi est principium agendi sibi simile; unde cum color sit quedam forma, ex se habet quod causet sui similitudinem in medio."

34. Thomas Aquinas, *In Sent. III* 3, 2, 1 c.: "Forma enim quae per se non existit, non agit, nec proprie patitur, sed compositum agit ratione formae, et patitur ratione materiae. . . ."

35. Aristotle, *On the Soul, The Complete Works of Aristotle* vol. 1, ed. Jonathan Barnes (Princeton: Princeton University Press, 1984), 674.

36. Thomas Aquinas, *In De anima II*, 24, 168, 18: "Set uidetur hoc esse commune omni paciente [. . .]."

37. Thomas Aquinas, *In De anima II*, 24, 169, 24–26; trans. Pasnau 1999, 282.

38. Thomas Aquinas, *In De anima II*, 24, 169, 27–29: "Dicendum est igitur quod, licet hoc sit commune omni pacienti quod recipiat formam ab agente, differencia tamen est in modo recipiendi."

39. Thomas Aquinas, *In De anima II*, 24, 169, 30–45.

40. Thomas Aquinas, *In octo libros Physicorum Aristotelis expositio* (Turin/Rome: Marietti, 1965), V, 4, 335–337; also *Commentarium in Libro De Generatione et Corruptione* (Rome, 1886), I, 4, 10.

41. See Thomas Aquinas, *In De gen.* I, 4, 10, 299a: "Alteratio est, quando manet idem subiectum sensibile: scilicet quando, nulla transmutatione in eius substantia facta, fit transmutatio in passionibus eius, scilicet in qualitatibus eius."

42. Thomas Aquinas, *In De gen.* I, 4, 10, 299b: "Alteratio est transmutatio in passionibus.—Sed dicendum est quod alteratio primo et per se est in qualitatibus tertiae speciei. . . ."

43. Thomas Aquinas, *ST I–II* 49, 2 c.

44. See Thomas Aquinas, *Sentencia libri De Sensu et Sensato cuius secundus Tractatus est De Memoria et Reminiscencia*, Opera Omnia t. XLV,2, (Rome/Paris: Commissio Leonina/ Vrin, 1985), I, 14, 77, 15–18: "Qualitates autem *sensibiles* que *passiones* dicuntur, ut dicitur in Predicamentis, sunt in corpore aliquo sicut in subiecto. . . ."

45. Thomas Aquinas, *In Phys.* VII, 4 n. 910, 465: "Omnis alteratio est similis alterationi quae fit secundum sensum."

46. Thomas Aquinas, *In Phys.* VII, 4 n. 910, 466: "Alterari autem secundum huiusmodi qualitates, est omnium corporum sensibilium, tam animatorum quam inanimatorum. Et quia in corporibus animatis quaedam partes sunt *animatae*, idest sensitivae, ut oculus et manus, quaedam autem inanimatae, idest non sensitivae, ut capilli et ossa; utraeque partes secundum huiusmodi qualitates alterantur, quia sensus sentiendo patiuntur: actiones enim sensuum, ut auditio et visio, sunt quidam motus per corpus cum aliqua sensus passione. Non enim sensus habent aliquam actionem, nisi per organum corporeum: corpori autem convenit moveri et alterari."

47. Thomas Aquinas, *In Sent. IV* 49, 2, 1 c.: "Constat enim quod omne quod recipitur in aliquo, est in eo per modum recipientis. . . . Ad hoc autem quod visus cognoscat albedinem, oportet quod recipiatur in eo similitudo albedinis secundum rationem suae speciei, quamvis non secundum eumdem modum essendi: quia habet alterius modi esse forma in sensu, et in re extra animam. Si enim fuerit in oculo forma citrini, non dicetur videre albedinem. . . ."

48. Paul Hoffman, "St. Thomas Aquinas on the Halfway State of Sensible Being," *Philosophical Review* 99 (1990), 77ss.

49. On the different modes of being see Thomas Aquinas, *In DA* II, 24, 169, 45–59.

50. Thomas Aquinas, *ST I* 14, 1 c.: "Considerandum est quod cognoscentia a non cognoscentibus in hoc distinguuntur, quia non cognoscentia nihil habent nisi formam suam tantum; sed cognoscens natum est habere formam etiam rei alterius, nam species cogniti est in cognoscente. Unde manifestum est quod natura rei non cognoscentis est magis coarctata et limitata: natura autem rerum cognoscentium habet maiorem amplitudinem et extensionem. . . . Patet igitur quod immaterialitas alcuius rei est ratio quod sit cognoscitiva; et secundum modum immaterialitatis est modus cognitionis."

51. Pasnau, *What is Cognition?*, 483.

52. See John Haldane, "Aquinas on Sense-Perception," *Philosophical Review* 92 (1983), 233–239.

53. Thomas Aquinas, *ST I* 7, 1 c.: "Forma vero finitur per materiam, inquantum forma, in se considerata, communis est ad multa, sed per hoc quod recipitur in materia, fit forma determinate huius rei."

54. Thomas Aquinas, *ST I* 84, 2 c.: "Unde manifestum est quod ratio cognitionis ex opposito se habet ad rationem materialitatis. Et ideo quae non recipiunt formas nisi materialiter, nullo modo sunt cognoscitiva, sicut plantae [...]. Quanto autem aliquid immaterialius habet formam rei cognitae, tanto perfectius cognoscit. Unde et intellectus, qui abstrahit speciem non solum a materia, sed etiam a materialibus conditionibus individuantibus, perfectius cognoscit quam sensus, qui accipit formam rei cognitae sine materia quidem, sed cum materialibus conditionibus."

American Catholic Philosophical Association Eightieth Annual Meeting

Minutes of the 2006 Executive Council Meeting

Denison University, Granville, OH
Friday, October 27, 2006

---

1. Call to Order
At approximately 9:00 am, Anthony Lisska (ACPA President and Local Organizer) welcomed the Executive Council to Denison University and provided a bit of history and information about Denison and the Granville area.

2. Secretary's Report
In the absence of ACPA Secretary Michael Baur, who is attending to his wife, Christine Baur (who was temporarily hospitalized), Timothy Noone suggested that Council members read the Secretary's Report to themselves and then pose any questions that might occur to them.

I. News from the National Office: Future Annual Meetings of the ACPA

a. The council expressed thanks to Howard Kainz and to Marquette University for their willingness to host the 2007 annual meeting of the ACPA.
b. Timothy Noone announced that he has confirmed one plenary speaker for the 2007 meeting, and is still working on getting confirmation from others.
c. William Desmond, as President-elect, mentioned that he is considering "Philosophy and Finitude" and "Forgiveness" as possible themes for the 2008 annual meeting.

II. ACPA Membership

Timothy Noone noted the drop in the number of associate professors who are members of the ACPA, and this led to a brief discussion about evangelization.

a. Judith Green made a suggestion about introducing new topics for discussion at annual meetings.
b. It was suggested that the ACPA President might send letters to appropriate colleges who might serve as hosts for future annual meetings.

III. ACPA Publications

It was noted that Robert Wood was unable to attend the meeting, and discussion of the *ACPQ* was postponed until later in the meeting.

IV. ACPA Annual Meetings

a. Regarding the 2005 annual meeting, mention was made regarding what seemed to be higher honoraria for invited speakers. Timothy Noone assured the Council of his commitment to observe the ACPA's usual practice regarding honoraria.

b. Regarding the 2006 annual meeting:
   1. Anthony Lisska moved to thank the ACPA's Program Committee;
   2. Anthony Lisska moved to congratulate William Jaworski for being awarded the Young Scholar's Award for 2006;
   3. Timothy Noone moved to thank Anthony Lisska for his hard work in bringing the meeting to Denison.

V. Thanks and Acknowledgments

The Council expressed thanks to Dr. Christine Baur and offered prayers for her health.

Patrick Byrne moved to accept the Secretary's Report as presented. John O'Callaghan seconded the motion, and the motion carried unanimously.

3. Financial Statement and Treasurer's Report

I. ACPA Treasurer William Jaworski reported a $4,000 increase in the ACPA's endowment, and noted the transfer of ACPA funds from a managed account to a TIAA-CREF account.

II. William Jaworski expressed thanks to Fordham University for its financial support of the ACPA.

III. Michael Gorman raised a question about a remark in the letter from the ACPA's Certified Public Accountant, Bill Eckenrod, in which Eckenrod notes that certain disclosures are omitted from the ACPA's financial statements. William Jaworski explained that the Certified Public Accountant standardly omits such items.

IV. Michael Gorman asked about increased spending from 2004 to 2005. William Jaworski explained that there were increased expenses for duplicating and office materials because of depleted supplies, and that there were increased hotel and travel expenses in 2005, as part of a large donation made by then-ACPA-President James Marsh in order to cover the honoraria he promised to speakers for the 2005 meeting.

V. Bernardo Cantens asked whether the ACPA might seek donations from institutions to help fund travel for students and foreign scholars in need of financial support. Timothy Noone noted that the suggestion had been made at a previous meeting to use ACPA funds for that purpose. Anthony Lisska appointed an *ad hoc* committee to study the question. The committee members are: Bernardo Cantens (chair), Alice Ramos, Judith Green, and Timothy Noone (*ex officio*). The committee shall work with William Jaworski as ACPA Treasurer.

Thomas Michaud moved to accept Financial Statement and Treasurer's Report as presented. Kurt Pritzl seconded the motion, and the motion carried unanimously.

4. Report of *ACPQ* Editor

I. It was suggested that it would be helpful if more submissions to the *ACPQ* could be encouraged.

II. John Deely expressed the opinion that the name, *American Catholic Philosophical Quarterly*, sounds more exclusive than the journal's previous name, *New Scholasticism.* There was further discussion about the history and the reasons behind the name change.

III. Michael Gorman moved to accept the Report of *ACPQ* Editor as presented. John O'Callaghan seconded the motion, and the motion carried unanimously.

IV. John Deely moved that Robert Wood be re-appointed as editor of the *ACPQ.* Kurt Pritzl seconded the motion, and discussion followed.

a. Anthony Lisska reported that Robert Wood has agreed to serve as editor for three more years, but no more after that.

b. Timothy Noone noted how important it is to start thinking soon about Robert Wood's replacement; Noone agreed to try to get a sense of whether or not any of the present staff at the University of Dallas would consider taking over as editor.

The motion to re-appoint Robert Wood as editor carried unanimously.

V. John Deely moved to make 170 pages the standard length for the *ACPQ,* as requested by Robert Wood. The motion was seconded, and discussion followed.

a. Patrick Byrne asked whether this would incur any additional costs. John Deely and Timothy Noone stated that in all likelihood the increase would not be more than $1,000.

b. Patrick Byrne proposed a friendly amendment: the addition of a request by the Executive Council for a financial report regarding the increased cost.

c. John Deely withdrew his motion.

d. John O'Callaghan moved that the Council approve the 170-page length in principle and conditionally, and refer the issue to the Executive Committee pending a financial report on the impact of the increase in standard length. John Deely seconded the motion, and the motion carried unanimously.

5. Pro-forma Election of New Members to the ACPA

Michael Gorman moved to accept the new ACPA members as presented to the Council. Kurt Pritzl seconded the motion, and the motion carried unanimously.

6. Executive Council Vote on Offer from the University of St. Thomas (Houston) to Serve as Host Institution for the ACPA's National Office

I. Patrick Byrne asked Thomas Osborne (the Secretary-nominee from the University of St. Thomas) whether he felt confident that accepting such a task would not interfere too much with his professional progress. Dr. Osborne assured the Council that it would not.

II. Patrick Byrne moved to accept the offer from the University of St. Thomas. Michael Gorman seconded the motion, and the motion carried unanimously.

III. Anthony Lisska moved to thank the University of St. Thomas for offering to host the National Office. John O'Callaghan seconded the motion, and the motion carried unanimously.

7. Election of Aquinas Medalist for the 2007 Annual Meeting

The Council voted to award Nicholas Rescher the Aquinas Medal at the 2007 Annual Meeting.

8. Future and Annual Meetings

I. The locations and hosts of future annual meetings of the ACPA were discussed when the Secretary's Report was reviewed.

II. Michael Gorman moved to ratify the Executive Committee's decision (as explained in the 2005 Secretary's Report) regarding the hosts and locations for the 2007 and 2008 annual meetings of the ACPA (Marquette University in Milwaukee for 2007, and Creighton University in Omaha for 2008). Kurt Pritzl seconded the motion, and the motion carried unanimously.

9. Election of Two Executive Council Members to the Executive Committee

The Council voted to appoint John O'Callaghan and Patrick Byrne as members of the Executive Committee for the coming year.

10. New Business

I. Anthony Lisska and Timothy Noone reported that the Executive Committee proposed the institution of the St. Catherine of Siena Distinguished Service Award as an occasional award for extraordinary service to the ACPA.

II. Anthony Lisska moved that Michael Baur be the first recipient of the newly instituted St. Catherine of Siena Distinguished Service Award, and that Michael Baur also receive a lifetime membership to the Association. Timothy Noone seconded the motion, and the motion carried unanimously.

III. David Foster reported on the work of the Committee on Priestly Formation, which is participating in the philosophy segment of the Guide for Model Curriculum for Seminary Education.

IV. Michael Gorman moved that, after the conference, e-mails should be sent to those on the Conference Program who did not register for the conference reminding them to do so. John Deely seconded the motion, and the motion carried unanimously.

The meeting was adjourned at approximately 12 noon.

Respectfully submitted,
Katherin Rogers, University of Delaware

American Catholic Philosophical Association

Secretary's Report (2005)

I. News From The National Office

A. Future Annual Meetings of the ACPA

The ACPA continues to encourage inquiries and offers from individuals who think that their institutions may be willing and able to sponsor a future Annual Meeting of the ACPA. The Executive Committee of the ACPA, in response to a very generous offer from Marquette University, determined that the Association's 2007 Annual Meeting will take place in Milwaukee, WI, and will be hosted by Marquette University. In response to a very generous offer from Creighton University, the Executive Committee of the ACPA determined that the Association's 2008 Annual Meeting will take place in Omaha, NE, and will be hosted by Creighton University.

B. Details Regarding the 2007 Annual Meeting in Milwaukee, WI

President-Elect Timothy Noone announced (and the Executive Committee of the Association approved) the following theme for the Association's upcoming Annual Meeting, to be held November 9–11, 2007, in Milwaukee, WI: "Freedom, Will, and Nature." The conference hotel will be the Hilton Milwaukee City Center, located at 509 West Wisconsin Avenue, in Milwaukee, WI. An announcement of this theme, along with the submission guidelines, was mailed to all members in the May 2006 mailing. The call for papers for the 2007 Annual Meeting is also posted on the ACPA's web-site: http://www.acpaweb.org.

II. ACPA MEMBERSHIP

In 2005, the ACPA roster included 1231 *active* members. The number of *total* members from 1996 to 1998, and *active* members in 1999 through 2005 (all segregated according to membership category) is as follows:

Membership Category	*2005*	*2004*	*2003*	*2002*	*2001*	*2000*	*1999*	*1998*	*1997*
Professor	201	209	198	185	198	198	209	213	208
Associate Professor	122	131	137	124	153	160	161	172	168
Assistant Professor	155	142	147	125	152	142	143	165	162
Instructor	74	73	68	53	64	63	50	37	32
Lecturer	38	39	41	37	43	41	44	35	35
Student	208	181	152	132	173	154	158	162	134
Emeritus/Emerita	131	132	129	122	139	134	133	122	120
Associate	97	97	91	80	100	99	102	147	141
Institutional	15	21	13	11	14	13	14	17	17
Library	60	66	60	58	63	62	60	55	55
Life	81	83	88	86	96	90	93	96	97
Exchanges	49	34	35	36	35	35			
Totals	**1231**	**1208**	**1159**	**1049**	**1230**	**1191**	**1167**	**1221**	**1169**

Please note that the membership figures for 1998 and earlier represent the "unpurged" *total* number of members in the ACPA database. The membership figures for 1999 and later represent only those members listed as *active* in the ACPA database; starting in 1999 the Philosophy Documentation Center (the ACPA's database manager) instituted the practice of purging non-active members from the ACPA database, in order to present a more accurate picture of the ACPA's actual membership. Please note also that the total membership figures for 1999 and earlier include "Exchange" memberships, but not as a separate category. "Exchange" memberships have been listed as a separate category only since 2000.

III. ACPA Publications

A. ACPQ

In 2005, four issues of the *American Catholic Philosophical Quarterly* (volume 79) were published. The journal is edited by Dr. Robert E. Wood, assisted by Drs. Philipp Rosemann and Lance Simmons.

The 1996–1998 distribution of the *ACPQ* to *all* ACPA members, etc., and the 1999–2005 distribution to *active* members, etc., are as follows:

Distribution Type	*2005*	*2004*	*2003*	*2002*	*2001*	*2000*	*1999*	*1998*	*1997*
ACPA Members	1182	1174	1124	1013	1195	1156	934	1221	1169
Subscribers	531	469	516	501	508	493	517	484	504
Exchanges	49	34	35	36	35	35	38	37	33
Totals	**1762**	**1677**	**1675**	**1550**	**1738**	**1684**	**1489**	**1742**	**1706**

B. Proceedings

Dr. Michael Baur edited volume 79 of the *Proceedings of the ACPA*, entitled *Social Justice: Its Theory and Practice.*

The 1996–1998 distribution of the *Proceedings* to *all* ACPA members, etc., and the 1999–2005 distribution to *active* members, etc. are as follows:

Distribution Type	2005	2004	2003	2002	2001	2000	1999	1998	1997
ACPA Members	1182	1174	1124	1013	1195	1156	934	1221	1169
Subscribers	120	129	132	147	143	150	132	92	107
Exchanges	43	47	66	75	39	35	38	37	33
Totals	**1345**	**1350**	**1322**	**1235**	**1377**	**1341**	**1104**	**1350**	**1309**

C. Acknowledgments

On behalf of the ACPA, the Secretary would like to thank Dr. Robert E. Wood, Dr. Lance Simmons, and Dr. Philipp Rosemann, all at the University of Dallas, for their work in producing the *American Catholic Philosophical Quarterly*. The Secretary would also like to thank the University of Dallas for its ongoing institutional support of the *American Catholic Philosophical Quarterly*.

IV. ACPA Annual Meetings

A. Seventy-ninth Annual Meeting (2005)

The Seventy-eighth Annual Meeting of the ACPA was held October 28–30, 2005, at the University of Notre Dame, in South Bend, IN. The conference theme, selected by ACPA President James Marsh, was: "Social Justice: Its Theory and Practice." The Program Committee included: Drs. Thomas Jeannot, David Kaplan, and Anne Pomeroy. Papers read at the meeting and reports of the official business of the Association were published in volume 79 of the *Proceedings of the ACPA*, edited by Michael Baur. The winner of the 2005 Young Scholar's Award was Bernard G. Prusak, of Villanova University, for his paper, "The Ancients, the Moderns, and the Court." The University of Notre Dame provided financial support to help cover the costs of registration services, coffee breaks, refreshments, and receptions, as well as the travel and hotel costs of invited plenary speakers. In addition, President James Marsh gave a large cash donation to the Association in order to provide honoraria, and to help cover the travel costs of invited plenary speakers. On behalf of the Association, the Secretary would like to thank the University of Notre Dame, James Marsh, and the Local Organizing Committee (chaired by Paul Weithman of the University of Notre Dame).

B. Eightieth Annual Meeting (2006)

The Eightieth Annual Meeting of the ACPA will be held October 27–29, 2006, at Denison University, in Granville, OH. The conference theme, selected by ACPA President Anthony Lisska, will be: "Intelligence and the Philosophy of Mind." The winner of the 2006 Young Scholar's Award is William Jaworski, of Fordham University, for his paper, "Hylomorphism and Post-Cartesian Philosophy of Mind." On behalf of the Association, the Secretary would like to thank the 2006 Program Committee: Drs. Michael Gorman, James South, and Douglas Rasmussen. The Secretary would also like to thank the Local Organizing Committee, chaired by Anthony Lisska of Denison University. Finally, the Secretary would like to thank the host institution, Denison University, for its very generous financial and organizational support.

V. ACPA Elections

The results of the most recent ACPA election (concluded on April 1, 2006) are as follows:

Vice-President/President-Elect:
William Desmond (Katholieke Universiteit Leuven)
New Executive Council Members:
Patrick Brennan (Villanova University)
Mark Gossiaux (Loyola University of New Orleans)
Judith Green (Fordham University)
Patrick Murray (Creighton University)
Brian Treanor (Loyola Marymount University)

On behalf of the Association, the Secretary would like to congratulate these newly-elected individuals, and to thank all who were willing to stand for election. Without the participation and enthusiasm of such people, the Association could not continue to thrive.

VI. Thanks and Acknowledgments

On behalf of the ACPA, the Secretary would first like to thank Eleanor Helms for her work as the Fordham-sponsored graduate student assistant to the ACPA during the 2005–2006 academic year, and Michael Caputo for his work as the Fordham-sponsored graduate student assistant to the ACPA during the fall of 2006. Secondly, the Secretary would like to thank the ACPA Treasurer, Bill Jaworski, for his dedicated work and his willingness to help out with various tasks at the National Office. Thirdly, the Secretary would like to thank Fordham University for its very generous financial and institutional support, without which the Association would not be in the healthy condition that it is today. Finally and most importantly, the Secretary would like to thank his dear wife, Dr. Christine Baur, for everything that she has done and continues to do for her husband and for the Association.

Respectfully submitted,
Michael Baur, ACPA Secretary

American Catholic Philosophical Association

Treasurer's Report (2005)

I. Financial Statement

The Financial Statement shows that 2005 was a very positive year for the ACPA. In 2005, the ACPA's total excess of revenues over expenses was $37,190 (as compared to $30,896 in 2004). The Financial Statement shows that at the end of 2005, the Association's total liabilities and net assets were $306,517 (as compared to $269,395 in 2004). Of this $306,517, $304,774 represents net (unrestricted) assets (as compared to $267,584 in unrestricted assets in 2004). Thus the ACPA's net assets grew by $37,190 in 2005.

II. Annual Revenues and Expenses

Between 2004 and 2005, total annual revenues increased by $14,376 (total revenues in 2005 were $92,542, while they were $78,166 in 2004), and total annual expenses increased by $8,082 (total expenses in 2005 were $55,352, while they were $47,270 in 2004).

III. Annual Meeting

A summary of revenues and expenses in connection with the 2005 Annual Meeting is attached.

The Association is very grateful to the local host institution—the University of Notre Dame—for its generous financial support (totaling $7,849) in connection with the meeting. On behalf of the Association, the Treasurer would also like to thank the host institution of the National Office—Fordham University—for contributing $4,872 towards this meeting, and James Marsh for contributing $4,000 towards this meeting.

The attached financial statements show that the 2005 Annual Meeting resulted in a $601 excess of revenues over expenses.

IV. Assets and Investments—Total: $306,517

The Statement of Financial Position lists our assets on December 31, 2005, as follows:

A. Cash and Cash Equivalents: $54,936

On December 31, 2005, the Association held $54,936 in a Chase Manhattan checking and savings account.

B. Inventory and Supplies: $875

C. Non-cash Investments: $245,431

On December 31, 2005, the Association's non-cash investment holdings with TIAA-CREF were valued at $245,431.

D. Accounts Receivable: $5,275

On December 31, 2005, the Association's assets included $5,275 in accounts receivable from Fordham University.

V. Liabilities—Total: $1,743

Account Payable: $1,743

The amount of $1,743 represents expenses incurred by the ACPA in 2005 (e.g., service fees attributable to work performed in 2005, etc.), but not yet paid-for until after December 31, 2005, i.e., after the closing date for 2005 statements from the ACPA's bank and investment manager. Accordingly, the ACPA carries these 'not-yet-paid-for' expenses as a liability.

VI. Reminder

The Association depends heavily for revenue on membership dues and subscription payments. Therefore, the National Office reminds members to be prompt in paying their dues and/or subscription charges.

VII. Donations

As always, the Association welcomes donations. Since the ACPA is a tax-exempt organization under section 501(c)(3) of the Internal Revenue Code, all donations to Association are tax-deductible to the full extent allowed by law.

VIII. Acknowledgements

On the behalf of the Association, the Treasurer would like to thank Fordham University for its generous financial support of the Association. In 2005, the Association received $37,536 in cash donations from Fordham University. In addition to this direct financial support, Fordham has also provided a substantial amount of non-cash, or "in-kind," institutional support, including office space, tuition remission for the graduate student assistant, and a course reduction for the Fordham faculty member in the office of Secretary. The Association is deeply grateful to Fordham for this generous financial and institutional support. Finally, the Treasurer would like to thank the Association's Secretary, Dr. Michael Baur, for his hard work and ongoing dedication to the Association.

Respectfully submitted,
William Jaworski, ACPA Treasurer

American Catholic Philosophical Association
Financial Statements

Years Ended December 31, 2005 and 2004

American Catholic Philosophical Association Accountants' Compilation Report

Years Ended December 31, 2005 and 2004

TABLE OF CONTENTS

American Catholic Philosophical Association
Accountants' Compilation Report

Years Ended December 31, 2005 and 2004

To the Executive Council
American Catholic Philosophical Association
Bronx, New York

We have compiled the accompanying statements of financial position of American Catholic Philosophical Association (the Association) as of December 31, 2005 and 2004, and the related statements of activities and changes in net assets and cash flows for the years then ended and the accompanying supplementary information contained in Schedule I, in accordance with Statements on Standards for Accounting and Review Services issued by the American Institute of Certified Public Accountants.

A compilation is limited to presenting in the form of financial statements information that is the representation of management. We have not audited or reviewed the accompanying financial statements and, accordingly, do not express an opinion or any other form of assurance on them.

Management has elected to omit substantially all of the disclosures required by accounting principles generally accepted in the United States of America. If the omitted disclosures were included in the financial statements, they might influence the user's conclusions about the Association's financial position, results of operations, and cash flows. Accordingly, these financial statements are not designed for those who are not informed about such matters.

Hutchinson and Bloodgood LLP

Glendale, California
October 18, 2006

American Catholic Philosophical Association
Statements of Financial Position

Years Ended December 31, 2005 and 2004

ASSETS	2005	2004
Current assets		
Cash-checking and savings	$ 54,936	$ 109,620
Accounts receivable—Fordham	5,275	—
Accounts receivable—PDC Royalty	—	5,553
Accounts receivable—Others	—	12,577
Inventory and supplies	875	912
Investments, at market value	245,431	140,733
Total assets	$ 306,517	$ 269,395
LIABILITIES AND NET ASSETS		
Current liabilities		
Accounts payable and accrued expenses	$ 1,743	$ 1,811
Unrestricted net assets	304,774	267,584
Total liabilities and net assets	$ 306,517	$ 269,395

American Catholic Philosophical Association
Statements of Activities and Changes in Net Assets

Years Ended December 31, 2005 and 2004

SUPPORT AND REVENUES	2005	2004
Annual meeting	$ 31,787	$ 29,087
Royalties	18,772	24,652
Donations from Fordham University	37,536	26,019
Donations from members	100	1,100
Miscellaneous income	53	7
Interest and dividends	4,772	1,092
Net realized and unrealized loss in investments	(478)	(3,791)
Total support and revenues	92,542	78,166
EXPENSES		
Salaries and wages	15,500	15,492
Annual meeting	31,186	21,067
Postage	657	589
Telephone/communication	510	303
Office supplies and expenses	416	1,852
Insurance	817	818
Investment expenses	894	3,682
Accounting services	2,900	2,900
Bank service charges	15	158
Web service charges	386	363
Duplicating expenses	711	46
Membership	1,264	—
Miscellaneous	96	—
Total expenses	55,352	47,271
Increase in unrestricted net assets	37,190	30,896
NET ASSETS, BEGINNING OF YEAR	267,584	236,688
NET ASSETS, END OF YEAR	$ 304,774	$ 267,584

American Catholic Philosophical Association
Statements of Cash Flow

Years Ended December 31, 2005 and 2004

CASH FLOWS FROM OPERATING ACTIVITIES	2005	2004
Increase in unrestricted net assets	$ 37,190	$ 30,896
Adjustments to reconcile increase in unrestricted net assets to net cash provided by (used in) operating activities		
Net realized and unrealized losses in investments	478	3,791
Net change in:		
Accounts receivable	12,855	15,600
Inventory and supplies	37	38
Accounts payable and accrued expenses	(68)	(1,014)
Deferred income	—	(45,887)
Net cash provided by (used in) operating activities	50,492	3,424
CASH FLOWS FROM INVESTING ACTIVITIES		
Net change in investments	(105,176)	(6,788)
Net cash used in investing activities	(105,176)	(6,788)
Net decrease in cash and cash equivalents	(54,684)	(3,364)
CASH AND CASH EQUIVALENTS AT BEGINNING OF YEAR	109,620	112,984
CASH AND CASH EQUIVALENTS AT END OF YEAR	**$ 54,936**	$ 109,620

American Catholic Philosophical Association
Schedule I: Revenues and Expenses of Annual Meeting

Years Ended December 31, 2005 and 2004

REVENUES	2005	2004
Registration and banquet	$ 12,290	$ 10,455
Book exchange, exhibits and advertising	2,776	2,122
Donations:		
Local institutions	7,849	11,572
Fordham University	4,872	4,938
Member—James Marsh	4000	—
	31,787	29,087
EXPENSES		
Hotel and travel	4,965	589
Banquet expenses	11,270	11,572
Invited speakers costs	4,000	3,638
Young scholar's award	250	250
Aquinas medal and engraving	83	80
Meeting registration services	4,508	2,866
Duplicating expenses	4,592	964
Postage expenses	1,518	1,108
	31,186	21,067
Excess of revenues over expenses	$ 601	$ 8,020

Available Back Issues of the Proceedings

Volumes

No.	Year	
29	1955	*Knowledge and Expression*
33	1959	*Contemporary American Philosophy*
35	1961	*Philosophy and Psychiatry*
36	1962	*Justice*
38	1964	*History and Philosophy of Science*
39	1965	*Philosophy of the Arts*
41	1967	*The Nature of Philosophical Inquiry*
44	1970	*Philosophy and Christian Theology*
45	1971	*Myth and Philosophy*
46	1972	*The Existence of God*
48	1974	*Thomas and Bonaventure*
50	1976	*Freedom*
51	1977	*Ethical Wisdom East and/or West*
52	1978	*Immateriality*
53	1979	*The Human Person*
55	1981	*Infinity*
56	1982	*The Role and Responsibility of the Moral Philosopher*
57	1983	*The ACPA in Today's Intellectual World*
58	1984	*Practical Reasoning*
61	1987	*The Metaphysics of Substance*
63	1989	*The Ethics of Having Children*
64	1990	*Ways to World Meaning*
65	1991	*Religions and the Virtue of Religion*
66	1992	*Relations: From Having to Being*
67	1993	*The Importance of Truth*
68	1994	*Reason in History*
69	1995	*The Recovery of Form*
70	1996	*Philosophy of Technology*
71	1997	*Virtues and Virtue Theories*

72	1998	*Texts and Their Interpretation*
73	1999	*Insight and Inference*
74	2000	*Philosophical Theology*
75	2001	*Person, Soul, and Immortality*
76	2002	*Philosophy at the Boundary of Reason*
77	2003	*Philosophy and Intercultural Understanding*
78	2004	*Reckoning with the Tradition*
79	2005	*Social Justice: Its Theory and Practice*
80	2006	*Intelligence and the Philosophy of Mind*

Please send orders to:

Philosophy Documentation Center
P.O. Box 7147
Charlottesville, VA 22906-7147
800-444-2419 (U.S. & Canada), or 434-220-3300
Fax: 434-220-3301
E-mail: order@pdcnet.org
Web: www.pdcnet.org

All back issues of the *Proceedings* are $40 each, plus shipping (see rates below). Make checks payable to the Philosophy Documentation Center. Please send checks in U.S. dollars only. Visa, MasterCard, and Discover are accepted for your convenience.

Shipping and handling charges for book orders are as follows:

Total Price	Delivery within U.S.	Delivery outside U.S.
$ .01–$ 50.00	$ 5.00	$ 8.00
$ 50.01–$ 100.00	$ 7.50	$ 12.00
$ 100.01–$ 200.00	$ 10.00	$ 16.00
$ 200.01–$ 300.00	$ 13.00	$ 19.00
$ 301.00–$ 400.00	$ 16.00	$ 22.00
$ 400.01–$ 500.00	$ 19.00	$ 25.00
$ 500.01–$ 1000.00	$ 22.00	$ 28.00
Over $ 1000.00	$ 25.00	$ 31.00

For international airmail rates, please contact the PDC.